cambridge
charles river
west end
back bay
south end
MEMORIAL DRIVE
LEVERETT CIRCLE
BEACON STREET
MARLBOROUGH STREET
COMMONWEALTH AVENUE
NEWBURY STREET
BOYLSTON STREET
ELIOT STREET
BOSTON & ALBANY RAILROAD

east boston
LOGAN INTERNATIONAL AIRPORT
north end
government center
boston harbor
fort point channel
U.S. NAVAL RESERVATION

AUNA BATH
UB DOWNS
TEAM BATH
ODERN GYM
2 BIG HITS
STALKING
MOON"
ON THE LA
SAVO
HAYWARD P ACE GARAGE
PARK
FIRST
NATIONAL
BANK
RADIO
SHACK
MOD
SCANNELL
Serving
BALTIMORE-WASHINGTON
TOW AREA
NO
PARKING
ANY
TIME
TOW AREA

This report is based on the work of Signs/Lights/Boston, a project of Ashley/Myer/Smith, architects and planners, acting as consultants to the Boston Redevelopment Authority. The project was carried out under a federal Urban Beautification Demonstration Grant from the U.S. Department of Housing and Urban Development.

Original edition published by the Boston Redevelopment Authority, January 1971.

First MIT Press edition, June 1973.

ISBN: 0-262-02087-4
Library of Congress catalog card number: 73-7647

Boston Redevelopment Authority.
City signs and lights.
Mass. MIT Press

June 1973 4-30-73

a GRANGE
Health Club
SAUNA BATH
RUB DOWNS
STEAM BATH
MODERN GYM
SAVO
CINERAMA
RADIO
SHACK
2 EXCITING
TOW AREA
NO
PARKING
ANY
TIME

CHAPTER TWO

Problems and Potentials of City Signs and Lights

City Signs and Lights

A POLICY STUDY

Prepared for

The Boston Redevelopment Authority *and*

The U.S. Department of Housing and Urban Development

Stephen Carr, project director

Signs/Lights/Boston, *a project of*

Ashley/Myer/Smith Inc. *Architects and Planners*

CREDITS

Project Office:	Signs/Lights/Boston
Project Director: Assistant Director: Coordinator:	Stephen Carr Barry J. Young MacDonald Barr
Project Contractor:	Ashley/Myer/Smith, Architects and Planners Fletcher Ashley John R. Myer Douglas Cole Smith
Participants	
Urban Design:	Michael Southworth Roger Pool
Prototype Design:	Robert Kramer Wayne I. Welke Constantine Karalis
Graphic Design:	Jack Gaffney Michael Csaky
Environmental Psychology:	Ursula Scherer
General and Local Review:	Jeffrey L. Steingarten Harold L. Stultz, Jr.
Field Survey:	Lois G. Stern
Research and Writing:	Rachel Glass Marilyn Sabin
Administrative Assistance:	Mary Ann Mazen
Technical Specifications:	Jay Cross
Research Assistance:	Barbra Apfelbaum Myra F. Bennett Marcia Ann Crawford Robert G. Gebhardt John W. Kelsey
Graphic Assistance:	John Perkins Susan Gaffney Peter Wilson Phyllis M. Whitson

Consultants	
Urban Design:	Kevin Lynch
Environmental Psychology:	Mary C. Potter
Graphic Design:	Herman and Lees
Sign Control Planning:	Philip B. Herr Associates
Electrical Engineering:	Maguire Engineering McGonigle Engineering
Structural Engineering:	Arthur Choo Associates
Report Editing:	Joan Taylor
Report Design:	W. Booth Simpson
Demonstration Contractors	
Signs and Signals:	Donnelly Electric & Manufacturing Company
Information Center:	Center for Communications Inc.
Slide and Sound Shows:	Stuart R. Cody Judy Namias
Maps for Center:	G. Mara Ogulis
Light and Sound Environment:	Yale Research Associates in the Arts (PULSA)
Lighting Experiments:	M. B. Foster Electric Company E. Powers Electric Company
Pavement Markings:	Marking, Inc.
Contributions	
Metering and Electricity:	Boston Edison Company
Films and Movie Projectors:	Ealing Corporation
To Yale Research Associates in the Arts	Goldston Family Foundation The Mard Fund
To Lighting Experiments for the Boston Public Library	Sylvania Lighting Products

Mr. Robert T. Kenney, Director
Boston Redevelopment Authority
City Hall/Room 900
One City Hall Square
Boston, Massachusetts 02201

Dear Mr. Kenney:

We are pleased to transmit this report to the Boston Redevelopment Authority and the U.S. Department of Housing and Urban Development. We take this occasion to thank the Authority for its interest in this study and for continued support throughout its development. Special thanks are due to Charles Hilgenhurst, Administrator for Planning, who supervised the work for the BRA and helped us in many ways, and to James Drought, Administrator for Staff Services. We also wish to thank former Directors Logue, Champion and Warner of the BRA and the other city officials whose cooperation made the project possible: Commissioner McGrath of Traffic and Parking, Commissioner Casazza of Public Works, Commissioner Thuma of the Building Department, Mr. Krekorian, State Traffic Engineer for the Massachusetts Department of Public Works, and Mr. Warner, when he was Commissioner of the Parks Department.

Many people assisted in the development of this project. No simple listing can convey an adequate sense of the talents that were brought to the work. Barry Young was the full-time principal for most of the project and thus bore heavy responsibility for its day-by-day direction. He made innumerable contributions to policy and his work was central in the development of the public signing system and the information center. The highly demanding task of coordinating our efforts with those of the BRA, other city agencies, consultants and subcontractors fell largely to MacDonald Barr, who also made many contributions to policy. During the demonstration phase, the work of Jack Gaffney on public signing and the work of Michael Southworth on the Park Square information center was critical. Southworth also developed an information analysis of private signs and lights and worked on the design of the field tests. Ursula Scherer developed and carried out the field tests and data analysis. Roger Pool worked on policy for private signs and lights. Robert Kramer developed the prototype designs and made the drawings in Chapter 4 for the Central Streets and Spaces section and for the Charles Street Rotary.

The principals of Ashley/Myer/Smith all made important contributions in both the design and administrative phases of the project. The ideas and criticism of my colleagues at MIT, Kevin Lynch and Mary Potter, were invaluable. Anyone familiar with the work of Lynch will recognize his influence. Another colleague, Philip Herr, made numerous helpful suggestions on the regulation of private signs and lights.

There were other advisors and consultants at various stages of the project. Eli Goldston, President of Eastern Gas and Fuel Associates of Boston, was instrumental in gaining local support in the early phases. Alex Ushakoff, Jr., President of the Center for Communications Inc., put the information center together in more ways than one: without his ideas and close attention to the project it might have been far less successful. John Lees, of Herman and Lees, helped us in many ways with the graphics for the public signing demonstrations. William M.C. Lam talked to us about public lighting early in the project and a number of our ideas on the subject were stimulated by his prior work. Robert R. Wylie of Sylvania was most helpful on lighting for the Public Library and Copley Square. Albert Wolfe gave us general advice on the legal problems of sign and light controls and reviewed the text of the section on Legal Issues in Appendix 3.

Many of the same staff team also assisted in preparing the report. Barry Young prepared drafts and preliminary layouts for parts of Chapters 2 and 4. Roger Pool drafted Chapter 5. MacDonald Barr drafted Chapter 7. Rachel Glass prepared most of the appendices, a major undertaking. Appendix 3 was written by Marilyn Sabin. Booth Simpson did most of the graphic design and layout of the report, and took many of the photographs. Much of what is good in the report is the direct result of the work of these contributors. The inadequacies and mistakes in the final draft are my responsibility alone.

The project has been always interesting, even if sometimes overwhelming in its complexity. It is intended as a first step in the process of planning and controlling signs and lights for purposes of improving the flow of information in the city. If this work proves useful to the City of Boston and the Department of Housing and Urban Development, we will be well satisfied.

Yours sincerely,

Stephen Carr
Project Director

FOREWORD

During the past century, the American city has become an increasingly complex "terra incognita" within which to live, work and travel. The simple days of Main Street as the one and only busy thoroughfare have long since passed, giving way to the confusion of vast and intricate systems of streets, alleys, transport, signs and lights.

The demands and opportunities for travel in today's city and in the society as a whole are continually thrusting people into strange environments where their only guides are the various signs and labels that clutter the buildings and lamp posts. All too often, these aids prove useless, and they are forced to rely on directions from the strangers they pass on the streets.

These problems are further compounded at night, when otherwise legible signs and landmarks become invisible or obscure under the confusing umbrella of city lights. To the motorist, lost in this nighttime labyrinth, the onslaught of signs, lights and signals often seems overwhelming.

Is it too much to ask (in this age of interplanetary communication) that desired information be presented to the motorist and pedestrian in a logical and coherent way? Must private interests be allowed to compete with each other on the basis of who has the largest sign and the most neon? Should private signs compete and interfere with public signs?

This book is the result of a unique demonstration and research project carried out by Ashley/Myer/Smith, Architects and Planners, under sub-contract to the Boston Redevelopment Authority. It is an attempt to analyze and comprehend these problems and it proposes workable solutions for them. The Authority has worked in close conjunction with both HUD and the sub-contractor reviewing the various proposals, suggesting avenues of research and formulating the project guidelines. It is our hope that city planners, officials, administrators and policy makers will find this report a most useful aid in confronting this facet of the urban crisis.

Charles G. Hilgenhurst, *Administrator*
Planning, Urban Design and Advanced Projects
Boston Redevelopment Autnority

CONTENTS

CHAPTER ONE

Signs, Lights, and Information

Signs, Lights, and Information

The more at home a man is, the less need he has for consciously designed information sources in his physical surroundings. In the preindustrial village there were no traffic control signs, no identification signs, no street lights, no information centers. People knew each other, the rules of life were clear, and the form of the environment was a direct physical expression of those rules. Only the stranger could be misled.

Today we are the strangers, in our own towns. We do not know and cannot see how things work. Our support systems — the vast networks of government, production, commerce, transport, communications, education, health services, power, water, waste disposal, law enforcement — are remote. The information supplied in the environment is largely irrevelant both to our immediate purposes or to an understanding of the world in which we live.

The streets of any large city relay thousands of conflicting visual messages. Red lights blink to regulate traffic and to attract us to the local bar. Arrows point out routes; they also flash for the nearest hot dog stand. Private messages are stamped on the face of the city with little concern for anything more than competitive advantage. Even street lights add to confusion by their unshielded glare. Whether these visual messages are valuable or trivial and, indeed, whether they can be perceived at all are questions for public policy.

People understand their environment through its overall form, not merely by signs and lights. That form bears a particular history and relationship with their life style. The character and arrangements of streets, buildings, and activities have deep cultural meanings. To develop processes by which people can discover and reflect on these meanings and then transform the environment so that it becomes more expressive of their own way of life is the central task for environmental planning. In such an "evolutionary" environment, information might again become so integral to the experience of daily life that there would be no need to talk about it.

This study takes the city as it is and develops explicit means for revealing its form, functions, and meanings more effectively. Its recommendations are limited to public policy for the design and control of a small but critical set of information sources in the environment: outdoor signs, lights, and other informational devices. The study does not probe deeply into the cultural symbolism of signs and lights, as important as this may be, but rather analyzes their more immediate functions as environmental information systems. It asks what are the problems and potentials of public and private signs and lights, suggests a set of criteria for improving their performance, recommends an administrative process and framework for dealing with them as an interrelated set, and develops a set of policies and a program to implement the criteria.

The term "environmental information system" appears frequently in this report. "Environmental" refers to the public spatial environment out of doors — the streets and public places and activities of the city. This definition corresponds to the limits of the normal realm of operation of the city agencies which deal with signs and lights; many of the principles and policies in this report could, however, apply equally well to non-public or to interior environments. "Information" is used rather than the broader term "communication" because the report deals principally with one-way transmission of messages — from sender to receiver. Signs and lights do not "communicate" with people in the usual sense of exchange; rather they inform people about rules, activities, and occurrences of various kinds. Of course, when informing does become communication it is particularly valuable. "System" as used here refers more to potential than reality. Although a few aspects of public signing and lighting are treated systematically now, this report insists that the transmission of information can be improved greatly by conceiving of public and private signs and lights and other outdoor information media as interrelated "environmental information systems."

The report is based on a two-year study of conditions in signing and lighting in Boston, Massachusetts. Its recommendations, prototype designs, and demonstration experiments were developed for Boston, but the operating principles and most of the designs should be useful to any other city with similar problems and opportunities.

Criteria

There are two types of criteria proposed in this report. Negative criteria, or controls, set limits on harmful messages so that overload is reduced and privacy is protected. Positive criteria specify information to be encouraged and establish priorities among different types of messages. Messages are favored which are essential for safety, improve orientation in space and time, increase knowledge of available public and private activities, goods and services, and improve the expression of diverse social issues and values. Further limits must be imposed on private messages which attempt to skew these priorities for reasons of competitive advantage. Whether these are the correct priorities is a question for public debate. The political process by which these values or others are legitimized is crucial.

Signs and lights which satisfied these criteria would have strong connections with some of the important social problems and opportunities: they would improve traffic flow and safety; increase people's knowledge of possibilities which the city offers them; make the city both more educational and more pleasurable; and, by rendering the city less inconvenient and ugly, might contribute to the mental health of its people.

Policies

Taken together, the policies for public and private environmental information systems would result in a reversal in present visual priorities. The scope and dominance of public signing, lighting, and other information systems would be increased. The private signs and lights which presently dominate critical zones would be strictly controlled, and public and private information would be spatially channeled to reduce interference and to make it easier for the observer to find the type of information he needs.

Policies for public signs and lights specify two major systems: one information system for people on foot and one for people in cars. The system for people on foot consists of major information centers located at transportation junctions where there is a high concentration of people, coupled with intensive development of pedestrian promenades and the insertion of information on history, ecology, orientation, changing conditions and issues. The system for motorists consists of traffic control, warning, and guidance information in typical urban conditions, presented by means of signs, signals, lighting, and pavement markings. These policies are illustrated by prototype designs, some of which were tested in the field.

There are two sets of policies for the control and encouragement of private signing, lighting, and advertising. The city is initially divided into two zone types: a small number of Special Information Districts, and General Information Districts consisting of the rest of the city. Special Information Districts are those in which public use and significance are high and the area is very sensitive to the effects of private signs and lights. In these districts the city retains centralized control but works closely with the affected groups to develop a set of specialized codes, guidelines, and incentives dealing with both public and private systems. In the General Information Districts, the city administers a simple restrictive code (like that in Appendix 3) and offers design aid and local control of sign regulations when petitioned by groups to form "Local Information Districts."

Continued evaluation of public needs and reactions to change are strongly recommended as an integral part of the city information program. Field testing was central to his project. A prototype information center was erected in downtown Boston; public use was measured and evaluations sought. Elements of a new traffic signing system were tested in two field locations and in the laboratory, and many of these signs remain in place. An experimental light and sound environment was tested in the Boston Public Garden, along with special tree lighting. An experiment in public lighting at the Boston Public Library will result in a permanent installation. Finally, two experiments and two surveys were conducted on the impact of private signs. Public policy recommendations in this report have been strongly influenced by the results of these and other field tests.

The field experiments represent a new approach to the development of urban systems. By investing the limited demonstration funds available to the Signs/Lights/Boston Project in mostly temporary experiments rather than more permanent improvements, a much broader range of policies could be tested. In the case of the new regulatory signs, which deviate from national and state standards, only temporary installations were possible. But the choice of experiments over permanent demonstrations was made on other grounds than necessity: they allow for learning and improvement on policy ideas before the city commits itself to a new program.

Official reactions to the experiments, like those of the public, were generally strong and positive. The information center and the new traffic signs were particularly well received. The policies in Chapters 4 and 5 for new signing, lighting, and information systems which grew out of these experiments are now under active consideration by the city agencies involved. The specific programs to be undertaken by these agencies (or by the city administration as a whole) will depend on many factors, including public reaction to this report and the availability of funding.

Action

To organize and carry out an environmental information program in Boston or any other city will require several types of public action. As a first step, a small team of professionals would need to be formed, preferably within the mayor's office. This special office would be a transition to a more general agency. It would have a number of tasks, including organizing a mayor's advisory committee with representatives of interested groups, contacting state and federal administrators of grant-in-aid programs, drafting and obtaining passage of new legislation, and setting up either a new agency or a new staff within an existing planning or development agency. This team could also promote early starts in the new citywide program by existing agencies using present powers.

The new agency or staff might begin operations with a limited, three-year program calculated to have a highly visible public impact. It should select some central area of the city for intensive coverage by new public signs and lights. Such an area would include several types of Special Information Districts where joint public-private development could be tried. The new code should be enforced throughout the area and at least one Local Information District should be organized. In addition, there would be area-wide improvements in information for people on foot and at least two permanent information centers. For adequate coverage of central Boston, such a three-year program would cost about $3,300,000 plus annual budget items totaling about $400,000 with prospects of about $1,800,000 coming from outside the city.

A serious cost-benefit analysis of the process, policies, and program recommended in this report cannot be made without further field experience. It is clear, however, that the costs in administrative time, dollars, and political controversy of achieving improvements in environmental information systems over large areas of the city are considerably less than those of other more conventional physical improvement programs.

The time required from start to finish is also much shorter. The demonstration experiments and prototype designs which illustrate this report indicate the highly visible and sometimes dramatic improvements which can be achieved with minimal disruption to the city fabric and threat to local interests.

The most difficult operational problems to be encountered are closely linked: funding and the control of private interests. There are presently available federal funds from various sources which can be applied to the development of public information systems, but substantial contributions at the local level will be required. The potential for this depends principally on the development of a public constituency. Businessmen will be an important element of that constituency and in many cases, for instance the information system for people on foot and private sign/light developments in Special Information Districts, joint public-private development is possible — if sufficient public control is maintained.

Herein lies the dilemma. Control of advertising interests is a key part of the general strategy; it might be better, for instance, not to have information centers than to have them become selling machines. The advertising industry constitutes a powerful, well-funded lobby which must be dealt with. In order to enact controls on advertising in the public environment, like those recommended in Chapter 5, a strong set of counter-interests — and especially a non-commercial public — must be organized. In addition, federal and local incentives to make code enforcement more feasible would be a highly desirable policy tool.

From most indications in this study and elsewhere, public reaction to improvements in environmental information systems is strong and positive. Our cities are confusing, frightening, and often depressing places. Inadequate public signing and lighting contribute to feelings of anxiety in carrying out normal daily activities. The visual overload caused by uncontrolled private signing and lighting heightens that anxiety and makes people want to minimize exposure to the public environment. Anxiety and withdrawal are disturbing symptoms in themselves, but they are especially troubling when contrasted with the potential benefits of improved environmental information systems.

By the deliberate extension of public information systems, coupled with controls on private signs and lights, cities can be made more legible, expressive, and meaningful. If the environment is organized as an information carrier, people can better find the information they need, and their experience of the city can become more pleasant and more engaging.

Problems and Potentials of City Signs and Lights

Signs and lights are out of control; they obscure the meaning of the environment as often as they clarify it. This condition is the visible result of a chain of causality which may be traced back to more basic difficulties in our economic and political systems. Unlike many other urban problems, however, most of the problems of city signs and lights can be dealt with directly.

In cities today, the observer is often overloaded by messages competing for his attention or else his view is dominated and his privacy violated by advertising messages which are irrelevant to his purposes. Often, useful or even essential information is missing; more often information is presented confusingly. Public activities and services are poorly identified and advertised. The form of communication is rarely expressive of the activity being communicated about and there is a lack of means for individual and group self-expression. Systems conflict with one another and the authority to deal with them is fragmented.

Beyond correcting these excesses and deficiencies, city signs and lights provide an opportunity to make significant improvements in the public environment. Good public and private information systems can markedly improve both the legibility and the expressiveness of the environment. They can enable people to better understand how the city fits together and how it functions, including how it got to be the way it is and its likely future development. Environmental information systems can express the structure of activities in the city: signs and lights can change their form with the functions they represent. Signs and lights can also provide a means for the direct self-expression of both individuals and groups. Priorities can be set for various types of information to reduce conflicts. Greater coordination may be possible even without changing administrative structure.

Thus, signs and lights are a potentially powerful but sadly neglected resource in making cities more meaningful and pleasurable. This chapter analyzes these problems and potentials; its examples are a cross-section of components of systems to be dealt with in the policy chapters. It argues that public and private signing and lighting should be planned as an interrelated set of environmental information systems. The chapter concludes with some of the difficulties in the current processes by which needs are analyzed, system components are designed, and hardware is purchased and installed.

OVERLOAD

In the typical American street each element appears as the product of somebody's rugged individualism. Privately owned signs and lighting are primarily designed and placed to capture attention, only secondarily to inform. Sign designers ignore buildings and architects ignore signs. The uncoordinated equipment for public signing and lighting results in a cluttered streetscape; illumination itself is haphazard.

As a result, the observer is often overloaded with stimuli. Human capacity for receiving information has sharp limitations. Attention which might be given to more useful or rewarding environmental experience is diverted by the abuses of the present landscape of signs and lights, and the information capacity of the public environment is wasted. Directional signs can be so numerous in a location that the important one is lost; many competing private signs can make it difficult to find one particular establishment; parking signs are often redundant or look like information essential to the driving task.

Photo: Nishan Bichajian

Sometimes, however, a concentration of signs and lights can become a message in itself. In Times Square, Piccadilly Circus and the Ginza, overload becomes "super-load" and other concerns give way temporarily to direct sensory experience of light, color, and motion. People may be both attracted by these spectacles and repulsed by their underlying meaning.

Concentrations of huge signs and bright lights have come to symbolize "downtown" for many people. Along with the entertainments that they advertise, these sign and light "spectaculars" are an important nighttime attraction of the center city for a growing number of people. That so many people take pleasure in them may be sufficient reason to preserve and intensify them as a matter of public policy.

The Times Squares are an expression of the commercial nature of our cities. They excite to sell. These displays are sometimes praised as a new art form. They are indeed living museums of our brand of materialism: capitalist realism for the masses and pop art for the elite. Nevertheless, they reveal the potential of environmental light and graphic displays as means of aesthetic expression and enjoyment. New uses of current technology for experiments in receiver activation and control of these displays might then find application in private signing. Stripped of their commercial intent and reborn in a public context, such displays can become a way of expanding the humane uses of our technology.

DOMINANCE

Where unlimited competition is the rule, the most powerful competitors will dominate. In private signing and lighting, these are the outdoor advertisers. Not only are their "super-signs" larger, better illuminated, and more attention demanding than those of local establishments, they are organized by a relatively efficient system which pre-empts the most visible locations.

Of all private signing, billboards most frequently conflict with the needs of the public. They skew communications systems so that local information is obscured and particular destinations are made more difficult to find. Unlike most other advertising, billboards cannot be turned off or ignored at will. They are thus a direct violation of the individual's privacy for someone else's profits.

Billboards located adjacent to complex, high volume urban highways and at major intersections are a safety hazard because they distract the driver's attention. In historic districts, such as those in Boston, the case against billboards and other large signs is clear. It is equally clear in residential areas. Businessmen in some shopping areas have taken joint action to remove billboards because they detract from local character. Arguments like those which apply to protection of natural scenery might also be made for protection of the city skyline from dominance by advertisements.

There is growing public concern with these super-signs. In order to preserve views of the natural landscape, the federal government now provides incentives for outlawing billboards along interstate highways. The State of Vermont has done away with them altogether on the grounds that they are bad for the tourist industry as well as highway safety. Many small cities, self-conscious about the appearance of their local environment, have passed anti-billboard ordinances.

The present "natural" domain of billboards and other super-signs is along the highways leading into the city, along the endless dreary "strips" on the fringes of the city, and increasingly on the skyline of the center city itself. For maximum selling effectiveness, billboards would dominate the skyline and the visual field at every major intersection and cluster at rhythmical intervals along all the main roads of the city. Fortunately, location by a purely economic rationale is constrained by the space available and the demand for this form of advertising; but the resulting scatteration is an important aspect of the billboard problem.

Where space is readily available and audience exposure is high, billboard concentrations sometimes develop which begin to have some of the visual interest of superload. If these posters could be dynamically related to one another on structures located in visually dull places like parking lots, away from dangerous intersections, they might enliven the urban scene. Limiting and "framing" billboards in this way might incidentally increase the effectiveness of the advertising.

UNAVAILABLE INFORMATION

Some information that is essential and much that is potentially useful is unavailable. Streets go nameless, street numbers are missing, road forks have uncertain destinations, rules of the road are not stated. We seldom display city maps and directories in our streets, and potentially valuable information about the functioning, ecology, history, and future of the city is missing.

Lighting has received considerable attention recently as a solution to some of these information needs. To walk through the city at night with a sense of security, one must know what and who is there. Data on the relationship between personal crime and street lighting may be ambiguous, but there is no doubt that people feel more secure on well-lit streets. All mayors are against "crime in the streets," and many have mounted ambitious street light improvement campaigns. High-intensity mercury vapor lights are being installed as rapidly as capital improvement budgets and tax rates allow.

Little thought has been given, however, to the resulting quality of light. Information is increased, streets feel safer, but human skin becomes a sallow greenish-gray. In addition, unshielded lights discomfort the driver and violate the privacy of upper-story bedrooms and apartments in residential areas. Apparent security is achieved, but the cost is a depersonalized local environment.

A Boston residential street.

Glare from new street lights in Back Bay.

Park area in Boston's South End

City Hall Plaza, Boston.

Piazza della Repubblica, Rome   Photo: William M. C. Lam.

Campidoglio, Rome   Photo: William M. C. Lam.

Light enhances the quality of environment in more dimensions than safety alone. There are light sources which produce a warmer light with nearly as much efficiency as mercury vapor. The techniques of stage lighting can produce a more natural skin color. Light color might even be used to complement seasonal changes: a warmer tone in winter, a cooler summer light.

There are other ways in which light can create new environmental information. At night, when lights are in perspective (and especially when they are closely spaced) the streetscape takes on a rhythmical cadence not present by day. Combined with architectural elements, such as canopies or arcades, a sense of unified composure can be created, as compelling as it is in parts of Paris, Bern, or Bologna. Such streets are far more than merely safe. They are beautiful and comfortable places for people to be.

There is an opportunity to create a new and life-enhancing night environment through conscious control of the medium of light as an information source. There are many comparable opportunities in our cities where new information is needed. The graphic form of new traffic control and directional signing can improve the appearance of the street as well as traffic safety and guidance. New sources of information for people on foot can also enhance the appearance and the life of city streets.

CONFUSING INFORMATION

Available information is often confusing. Naming systems, for instance, are unreliable. In Boston, minor intersections are often named for honored dead, but these designations cannot be found on any street map or directory. Paradoxically, major intersections such as Dewey Square often go unidentified except on maps.

There are other common confusions in terminology. Curb signs use the terms "loading," "stopping," "standing," and "parking," but these distinctions are not clear to most people and are usually ignored. Route "C9" is used for several different roads through central Boston (fortunately, they do eventually converge).

As frequently, message systems are inconsistent and the same route is designated differently in different places. The driver is led past a series of signs displaying his destination; then the original name is abandoned — often at some particularly confusing decision point. Lack of follow-through information is most obvious when a driver exits from a relatively well-signed expressway into the maze of city streets. Also, when entering or leaving a city, it is difficult to know which road signs refer to local city destinations and which to distant places.

1

2

3

4

5

6

7

8

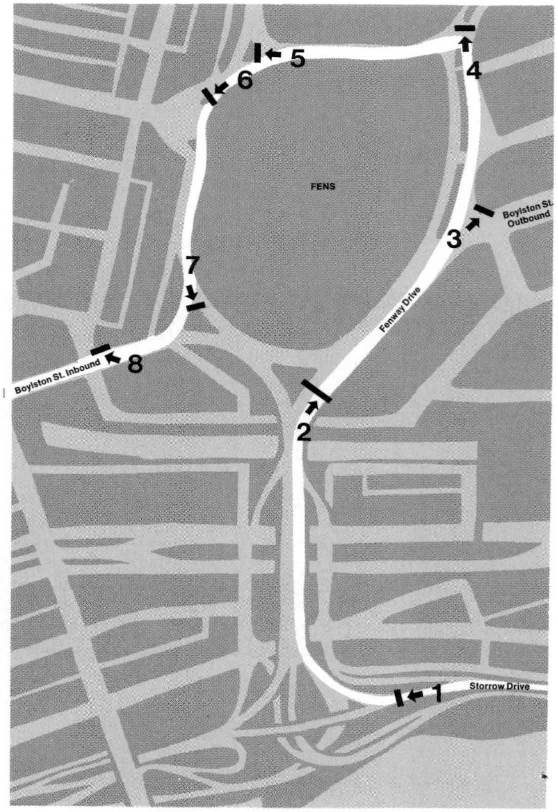

The motorist who wants to go from Storrow Drive to Boylston Street, a major commercial street in Boston, encounters this inconsistent sequence of guide signs: Boylston Street is indicated at the first three decision points; at the fourth and critical left turn the indication changes to "Downtown Boston"; at the seventh sign two destinations on Boylston Street appear; the name itself does not reappear until the street name sign. For someone who knows Boston well, this might be just tolerable but for the visitor it is impossible.

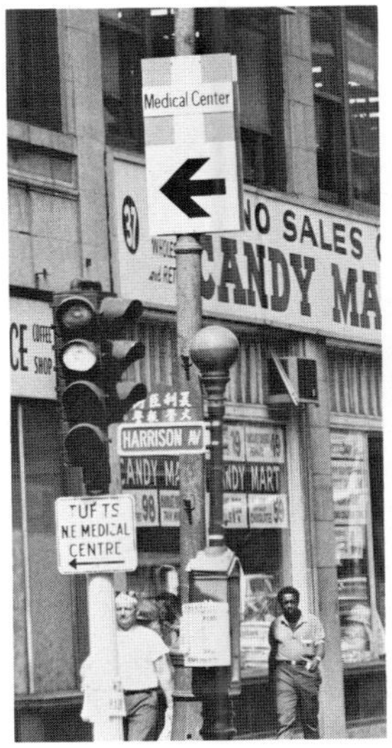

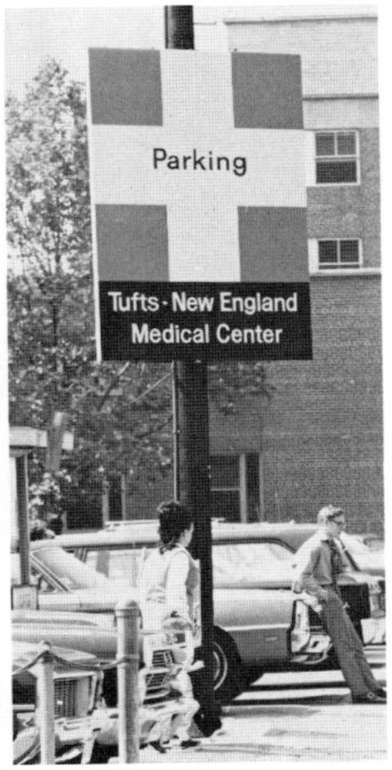

An early design for a "go slow" pictograph.

Principles of visual order are generally straightforward, and means for clarification of the environment are ready to hand. Shape, color, and illumination can be used to organize public signs into systems and sub-systems by type of content. Messages themselves can be expressed in words or graphic symbols ranging from pictures associated with the thing or activity symbolized to abstract forms. Well-known symbols such as the arrow are helpful for messages which occur with high-frequency and demand quick recognition. Graphic symbols are not always better than words, however, especially when they must transmit abstract or complex messages. Once the basic systems for signing and lighting have been clarified, sizes and locations of signs will be governed by viewing angles, stopping distances, and the logic of sequence for observers in motion.

It is important to note that the legitimate desire for order and clarity in public signing and lighting has its dangers. At the other extreme from the present muddle is the world of Big Brother. Public information policy could aim to tell everyone where he is at all times, what is good about the place, and how he should conduct himself while there. Every building, place, and activity would be clearly labeled; every street lit to a uniformly high level; signs and signals would describe all possible movements. This caretaker environment might be far more disturbing than the present confusion. The line between essential organization and clarification and such "institutionalization" of the city is fine but important.

OBSCURE PUBLIC SERVICES

Street communications services such as telephones, mail boxes, fire alarms, and police call boxes are inconsistently located and poorly identified. They are scattered in seemingly random locations. At night they are often unlit.

Major services such as public transport are also poorly identified. Transit stations are normally not visible from a distance, although under Boston's present improvement program large, illuminated, highly visible "T" markers are being installed. In most cities, bus stops give no information about schedules or destinations. Connections between public transport and taxis, long-haul buses, trains and planes are also obscure.

Identification of other public activities and facilities is often discreet to the point of invisibility. City events are seldom announced in the public environment. Police stations may have blue lights, but hospitals and government offices of all kinds are poorly identified. Even when there is identification in the immediate locale, there is normally no signing system to guide people to these important locations. In Boston, it seems, only historical sites are worthy of a special guide signing system; but even the "Freedom Trail" is confusing to follow and loses many a discouraged tourist.

A fire alarm box lost in the clutter of street hardware.

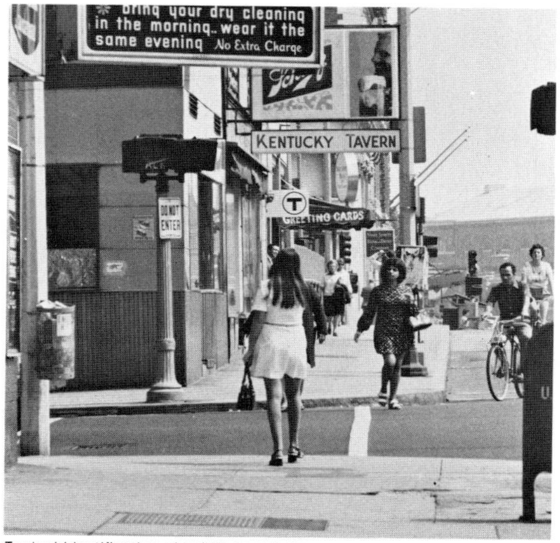

Typical identification of public transit stop.

Entrance signs for the Massachusetts General Hospital.

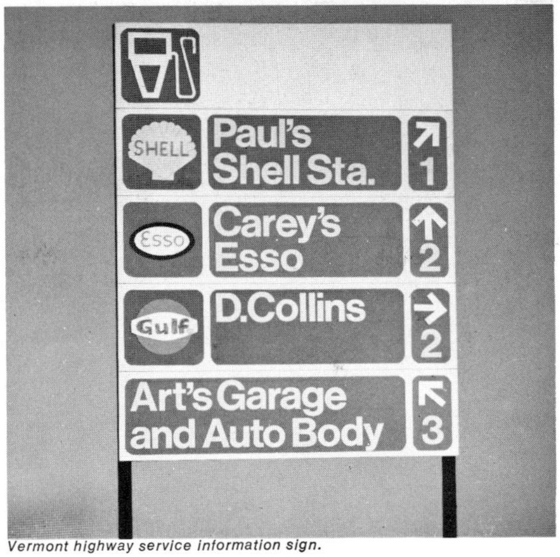

Vermont highway service information sign.

Public service signing for Mexico Olympics, 1968.

Chicago poster kiosk.

Public services, activities, and facilities of all kinds can have visual identity. The city government could have an overall graphic identity, within which each agency would have its own variant on a general theme. An overall scheme would include signs (logos) to identify the agencies, letterheads, color schemes, identification of official vehicles, a special graphic character for official publications, posters, and the like.

In Zurich, Switzerland, graphic coordination already exists among city offices and in public announcement posters. In our less centralized city governments, it might be more difficult to achieve, but it should not be impossible. In Chicago, for instance, a series of fine posters advertising public activities is displayed on kiosks designed for the purpose.

World fairs and Olympic events have set up complete guide signing systems for their visitors which locate public facilities and events by color and symbol codes. The public services and facilities like telephones have been given visual identity. Vermont developed a sign, map, and directory system to provide roadside information about services available to its summer and winter visitors. These signs and kiosks will replace the incomplete information previously provided by billboards and other highway advertisements. Guide systems of this type can be developed within cities for all public services and facilities, and the services themselves can be graphically identified.

ACTIVITY POORLY EXPRESSED

Good signing and lighting should go beyond minimal provision of basic information. Meaningful messages touch our consciousness on many levels, and the best signing and lighting will be expressive of the thing signified with all its overtones. An entertainment sign will look gay; a danger sign, dangerous.

Our cities are notably lacking in messages which express the activity symbolized. Signs and lights have increasingly standardized and repetitive forms as larger manufacturers dominate the industry. Signs look alike whether for restaurants, gas stations, supermarkets, or mortuaries. In Boston there are still many examples of the more diverse and expressive signing of the nineteenth century, but these fine old signs and symbols are gradually being replaced by the back-lighted plastic uniformity of the twentieth century.

Our present dreary signs and lights do express the commercial, non-public nature of our cities. This is nowhere more noticeable than in outdoor lighting. Lighting in American cities is currently designed to serve two functions: to allow people to get about at night with some minimum standard of visibility and safety and to announce salable goods, services, and diversions. Incidental additional light is produced by night functions in commercial buildings. Cities at night consist of long, dark stretches (since even minimum standards are not achieved) alternated with scattered brighter elements like gas stations and used car lots.

Different functions, similar signs.

The 1970 standard model.

Urban nightscape.

There are many cities in the world where the design of the public environment exploits the delights of changing light and color. The fountains of Rome demonstrate this potential developed as a high art. The fountains and their surrounding piazzas become collecting places for people where the sound and sight of water and the soft flicker of light may activate deep associations with firelight and the village well. Parks in our cities might be lit to achieve some of these qualities.

Streets need not be lit uniformly. An adequate standard for safe visibility must be assured but that need only be a baseline for enhancing the expressiveness of the street by night. Light could change as activities change. A street could combine public and private lighting to express its changing character: In some areas, public lighting including special lighting for pedestrians might predominate, expressing the flow of people — shop windows and canopies would provide the light. Elsewhere, promenades of trees would carry lanterns.

Signs may also be designed to be more expressive by drawing on common associations to reinforce their message. Direct views of the activity itself are usually more expressive than any abstraction or symbol. Messages normally suffer a loss in immediacy and associative power as the connection between the sign and the activity it symbolizes becomes less direct: compare a view of an open market with that of a sign saying "produce sold here." The signscape would be more expressive if most signs were associated directly with activity — if beer signs only occurred on breweries or bars. It might also be possible for a signing policy to encourage non-verbal signing in the tradition of the barber pole and the three golden balls of pawn shops, or even poetic forms of verbal signing.

LIMITS ON SELF-EXPRESSION

Individuals and groups can express themselves by means of signs, lights, and other media in the city. The peddler and the market vendor hawking their goods in their own personal style have all but disappeared from our streets, but handmade signs still appear in local shops and often have a graphic flavor which is expressive of the personality of the shopkeeper.

For the most part, direct expression by individuals is now limited to illicit forms such as the graffiti of teenage gangs or, increasingly, political protesters. Except where protesting groups have the funds to mount billboard campaigns (to impeach the Chief Justice or to stop urban renewal), their expressions usually involve defacing buildings and are discounted by most people as acts of vandalism committed by "irresponsible extremists." Thus, the use of an "illicit" medium can defeat its own purpose. The attempt to create legitimate channels for such protest is also problematic; protesters against the institutions of government are unlikely to limit their expressions to publicly provided graffiti space. The speaker's area in Hyde Park in London, however, seems to serve a similar function well.

Many other forms of self-expression besides protest are presently discouraged. It is expensive to send messages in the city. The small businessman is likely to be out-shouted by the large corporate senders and to fall into the hands of the national firms which distribute stock signs with product advertising built-in. Standardized commercial signs preclude personal expression, and lighting, despite its great potential, is rarely used as a medium of expression in the outdoor environment. As a result, neither individual establishments nor commercial areas express identity through signs and lights. A commercial everyman's land stretches from Boston to Los Angeles.

Photo: Tony Lob

Photo: Nishan Bichajian

If personal and group expression is to be encouraged as a public good, policy will have to deal explicitly with the means. Kiosks and message boards could be used, along with public wall space which allowed graffiti but had a regular program of repainting. Policies limiting certain forms of commercial signing might encourage more reliance on the handmade temporary variety. Ideally, policy would also encourage custom made signs and the use of skilled designers to develop signs expressive of each establishment.

Private signing and lighting, one of the most dominant and easily changed parts of the visual environment, can reinforce area identity; there are a few places in Boston in which commercial signing and lighting begin to support and enhance character. The intensity of competitive signing in the "combat zone" of lower Washington Street gives it an aspect of its own; commercial signs in the Chinese community are unmistakable and in other areas too the names of shops suggest ethnic character; signing in the old produce market area retains the black and gold nineteenth century character and is thus expressive of the continuity of use; in Back Bay there is a restrained graphic elegance that is congruent with its boutiques and art galleries. On the other hand, efforts to "colonialize" Charles Street on Beacon Hill (reaching their zenith with a proposal for colonial parking signs) are incongruent with the actual antique-speciality-hippie use of the street.

Intensity, ethnicity, history, and character of activity are all aspects of area personality that can be developed to give places in the city their own identity. Signing and lighting which expresses the real diversity of individuals and groups will have character without the need of superficial or phony "images."

CONFLICT

Messages are organized and presented in ways that are often in direct conflict with public information needs. Motorists face a task increasingly like trying to read a newspaper and a novel, watch television and listen to the radio all at once. A car driver must pay attention to other drivers and pedestrians, watch for signs and signals describing the rules of the road, and at the same time look for clues to his direction and destination; while he is doing this, he will normally be distracted by advertisements to entice him into local shops or to buy a national product or service.

Although under most circumstances people can screen out information that is not needed, many private signs are designed to frustrate this. Size, placement in the visual field, motion, and the contrast of a sign with its background determine the focus of visual attention: when the size of a sign is increased, the message seems more important; messages which occur near the center of the visual field tend to dominate those at the edges; moving objects and flashing lights are more engaging than stationary ones; high-intensity lighting and color increase the relative contrast of a sign with its background.

At major intersections, drivers are often faced with billboards which dominate the visual field by size, location, and contrast; in these same locations, it is common to find huge facade signs advertising local businesses. At night, all these signs are brightly illuminated, even flashing. Public signing, on the other hand, is often dominated by a welter of parking regulations, with important information such as street names or destinations reticently presented by comparison. Even traffic signals may be difficult to find or see against competing backgrounds.

The resolution of conflict among and within environmental information systems will necessitate a public effort to establish priorities and appropriate rules of order. This will involve both improvements in public systems and also limits on private initiative. Increasing the dominance of public messages, while continuing to allow private senders free sway, could result in street names the size of billboards.

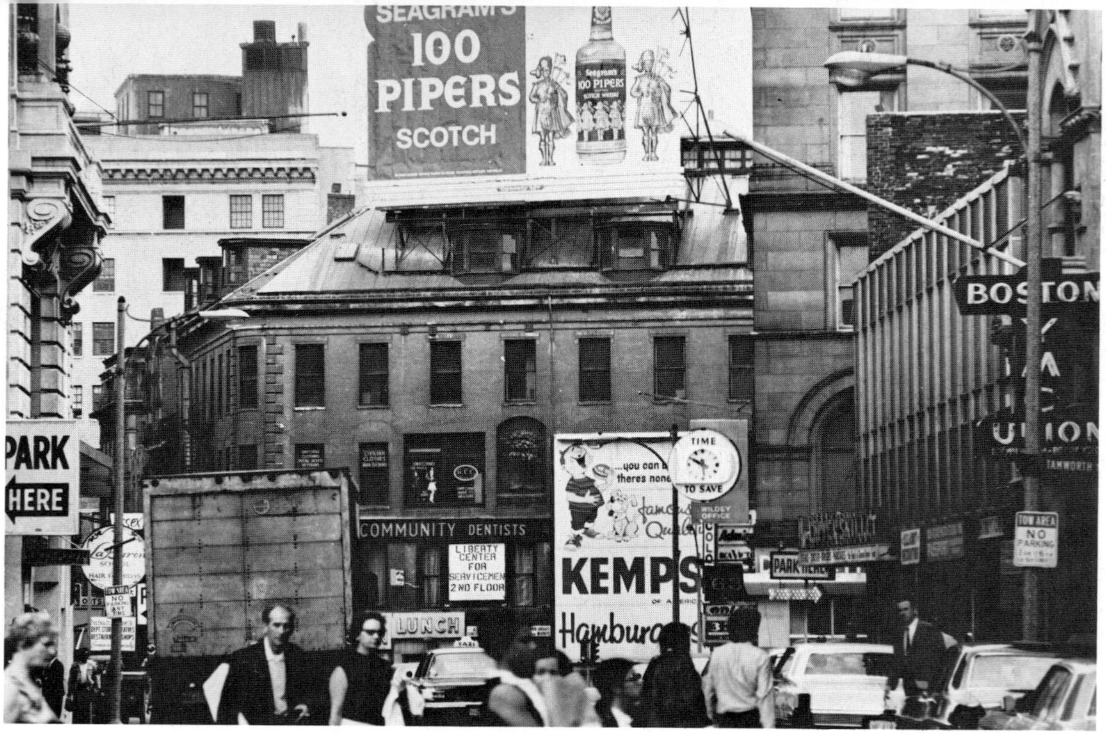

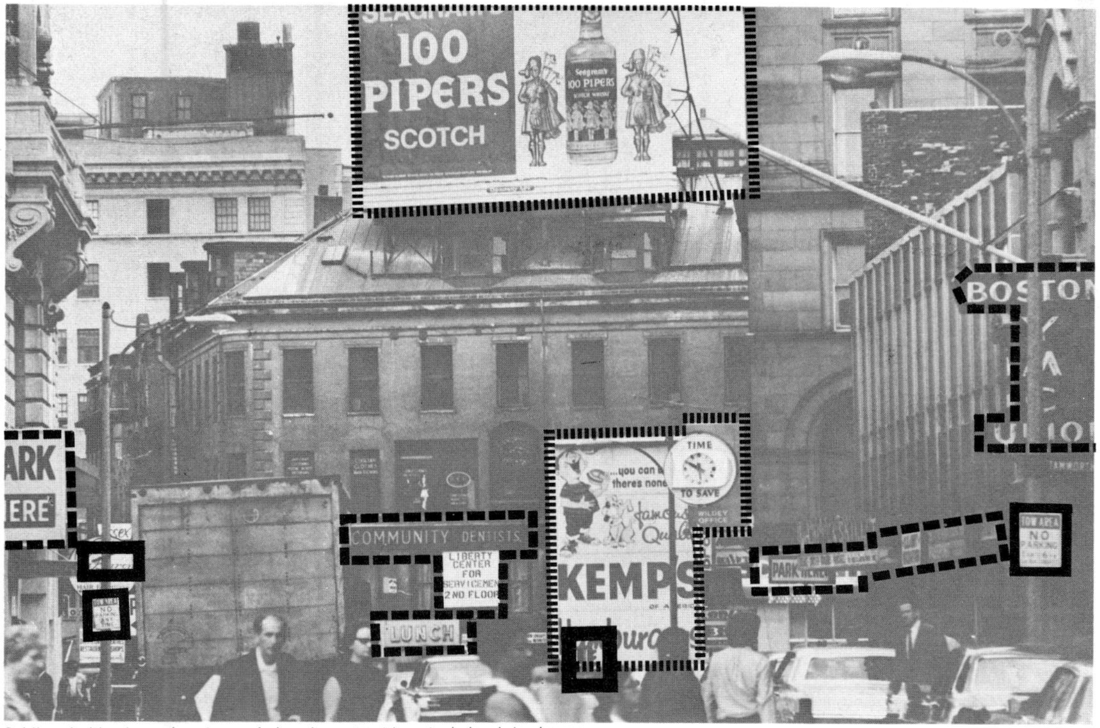

Public priorities for various types of signs in contrast to actual visual dominance.

Most important.

Stop Light and Turning Regulation

Street Name (missing)

Parking Regulation

Identification

Advertising

Least important.

Once priorities are established, one method for avoiding conflict is by visual channeling in relation to familiar patterns of looking. By this system, each type of information would have its own environmental zone with the most important information centrally located in the visual field. Such a system would be designed to reflect public priorities; it would also enable users to be efficient in finding various types of information. Channeling is already a familiar principle for dealing with conflicting traffic flows and regulating the use of radio and television frequency bands.

FRAGMENTED AUTHORITY

Current processes for determining needs, programming information, designing signs and lights, regulating their form and use, and installing the necessary hardware are extremely fragmentary. Since information systems have not yet been seen as interrelated, the responsibility for dealing with them at the city level is normally divided among a number of agencies. For example, in Boston, street lighting is under the control of the Public Works Department, park lighting under the Parks Department, highway lighting under several different agencies at the state level, traffic signing is under control of Traffic and Parking and several state agencies; Public Works, the Building Department and the Zoning Board all have some jurisdiction over private signs; and the Redevelopment Authority advises the Zoning Board. In renewal areas, the Redevelopment Authority may attempt to change all of these elements and may control the funding to do so. Where traffic control devices and lighting are concerned, there are national standards and also regulations which originate on the state and local levels. Private signs and lights are usually subject only to minimum safety regulations.

The present situation in urban guide signing illustrates the problem as it comes down to the driver. The national Manual of Uniform Traffic Control Devices does not set standards for urban guide and information signs. Each agency responsible for such signs has its own system of establishing needs and priorities, develops its own designs, and has its own standards for hardware and installation. These agencies operate on different levels—city, metropolitan, and statewide—so there is little pressure toward coordination of their activities. The driver is confronted with a confusing welter of scattered signs conveying similar messages in dissimilar ways.

Even when the decision-making agencies are all at the local level, cooperation in programming, budgeting, and implementation is rare. Each agency has its own institutional perspective and set of procedures. Public works departments do not normally see lighting as an information system which has effects on traffic flow, control, and orientation. Traffic departments have no control over interference from private signs and lights. Although such coordination is only one of a number of problems, the present decision-making structure militates against it.

Fragmented authority results in uncoordinated systems of equipment in the street. Major breakthroughs are sometimes sought in the development of integrated hardware, as if necessary interrelation among information systems could be achieved through hardware. In nearly every case, the problems described in this chapter can be dealt with by appropriate uses of presently available hardware. The problem of fragmented authority is no exception. Indeed, few environmental information problems require large shifts in hardware design or production. Where innovation is required, as in information systems for people on foot, components either can be adapted from standard ones or are too specialized to local conditions to be manufactured on a national scale.

Efforts to achieve "total integrated hardware" solutions are questionable on a number of grounds. A systematic combination of street fixtures within a single unit would need to be based on integrated planning and programming of the several different information systems which require street fixtures. Not only is each system lodged in a different agency, but also it is governed by a different rate of technological change. If — as in the recent 53rd Street prototype proposed in New York — traffic signing, signal, lighting, and street service systems were fully integrated within "simple" rectangular pylons, subsequent shifts in national traffic control standards (which might require a different spacing of signs or signals) or a new lighting or signal technology (requiring a new system of mounting) would be much more expensive to achieve than if each system were to remain independent. Further, in Boston and in many cities, irregularities in the street pattern make such total integration impractical because of the need for flexibility in adapting to existing field conditions. While some partial integration may be desirable, it can be achieved by minor modifications in existing hardware and, indeed, is already achieved in a number of cities — though not always elegantly.

MDC Green Guide Sign   Garage Trailblazer   State Highway Route No. Sign   City Route No. Sign

The present confusion and clutter of the streetscape need not be accepted as another of the unpleasant facts of urban life. The principal need for integration is not in hardware but in planning, programming, and controlling environmental information sources as a set of interrelated systems. The types of coordination which are necessary will come about through initiative from the mayor's office rather than through hardware. The real potential for change lies in building political support through demonstrating the benefits of new environmental information systems.

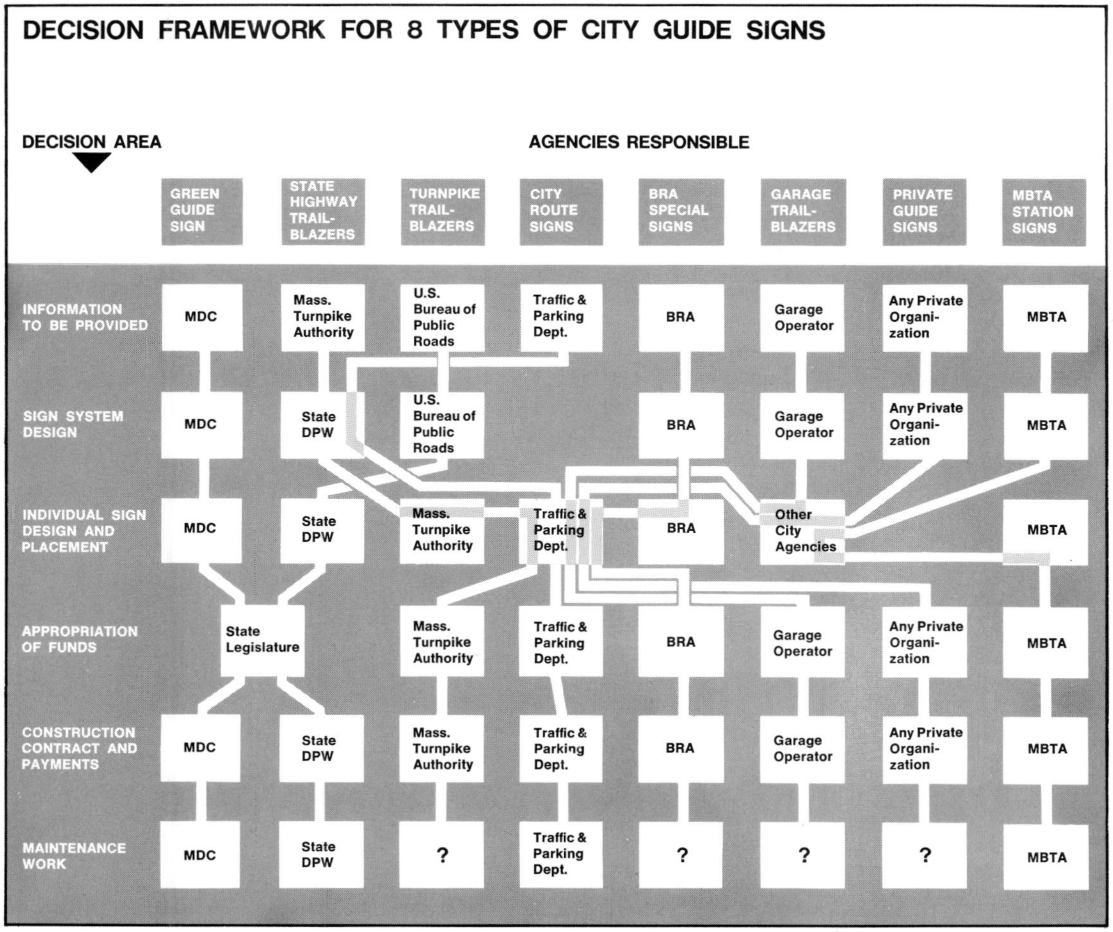

CHAPTER THREE

An Environmental Information Policy

An Environmental Information Policy

The development of an environmental information policy is a new undertaking for city government. While all cities install public signing and lighting and engage in some form of control over private signs and lights, none presently treats these components as a set of environmental information systems. Cities will need to establish criteria, a process for analysis, planning, implementation, and evaluation, and an organizational framework to house new functions.

Information policy can benefit a city in many ways. Environmental information systems can be a means of public education. They directly affect the efficiency and safety of traffic flow. Signs and lights are critical to orientation and to achieving a sense of security in moving about the city. The design of public information systems and the control of private signs and lights can make a city more attractive and reduce visual overload. These benefits and others are illustrated by the policies and prototypical designs described in Chapters 4 and 5. This chapter recommends a set of general criteria, describes the necessary new administrative functions, and discusses alternative frameworks within which these benefits can be realized.

Many conflicts of interest must be faced in establishing environmental information policy: the necessary balance between centralized and decentralized authority, between public and private interests, between receiver and sender control and between big and small senders will only be achieved through a political process which involves both the mayor and the city council. To deal with vested interests which will oppose the policy, the mayor and the council must gain sufficient support both from the public and from agency heads. The outdoor advertising industry, for instance, is not accustomed to being strongly regulated in the large cities and will lobby strongly against such regulation. Rights of private property are often confused with the privilege of using the public environment as a channel for advertising. Further, the public is not generally aware of the benefits a good public information system provides and may oppose new expenditures. Support will be needed from businessmen and, most important, a non-commercial client; this will depend on the success of initial actions and on graphic demonstrations of potential benefits, especially in the area of sign control.

This chapter is written with Boston in mind, but its recommendations are not limited to Boston. Each city, however, will need to make its own analysis of needs and priorities and determine what is viable within its own governmental structure. The task of deciding which criteria, process, and framework are most appropriate and feasible will fall to the mayor, the city council, and the neighborhoods of the city.

CRITERIA

The set of basic general criteria which follows is a guide to developing policy. The particular form and relative weighting of the criteria are matters for public debate. These discussions can be informed both by prototype designs illustrating the environmental consequences of the criteria and by the results of field demonstrations like those carried out by the Signs/Lights/Boston project (see Chapters 4, 5 and 6). Further testing can refine these criteria into operational performance standards by which information planners can evaluate alternative actions. Chapters 4 and 5 include a number of examples of such standards.

Reduce overload — Extreme visual competition for the observer's attention, especially at points where he must make critical driving decisions, should be eliminated. Human capacity to process information is sharply limited. Though the precise number of messages that people can handle under differing environmental conditions is not known, it is certain that people are confused by present message levels at many visually busy intersections. The degree of confusion can be observed and the effectiveness of policy in reducing this confusion can be tested empirically (see Chapter 6).

Respect privacy — Individuals and social groups should be protected from signs and lights which violate their privacy. Preventing unnecessary intrusions into people's private lives is a general and growing problem. Television can be turned off, but environmental advertising often cannot be ignored. Attention demanding features such as large size, high brightness contrast, flashing lights, and the like are so strongly associated with importance that ignoring them requires enormous effort. Sometimes, there is direct intrusion when light spills over through bedroom windows. This type of violation must obviously be prevented; but the city should limit the visual intensity of all public and private messages to levels which are appropriate to the social purpose which they serve (see final criterion).

Clarify control information — Signs and signals necessary for traffic control or emergency must be clear and visible in time to take the necessary action. Ambiguous messages of this type are worse than none at all: at the moment of a life or death decision, it is better to be wary and ignorant than misled. These messages should be conveyed in several ways simultaneously by shape, color, symbols, and by learned associations — red for danger, yellow for caution, green for go, an arrow for direction, and so on. While all of these graphic devices are used in present traffic signing, they are used inconsistently and many words are wasted where arrows or other symbols would do.

Wherever complicated decisions are to be made, there should be an early warning followed by a confirming message at the point of decision. Where the safety risk or social cost of violation is high — entering an exit ramp, for instance — environmental alarm systems should be developed. The bumps in low speed residential roads or the bells at automatic toll booths are examples. Automatic positive reinforcement — like the toll booth "thank you" light — should generally be avoided, since the impersonality of the medium contradicts the message.

Orient in time and space — Signs and lights should provide basic guidance in way-finding and should aid in identifying locations in space and time. Cities are large and complicated and people are increasingly mobile; common knowledge won't suffice. In New England, main streets are often without street-name signs, presumably as an economy measure, on the assumption that everyone knows these streets. Such practices are infuriating and disorienting to the visitor or short-term resident.

Of course, there is far more to orientation than naming streets. A guidance system is needed which covers all major decision points in the city: directions may be given by major streets, districts, nodal points or some combination of these, depending on local custom.

Orientation is easiest when these streets, districts, and nodal points have distinct identity. Signs and lights should reinforce the uniqueness of places in the city. The forms of signing and lighting should directly reflect the flow and activity of people and the spatial structure of a place. For instance, in entertainment districts where people cluster densely together for the fun of it, signs and lights can do the same. In parks where people come together for rest and relaxation, signs and lights should generally be designed and controlled for repose.

Expression of seasonal or other cyclical change also contributes to the expression of place. Except for weather and foliage, our cities show little evidence of cyclical change. Lighting suddenly becomes an expressive element at Christmas time, but for the rest of the year it is merely utilitarian or commercial. Temporary signs, banners, and posters announcing changing events are welcome but infrequent occurrences. The developing technology of outdoor projection and programmed light grids will make it easy to change signs and lights with the seasons, with the weekend, and with the time of day. Although this already occurs at nightfall and again at midnight when most signs go out, it should become a matter of conscious policy.

Beyond cyclical changes, signs and lights should express past, present, and future time; orientation is improved when signs are located appropriately in time as well as space. This does not imply that signs should have "colonial" formats in areas of colonial architecture; this is false expression. There is more, too, to the expression of history than plaques and floodlighting. Boston has numerous signs, traces, and symbols which are genuine relics of the past and should be preserved and enhanced. Large sections of the city are being rebuilt, yet little is done to explain the process and expose the future by means of on-site displays or signs.

Express city functions — The location and flow of people, goods, and services should be expressed, with as much immediacy as possible. Signs and lights should be used to help identify who is active in a place, how, and for what purpose, within the limits of violation of privacy. Often the best way to do this is through direct exposure of the activity or thing itself; the observer can then experience it in several different ways if he chooses. Other devices include a trace of a hidden activity, like the odor outside a restaurant of food being cooked, or a symbol directly evocative of the activity, like the optometrist's eyeglass sign. The final section of Chapter 5 presents some guidelines for expressive signing and lighting.

The basic principle of expressive messages is that visible form should "fit" with the activity and its meaning on as many levels as possible. Thus, as its fullest expression, a bus stop sign would have a picture of a bus, say "stop," give the bus number and stop number, include a map of the route and the scheduling of the bus, and light up as the bus approaches. It would also have a recorded message of public activities and services available on the route, allow patrons to register complaints, look menacing to cars and make an alarming noise if a car tried to park there.

Encourage diverse and responsive communication — Signs, lights, and other informational devices should enable the government of a city and groups and individuals within it to express collective and individual views and values. This is the most sensitive aspect of information policy, since the ability to define issues and express values is a fundamental basis of power. This power now rests mainly in the hands of the mass media and advertisers; though the urban environment is one of the last refuges for individual and small group expression, it is being subjected to increasing constraints.

In part, the problem is to provide more opportunities to small senders and especially to poor or fringe groups which are presently shut out from use of the media. Simple devices such as bulletin boards and poster kiosks are a step in the right direction, but much more should be done to encourage other forms of expression: more personal identification signing and lighting, opportunities for slide and movie presentation in the street, street theater, speakers and teachers, and the like. All of these measures require management to ensure equal time and some form of collective control at the city or local level, depending on the nature of the information.

The problem is also one of responsiveness: signs and lights should increase the ability of the receiver to shut off undesired messages or to get more information or to tailor it to his needs.

Skilled informants are the most responsive source of information, since they can shape answers to the needs and abilities of questioners as well as record their reactions for future reference. Information booths in department stores and transportation terminals are familiar examples. In the future, computers may be able to perform this service. The information system should become adaptive, growing and changing in direct response to issues and values defined by the people who use it — like a good school.

Seize opportunities for education — Environmental information systems should be used as means of public education. They are especially suited to educating people about the environment itself, its structure, function, history, ecology, and possible future development. But they may also be used, like the press and television, to provide information on the nature and occurrence of conflict and cooperation: politics, crime, collective action, meetings, and celebrations. Beyond that, they may be used to educate people about the culture in general, about the variety of ethnic, economic, and social interest groups, and something of their nature and interrelationships. Relations between people and their natural environment can also be described.

Orientation, expression of city function, diverse and responsive communication all contribute to the educational value of information systems. Understanding the basic structure and function of the city is central to learning about its social life. Providing more opportunities for small senders and fringe groups and increasing receiver control over information will improve the educational value of the environment. Responsive information systems and devices can also be programmed for explicit educational purposes.

Establish priorities — To mediate conflicts of interest, environmental information policy must set priorities among various types of information, provide non-overlapping channels for each where possible, and establish controls for the uses of those channels. This is an allocative criterion which affects many of the others.

Some conflicts, like those between public agencies conveying traffic information in inconsistent or contradictory ways, must be eliminated altogether; others, such as those arising from competition among private interests, need only be controlled to reduce dominance of larger senders and to assure more equal distribution of the right to identify a place or activity. Privately controlled messages should not interfere with the transmission of public information; less important public messages should not interfere with more important ones. Certain radio frequency bands are restricted for official use. The same principle should be applied to the public environment: since the motorist's attention is principally straight ahead and becomes more focused as speed increases, traffic control and guidance information should be located as centrally as possible within this cone of vision and the intrusion of private signs within this field should be minimized. Among public messages, those controlling intersecting flows of people and cars should dominate, using centrality, intensity of color, uniqueness of shape, simplicity of message form, figure ground contrast, and illumination. Streets must be lit well enough to silhouette pedestrians and obstacles at safe stopping distances, depending on the class of street. Orientation information is next in importance and should be next in visual dominance. Policy should also give high priority to messages which express basic city function, especially the location of goods and services, public and private. Next would come general educational messages and those which express social issues and values, including — as the lowest priority — advertising messages.

When private signs and lights are uncontrolled, locations having the highest visibility are usurped by large advertisers for billboards and other super-signs. This domination has its limits — availability of leasable space and the market for such advertising — but since by location and design these signs are all but impossible to avoid and since people's attention capacity is easily overloaded, they constrict choice. If the attention seizing features of signs and lights are appropriate to the information needs of people, no one sign will so dominate as to obscure the others. The observer should be able to search freely among messages to select those he needs. The right of identification of an activity should be based on the principle of sufficient visibility of signs to enable passing motorists to stop safely, rather than being determined by length of frontage and ability to pay for signs or lights.

For a city administration to adopt a set of criteria such as these implies that it is ready to make changes in present practice. The city must be prepared to treat signing and lighting as interrelated information systems. The priorities among types of information recommended here represent a reversal of present practice. The emphasis given to orientation, expression of city functions, the encouragement of diverse and responsive communication, and education will be new to most cities. Chapters 4 and 5 show how these criteria can develop into detailed performance criteria, many of them illustrated and tested by programs and prototype designs for particular locations in Boston. Chapter 6 describes how the success of particular policies can be evaluated by field tests of public response, which can result in modifications of the policies, the criteria, or both.

PROCESS

To meet criteria like these, particular changes are needed in the processes by which environmental information systems are evaluated, planned, programmed, and installed. Overall, the process must be made more politically accountable to public needs and less a function of conventional bureaucratic procedures. The necessary first steps are in public education and analysis of needs and priorities to validate a set of criteria like those suggested. Chapter 7 describes one possible sequence for this organizing phase. Besides legitimizing new criteria for environmental information systems, the expected outcome of this initial phase is a new definition of necessary information planning functions.

Setting basic criteria, analyzing and defining needs, and establishing priorities are highly political phases of the process, even if they are not currently treated as such. As with many urban problems, issues in the planning and development of environmental information systems are largely defined by existing functional divisions within the city's organizational structure, in the context of past practices and hardware. Professional and trade organizations, industry, and the federal government in the case of traffic signing, influence or even determine these definitions and priorities, but as usual no one speaks for the needs of the people who must use these systems. Cities establish codes, ordinances, and departmental practices based on these professional, industrial, or federal standards as modified by local expert opinion and experience. There is little else that a city administration can do, since they have no access to public perception of needs and priorities except as they are occasionally interpreted by the local press or TV.

One new function will be on-going analyses of public information needs, coupled with continuing evaluation of the effectiveness of present and future systems. One part of this should involve working with local groups to learn how signing and lighting problems are perceived in local communities. But this type of analysis will prove difficult or impossible in cities where planning advisory groups do not already exist at the community level. In a few communities, special purpose groups of residents and businessmen might be organized to deal with local information systems, but not on a city-wide basis.

For most public signing and lighting, local needs will be little different from general needs, so that field analysis by professionals, like that described in Appendix 4, should be sufficient. This identification of problems and potentials in relation to general criteria must be supplemented by field inspection and inventory of existing systems as the work goes into the programming phase. Such inventories are already made, albeit with little or no coordination between agencies, and no new skills will be required.

The same staff which is involved with field analyses of problems and potentials should also be studying public reaction to new systems as they are installed, and here new skills are needed. The Signs/Lights/Boston project had its own psychological testing function and many of the proposed policies were modified as a result of it. There is no way to fit information systems to peoples' needs except by continually evaluating public effects. Feedback and evaluation skills naturally combine with analytical abilities; there would need to be a substantial staff concerned with these functions, in constant touch with design and planning staffs in the development of policies. All these new functions will have to be integrated with normal programming, budgetary analyses, and implementation.

Setting priorities will not be a direct result of analysis of public needs. Rather, it must result from dialogue among information planners, agency heads, community and other interest groups, and ultimately the mayor and city council. Since environmental information systems are currently not seen as interrelated, there is no coordinated program of development. Priority setting occurs in the final preparation of the budget for submission to the council and is thus in the mayor's (or manager's) hands. At that point, however, it is too late to develop an integrated approach to the problem since the definition of need and the development of specific priorities, policies, and standards has already been done on a fragmented basis. Thus, a second principal process need is for a coordinative function at an early stage in policy development.

National action is needed to aid cities in implementing information policy. Basic changes in traffic signing, like those recommended in Chapter 4, should be tested over large parts of several cities before changes in national standards are made. Demonstration funds are currently available through the "TOPICS" program of the U.S. Department of Transportation and use of these funds for such tests could result in a significant advance in general highway signing. Lighting improvements can also be partially supported under existing programs like the Crime Control and Safe Streets Act of 1968 administered by the U.S. Department of Justice and the Urban Beautification and Improvement Program of the U.S. Department of Housing and Urban Development. Economies of scale introduced through schemes like the Urban America five-city consortium could be significant in reducing the cost of public information hardware.

New programs are needed to support the development of information systems for pedestrians and improvements in private signs and lights. A program to fund a system of information centers and other communication devices to aid pedestrians would be an excellent way to redress the balance with support for motorists. This might be done by matching funds with private contributions, under the control of the city, as in the Urban Beautification program. Rapid improvement in private signs and lighting could be achieved through a roadway rehabilitation program by which property improvement grants and low interest loans are made available as in "concentrated code enforcement programs." Even limited funds of this type could have a significant impact in a few key city areas. This program might include compensation payments for condemned sign or lighting development rights to be discussed in Chapter 7.

While much of the funding for these new functions will necessarily come from new or existing federal programs, there are also some attractive possibilities for joint public and private development (see Chapters 4 and 5). The city might design and test prototypes for private signing and lighting, with the assistance of private contributions, to demonstrate ways to improve the character of local shopping areas. As another instance, the pedestrian information system described in Chapter 4 has obvious potential for local advertising. Parts of such a system might be an attractive venture for certain private developers even though the city would retain control over information content and presentation.

FRAMEWORK

The new environmental information functions could be housed in various ways, each with its own implications for policy. There are three general approaches.

The line of least resistance is to leave system responsibilities where they are — in several agencies — adding new staff and functions where necessary. This approach puts the planning and evaluation where the money and action capability already are. Moreover, it doesn't rock the boat: administrative territories and decision structures remain essentially intact. Political and bureaucratic resistance would be minimized.

On the other hand, the usual problems in coordinating the planning and action of several agencies would persist. This report argues that public and private signing and lighting are best considered and developed as a set of related systems, especially in central areas where public use is intense. The problem illustrated in Chapter 2, where a single system (guide signing) is dealt with by several agencies, represents an extreme form of the general coordination problem. Nevertheless, some gain would normally result from improving one system even without improving the others.

The inertia of present attitudes and procedures within agencies is another serious difficulty in this first approach. Established patterns in defining needs, planning, and budgeting, and in selecting, purchasing, installing, and maintaining public equipment will naturally be resistant to change. To treat public lighting as an information system involves a shift in perspective and, more important, a shift in the procedures by which needs are assessed and performance is evaluated. In public signing, significant shifts are required to make guidance and identification systems central concerns and to deal with them adequately. Similarly, the information system for pedestrians proposed in Chapter 4 and the informational controls in private signing and lighting proposed in Chapter 5 do not fit neatly within the concerns of most existing development or zoning agencies.

For existing line agencies to take on these additional functions will require new staff for analysis, planning, design, and evaluation. In most cases the new staff would be a small increment to the existing staff and would likely encounter substantial resistance to its proposals if they involved shifts in approach and procedure. Informally, these "information planners" could be expected to be in touch with each other across agency lines, and this contact may be formalized in cities which have a development coordinator in the mayor's or manager's office; but their ability to reinforce each other would be limited by their necessary loyalty to their own agencies. So while this line of least resistance alternative may be a reasonable choice for many cities, there is a real risk that it will not have much effect on environmental information systems.

The second approach for an organizational framework is to centralize the analysis, design, and planning functions and resources within one existing agency or office. This should be an agency which already has some of the desired functions and can deal on an equal basis with agencies responsible for installation of information hardware or the enforcement of regulations over private media. In most cities, the likely contenders will be the planning and development agency (or the planning agency, if these functions are split), the public works department, or the mayor's office.

The choice of the planning or development agency as a locus for new staff and resources has one major advantage. It is the agency most likely already to have people carrying out functions relevant to developing and monitoring environmental information programs. Although the development of a new city-wide information policy will require additional staff, and probably the establishment of a new section, incremental phasing is simpler where people with relevant skills already exist. Some designers and planners who have been working on physical change at a large scale may find it difficult to shift to the incremental approach appropriate to environmental information policy, but many have worked incrementally and others will be able to change.

Unfortunately for this alternative, planning and development agencies lack the power to implement city-wide environmental information policy. Even when the agency has development powers and controls funds, as in urban renewal areas, most improvements in public signing and lighting are programmed and implemented by other agencies. This divorce between planning and implementation has been the cause of many of the past failures of planning agencies. Even a public works department does not control all components of the systems and would have difficulties in implementation. It would also suffer severe problems in staff orientation and skills if assigned full responsibility for environmental information policy.

New planning, programming, budgeting, and evaluation functions located in the mayor's office create a quite different set of implications. This alternative emphasizes the political aspects of the policy and maximizes its potential for rapid, visible, and relatively low-cost environmental change which would win approval of many voters while alienating comparatively few. If the mayor is strong, a new group lodged in his office may be in a good position to influence the operations of the action agencies. The group would be politically more accountable for its programs and highly dependent on the political fortunes of the mayor.

In most cities, locating information policy functions in the mayor's office would imply a short-term task force operation. On the other hand, a number of cities are establishing development coordinators in the mayor's office. In Boston, the mayor has recently proposed that general planning, budgeting, and evaluation functions be consolidated in a new "Executive Office of Administration."

In any event, the success of information policy will depend on a long-term commitment allowing for continual feedback and revision. This continuity might be accomplished by shifting the operation to an existing agency or to a new one when the initial programs are underway. In this strategy, the mayor's group is the seed for the growth of a major new program. A measure of accountability to various interest groups could be achieved by the establishment of an advisory board including a wide representation — district representatives, businessmen, educators, historic conservationists, architects, planners and designers, and representatives of the various agencies. However, even the initial housing of the program in the mayor's office may be resisted where the city council is reluctant to assign new powers and resources to the mayor. (For the full development of this strategy, see Chapter 7).

The third approach is to centralize analysis, planning, implementation, and evaluation within a single new agency conceived at either a city or regional level. It might prove easier to shift existing responsibilities to a separate agency, justified by the need for this broad function, than to add them to any existing agency. Such an agency would be charged with more than the development of policy and programs for environmental information systems. It would be an educational agency, exposing and amplifying environmental information and increasing channels for new information, as well as improving and controlling the means of information presentation. It would also be concerned with encouraging, developing, and testing experimental and responsive information outlets. It might deal with public information and education through conventional outlets such as television, radio, the press, and other media. The urban environment is potentially a vast underdeveloped resource for educational experience and an agency of this sort would be better able to exploit it than any other.

The new agency should be directly responsible to the mayor and the city council, rather than an appointed board. The appointed board can be a useful device, but lacks both the power of the mayor and the political legitimacy of the council. However, the powers of the agency will need careful definition and protection in order to avoid creating a new monopoly which could be subverted to distortion and suppression of information. Its relation with the school system will be a sensitive issue; and when the information function is thus centralized and made visible, political and commercial interests will immediately press to capture it.

The new "Department of City Information" should have all necessary powers of analysis, planning, and implementation to create and maintain a public system of signs and lights and supplementary information sources, such as information centers. While the control of private signs and lights is best accomplished through existing zoning mechanisms (see Chapter 5), the DCI should draft the regulations, work with local groups, monitor, and review. It should be able to conduct limited experiments and prototypical demonstrations of new or unrealized potentials in both the public and private sectors.

The central difficulty with this last proposal is of course the administrative *tour de force* necessary to shift programming and implementation functions from existing agencies to the new agency. While many of the existing people might go along with their responsibilities to the new agency, many established working relationships would be broken or badly strained. The desirability of the broad educational function that the DCI would perform is not yet widely recognized. City councils are rightfully wary of creating more bureaucracy, especially if it seems to increase the mayor's power over something as politically important as the flow of information. To establish the new agency would require strong initiative from a strong mayor and agreement from existing agencies about its powers and responsibilities. The new agency must be on an equal footing with other line agencies if it is to relate to them properly; if it is to be effective, it must have the continuing support of the mayor and be responsive to his concerns.

The issue of who will control a city information process could become a highly sensitive one. Control over information is a source of power; information and propaganda cannot be easily separated. The present confusion and lack of control clearly favor the large private senders at the expense of receivers and public senders alike, but on the other hand centralized, politically-motivated control could be even more destructive to receiver control, education, and self-expression. If any city information program is to be mounted, greater centralization of authority in one public office may be a necessity, but there must be checks on the potential abuse of that authority for purely partisan purposes.

A workable information process will have to combine centralized and decentralized control, and the determination of which kind of control is used will be based upon the type of information, the type of channel, and the predominant type of receiver. Information dealing with orientation or with the regulation of traffic clearly should be centrally controlled (starting at the national level), and regulation of private signing and lighting must be done on a city-wide basis (although such regulations must be sensitive to the individual character of city zones). It is also clear that some types of centrally provided information — such as that on ecology and history — strengthen local identity.

Local control over locally significant information policy could be achieved within any of the several organizational frameworks. The necessary condition for the decentralization of authority is the existence of locally accountable organizations with geo-political legitimacy. Groups which are accountable to real communities with sociological, spatial, and historical integrity have a legitimate claim to control environment information in their own areas. In Boston, the new Local Advisory Committees now being established by the mayor's Office of Public Services may meet some of these conditions. Thus, information on local issues, organizations, and programs can and should be handled locally by such committees, with technical and financial assistance from the central authority. These groups could also choose their own type of public lighting, as long as it meets city standards, and propose additional regulations on private signs and lights if they so choose.

This report intentionally stops short of a particular organizational recommendation for Boston, since the necessary analysis of Boston's government and politics was not a part of the study. If the mayor's recently proposed reorganization of city government* were put into effect, there would still appear to be three organizational alternatives for information policy: the new Department of Development, the Executive Office of Administration, or an additional new agency. Although a new agency with broad educational functions may be the most desirable choice for many cities, in Boston it may not be a politically viable proposal at this time or may not even be the most appropriate framework for action.

Administrative organization is an essential part of a policy for environmental information. The feasibility of most of the particular policies and programs recommended in the chapters to follow will be strongly affected by the organizational framework as will the overall success of information policy. Where it has been necessary to make administrative assumptions in the rest of this report, the choice has been made in favor of a new Department of City Information.

* The mayor has proposed to reallocate the functions of more than a dozen existing agencies into four new action departments plus an Executive Office of Administration to do analysis, planning, budgeting, and evaluation. The four new departments would be called the Department of Development, the Department of Housing Services, the Department of Building Regulations, and the Department of General Services.

CHAPTER FOUR

Public Environmental Information Systems

Arlington St
81-50
Berkeley St
Providence St.

Public Environmental Information Systems

Public information systems carry a critical part of the vast quantity of information in the urban landscape. Public signing and lighting transmit messages which are essential to the efficiency, security, meaningfulness, and pleasure of city life. Sometimes, as at intersections, this information can be a matter of life or death. It is typical of public systems, however, that they are haphazardly designed and that the information is meager and inconsistently and unimaginatively presented. This chapter describes a set of concrete policies for improving the transmission of essential and desirable public information, to increase its scope and its relevance to the needs of people.

Much of the information in the public environment is there to serve the purposes of private individuals or organizations. The regulation of privately owned signs and lights is the subject of the next chapter but these information sources cannot be ignored here. Privately and publicly owned signs and lights sometimes conflict and sometimes complement one another. Some of the policies in this chapter indicate how public agencies can intervene to increase the effectiveness of private signs which serve a public purpose by identifying and expressing activity. However, a necessary complement to many of the public information policies is the exercise of greater public control over visual intrusions of privately owned signs and lights.

As a first priority for public systems, the network of streets, intersections, and open spaces must be made understandable and memorable. Unless we are able to get around the city with a sense of well-being, much of its potential for serving and enriching our lives is lost.

People need to know the destination choices available to them and the best ways to get there; en route, they must know the rules of the road and be able to travel safely. Improved informational devices can do much to simplify the movement systems in operation, through clearer and more complete signing, marking and signaling, and by lighting which aids in understanding the system.

There are two broad groups with different requirements for the presentation of information: people on foot and people in cars. Under most circumstances, people on foot are able to stop and delve into information. Like a good painting, a good book or a good building, an information system for people on foot should be designed to sustain both a casual glance and a prolonged involvement. Information systems for people in cars, on the other hand, must strive for extreme simplicity and high immediate visual impact. Subtle effects cannot be appreciated from a moving car and may be dangerous.

Policies for people on foot include specifications for a city-wide basic system and policies for increasing the informativeness and expressiveness of central streets and spaces. Policies for people in cars concentrate on prototypical sign, signal, marking and lighting systems, and interchange design. Sometimes the systems overlap — as at intersections. In Boston, responsibility for development of the two systems presently falls within the domain of different agencies: for people on foot, the Redevelopment Authority and the Parks Department; for people in cars, Traffic and Parking and Public Works Departments.

Wherever possible, for the most general and most critical policies, field tests were conducted by demonstration experiments, and their effects on observers were evaluated in detail. For some of the less critical policies, field demonstrations were carried out but were evaluated only by professionals. Sometimes the findings from the tests were inconclusive, but in general the effectiveness of the principal proposals for public information systems was confirmed by evaluations of public response. In many particulars, these policies were changed by the results of these tests.

Within the broad division between the needs of people on foot and people in cars, the policy proposals consider some special groups. Several policies for central streets and spaces aim to increase and improve the information available to shoppers as well as to make the shopping experience more pleasant. The policies also provide greater support for communication among people downtown and create opportunities for education and public celebration in the street. Other policies aim to increase the enjoyment of people seeking entertainment downtown. Foreign travelers, the illiterate, and children would benefit from a traffic signing system which relied more on visual symbols and less on words. Younger people seem to find experimentation with light and sound particularly appealing. Transit riders need better signs. Tourists need to learn how to get around and what there is to see and do. The needs of people in low-income communities also place special requirements on information systems.

Still other groups whose needs might have been analyzed were ignored for reasons of time and cost. What, for instance, are the special needs of children or the aged? What are the special needs of various ethnic groups or of particular communities? Further field research, conducted with the full participation of the people affected, must be an integral part of carrying out these policies, especially in the development of the system for people on foot.

Information Systems for People on Foot

CINEMA
MERCHANTS
MUTUAL
INSURANCE
COMPANY

Information Centers: An Experimental Demonstration

On April 25, 1969, in Park Square in the middle of downtown Boston, Mayor Kevin White inaugurated an experimental information center. It was a full-scale working model, built to demonstrate and test a set of ideas for permanent centers. It was evaluated over 33 days of continuous 24-hour operation.

The center was a new public place, created by re-paving an under-used area of the street to sidewalk level and erecting a cluster of eight brightly colored information kiosks topped by 12 foot translucent plastic balloons. Each kiosk served a different purpose and had its own type of information. All information was designed to be on call, easily available when and if someone wanted it, but otherwise unobtrusive.

Large, constantly changing groups of people were attracted at all hours from nearby bus and airlines terminals, a major hotel, and a transit stop. During its four weeks in Park Square the center was visited by more than 80,000 shoppers, office workers coming and going, lunch-time strollers, people on their way to and from nearby places of entertainment, and tourists.

The center was designed to test three main hypotheses:

1 Basic information on the city's diverse activities, its physical structure, its history and culture can be presented in a manner that people will find both useful and engaging.

2 An information center can become a local forum for communications of all kinds and can itself stimulate people to talk with each other.

3 Information centers can be designed to evolve by means of feedback mechanisms which enable content to continually be made more relevant to the needs and interests of the people who use it.

In its location, form, and content, the Park Square experimental center was a prototype for a proposed network of centers which would be the backbone of a city-wide information system for people on foot.

LOCATION

Every city has major junctions where several movement systems interlock. Here people begin or end trips or transfer from one type of transportation to another. In the greater Boston area, historic junctions such as Harvard Square, Dudley Square, and Fields Corner are both gateways and centers for the activities concentrated in their surrounding areas.

Park Square is an important junction. It is an ideal location to transmit information to people

1

4

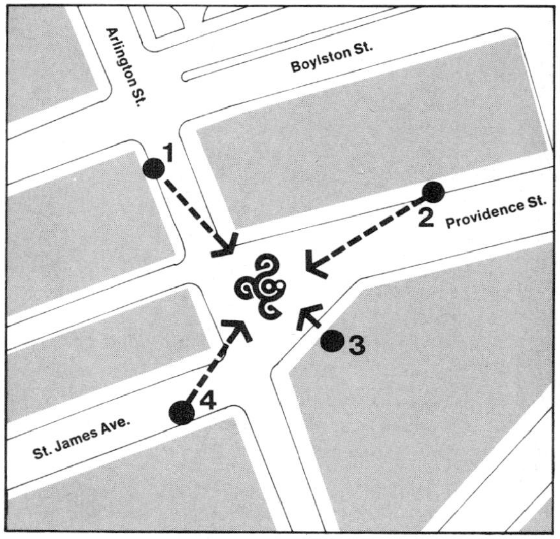

2

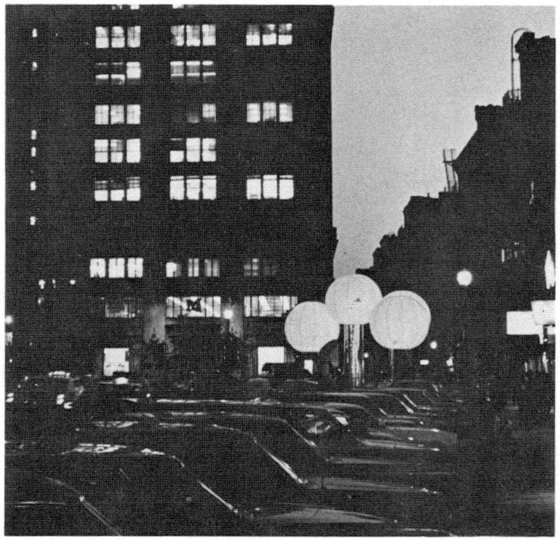

on foot, except that it lacks a focal point where people can gather. There are two long-haul bus terminals (Trailways and Greyhound), an airline terminal, a major taxi rank (Statler Hilton), and a subway stop (Arlington). The reclaimed portion of the street was located in full view of people leaving these terminals.

3

FORM

The balloons, bright colors, and reflective surfaces were attractive from a distance and, along with the information content, created a pleasant and interesting place to stop and talk. Many people received explicit new information and many left the center with a new sense of what public space in the city can be. According to one observer of many who made similar comments: ". . . it adds an extra dimension to the city, and I'd like to see more projects like this displayed around the city so other people can stop and enjoy themselves now and then."

The center allowed for free movement through it. It became an "eddy" in the flow of people. Given the extreme shortage of public space not given over to cars in our cities, an open form will not always be easy to achieve while maintaining necessary traffic connections. In Park Square, an existing island with a raised planter and a small tree added some additional potential for creating a gathering place. Moveable seats and platforms were provided.

CONTENT

What is Nearby?

The center was designed to serve the people who would ordinarily be in Park Square. Three of the kiosks presented detailed information on activities within easy walking distance (ten minutes, or about one-quarter mile).

The information came from questionnaires which were sent to every activity listed in the city directory within the quarter mile radius. Questionnaire replies normally included a description of the activity, the groups of people likely to be interested, and any special facilities, programs, or services (available to whom, when, and at what cost). This information was sorted into classes of similar activities and reproduced on revolving directories. The descriptions were in the words of the person answering the questionnaire (he was identified by name and phone number). Each activity was keyed to a grid location on a map above the directory. The maps were drawn three-dimensionally to give a sense of the "look" of the city. The map and directory allowed people to mentally explore the area in terms of its shopping, entertainment, transportation, and other public and social services.

Each kiosk also offered a series of vivid impressions of the experiences associated with the activities on the directories. Slide and sound shows presented an unorthodox view of Boston which often seemed to give people a new sense of the city's possibilities. Slide-sound "chains" are an effective and relatively inexpensive form of presentation which allow for frequent changes of content. Several private and semi-public groups spontaneously requested the opportunity to say their piece through this medium. Further developed, the technique could make use of a coding system on the slides and random access projectors: an observer could locate a particularly appealing place on the map — perhaps by a flashing light — or he could immediately see a slide of a place listed in the directory.

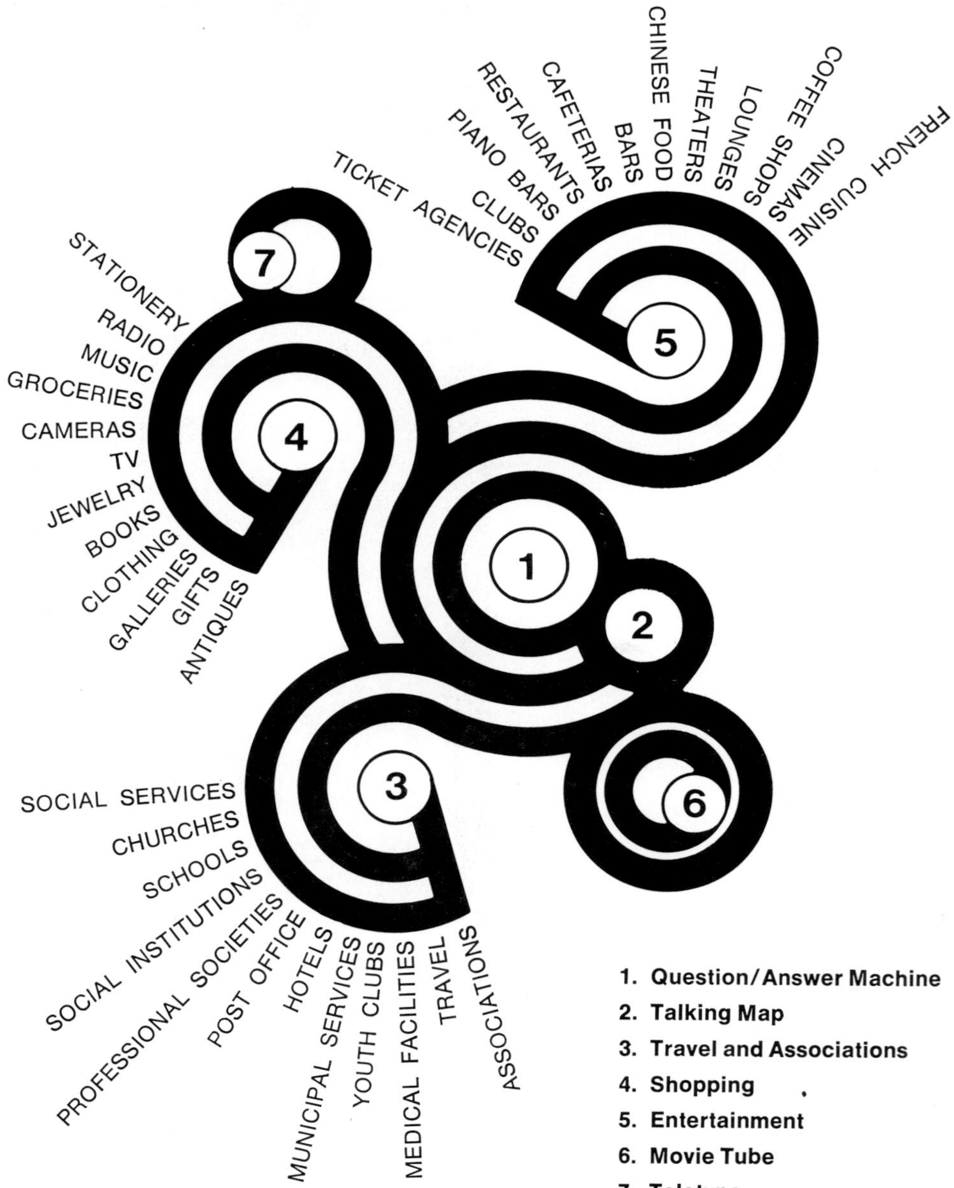

1. Question/Answer Machine
2. Talking Map
3. Travel and Associations
4. Shopping
5. Entertainment
6. Movie Tube
7. Teletype

associations

D-5 DRUG ADDICTION REHABILITATION BOARD
80 Boylston Street =1201 phone/542-4664/65

Information from Lawrence D. Gaughan, Administrator
Activities/Treatment and rehabilitation units providing in-patient and out-patient services for persons having a problem with drug dependency; intensive after-care services; research program into drug dependency; educational and preventive programs; training and orientation for profesisonal and civic groups.
Services available without fee at Boston State Hospital, Department of Mental Health, Mattapan, Mass., Drug Addiction Treatment Unit, Department of Mental Health and Hospitals, 20 Whittier Street, Roxbury, Mass.
Services limited to particular groups: for information consult Administrative Officer of the Drug Addiction Rehabilitation Board.

D-4 CARE INC./NEW ENGLAND REGIONAL OFFICE
120 Boylston Street = 305 phone/542-5387

Information from Richard J. Calandrella, Assistant New England Director
help themselves to a decent future; sends MEDICO doctors, nurses and medical technicians to practice

There are many other possible extensions of this directory service. The shopping tube, for example, could present changing information on sales as a part of the slide shows. The kiosk should also incorporate a free telephone to register complaints with the Better Business Bureau or a city *ombudsman.* Value information from *Consumer Reports* and other sources should be available at the push of a button on a time sharing computer terminal.

The travel and associations tube should also have its free telephones with direct connections to the Tourist Information Center in the Common and open lines for hotel and travel bookings. A battery of taped messages or the same computer terminal should be available for more information on services and institutions. This could also be done by open telephone lines. Airline, train and bus schedules, cost information, and local guides should also be available on call.

The entertainment tube should incorporate a system for displaying (visually or audially) the changing schedules of floor shows, movies, and other performances. By means of the computer terminal, a selection of reviews from various sources could also be on call. The system could also operate movie projectors in the film tube (described later) which would make it possible to preview current attractions. Here also there should be a phone to register complaints.

What is Boston?
Information at the center also aimed to increase people's understanding of the city's structure: physical, governmental, economic, cultural, and social — past, present, future. Explaining things about the city need not be boring. People in the street are not likely to spend hours perusing a general plan or a history book, but they may want to take advantage of succinctly presented facts.

An available device for doing this is the question/answer machine (Directomat). It is a random-access information retrieval machine with a capacity of 120 answer plates that will select and print a take-away card when any of the question buttons on the face of the machine is pressed. The question/answer machine in the center included information on general orientation ("Directions from Park Square," "Untangling Boston," "Directions to Major Destinations"), things to do ("Suggested Activities in Boston," "Excursions out of Boston"), facts of Boston's history and culture, information on public services and on future plans for the city.

The question/answer machine was the most popular display in the center. The number of times the buttons were pushed indicates the relative popularity of the various types of information:

Total number of questions asked over 32 days:	84,940*
Average daily figure:	2,654

*An average of 2 questions per minute for 32 days.

Categories of questions, listed in order of popularity:

1. General Knowledge — questions on sports, voting habits, cultural, regional and geographic points of interest
2. Directions from Park Square
3. The New Boston
4. Boston History
5. Excursions out of Boston
6. Cultural Boston
7. Suggested Activities
8. Associations, Institutions, Agencies
9. Untangling Boston
10. Directions to Major Destinations

welfare and family service agencies?

110. Can I take evening courses in the area's major universities?

the new boston

111. What is happening to Copley Square?

112. Where has progress already been made in renewing a blighted neighborhood?

113. Where can I see the first examples of a new concept in subway station design?

114. What are the distinguishing features of the new City Hall? Who designed it?

115. Where can I see Le Corbusier's only North American building?

116. What are some good examples of contemporary architecture in the Boston area?

Specific questions most asked:

How many pennants and World Series championships have the Boston Red Sox won?	4,035
Where did Boston get its name? What was the Indian name for the area?	3,266
What would be a good 20-minute drive to begin to know the city?	2,697
What is happening to Copley Square?	2,593

Specific questions asked least:

Directions to Old Downtown	128
Directions to Copley Square	158
Directions to Dock Square	165

In general, there appeared to be a strong preference for information dealing with history, change, and other dynamic issues and a low demand for specific directions, better conveyed by maps.

This experience represents a small step in a promising direction. But the Directomat, unfortunately, is stupid: it has a tiny memory and no flexibility in question or answer. A more developed system would make use of a time sharing computer with its vastly larger capacity, attached to a local console and teletype, TV display system like those used in airports, or an X-Y plotter which could make maps. Many more questions could be asked. With more development, it would be possible, though costly, to enter into dialogue with the machine, which would search through its memory on the basis of key phrases until relevant information was found. Computerized library information systems already under study could be adapted to this use.

What's Happening and How Do I Get There?

Talking maps

The most convenient map of the city is one that you can carry with you. The available fold-up maps, however, generally fail to give a sense of city form apart from the street pattern. For this purpose, isometric maps are better; they can show the three-dimensional form of the city, picking out key landmarks realistically and indicating the general building and open space texture.

Maps such as these should be spread throughout the center city at rapid transit stops, large parking garages, parks, public buildings (State House, City Hall, hospitals), and high-use commercial buildings. These maps refer the viewer to the nearest information center. Similar street maps, with perhaps only the major public buildings in three dimensions but including the street numbering system, should be distributed as a free city service and would be a very useful addition to the yellow pages of the telephone book.

The map in the center itself had an audio system describing city events of the day at the punch of a button. This "talking" map was much used. The principle could be extended by a system of lights on the map, which would be coded to flash at the locations of events mentioned on the sound tape. The computer system could then produce simple computer graphic maps to these destinations.

Local events

The small poster seems to have passed from city streets. These posters can make a lively display and allow institutions, small groups, and individuals to send messages to the public. Free space in an established center could be filled with continually changing information on local theatre groups, art shows, rallies, meetings, speeches, and the other small events that make up city life. Personal messages would also be given space; only product advertisements would be prohibited.

Such space must be managed by the city. Size and location of posters and other messages must be controlled to assure equal exposure. Where space is restricted, redundancy should not be allowed. Messages must be dated and removed after an appropriate period to prevent staleness.

Backtalk: What Do You Think?
An opportunity to say what you think and hear what others think is essential in an information center. Information need not be transmitted in one direction only. Attendants are important but machines can also help.

People were invited to talk into a telephone handset linked to a recording and playback device. The intake tape (minus obscenities) was played back to anyone lifting the handset. This response phone was in use continually and was an important source of spontaneous criticism and suggestions for improving the center.

The comments were overwhelmingly positive. For instance, on one 40 minute tape with 216 comments, 141 were favorable. Thirty-six people responded negatively: of these 15 thought it a waste of money, and the rest didn't like it for other reasons. The other 39 comments were a mixture of opinions about Boston and life in general.

Some comments from the tape:

This is one of the greatest, most fabulous, progressive things that's ever happened in Boston in my entire lifetime.

It's a damn waste of money and time.

I think this is the greatest thing since coca cola. I think with taxes out of our own pocket money we should have a unit like this installed on every other street corner in downtown Boston. No matter what it costs, we need it.

I think the renewal department and the housing department, or the ones responsible for something like this — it's really tragic. There are people out of jobs and there are a lot of things they could do for people who really need the money.

Why shouldn't I get a chance to say something when everybody else is saying something and I think I should be listened to. I'm very happy to have this occasion and be out here on this beautiful day and these balloons floating all around and ask a million questions and get a million answers. Very interesting.

What's New in the World

Instant news

News, even hotter than off the press, can be engaging even when it is trivial. News print-out was fed from a UPI teletype machine into a basket and could be torn from the spout and taken away. The basket was always empty; people seemed to want these scraps of news. As one observer said: "You don't have to go and buy a newspaper. You can just read what's happening. Also, it's fun to watch a teletype machine, 'cause I never saw one before."

A permanent information center might also incorporate a regular newsstand, with national and international newspapers and magazines and browsing space. Television and radio news programs, news reels and international slide shows of various kinds would also be desirable. Current and changing information on time, weather, and on traffic conditions for various forms of transport could also be provided. A special telephone could connect people to appropriate sources for answers to direct questions like, "What is the weather *now*?"

Cities and other things
The movie tube was a viewer-activated multiple display of silent films mostly about cities and particularly about Boston. Some of these were prepared by the project staff, but educational loops on many topics are available. The standard 8 millimeter film loops were four minutes long and were projected on six tubular screens in any combination, at the choice of the viewers. Given a network of centers, a microwave TV system would allow films of general significance to be seen simultaneously at all of them.

The loops are not expensive and could be changed frequently. Institutions and service groups who produce their own films to explain their activities to the public could show them here. Amateur film-makers could present short impressions and expressive commentaries on city life through this medium. Like the poster kiosks and the slide-sound shows, the movie tube provides another opportunity for small senders of information.

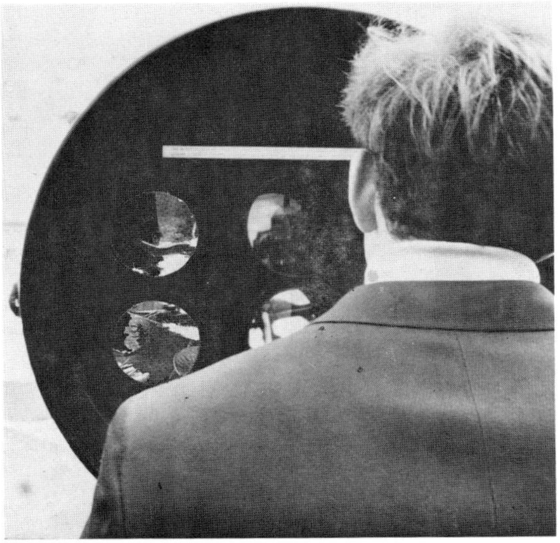

EVALUATION

A Place To Be

The most encouraging response to the center was that people chose to spend time there. The average was 20 minutes per visitor which means that many people were there longer. Apparently, an occasion to idle, to talk and to watch, offers welcome contrast to the businesslike nature of our streets. Moveable seats allowed people to make conversational grouping. Children used the bright-colored platforms, originally provided for theater, musical performances or speech-making, as impromptu play sculpture.

An information center should also offer food, drink, and shelter. It is an ideal location for pretzel sellers, hot dog, soft drink, and coffee stands. Protection from wind and cold can be provided by simple and unobtrusive means — radiant pavement heating and temporary wind screens. Permanent overhead enclosure is unnecessary and undesirable; operation during heavy rain and snow can be temporarily suspended. A center should be of the street and must not become just another building.

Many visitors commented on the attractive appearance of the center and especially on the balloons. These "signal balloons" were sun traps by day and lanterns by night. With its multiple reflections of the surrounding environment and its movies, slide shows and sound tapes in action, the center was itself a novel light and sound experience, particularly at night. The changing spectacle of people using the center at all hours and reacting to its form and content was good reason for being there and reason enough to talk to a stranger. The vibrant quality of the place was an essential ingredient of its success.

Visitors expressed it in various ways:

It completely surrounds you. It gets you into the entire feeling of Boston.

All kinds of people mingled around the space, unparanoid, relaxed, together feeling their city, their environment . . .

Adults and children in our family found it intriguing, and it was an oasis at which people seemed to linger and become friendly . . .

After Park Square

By all available measures, such as number of visitors and their recorded responses, the Park Square center was a success. It was a place where people both enjoyed themselves and found specific information which was useful to them. On the basis of this experience, a program to develop permanent information centers for pedestrians would achieve broad support and contribute to the quality of street life in Boston or any other city.

A summary of observations, interview results, and recorded opinions of people at the center appears in Chapter 6 and a full report in Appendix 5. In general, people were highly favorable to the center, thought that there should be more centers like it, and made a number of suggestions for doing it better next time. Many of these comments imply further development of the idea of a local forum, a two-way communications center.

The social communication generated by the experimental center was striking. The place seemed to draw people, many of whom returned a number of times. There are precious few such places in our cities.

To develop this aspect of the center would suggest increased emphasis on the creation of public channels through which small senders — individuals, small groups, and institutions — could speak to a wider public. These channels should allow for any kind of speech, display, or performance which is legal in the street. At the least, there should be an improved version of the movie tube allowing for larger audiences and sound, better accommodations for small performances, and more space for posters and notices. People will need to learn to use these channels, and a program for making the opportunity known and for scheduling and managing their use will be necessary.

About one-third of the people who visited the center made some specific criticism. The most frequent criticism was that the center was crowded and confusing when it was in full operation. This suggests that the space was too restricted for the crowds, but poses a dilemma since the intensity of the place, even when it was not full of people, was one of its most attractive qualities. In a larger center, both dense and more open areas could be created.

The Park Square experiment also suggests some limitations on the use of information centers. They have special operating expenses for management and policing (see Chapter 7), including continual up-dating of content, special cleaning of the area, maintenance of the audio-visual equipment, and a night watchman. A center in the street is not a good place to present complex or detailed information which requires concentrated attention to comprehend. Subtle points would be lost in the noise and activity of the street scene. They also would not normally be suitable locations for major speeches or performances attracting large crowds: the intimacy of the center was one of its most attractive qualities, and future centers should be more appropriate to story-tellers than to orators.

Finally, the centers must be public institutions. Despite the attractions of private funding, they must not become merely selling machines for advertising promoters. As such, they would be more likely to repel people than attract them.

How To Do It

Cardboard tubes, normally used for forming concrete, provided inexpensive ready-made kiosks which were relatively easy to modify for display purposes and sturdy enough for a short-term experiment. The balloons were anchored through the tubes into concrete pads and were inflated by small blowers. Permanent tubes could be made of translucent fiberglass or steel. The polyethylene balloons could be permanent or they could be replaced by rigid plastic or geodesic spheres. A more attractive paving than painted asphalt might incorporate radiant heating.

The audio-visual techniques relied on modifications of conventionally available equipment. The slide-sound show synchronized normal projectors with continuous tape decks. The movies were shown by standard loop projectors. Projecting slides in daylight is difficult; each projection screen with its associated lenses became an optical element, hooded against ambient light and aimed away from direct sunlight.

Although there were maintenance problems, most of the equipment was quite reliable. The use and environmental exposure was more severe than encountered at a World's Fair: the equipment was running 20 hours a day and there was no preventative maintenance program. Each slide projector went through more than 300,000 cycles with no jams. The tape units did jam (and cause the projectors to stop), but this problem was due in large part to dampness at the site. The movie projectors were "off the shelf" units designed to be used 20 hours a *year* not 20 hours a *day;* they often jammed and broke film loops. The question/answer machine broke down occasionally under its constant use.

These problems can be resolved by further modifications in standard equipment, coupled with a regular preventative maintenance program. Given multiple centers, an information retrieval system based on a central computer could offer a number of additional services: It could answer questions typed in by the visitor, enter into dialogue with him, draw pictures, maps, and directions for him, and operate random access slide and movie projectors.

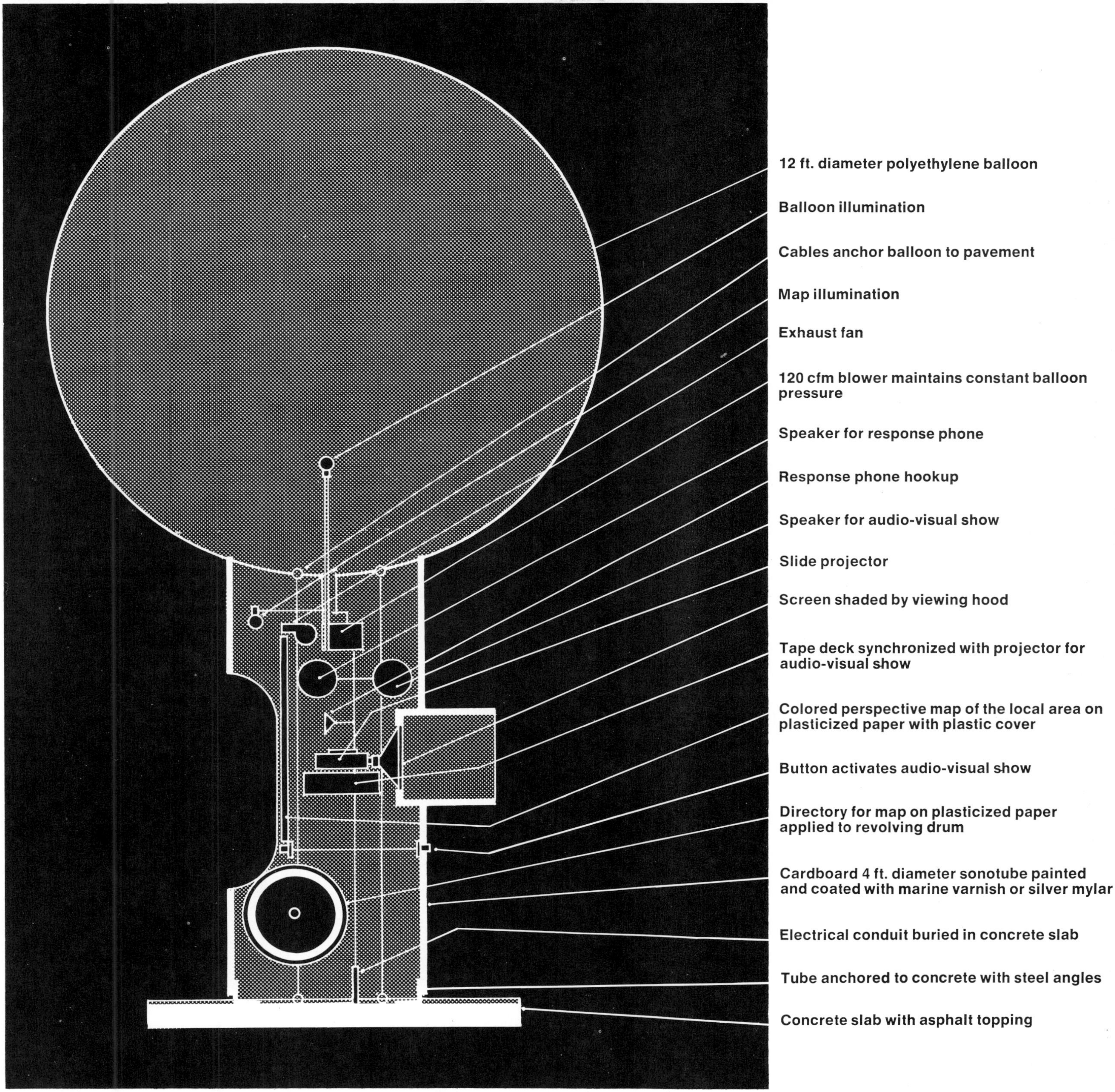
12 ft. diameter polyethylene balloon
Balloon illumination
Cables anchor balloon to pavement
Map illumination
Exhaust fan
120 cfm blower maintains constant balloon pressure
Speaker for response phone
Response phone hookup
Speaker for audio-visual show
Slide projector
Screen shaded by viewing hood
Tape deck synchronized with projector for audio-visual show
Colored perspective map of the local area on plasticized paper with plastic cover
Button activates audio-visual show
Directory for map on plasticized paper applied to revolving drum
Cardboard 4 ft. diameter sonotube painted and coated with marine varnish or silver mylar
Electrical conduit buried in concrete slab
Tube anchored to concrete with steel angles
Concrete slab with asphalt topping

A City-Wide System

BASIC ELEMENTS

Information centers would be more effective as part of a city-wide system. They should become a basic information channel between people trying to use the city more effectively and individuals, small groups, and institutions trying to make contact with people. A good system would be located at points accessible to most of the population at some time in their everyday routine.

These would be the major policies and criteria for a city-wide public information system for people on foot:

1 The system should consist of three subsystems:

a. Junction centers located near major transportation facilities.

b. District centers at district focal points, under local control.

c. Map displays and display kiosks at dispersed locations where there are high concentrations of people on foot.

2 All three subsystems should provide basic information on activities within walking distance, on connections to the larger area, and on current events.

3 The entire system should provide channels for small senders and opportunities for individual or group commentary.

4 Centers should function as both high identity landmarks to attract people and as places which provide support and stimulus for people while they are there.

5 Presentation techniques should be simple and direct, combining words and pictures whenever possible, and always allowing the receiver to select the information he wants.

6 The system should incorporate a process for feedback and evaluation so that both the content and the form of presentation can be continually revised to satisfy evolving needs and interests.

Junction Centers

Information centers at major junctions would be the backbone of the system and would serve a city-wide population. The scale and character of the major centers would be based on the size and mix of the pedestrian population and the nature of the surrounding district. Basic content would always include detailed descriptions and locations of all nearby activities plus information on city-wide orientation and transportation. Supplementary information would vary in accordance with the particular interests of the population using the center.

The information system for pedestrians should be phased so that at least one junction center, located in central Boston, would be built first. Locations for centers might include North Station, Government Center and upper State Street, Park Street and the Summer-Winter-Washington Street crossing, South Station, Park Square, Copley Square, the intersection of Boylston and Massachusetts Avenue, and perhaps Symphony Hall. The ultimate desirable number of junction centers is indeterminate: by building them one or two at a time, the overall program can be adjusted to the demand and the form and content of each center can be progressively better adapted to need.

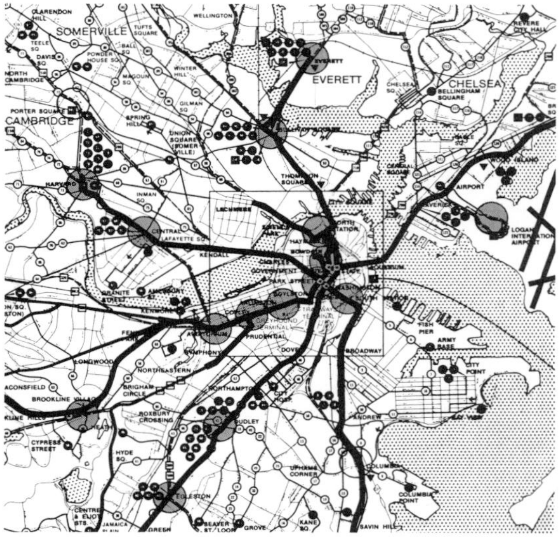

INFORMATION TRANSPORTATION NETWORK

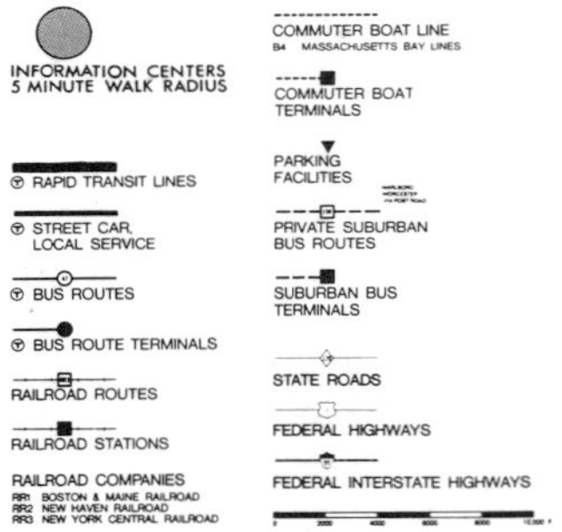

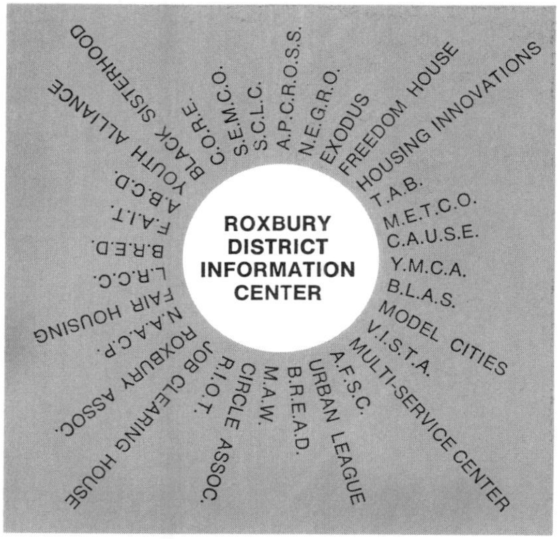

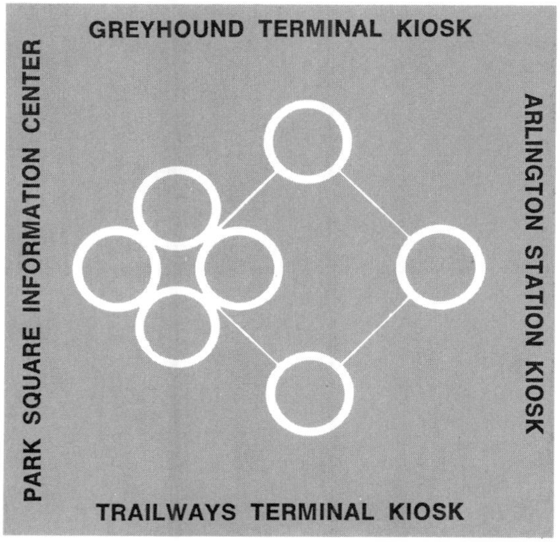

District Centers

A second level of centers would be developed for local districts. These would be located at places where people gather, but not necessarily at major transportation junctions. The focal point of a large shopping area within a residential district would be a likely location. These centers would be under local control in terms both of initial content and continuing policy. Much of the information would be collected or generated by local groups.

Basic information might be similar to that of the major centers. Other information would probably concentrate on past, present, and future plans and events that affect the way of life of local people. It should reflect the interests of various groups and organizations within the district, even (or especially) when they are conflicting. To encourage this, these centers should rely principally on simple and inexpensive techniques of information presentation: notice boards, hand-painted signs, and the like. In many areas, the presence of local people working in the centers may be the single most important factor in establishing their local function.

The district center should provide a central communications outlet for all of the activities in the district and a place for local people to get together informally to exchange opinions on things that are happening or might happen to their community. An opportunity for dissent, persuasion, or clarification of issues would be an essential part of these centers. As the district centers developed, so would possibilities for communication between different populations — for example, a "black" movie shown to the Irish in South Boston.

The district system should be developed incrementally under the control of local representative bodies locally accountable for their management policies ("equal time"). Because of the political nature of information that concerns local organizations, city government cannot locate, build, and manage district centers on its own initiative without courting failure. The city can offer technical communications services, including basic information packages, and may offer financial assistance as funds are available.

Local Kiosks

The third level of the system would consist of map displays dispersed throughout the city above ground — at transit stops, at major parking garages, or at high-use buildings. These would contain city maps for general orientation, an enlarged three-dimensional map of the local area, plus maps and schedules of alternate transportation services available from or near that point. They might include shortwave radio messages on daily events and would definitely have a local bulletin board and poster displays of local and city events. The most intense pedestrian zone of the center city should be covered by a network of these map displays, notice boards, and poster kiosks.

Many of these kiosks would naturally be located at or near street corners. Wherever possible they should be coordinated with locations of fire and police call boxes and public telephones. Locations of these important street communication services should in any case be made systematic and the new information system would provide an opportunity for reorganization. Other emergency information, such as first aid symbols and instructions (including emergency numbers), should be posted on each kiosk and when necessary, warnings could be broadcast over the shortwave current event system.

The information system should be of the street: the public ways are the only collective territory of the city. A building is the territory of its occupants and everyone else is a visitor — the streets belong to the people. Beyond the basic system represented by the Park Square Center and kiosks, there are other possibilities for new dispersed sources which should be tested: display structures for projected images, display screens for parking lots, and some special means for presenting information on local history and ecology.

SUPPLEMENTARY SOURCES OF INFORMATION

Projection Structures

With the use of multiple screens, projected images have become a more interesting medium. One of the finest examples of the art was seen at the Czechoslovakian Pavilion at Expo '67, but no discotheque or dance hall today is without its own version. Projected images have already become an outdoor advertising medium. If the images are multiple, as well as changing and intense, they will be a dominant part of any night scene. This medium should be captured for public purposes.

The film tubes in the prototype information center gave some indication of the potential of multiple projection in the display of public interest films. The projection structure shown here would be a much more dynamic and dominant part of the scene, and its deployment should be limited mainly to key junctions like those of the major information centers. It should be used for films and slides with an educational purpose, for news and other public announcements, and for the display of expressive commentaries on the city. Proliferation of these display units throughout the city for advertising use should not be allowed.

The structure described here is designed for rear projection of slides or movie images on several sides of translucent modules, contained within a light steel frame. Though originally designed for the prototype center, it was too costly and required too much pretesting to be used.

Such structures could be built by joint public-private development and used in part for some types of advertising. The criterion — admittedly a slippery one — could be set in terms of appropriateness of the material being presented to the location. Thus, in Park Square, an appropriate display of international travel slides might be presented by the various airline offices located there. In the *Central Streets and Spaces* section, other controlled uses of projection structures will be described: the intensification of the character of shopping and entertainment zones.

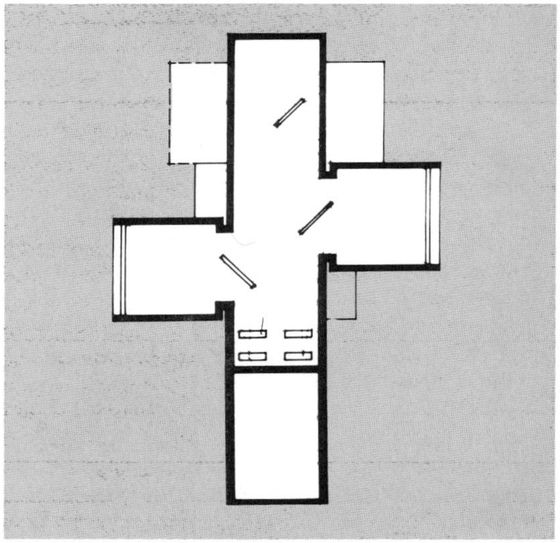

Section showing projection system.

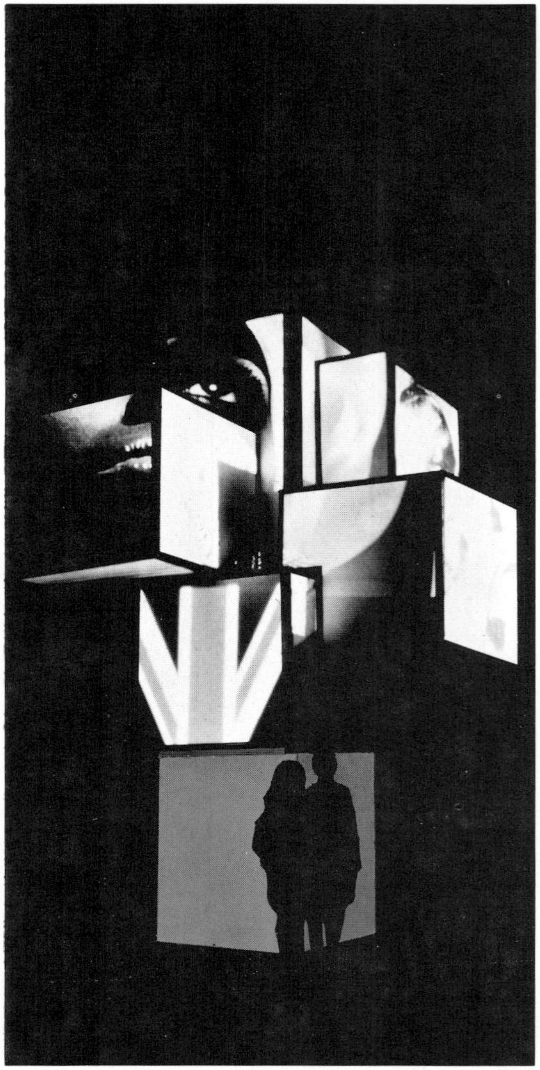

Parking Lot Display Screens

Presently, open parking lots in downtown areas have an entirely negative impact — gaping holes, undefined edges, and masses of metal. However, they are apparently here to stay; the demand is high, so are the profits. They have an important function as transfer points, where large numbers of motorists become pedestrians.

Screens for parking lots, especially in areas of high pedestrian use, could reduce the visual nuisance and also become attractive display structures. They could become part of the general information system by displaying city maps, local area maps, descriptions of local activities, bulletin boards, posters describing local theaters, exhibitions, entertainments and events. Information on time, weather, and levels of traffic on major roads and congestion points could be incorporated into the displays. Large changeable signs, making use of light patterns, should display the capacity of the lot and the current load. (These signs should also be required on parking garages.)

Parking lot screens could also be used for public murals, like those which sometimes appear on construction fences. School art classes might paint them, or the city could sponsor competitions for posters advertising public activities (like the posters on buses in New York City), or they might be done by artists' workshops, like the one sponsored by the Institute of Contemporary Art in Boston, to bring art into the streets. The basic structure need cost no more than $10 per lineal foot. The screens could be a simple and relatively inexpensive way of changing and humanizing the appearance of the central city.

Parking lot operators will not rush to build such screens. They will have to be legislated into existence, probably by means of zoning, and they will require some public support for the display material and its maintenance. It may be that operators will have to be allowed to rent some of the space for controlled local advertising — such as theater posters — both to fill the space and to help pay for the screens.

Supplementary Environmental Education

There are many other means of informing people about the city which could do much to help transform the environment into a place for learning and growing. Policies for private signs and lights in Chapter 5 indicate how they may be designed and regulated to increase the flow of information on the economic activities and processes of city life. Public systems should illuminate the visible history of the city by showing the connections between the present and the past, current processes of change, anticipated or possible future changes, and the ecological adaptation of the city to its site.

Historical markers and trails, like the Freedom Trail in Boston, are a step in this direction but could be much improved. Usually historical markers are hard to find, dull, and do not give enough information about the site and its historical context. Many historically important buildings and places are unlit at night. Besides more complete verbal descriptions, signs could include outdoor displays of etchings, drawings, photographs, maps, or models showing what the place was like at different periods in history. Recorded messages could also be used at particularly important sites, accompanied by lights programmed to show who did what where ("Ben Franklin gave his famous speech from the balcony which is now being illuminated," followed by a part of the speech). Such techniques should be used with restraint to avoid the Disneyland effect.

Similar techniques can be used to explain the topographic and ecological development of the city. In Boston, markers in a few highly visible locations could show the locations of the first housing or center or the old shoreline, before filling. Street name signs could indicate when the street was laid out. Subway stations could directly expose geological structures and levels of fill. Locations of major subsurface utilities could also be marked. Recorded messages and visual displays in the Boston Common and along the Charles River Esplanade could describe the diverse plant and animal life which originally inhabited the site and tell what has happened to it with urbanization. These displays could be dramatically related to pollution abatement and recreational development programs.

Other aspects of nature still visible in the city could be made more visible. Sun, star, planet and moon positions, motions, and composition could be marked and explained at the harbor-front and on the banks of the Charles. Seasons and hours can be marked by sun and water clocks. Astronomical influences on surface life such as solar flares, cosmic rays, and gravitation could be dramatized, along with the mechanisms of cloud formation and the macro and micro-climate.

Describing current and future change is more difficult and certainly involves more risks. "Artists' conceptions" of future buildings are increasingly common for large buildings, but displays which describe the process of construction are far more interesting and informative; they should be required at all large construction sites. Plans for new developments should be displayed only where it is certain and soon. Doubtful or delayed promises are risky. Plans for changing areas of the city should be displayed to emphasize alternative possibilities and to explain the process for achieving the various outcomes. Such displays should be an integral part of a participatory planning process.

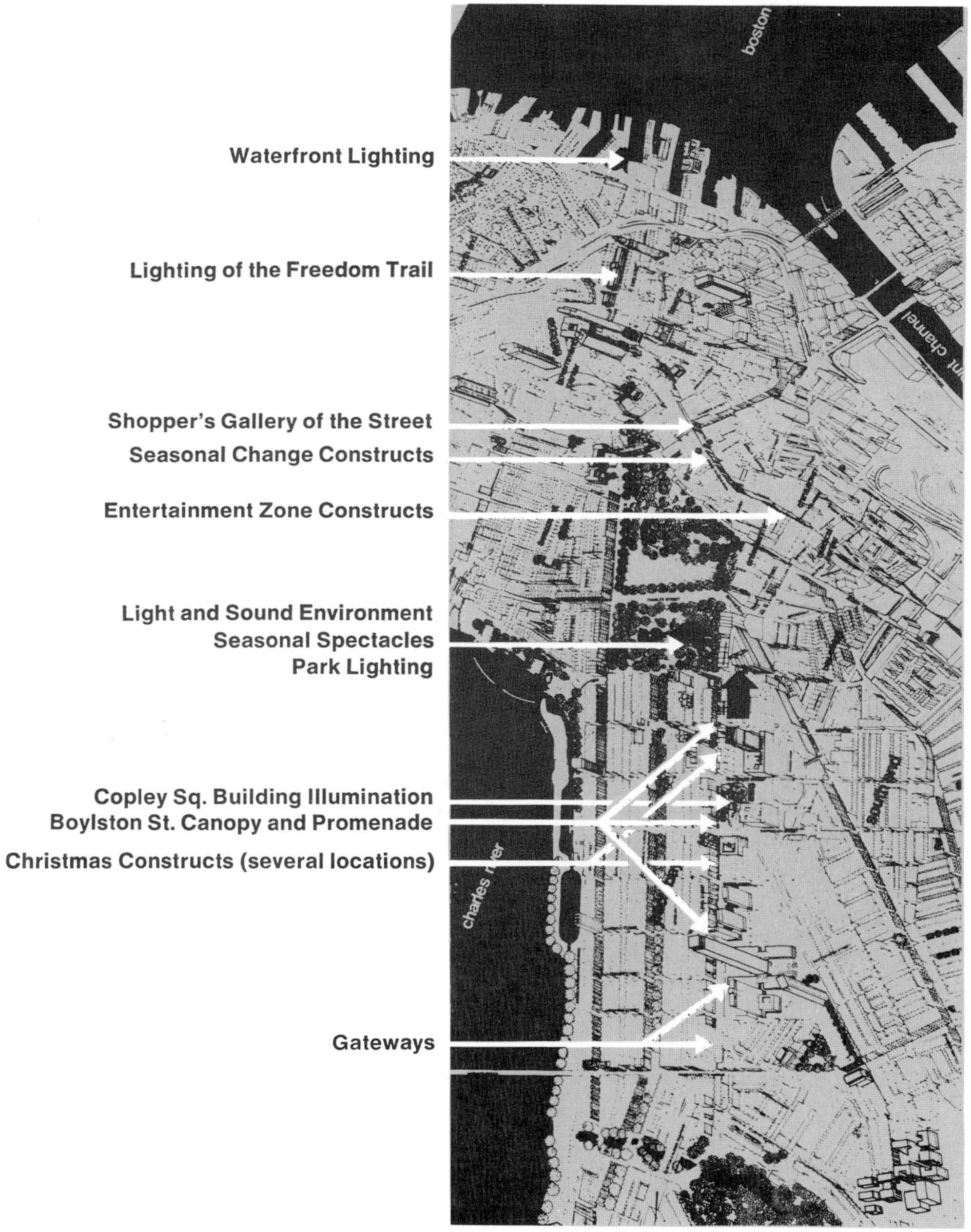

Central Streets and Spaces

Streets and public open spaces are the most basic environmental information system. It is in the streets that public life takes form and is revealed. Here, the atmosphere and life-styles of a city may be experienced. Here also, public celebration must take place, if it is to occur at all.

Our streets do not support public life for many reasons, not the least of which is their subjugation to the automobile. In the near future — on most streets at least — cars must be lived with, but the street need not be merely a functional adjunct to these machines. Inside the machines are people and a small portion of the street space is still reserved for pedestrians. To reclaim some part of these central streets and spaces for shared public life is both important and possible.

This transformation will require dramatic counter-functionalist changes in the mood of the street. These changes must be at a scale and intensity which can successfully compete with the compelling dynamic of streams of vehicles, yet they should be inexpensive and nondisruptive to existing activity. In addition, the means for counter-functionalist transformation could provide opportunities for a variety of artists to work at an urban scale. These means of transformation should themselves convey the notion that further changes are possible.

The prototype designs and demonstrations described on the following pages occur along the commercial "spine" of central Boston. Beginning at Massachusetts Avenue the route follows Boylston Street, the commercial center of Back Bay, then goes past the Public Garden and up Washington Street, the nighttime entertainment and shopping center of Boston, to the historical Quincy Market area and down to the new harborfront.

GRAPHIS

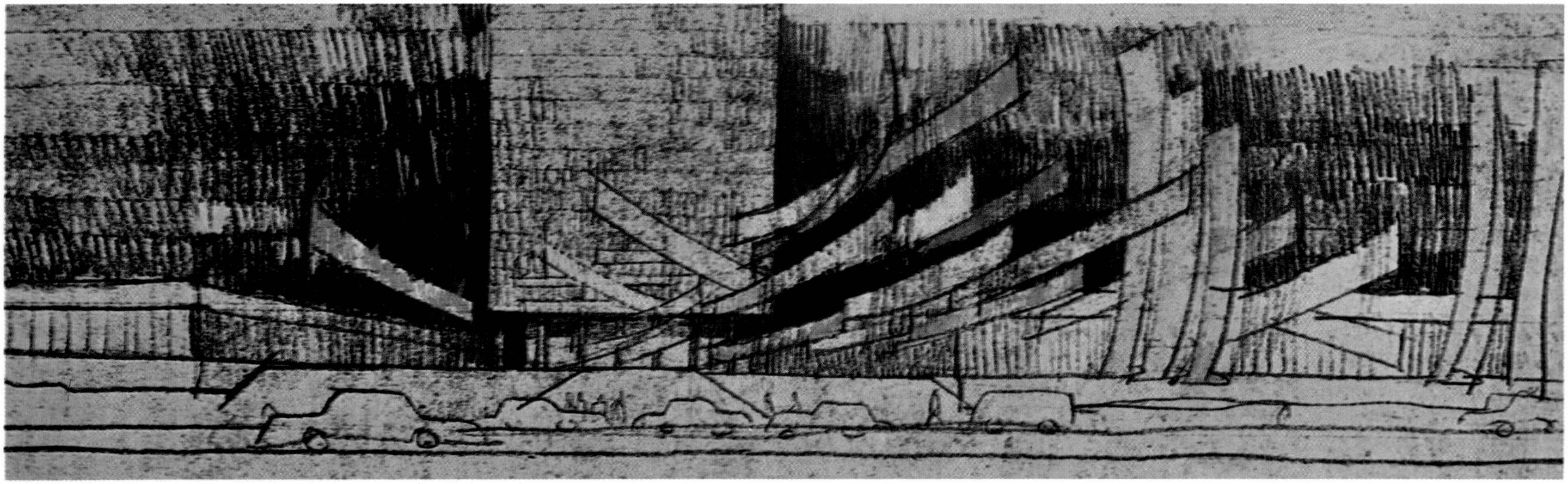

Dragon designed by Ann Kramer, age 6.

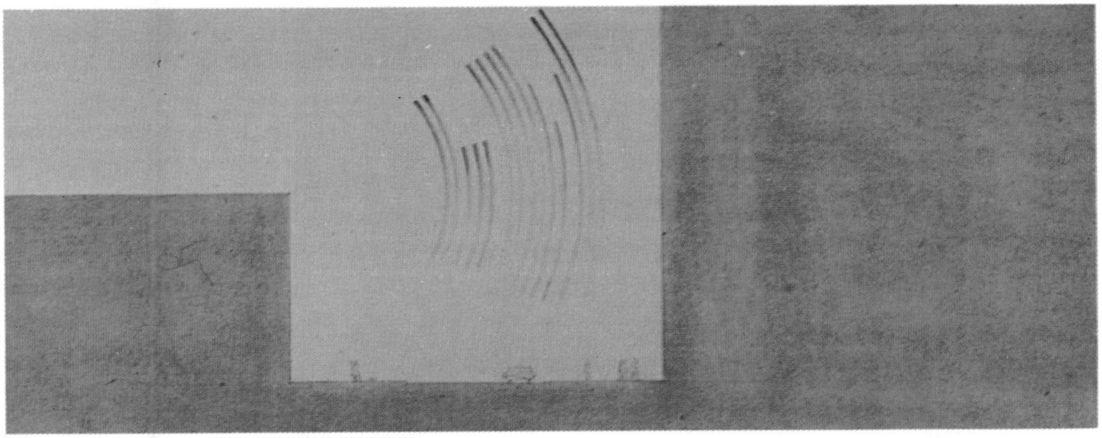

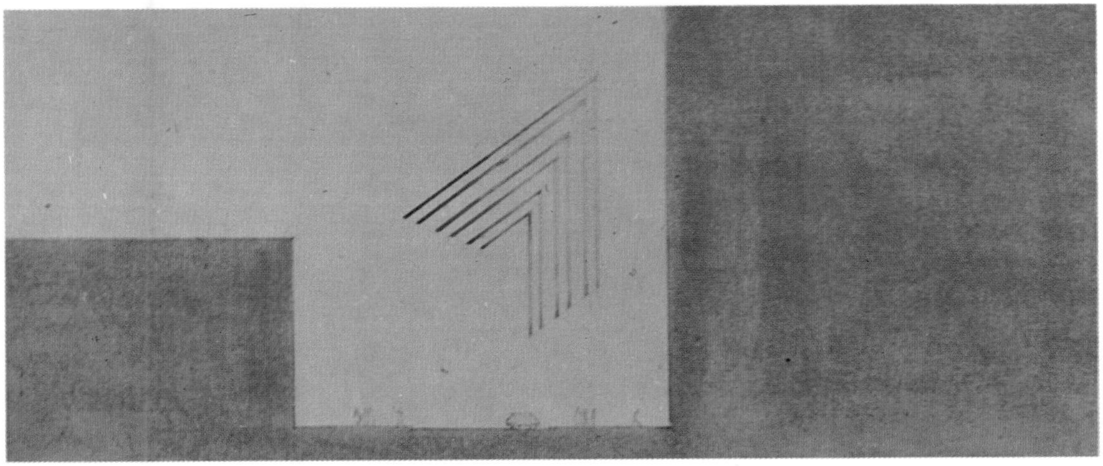

SHOPPING STREETS

Gateways and Constructs

Boylston Street is a rapidly changing office, entertainment, and shopping street linking such divergent buildings and spaces as the Prudential Center, Trinity Church, and the Public Garden. The street begins awkwardly at the wide open intersection of Massachusetts Avenue and the Turnpike and then passes the cold and monumental facade of the Prudential Center. Gateways above the street and at the entrance to the Prudential plaza could employ public street graphics — signs and banners — to counter the deadening effects of openness and monumentality. Graphics would change continually, announcing sales and events in the area.

Other "street constructs" could come and go with holidays; those illustrated here are for Christmas. They are composed of light foam-core shapes encased in cloth or mylar sleeves, tied onto great triangular nets or webs and hung over the street. These webs are spaced at 30 foot intervals and clustered in groups of four and six. The bright, minimal shapes in planar sections perpendicular to the street assume complex patterns of overlap in groups. The shapes may be tied to the webs before erection or can be assembled after the web is in place (and therefore composed within the context of their urban setting).

The webs are constructed of high strength monofilament strand with grid intervals running at one foot centers and are capable of carrying wind loads of up to 60,000 pounds. Attachment to structures on both sides of the street is made at the apices of the web with bolts anchored into the floor system of the buildings (loads are distributed evenly through the diaphragm action of the floor planes). The webs are designed to "break away" under sudden impact loads (hurricane winds) and would be held off the street with a network of secondary support cables. These webs triangulate the space in which they are placed (being a function of the heights of the buildings to the width of the streets) and become sculptural elements proportional to their urban setting.

Promenades

Shopping in American cities is, more often than not, grueling and unrewarding. Our shopping streets offer little support for informal communication among people and little relief from the oppressive atmosphere of stores and sidewalks. The unremitting commercial functionalism seems suitable only for some imaginary "efficient consumer."

Since the building of the Prudential Center with its huge office, convention, apartment, and shopping complex, Boylston Street has become the leading edge of central Boston's commercial growth. Many other new activities are locating on the street — stores, restaurants, movie theaters, bars, and nightclubs. There is a new intensity of day and night street life but no reflection of it in the form of the pedestrian space.

Sidewalks are wide (30 feet) and unrelieved. There is a tree planting program under way, but it will take years for the trees to significantly alter the functional character of the streetscape. A transforming device is needed to create a new character for the pedestrian space and a new, more appropriate identity for the street.

A light steel and plexiglass canopy extending over 12 feet of the sidewalk would create a pedestrian promenade with a sense of intimacy and shelter. The plexiglass should be tinted in a range of warm colors to produce patterns of filtered light during the day and to allow each establishment to assert its own identity. At night the canopy would be floodlit from above to produce a warm glow of light on the sidewalk. The leading surface of the canopy could be used as a screen for changing advertising images projected from inside show windows. Stores, restaurants, and the Department of City Information, individually or jointly, could establish resting and eating places between the canopy and the trees, mingled with display kiosks and screened from the traffic by shrubs. Many of these sidewalk amenities could be paid for by the rental of advertising space in or on the kiosks. Where the canopy is inappropriate (for instance, in front of a church) strings of small bulbs in the foliage of the trees ("glitter" trees) can be used to extend this humane and festive character.

Projected images seen from under the canopy.

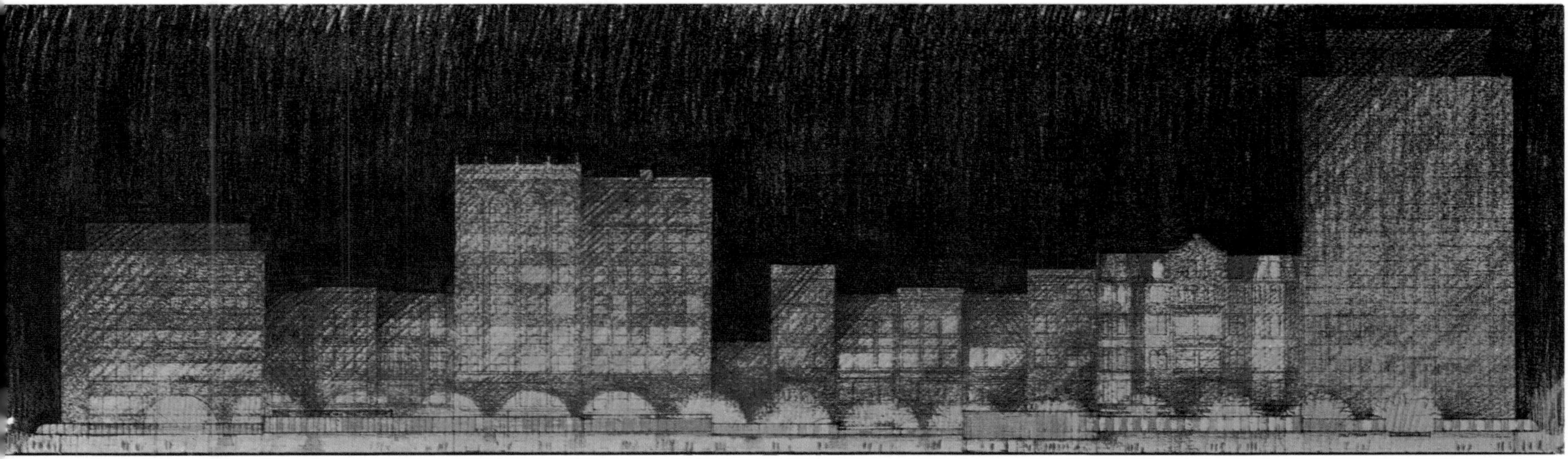

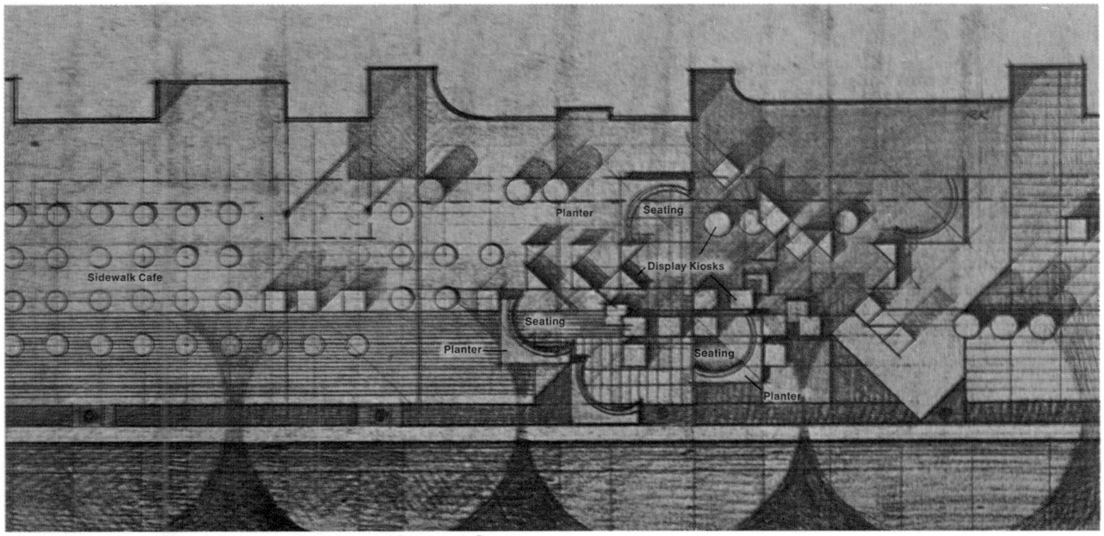

Partial plan of the promenade between Clarendon and Dartmouth Streets.

PUBLIC PLACES AND EVENTS

Copley Square Building Illumination

Many of the landmarks which make urban places distinctive by day disappear in the general low visibility night field. Such differentiations as occur are chiefly commercial — shop fronts, restaurants, movies, gas stations, and illuminated signs. Illumination of public buildings and places, along with major private institutions, can redress the balance by establishing a sense of public identity in the nightscape. The most important landmarks to light will be those on major streets, at major intersections, or fronting on public open spaces, as well as those with historic value or nighttime functions. Illumination of commercial buildings can also be valuable in some parts of the city, but the growing use of floodlighting to create corporate identity should not be allowed to dominate the nightscape as a simple function of economic power. These sign-buildings should be controlled by the same rules as other "super-signs" (see Chapter 5).

Techniques of illumination for particular buildings will vary, but in general lighting should be designed to express the activity system of a building and to articulate parts. Thus, entrances and spaces which are used at night should be emphasized, along with architectonic elements which can give unique nighttime character to the building such as columns, cornices, stair towers, and roofs. Buildings cannot look the same at night as in the day and overall floodlighting will generally not be appropriate.

Copley Square, with its superb nineteenth century buildings — the Boston Public Library and Trinity Church — has recently been reconstructed as a monumental plaza and lit with mercury vapor of a color and intensity appropriate to a highway interchange. Illumination of the Public Library, Trinity Church, the Sheraton Plaza Hotel, and Old South Church should contribute to a different nighttime image for the square, one in keeping with its nineteenth century character.

Experimental lighting of small parts of the library was demonstrated on several occasions to the director and a group of people involved with the reconstruction of the square. The final design evolved through this process of trial and error.

The library will be illuminated principally from inside and from the bases of the window arches on the second floor, the location of the main reading room; an overflow of light from the arches will softly light the cornice. The three arches of the entrance will also be lit. The building will seem to glow warmly from within, like a lantern (see Appendix 7 for technical details).

Similar policies are recommended for Trinity Church, emphasizing its rich and mysterious jewel-box quality. Stained glass windows in the facade, the facade towers, and the main tower can be lit from inside. The inner porch of the main entrance should also be intensely lit. The surfaces of the roofs should be gently washed with light from concealed sources.

The hotel should be lit principally at the entrance and in the first floor arched windows, the location of the function rooms. By changing the window awnings to a translucent material of a warm color, the hotel could create a strong sense of welcome and warmth at street level. In addition, a fluorescent strip on the seventh floor ledge would delineate the cornice.

Similar principles apply to lighting Old South Church on the northwest corner of the square, across from the library (see the Boylston canopy drawing and Appendix 7).

Lighting these four buildings will do much to enhance Copley Square at night, but to do justice to the square, the street lights around it should be changed to shielded high-pressure sodium vapor, with its warm golden color, and the new globe lights within the square changed to incandescent sources. Completed by the Boylston Street canopy, Copley Square could become one of the most beautiful nighttime places in America.

Library lighting test.

Trinity Church.

Boston Public Library.

Sheraton Plaza Hotel.

Lighting Parks

Parks should be as inviting by night as by day. A fine park is a sanctuary of the natural garden in the city; ideally it might also be a sanctuary of natural darkness, lit only by the moon and the stars. In our cities parks must be artificially illuminated, but this could be the occasion for the creation of a beautiful nighttime environment. Instead, parks are often ruined for night enjoyment by glaring mercury vapor street lights. Broad areas are flooded with unnecessary blue-green light, driving away the very population of nighttime strollers which would be the best source of security.

The sidewalk at the edge of the Boston Public Garden along Boylston Street is similar to many park pathways. Large elms shelter it from both sides. It is a wide pleasant way, intensively used by day for both strolling and sitting. At night it is gloomy, forbidding, and little used.

With the cooperation of the Boston Parks Department, the lower foliage of the trees along this path was up-lighted as a demonstration of an alternative to the conventional street lighting approach. The method is simple and inexpensive. Outdoor floods with built-in reflectors (PAR's) strapped to branches are unobtrusive and out of reach of vandals. This dramatic lighting reverses normal expectancies. Where there was a dark tunnel of foliage, there is now a tunnel of leaf-reflected light.

Although many people, including city officials, liked the demonstration, there are some serious drawbacks to this technique. Mounting the lights on the lower branches throws the skeletal structure of the trees into sharp relief at a seemingly arbitrary point. If trees could scream, these would have done so. The effect was particularly garish in the winter when the leaves were gone. In addition, the strapping does not allow for normal growth and thus can only be a temporary mounting. Such fixtures can be mounted on independent poles, which allows the light to be directed away from the lower branches; but like any theatrical technique, this form of park lighting should be used with restraint.

Park lighting techniques should be as subtle and varied as the plant life itself. In the Public Garden, these might range from warm shielded down-lighting of sidewalks combined with large plastic lanterns hung in the elms on the edges of the park to small glass globe lights floating in the water of the central pond. The lighting should be both intimate and festive. The soft textured surfaces of the plant life and the dark sheltering volumes of the trees must be respected. Trees near the pond could be lit with strings of tiny clear bulbs, like clouds of fireflies. In other areas, between the pond and the surrounding streets, the dark silhouettes of the trees against the night sky should be protected, with necessary security lighting provided by low shielded sources along the paths and near resting places. The suspension bridge across the pond should have lights strung along its cables, in addition to the existing globe lights mounted on the piers and abutments. So that people could better enjoy this new light environment, the swanboats should be operated at night during the summer. In the winter the pond should be opened for skating around bonfires.

None of these policies is costly or requires elaborate technology. Great effects can be simply achieved by appropriate lighting.

Park lighting in San Antonio, Texas.

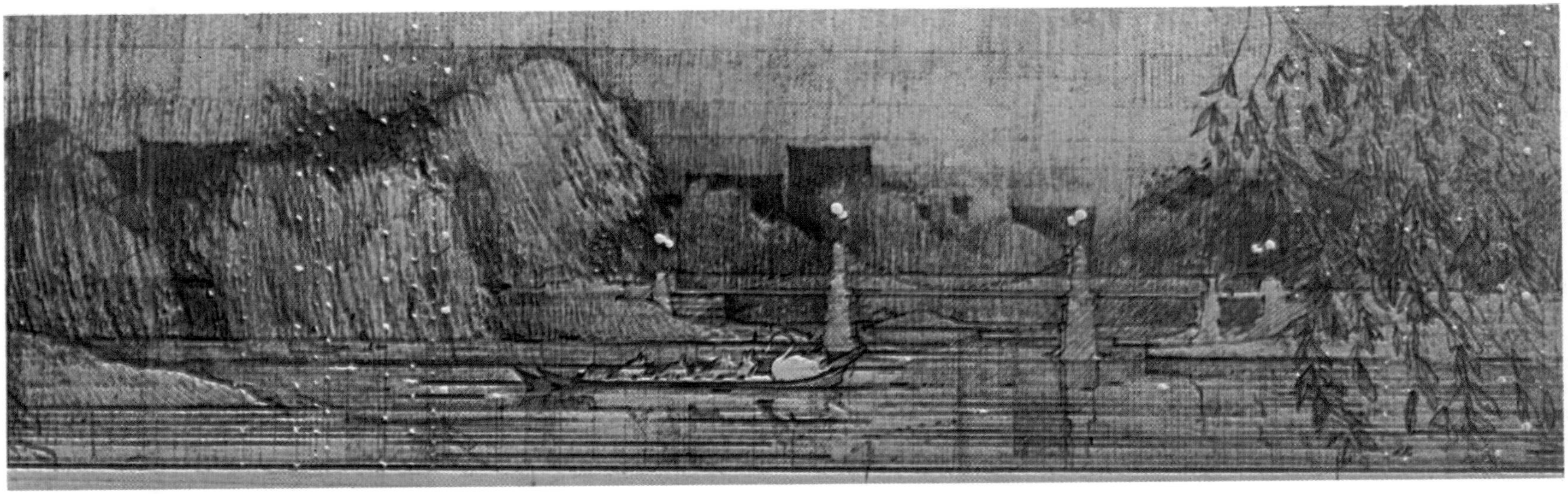

The Light and Sound Environment
For twenty nights in October, 1968, another demonstration experiment — again under the auspices of the Parks Department — transformed the pond in the center of the Public Garden into a continually changing light and sound environment. The experiment, designed and installed by Yale Research Associates in the Arts (Pulsa), deployed sequenced xenon strobe lights, flashing just below the surface of the water, played in concert with sound programs emanating from floating polyplanar speakers. The light flashes reflected on particles suspended in the water, creating a corona of light without disturbing the reflecting plane of the surface. The concerts were controlled by a console and sound synthesizer which permitted the strobe lights and electronic sounds to be sequenced in many combinations.

Such experimentation in the creative use of light and sound for the enhancement of existing nighttime environments or the creation of new ones would be good policy in many public places. It can open up places that may otherwise be little used. It can be a novel and interesting form of nighttime experience. It offers opportunities for artists to work in the public domain and to talk with a great diversity of people about their reactions to the work so that it can be improved incrementally. A small commitment of public resources (the cost of arrangements, electrical connections, and wiring in this case) can stimulate private contributions from industry and other sources to cover most of the costs. Many artists are now attempting to work at an environmental scale after years of withdrawal into the ivory tower of the studio. Temporary publicly aided experiments like this one can contribute significantly to the development of a new environmental art for our time.

Public reaction
The experiment increased the number of people using the park at night. People were attracted to the pond from nearby streets and strolled more freely than usual around the Garden. There was no vandalism during the twenty nights of the experiment. The composition of the audience reflected the population composition of the surrounding residential areas: there was relatively little publicity of the event and the evenings were cool.

Observation and interviewing during the experiment indicated strong interest among young people, but less interest among those 35 and over. The "less conventional" in dress and hair length, were unanimous in their intention to stay, often through the whole performance. Almost half of the people interviewed visited the Garden at least twice and most of those said they came back because they liked the experiment. Most of the respondents were first attracted to the experiment as they walked by or through the park for other reasons; very few came because of publicity. The average time spent in the Garden during the experiment was 45 minutes. Apparently a large nighttime population might use the park if it offered an appealing night environment.

The experiment was generally liked by those interviewed. For most people it was an interesting innovation, stimulating to the imagination, aesthetically involving, and appropriately located. Many people were confused about its purpose. Many found the repetitive programming boring after a time and there was a general preference expressed for "nature" and an antipathy toward "technology." Most people agreed with the suggestion that similar light and sound experiments should be conducted every year in the Public Garden.

Despite the generally positive comments, the experiment was not entirely successful. It failed to draw the large crowds expected, partly because of cold weather and lack of publicity, but probably mainly because its appeal was limited. Although the multiple-speaker electronic sounds were often arresting and beautiful, especially in combination with the ambient noises of the city, the strobe lights were often less compelling than the reflections of the city lights, both because of the very brief duration of the flashes and because of the brown water. Programmed patterns were sometimes either too complex to perceive or boringly simple, a defect easily overcome by further programming developments. The brilliance of the last performance, when the water was drained and the lights emerged, suggests that additional lights located above the water or in the trees would have been desirable.

The shortcomings of this experiment in no way invalidate the underlying policy. Light and sound in the city must not be limited to merely utilitarian functions. Boston might again achieve some of the acclaim it has lost as a center for the creative arts if it were to establish a yearly tradition of such experiments in environmental art, perhaps as part of "Summerthing." The Charles River Basin and the new harbor-front would be ideal settings for further developments.

ENTERTAINMENT ZONES

In these four prototype designs for lower Washington Street, sign and light infrastructure is used to enhance and intensify the honky-tonk atmosphere of Boston's "Combat Zone." The mood here is strictly commercial: amusements of all kinds are bought and sold in the marketplace of the street.

The "Street of Coming Attractions" uses projection onto screens suspended over the street to display slides and film clips of current or imminent night club shows or movies. Music and soundtracks would be projected along with the visual images. Between commercial announcements, the hardware could be used for experimental light and sound shows.

The "Loom of Aggression" is a light steel space-frame spanning the street and providing additional display spaces for graphic and neon advertisements. The commercial messages would change frequently and the loom could also be used to display the creations of light and graphic artists.

The "Reflective Light-Space" is a construct of hundreds of reflective mylar strips suspended above the street from building to building. This is the least expensive way to intensify existing character, simply by fragmenting and multiplying it in a myriad of mirrored surfaces, shimmering in the wind. The street would be especially spectacular on a rainy night.

The "Cybernetic Light-Space" is created by programmed serial progressions of flashing lights, arranged in grids and suspended above the street like the Back Bay Christmas constructs. The light bulbs would be tinted in a range of bright warm colors. Light would pulse in various rhythms or move in waves along the street, depending on the intensity of the crowds; it could also be activated by the movement or sounds of people and cars.

In all cases, cars in this intensified zone would be limited to speeds of ten miles per hour during the active nighttime period (this is not far different from present weekend conditions). Thus people in cars and people on foot could safely mingle and enjoy the show.

The Street of Coming Attractions.

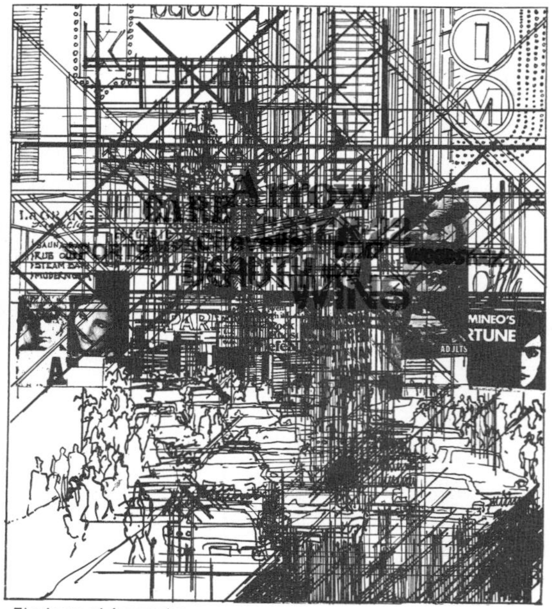

The Loom of Aggression.

The Reflective Light-space.

The Cybernetic Light-space.

Spring.

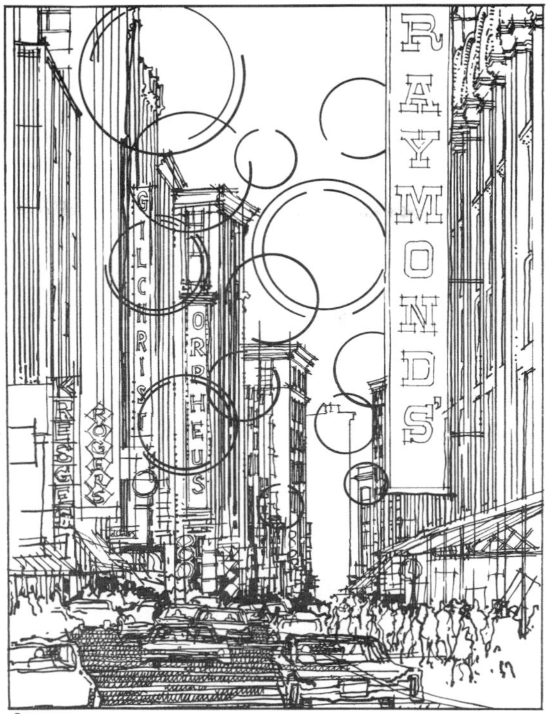

Summer.

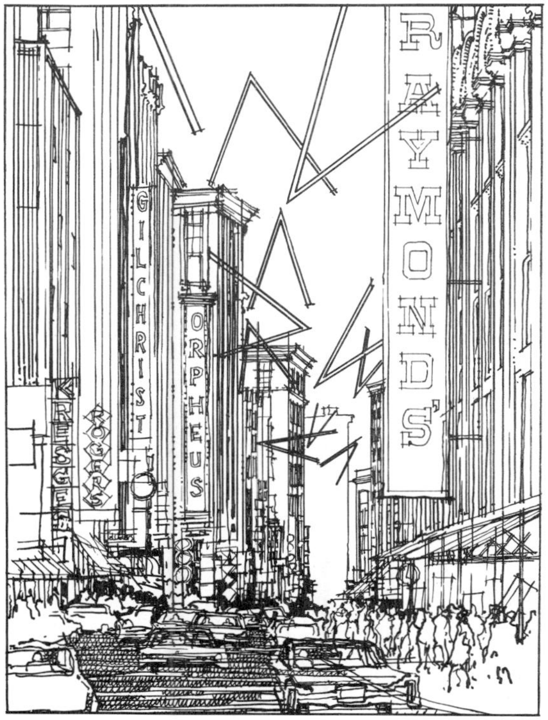

Fall.

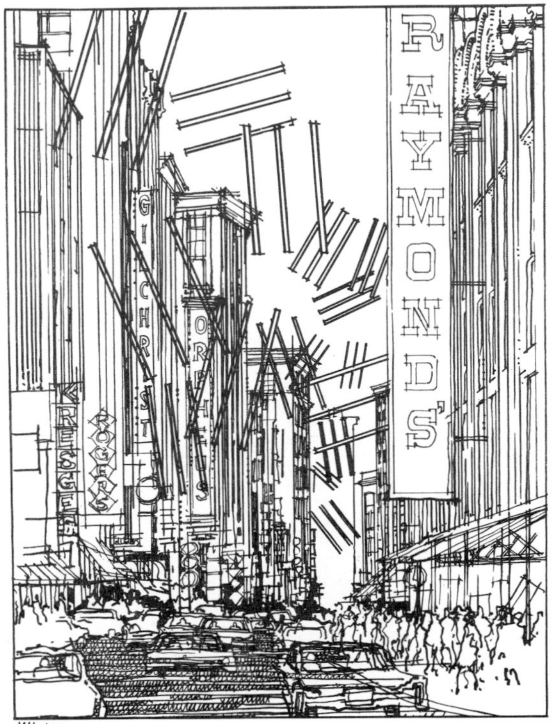

Winter.

SHOPPING CENTERS

Seasonal Change

To change the oppressive, sometimes nightmarish atmosphere of downtown America on any significant scale, we need simple devices for transforming the shopping street into a more habitable urban place. Massive renewal schemes which require large-scale rebuilding and major shifts in the pattern of circulation are extremely costly, take many years to accomplish, and are becoming politically infeasible. Moreover, most of these grand schemes have been aimed at suburbanization of downtown, aping the regional shopping center in the creation of long anemic malls, inappropriate to the dense urban character of the center city.

As one step in this direction, counter-functionalist street constructs could also be used downtown. Here in the canyon of the Washington Street shopping center, they could become permanent features, changing regularly with the seasons. The monofilament webs would be rigged to be lowered once each season for the attachment of new constructs. An association of Washington Street or downtown merchants could commission a different artist every three months to do a new set of constructs, in celebration of the coming season.

A Gallery of the Street

In certain parts of downtown more dramatic changes are possible. This prototype proposal describes a new climate-conditioned urban place at the core of the region: Boston's 100% corner — the location of the two major department stores — where Summer and Winter Streets intersect with Washington Street. This transformation of public space would create new opportunities for education and the encouragement of informal communication.

Summer and Winter Streets can be closed to vehicles without a significant disruption of downtown traffic. Then, using the new technology of high strength plastic membranes and extruded steel in tension, a webbed transparent canopy can be hung from building to building overhead. The main strands of the web can be attached on both sides of the street by a support system anchored by long bolts into the floors of the buildings. Steel strands fastened to the ground would be attached to a continuous tube at the lower vertex of the network overhead and put into tension to give the structure its final form and check uplift wind action (they also act as drains). Radiant heating coils would be laid curb to curb for the two reclaimed blocks of street and the whole repaved to existing sidewalk level. Radiant heating within the canopy itself could be energized when necessary to melt heavy snow. Lighting can be provided by simple strings of bulbs attached by a pulley system to the steel strands so that what is by day a web against the light is by night a web of lights. The canopy can be fabricated off the site, then rigged and unfurled in less than a month. The cost is low relative to the value of the space reclaimed and by comparison with any conventional galleria structure.

Many uses are imaginable for this new central place. Perhaps the most attractive is that it become a shopper's gallery of the street, a place where artists working on large scale environmental constructions, employing light, graphics and space, can try out ideas. The place might become a continually changing landscape of fantasy: diaphanous banners and light constructions — some of them signs — would be suspended

Winter Street in 1969.

The Gallery from Summer Street, looking over the Washington subway concourse.

Looking toward the Washington Street fly-over and information center from Winter Street.

from the rigging above, light and color environments would occupy real ground space or be created by projection on the building facades or on hanging screens. This kaleidascope of urban ephemera would be a cradle for the development of more permanent works to be placed elsewhere in the city.

Abutting owners and entrepreneurs should have a share in the management of the space, along with the institutions which support the visual arts and the people of the city who use these streets. This multiple control could be achieved through a board of directors appointed by the mayor. The charter governing use of the space might secure some part of it as a gallery for major exhibitions of institutions such as the Institute of Contemporary Art. However, except for this sanctuary, the space would be fully public and thus the people who use it should be able, by some means short of physical destruction, to compel removal of works which seriously offend them, after some minimum guaranteed display period.

Given the overhead protection, the Washington subway concourse could be opened up to the place above and connected more directly with it. New usable space and activity could be created on still another level by a partial pedestrian fly-over on Washington Street, above the traffic and giving access to the mezzanine levels of the adjacent stores. This platform would be an ideal location for a major city information center, perhaps a multi-media presentation of the history, function, structure, and future possibilities of Boston.

Other more conventional uses are also important. There must be many places to sit and talk and places to eat and drink. There should be provisions for street musicians, street teachers, and street theater. It is not difficult to imagine that such a place might achieve some of the sense of abundance, diversity, and interest of the old European marketplace or the oriental bazaar. But far from imitating these examples, Boston's gallery of the street would have a unique style and character proper to this space and this time.

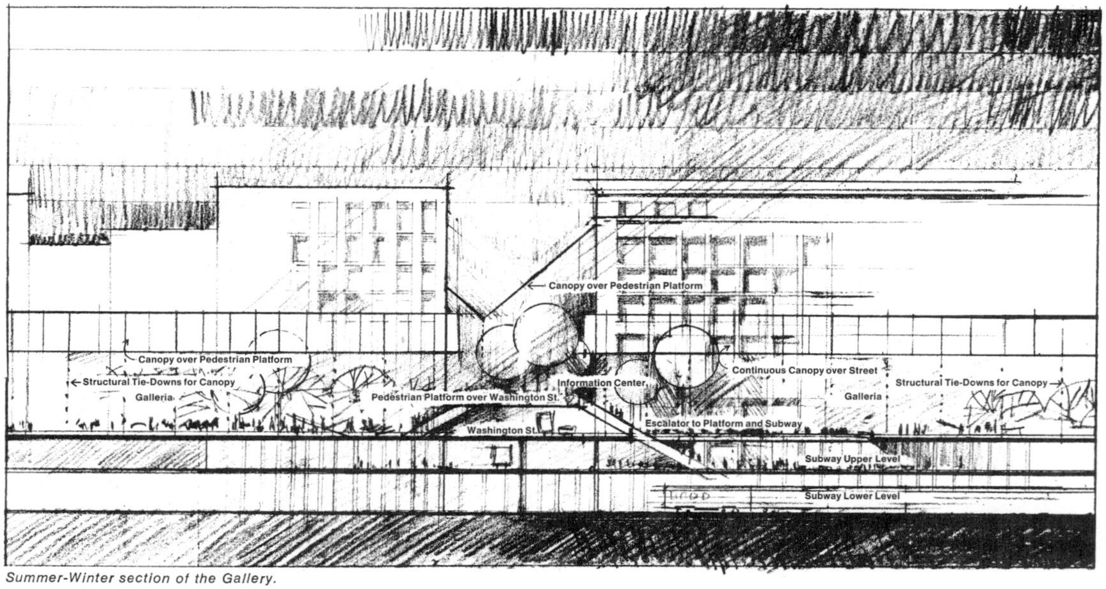

Summer-Winter section of the Gallery.

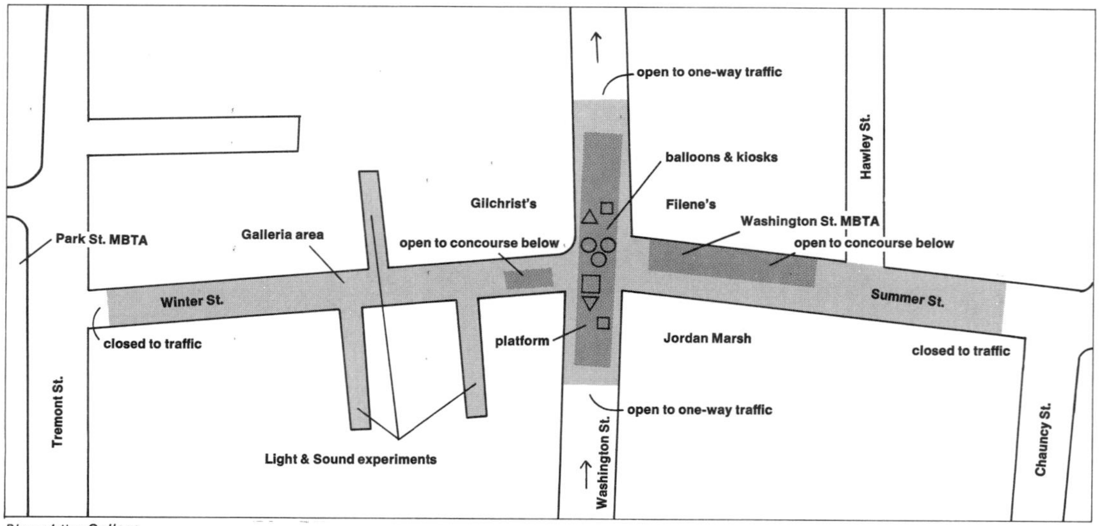

Plan of the Gallery.

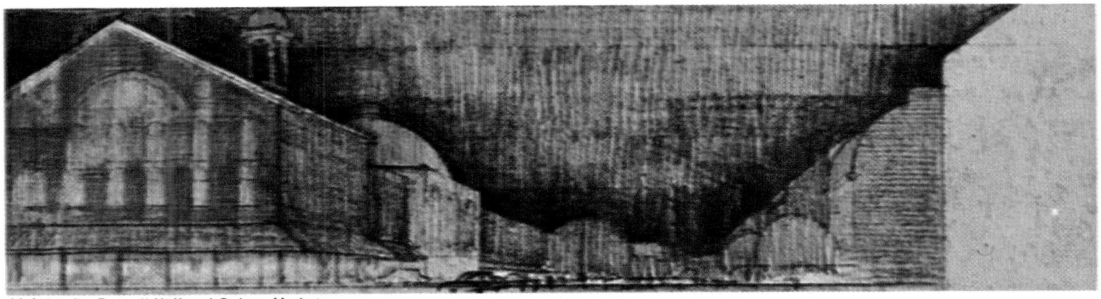

Lighting for Faneuil Hall and Quincy Market.

Old South Market Street.

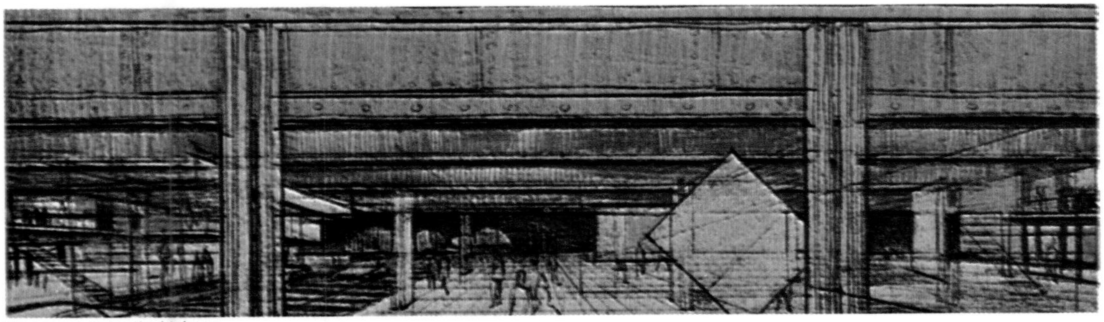

Workshops under the highway.

Lighting the new harbor-front.

HISTORY: LIGHTING THE FREEDOM TRAIL

Boston's Freedom Trail is already a unique path, principally for tourists, which links many of Boston's famous historic landmarks and passes through some of her more colorful districts. Many improvements are needed to provide much more and better presented information and to make the whole a more comfortable experience, but there is also great unexploited nighttime potential.

Overall floodlighting of historic buildings should be avoided in favor of more subtle re-creations of the character of the buildings in use. Faneuil Hall, with its ground floor market and the town meeting hall above, should be lit from within and from under the first floor canopy. The cupola should be softly floodlit. Quincy Market, immediately behind Faneuil Hall, should receive the same treatment but omitting the light from within.

Old South Market Street, soon to be a pedestrian mall, could be a summer location for temporary outdoor restaurants and cafes. An appropriate technique for this development, given the historic function of the place, would make use of antique trucks with their handsome form and graphics as roll-in kitchens and bars.

The trail should be extended to include a loop under the Fitzgerald Expressway out to the new harbor-front and back. Passage under the expressway is at present an unpleasant experience, likely to be depressing. The covered space under the road might be used for workshops where artists making large scale environmental constructions could have free space in exchange for public exposure of the process. Such activity under the highway could reverse the negative image.

The powerful meeting of granite-edged land with water requires restrained lighting. Light emanating from waterfront buildings should be supplemented by low light from ballards at the edges of the quays. Floating lights in the water can delineate its edge. The rigging lights on the U.S.S. Constitution, "Old Ironsides," would provide an appropriate focal point. Another cluster of lights might occur on the proposed mast museum.

Summary: Information Systems for People on Foot

Information systems for people on foot include a wide range of street hardware which should be developed and paid for in different ways depending on its purpose and who principally benefits. The city-wide system consisting of junction centers, district centers, local kiosks, and other supplementary sources is clearly intended to benefit all groups in the city. It should be paid for mainly by public funds, although it might well receive private donations, especially from merchants' associations which stand to benefit heavily. While some advertising devices might be incorporated under strict control of the city as a means of deferring the operating costs of the centers, it would be a serious mistake to rely on advertising sales to individual merchants (for example, a fee to have one's name on the directory) as the sole device for funding the centers. This procedure would quickly lead to commercialization of the content.

The policies and prototypes for central streets and spaces, for the most part, benefit some groups far more than others. Some of the prototypes contribute to the general nighttime public form of the city (Public Library, Public Garden lighting, and the Freedom Trail lighting) and thus are legitimately done with public funds supplemented by private contributions. However, most of the rest should be supported principally by private funds or contributions from those groups most directly interested or benefited. Often these will be merchants' associations or the particular owners and entrepreneurs abutting the space to be transformed. Where possible, of course, matching public funds from programs specifically set up to support such improvements should be sought (for instance, the Urban Beautification program or the National Endowment for the Arts).

How realistic, then, are these proposals? Can they be funded and carried out? Chapter 7 describes the process by which such policies might be initiated for central Boston and describes the estimated costs to the city. These are low by comparison with the public impact of the policies as demonstrated by the experiments already done. The critical question is the availability of private contributions, and here the city agency in charge would need to undertake a program of education to produce a spirit of enlightened self-interest. The Christmas constructs proposed for Back Bay would cost no more than a heavy treatment with standard Christmas decorations, yet they are also public works of art and could be paid for by a combination of local merchants and a joint public-private winter version of Boston's "Summerthing" (50% city and 50% private contributions). The Combat Zone proposals are a more strictly commercial venture to be paid for primarily by local businessmen. They can be sold, like any advertising device, in terms of people attracted to the area who might otherwise go elsewhere for their nighttime entertainment. The "Gallery of the Street" could no doubt be paid for in short order by increased sales of the abutting merchants, though its use as a gallery and information center would justify contributions from other sources, public and private. The same economic argument could be made for the Boylston Street promenade, although the pay-off period would be longer. Nonetheless, economic rationales are not the only arguments which should be used for such dramatic improvements in the appearance and informativeness of the central city.

Information Systems for People in Cars

Purchase St.
201-271
NO ENTRY
ONE WAY
Waterfront
So. Boston

Experimental Demonstrations

In mid-April, 1969, experimental components of information systems for people in cars were installed in Dewey Square and Park Square, two complicated and confusing traffic areas in downtown Boston. The demonstrations included guidance and traffic control signs, as well as modifications to traffic signal units and a pavement marking system. Field and laboratory evaluations tested the effectiveness of the new signs. More than half of them still remain in place. The experimental demonstrations tested principles in the field which were derived from other research and precedents. These principles then became the basis for a set of comprehensive recommendations. These principles are:

1 Information requiring different types of action by the driver should be conveyed differently.

2 Color, shape, message form, and location should be consistent for signs, signals, and markings conveying the same type of information.

3 Each type of information should be ranked for its importance to the driver, and this hierarchy should be expressed in the choice of color, shape, and message form and in rules governing location.

4 The system should prepare the driver in advance for turning decisions and oncoming road and traffic conditions.

5 All parts of the system should be designed to be visually distinctive against complicated urban backgrounds.

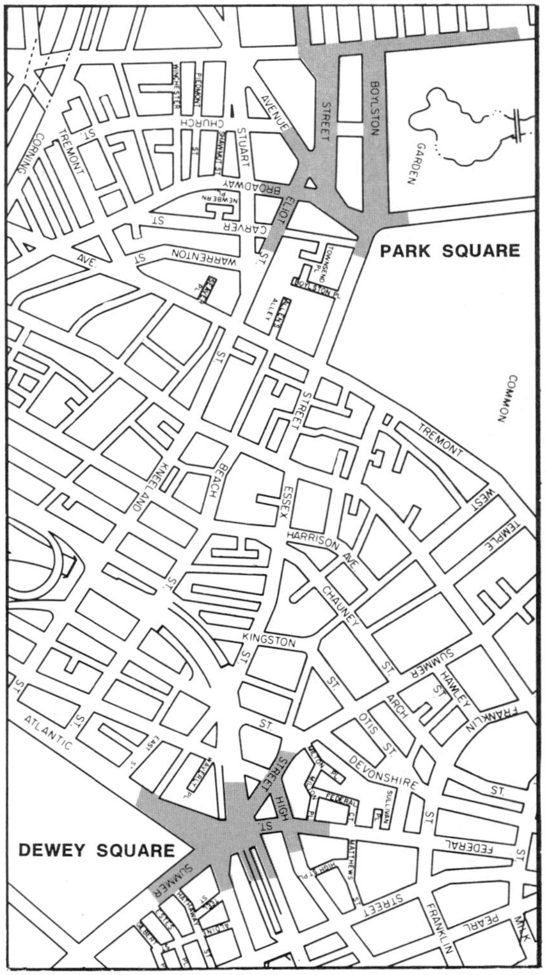

Demonstration areas.

SIGNING PRINCIPLES

Shape and Color Coding

Shape and color coding are the means of distinguishing the main classes of message for the driver in motion. Shape is seen first and should indicate the general class of message:

Circle	Critical rules: stop, yield, turn
Rectangle	Guidance, lane and curb usage, and speed regulation
Diamond	Warning

Color and shape combined should indicate the specific class of message:

Red circle	Braking rules
Green circle	Turning rules
Blue rectangle	Local guidance
Green rectangle	Distant guidance
Yellow diamond	Warning

The particular message is seen last and the driver has been prepared for it by the shape/color code. The choice of shape and color for each type of message is based on previous research (see Appendix 1), current usage, and an analysis of the problems of the present regulatory system. The principal need is to differentiate critical regulatory signs from all others (and from most signs in the urban environment): hence the circle, which also corresponds to the European "International" system. The diamond for warning signs is already distinctive and well learned, as is its color: yellow for danger. Within the critical regulatory system, red braking signs are further distinguished from green (for go) turning signs. Within the guide system, the use of green for distant destinations and blue for local ones is already well established on interstate highways.

For maximum "target value" against diverse backgrounds, all signs are given reflectorized surfaces and substantial borders of a contrasting color value: dark for light signs and light for dark colored signs. For dangerous intersections in areas of intense private signing, internally illuminated plastic faced box signs should be used.

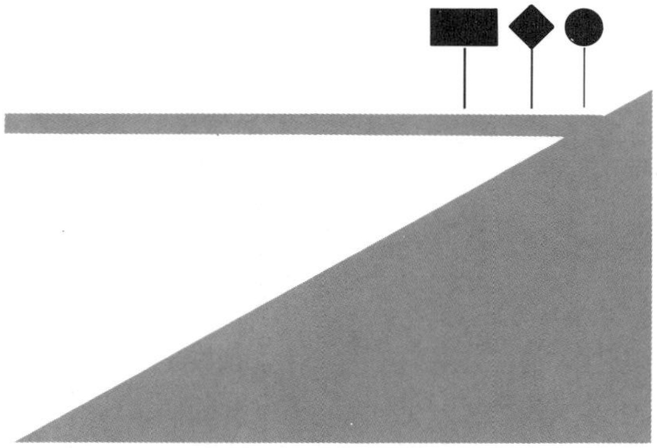

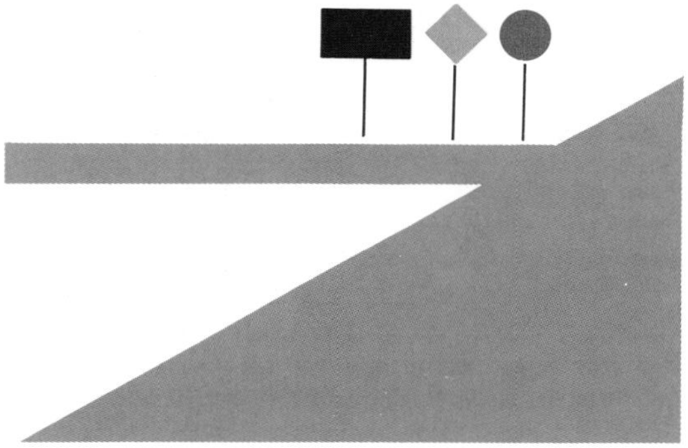

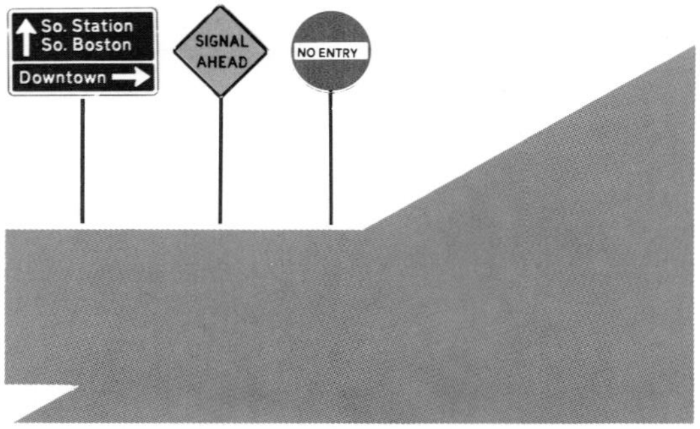

Message Form

The visibility of specific sign messages is determined by the choice of legend. While some types of messages are better conveyed by abstract symbols or pictures, most signs will require verbal messages: lettering is a critical variable. Assuming that the words are placed within a comfortably large, uniform background of maximally contrasting color value, their legibility will be determined by the form and size of lettering. (Research on the subject is reviewed in Appendix 1.)

The lettering used in this project is the same as that used by the British Ministry of Transport. It is an alphabet which was developed by Jock Kinneir, based on the best present evidence of performance. It is derived from the classic group of modern sans serif type face alphabets which includes Helvetica and Univers. Height to stroke width ratio is 6:1 (similar to series E of the U.S. standard alphabet). Condensed lettering is not used in the system for reasons of legibility and appearance.

An upper-lower case combination is used for all guide signs and upper case only is reserved for regulatory and warning signs. There is no conclusive evidence that either way is more legible, but it is generally thought that capital letters are more commanding and more appropriate for terse legends which demand respect.

Letter height is based on evidence that (for this type of letter) 1 inch of letter height gives about 50 feet of visibility. A 4½ inch "x" height is used for all directional signs, regulatory and warning signs. A 2½ inch "x" height is used for street name signs.

Pictures are useful for rapid and sure communication when they have become universally understood symbols. The arrow is one such symbol and is used for all turning regulation signs and retained for the one-way sign. Other less symbolic pictures — "pictographs" — can be useful where there are language difficulties but they often require special learning, are frequently ambiguous, and may get out of date (locomotives, airplanes). Nevertheless, they normally appear in signing system proposals, probably because graphic designers are fond of them.

TESTING THE PRINCIPLES IN BOSTON

The experimental signs were derived mainly from British and Canadian systems now in use, with some modifications. The British arrowhead, for example, does not work graphically in the slashed circle signs and tends to restrict arrow size in signs with two allowable directions; an arrowhead similar to current U.S. usage fits into all signs. The Canadian system was modified to make all turning movements positive rather than utilizing the negative red slashed circle. Legends were made consistently mandatory by using "only," rather than messages such as "no left turn" under a mandatory arrow sign. No significant changes were made in the U.S. "stop" sign, but the red circular "no entry" sign and a red triangular "yield" sign were tested. Some pictographic warning signs, set within the European red triangle, were demonstrated.

The recommended guide signing system also drew extensively on British experience (again the work of Jock Kinneir for the Ministry of Transport). A full range of guide system components was tested, from street name signs incorporating building numbers to large map diagrams giving advance directions for complex intersections. Besides being consistent with the Interstate system and highly legible, these bright blue reflectorized signs with their white borders and lettering are very handsome additions to the streetscape.

Both field and laboratory tests accompanied the demonstrations. The main findings are reviewed in Chapter 6 and full accounts are in Appendix 5. The demonstrations made clear that the color coded symbolic regulatory signs were considerably better than the corresponding rectangular legend signs currently in use throughout the United States. They were quicker and easier to read and understand; they looked better and helped reduce the visual clutter of the streetscape; and they were preferred both by the general public and professionals in motorist problems. It also became apparent from the tests that visual symbolic messages should be either well-known abstractions, like the arrow, or unambiguous pictorial representations. Thus, the cross of the "no stopping" sign has no visual relation to stopping and may even be confused with the better-known symbol for a railroad.

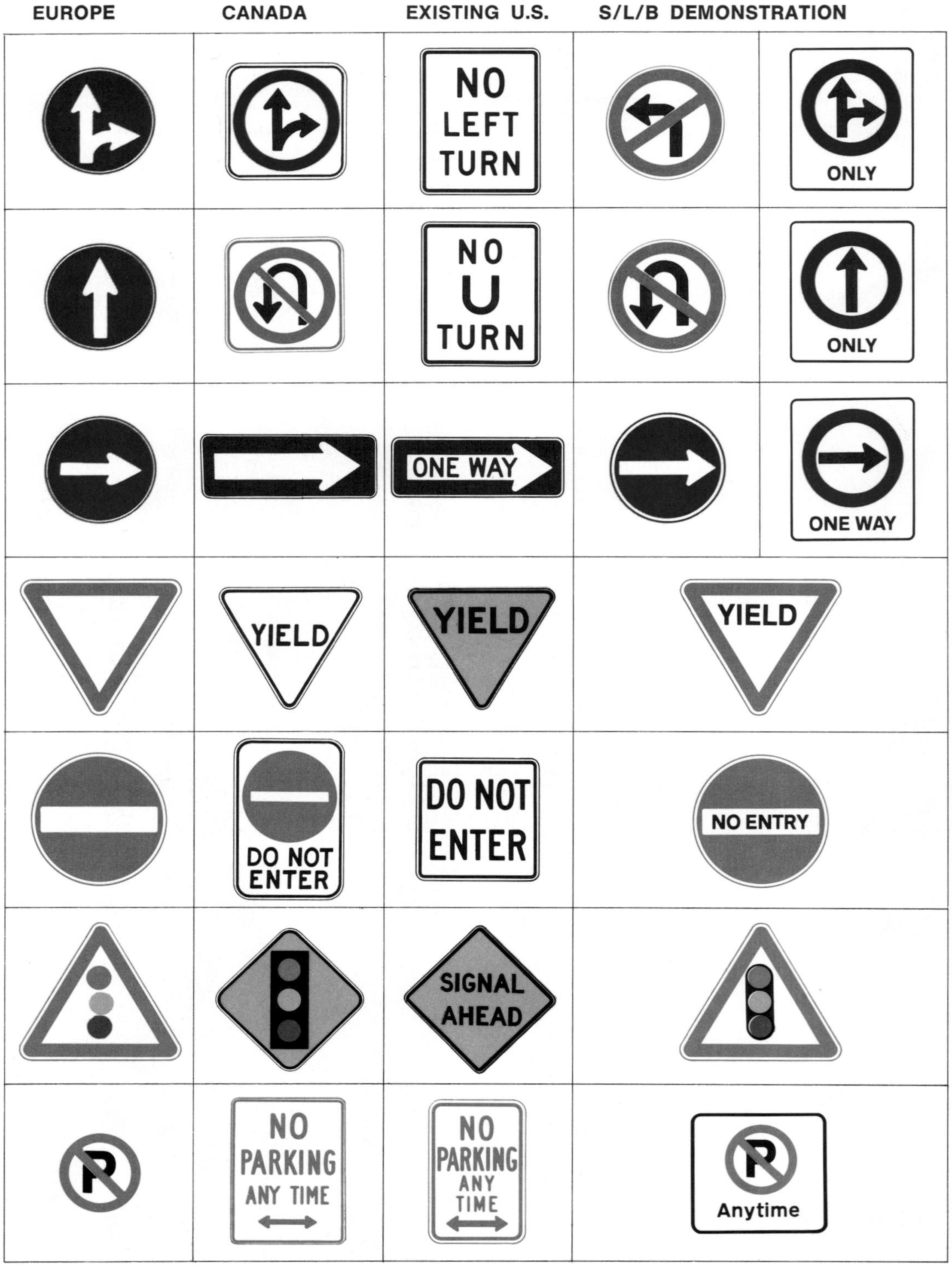

The guide system was partially tested by before and after driver confusion counts at several locations. In all cases, confusion appeared to be reduced but the meaning of these results is confounded by changes in the regulatory system and by the inadequate prior signing. The improvement in ease of movement and way-finding was remarked repeatedly, however, and hardly requires vigorous statistical proof to be appreciated.

The next step was to further systematize information giving, so that following the rules of the road becomes a more automatic process for the driver, freeing his mind for planning and strategy decisions as he tries to find his way about the city. The best sign systems will be those that require least learning and least effort to understand. They must be simple and logical and, where possible, derived from known symbolism. For example, the three basic rules conveyed by the red, yellow, and green of traffic signal lights are so well known that most drivers follow them without effort; this coding can be a model for similar rules of coding using shape, size, and location as well.

A City-Wide System

TRAFFIC CONTROL

System Identity
The chart is a compendium of current regulatory signs. It reveals that there are in fact several systems which should be separated out and treated differently. This reorganization is based on an analysis of the driving task, the driver's perceptual needs, and the groups at which the messages are aimed. The different classes of sign are indicated by the over-printed symbols.

The circular sign shape is reserved for critical regulations involving braking and turning actions. Other important signs regulating lane usage are increased in size and gain a contrasting border. Parking signs retain their rectangular shape but are made smaller. There are several signs that are currently classed as regulatory but which should be transferred to the warning system. Red and green are used in their conventional negative and positive meanings (all turn signs are made positive).

The chart also gives separate identity to signs aimed at truck drivers and pedestrians. Here, obvious pictographs might be used. Black on white should be retained to avoid confusion with signs for automobile drivers.

A system not dealt with here but which is presently in operation on some highways involves changeable flow state information and regulation. By means of centrally programmed light grid signs, levels of traffic on major streets, congestion points and alternate routes, dangerous road conditions and special speed limits could be signaled at major intersections.

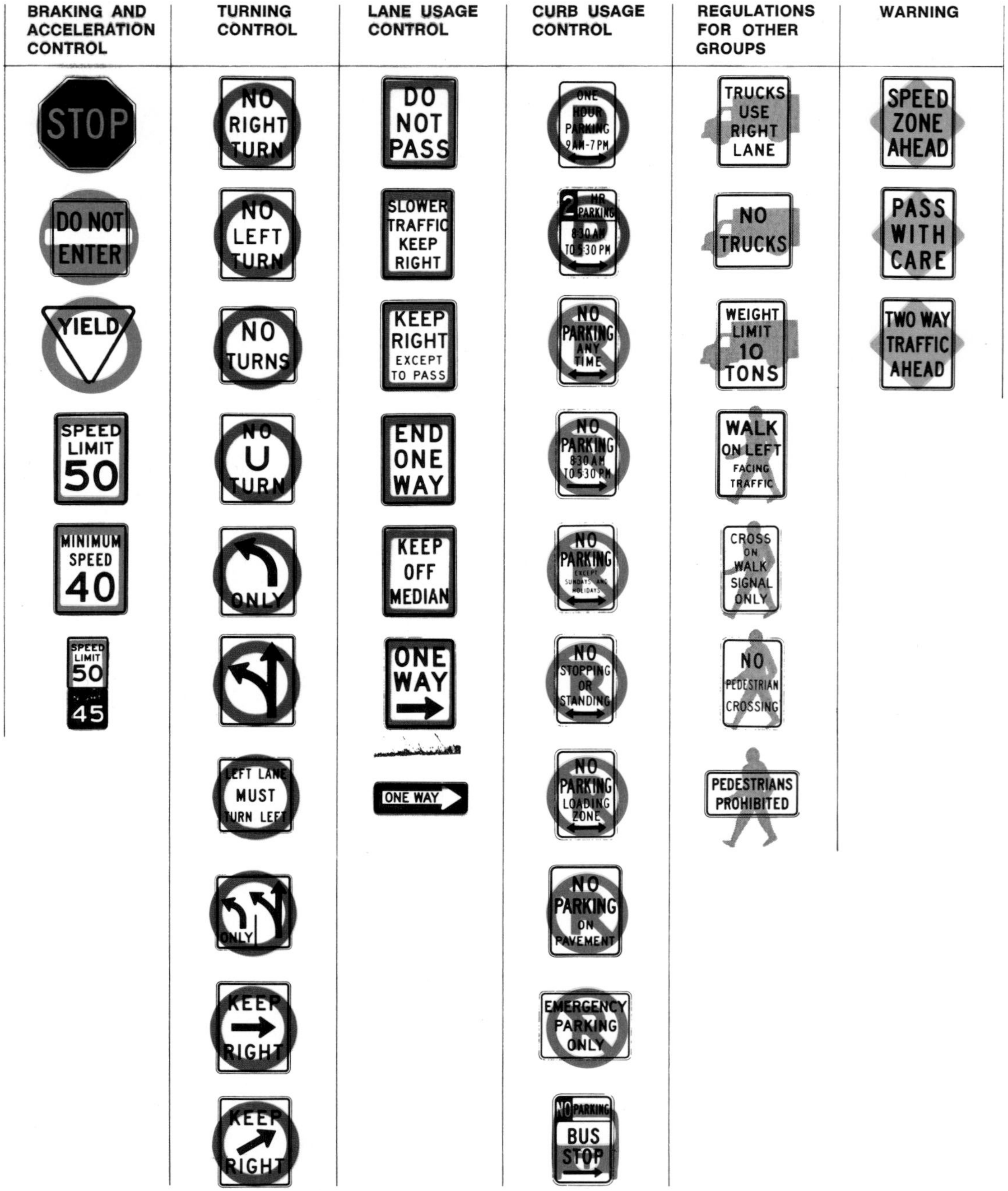

Signal Lights

Signal lights are probably the most effective traffic control devices: they are easily understood and generally obeyed from the age of four onward. Nevertheless, recognition of signal lights, and particularly of turn arrows, can be difficult against a cluttered background of private signs and lights. Increasing the size of the lights may help (from 8 inches to 12 inches is common). New high-intensity, long-life lamps could produce significant gains in contrast. Another aid is a neutral background provided by a baffle plate. The demonstration unit shown here has a reflecting border as well.

The driver's visual task at intersections would be considerably simplified if regulatory and street name signs were combined with signal units or attached to the same pole. Various arrangements of these elements are possible. In many cities it is common (and good) practice to attach all these elements to a street light pole.

The horizontal unit shown here should be developed as a coordinated regulatory, street name, and light pole unit. This unit gets the signals closer to the center of the driver's field of view, but avoids the grotesquely heavy superstructure of some current signal support arms. Turn arrows are larger. It provides a visually-dominant location for street name signs (which could be rear-illuminated from the same wiring system). The horizontal signal unit is available (and used in Canada) and could easily be adapted to incorporate the street name signs. Only minor modifications in light poles, such as the addition of threaded sleeves in Boston's current standard concrete pole, would be necessary to allow for attachment of the units and regulatory signs.

This policy requires a new level of coordination among city departments, but the gains in effectiveness of public information systems by integration at these relatively few critical points would more than justify the effort. The overall cost to the city should be less than that of current uncoordinated practice which results in a clump of corner fixtures, each with its own pole, base, and wiring.

Braking Signs
The current regulatory sign system does not consistently identify required braking actions: the STOP sign is in white lettering on a red octagon; the DO NOT ENTER sign is in black lettering on a white rectangle; and YIELD is in black letters on a yellow triangle. But these three signs are in the same category as the red stop light and should be so identified. Since red is firmly established as the color cue for both the stop light and the stop sign, DO NOT ENTER and YIELD should be similarly coded. The three signs should also have related shapes.

Other signing systems have identified the stopping category and offer some alternatives. The British system uses the red color coding, but its use of both a triangle and circle for the STOP sign seems unnecessarily complicated. Red could replace yellow in the YIELD sign and the international convention, a red circle with a white bar, adopted for NO ENTRY.

A more consistent solution would be to adopt the circle for all three signs, in accord with the signal light. YIELD, in this system given a white border, would be less emphatic than the all-red circle, since it requires a braking but not a full-stop response. Thus, any red circle requires a braking action to a greater or lesser degree. This is a very simple rule to learn and demands less of the driver than the disparate signs that are currently used.

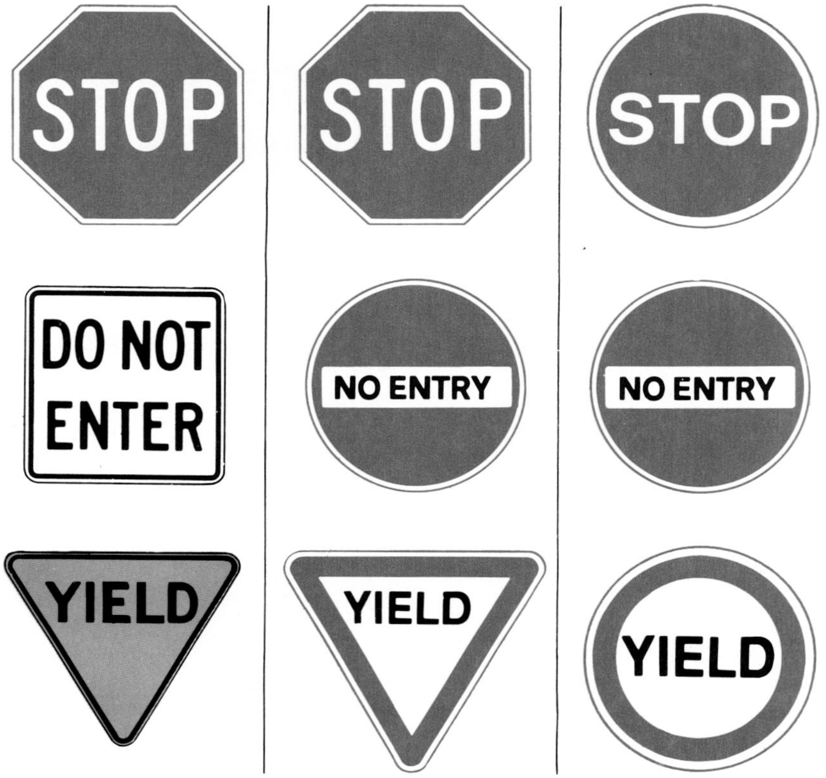

Turning Signs
Rules which require turning actions also follow no consistent system of presentation in current standard signs. Signs have black legends on a white background, but they may be square or rectangular and they vary in size and legend. Some messages are negative (NO LEFT TURN); some are positive (KEEP RIGHT). The driver must read and translate each legend every time he sees it, whether he needs the information or not.

The recommended system has been made as direct and immediate as the braking system. It is coded by shape, color, and symbol to tell the driver that: **1** it is a critical regulatory system (circle); **2** it is a turning, as opposed to a braking action (green); and **3** that there are only certain permissible movements (arrows). Green color coding is an extension of the known symbolism of the GO signal light, appropriate for these consistently positive messages which tell the driver what he may or must do. Arrows are better than legends, because they are quicker and easier to read and comprehend. Signal lights have themselves evolved from a simple green circle by the addition of arrow symbols which contain turning messages. The particular arrow form chosen is twice as legible as any other since it conveys information for its whole length. (The same arrow should be adopted, without the unnecessary legend, for the ONE WAY sign — a lane usage sign — shown here.)

This is a simple, legible way to present the complicated turning rules that occur so frequently in city areas. The system is also economical, since it reduces the number of different signs to a minimum.

Curb Usage: Signs

Rules of curb usage conveyed by ubiquitous NO PARKING, LOADING, BUS STOP, TAXI STAND signs are not as important to the safe and efficient movement of traffic as regulatory and warning signs and should be less dominant in the streetscape. Curb usage signs should not be jumbled together with the stopping, turning, and warning systems.

One way of clarifying parking information would be to meter all parking in areas of high demand. The number of signs would be drastically reduced. In areas of less intense demand, with no or occasional meters, color-coded signs (red, NO; green, YES) would simplify the search process. In Park Square, one street was re-signed with the curb usage set shown here.

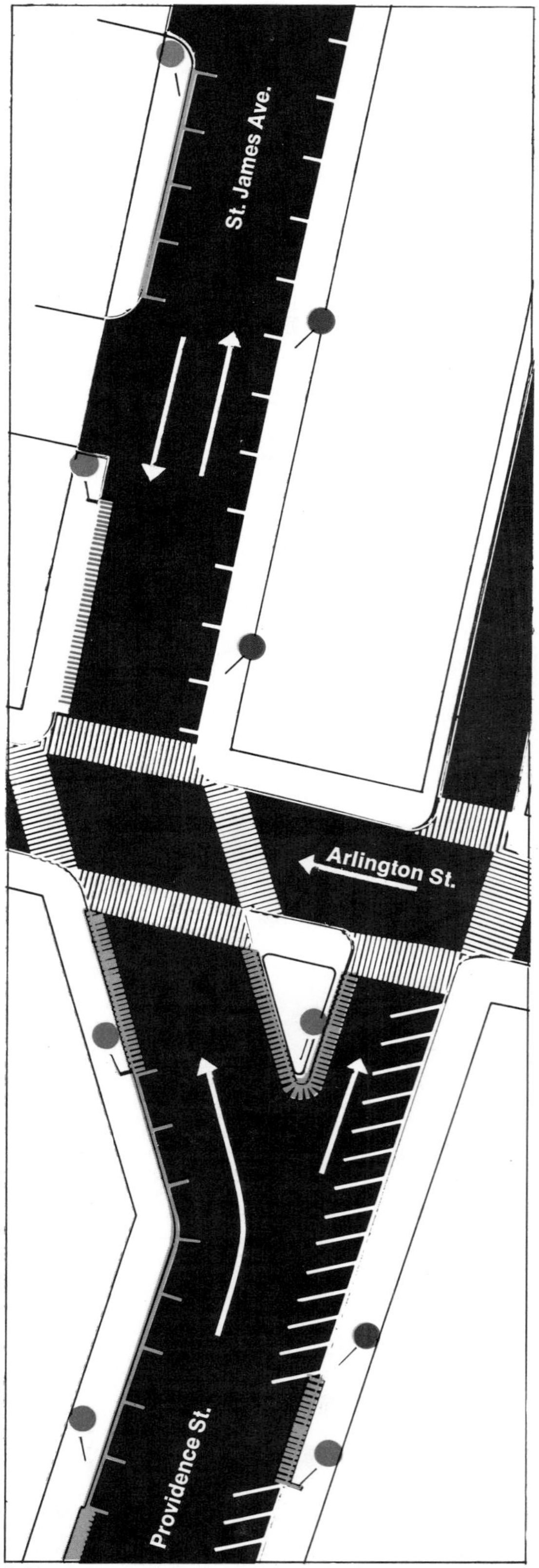

Parking signs and curb markings demonstrated in Park Square.

Markings

Curb usages can be further clarified by a pavement marking system, as demonstrated in Park Square. Color coding and pattern were used to show the various possibilities. The pattern — striping — was chosen for its vividness. It extends from the curb itself halfway into the parking lane to act as a visual barrier: a car will not fit comfortably on the pattern. With normal snow clearance, the pattern should remain visible during most of the snow season.

The color coding is simple: red (and white) stripes mean no parking at any time; yellow stripes, restricted parking (taxis only, loading, etc.); white, car-width bays show permitted parking. (Thermo-plastic tape or powder is recommended over paint for durability.) Signing would be reduced to one at the beginning of each restricted section, instead of one at each end. Pavement markings are at their best in defining zones (lanes, crosswalks, parking). They may be dangerous for more particular messages (words, arrows) since too much attention to the road surface can mean missing a car or pedestrian just ahead. Any use, of course, must be regularly enforced to be effective.

MESSAGES FOR PEDESTRIANS IN THE RIGHT OF WAY

Crosswalks, Signs, and Signals

The standard method of delineating pedestrian crosswalks is visually weak. If a crosswalk is to serve its purpose, it should be obvious to the motorist as a barrier and persuasive to the pedestrian as his turf. The marking system demonstrated in Park Square produces visually dominant paths that command respect.

A vigorous law-enforcement program would be a necessary complement to show motorists and pedestrians alike that the markings really mean what they appear to say. Even when enforced, as in London and California, the results for pedestrian safety are ambiguous. Some studies suggest that accidents may actually increase (at least temporarily) due to a combination of pedestrians becoming more assertive of their rights — resulting in quick stops and rear-end collisions — and relaxed vigilance. These are probably short-term adaptation problems, however.

Signs and signals regulating the flow of pedestrians are not treated here. WALK/DON'T WALK signals appear to be adequate to the task. Pedestrians have time to read current regulatory signs, but identification could be aided by the addition of a pedestrian pictograph. In the new system, they would be distinctive by virtue of being the only remaining signs in black on white.

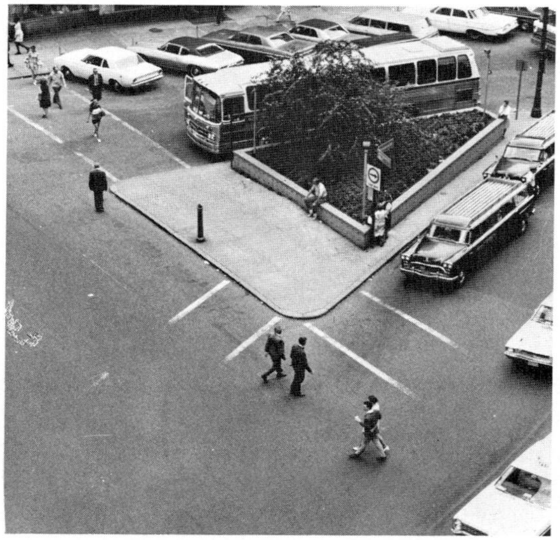

Transit Stops
Until recently, prospective transit bus passengers had a hard time even identifying bus stops in Boston. The bus user had to look for a "No Parking" sign and hope that it would say "Bus Stop" in a subsidiary message. The MBTA has recognized the problem and has begun to install "T" signs for stop identification. The bus user has his own needs and should not have to rely on signs which are part of the regulatory system for motorists.

The bus sign illustrated performs a number of functions. It identifies the stop from a distance. The route number gives specific information within the target symbol. The sign also includes a map of the route and schedule information. As a further development, there should be a signal light on the sign which lights by remote control when the bus is within five minutes of the stop. The intensity of the light might indicate loading.

The needs of the passenger on the bus are also provided for by the sign, which shows a large stop number. This number would be keyed to route maps in the bus which would identify stops by street name. Even in peak-hour crowds, the passenger would have a reasonable chance of occasionally spotting the large stop numbers and could thereby calculate his progress toward his destination.

The same principles also apply to signing for rapid transit stops. Here Boston, along with several other cities, has already made progress in adopting new standards which include use of color coding, local area maps within the stations and symbolic simplified maps showing the whole system (these unfortunately lack topographic reference). A large illuminated "T" will mark the locations of station head houses from a distance.

LIGHTING FOR SAFETY

Street lighting makes essential information visible to people abroad in the city at night. The level of illumination must be sufficient for people to perceive a potential hazard and evaluate it in time to plan and carry out an appropriate action with a minimum of stress. This requirement is a matter of debate among illumination engineers and researchers. It will vary with the speed of the traffic, the reflectance of the road surface, the presence or absence of oncoming headlights, and the light from surrounding buildings and activities.

Current standards range between 0.2 foot-candle for outlying residential streets and 2.0 foot-candles for major downtown streets and expressways. If these levels are adequate for driving safety, they should be more than adequate for people on foot who have more time to see a potential danger. A few cities have created levels up to 20 foot-candles in downtown areas. Cars could run safely on parking lights at these levels, which might increase safety by reducing the confusion of headlights, but they are far higher than can be justified by anything that is known about the relation between crime and light (see Appendix 2) or light and business. Despite a trend toward higher levels there is insufficient evidence as yet to conclude that present standards are too low for driving or walking safety.

Glare is another matter. Unshielded high intensity lamps, especially when mounted at levels below 35 feet, glare uncomfortably. Drivers have a right to be protected from this additional source of distraction and potential visual overload. Shields also protect the privacy of occupants of upper stories in adjacent buildings. This project demonstrated semi-cut-off shields on one block of Boston's standard 400-watt mercury vapor lamps, mounted at 29 feet. The shields are inexpensive and the increase in driving comfort is noticeable. Full cut-off fixtures, like those shown at Logan Airport, would be even better but imply somewhat higher system costs because closer spacing or higher mounting would be necessary to meet illumination uniformity standards.

Glare from standard double mercury fixture.

Semi-cut-off shields demonstrated on Boylston Street.

Full cut-off fixture in use at Logan Airport, Boston.

ORIENTATION SIGNS

System Identity

The system of guide signs must convey unambiguous directions and destinations and give systematic preparation for turning decisions. This is not only so that the motorist can go from one point to another within the city without undue confusion or false turns, but also so that he can develop an accurate mental image of the layout of the city. In Boston, of course, this is a formidable challenge. But in any city, however clearly and simply structured, guidance information is an essential public system.

Expressways, for the most part, are clearly signed in accordance with national standards for highway guide signs. But when the driver leaves the exit ramp in Boston, he is confronted by a very confusing street system and is given little help in reaching his destination.

The recommended in-city guidance system is color-coded blue, which distinguishes it from the green highway system but also relates to the existing highway practice of coding local service signs blue. The driver approaching urban areas can quickly separate local (blue) from distant (green) destinations. In leaving the city, green means exit, as opposed to local routes.

Sign Sequence
The guidance system shown here organizes the city by district, an appropriate unit for Boston. Lynch found in *The Image of the City* that districts in Boston are generally well-defined physical, social, and activity areas and seem to be widely used in orientation. In other cities, districts may be ill-defined, too large or too little-known to be meaningful units; in such cases major streets, or nodes (centers or intersections), or both, may be the meaningful units for the guidance system. In each city a special analysis, including citizen interviews, will be required to determine the most appropriate local system of orientation.

The recommended guidance system would provide information at intersections and at points along the route. Generally, only immediately adjacent districts (or whatever unit is being used) would be identified, and the successive naming of these at each decision point would increase understanding of city structure.

Prior to major intersections (at mid-block), advance information is presented to prepare the driver for oncoming decisions. This may be done by map diagrams, or normal stack type directional signs, identifying districts or by trailblazers to major specific destinations. At the intersection, improved street name signs state the driver's immediate location, including the building numbers on that block (the number nearest the sign appears in the white box), and the next major street. Information previously presented on the advance directional signs is repeated at the intersection as confirmation to the driver.

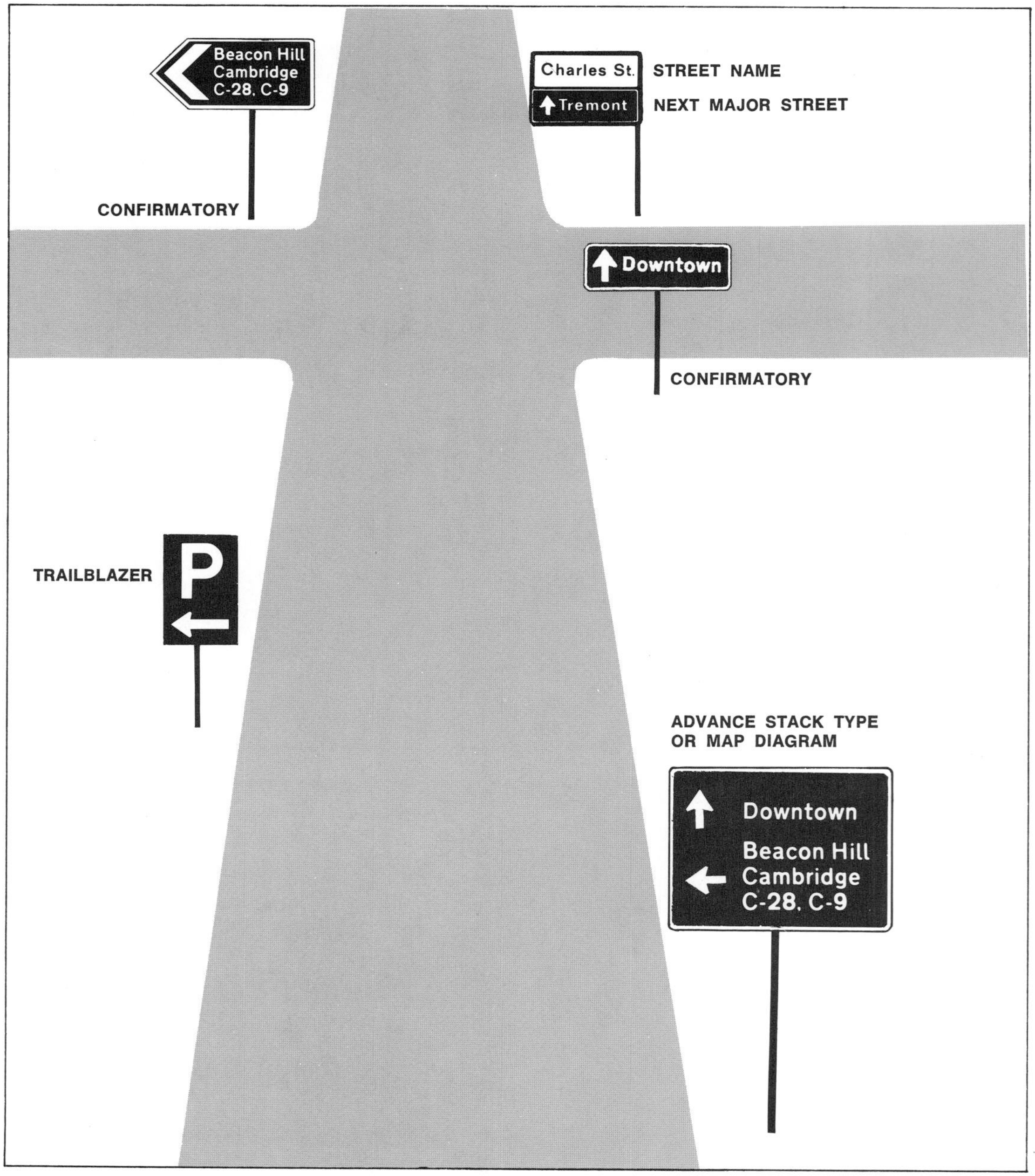

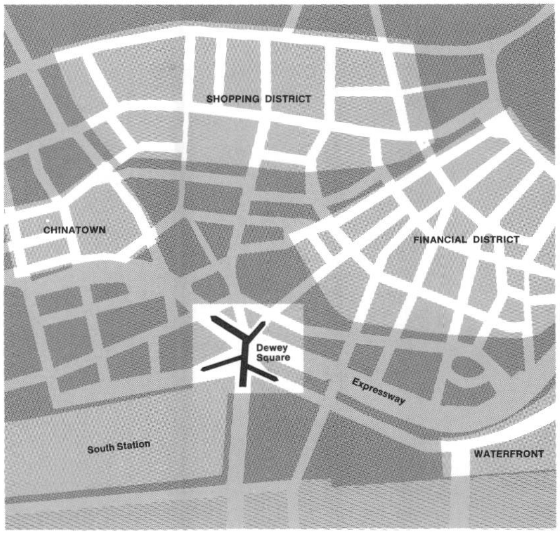

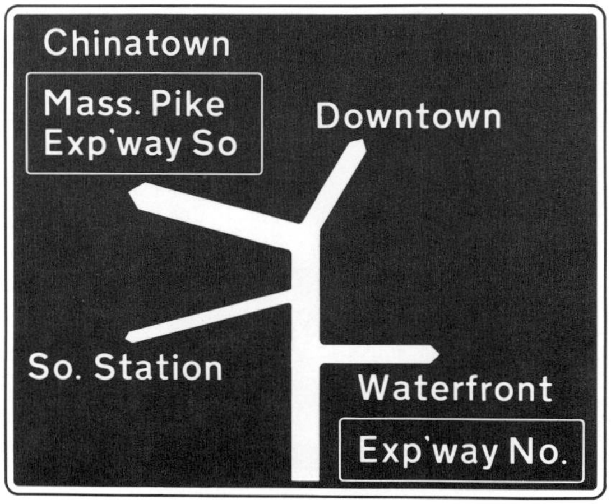

Complex Intersections

Intersections are the most important decision-making points. At its simplest, the guide system would show street names (in properly-sized lettering, including block numbers), and the next destination points. However, at complicated intersections — such as Dewey Square in the demonstrations — there must be more, and more complicated information. Here, where there were multiple intersections, not all at right angles, not all two-way, advance map diagrams of the situation were installed. Such diagrams are in use in Britain and Europe and are both helpful and problematic.

Unlike ordinary stack signs which can only deal with simple right angle crossings, map diagrams can give a complete picture of an intersection. At their most elaborate they can show the relative importance of each road that may be entered (by making it narrow or wide) and indicate also roads which cannot be entered (by stubs or no-entry symbols). All this valuable planning information makes a complicated picture, however, and unless the driver has ample time to read the sign, a simpler diagram, like the one below, is preferable. Map diagrams have the further liability of being costly and large and therefore difficult to place in the streetscape, especially in older cities like Boston where sidewalks are narrow. This study demonstrated but did not test them, and although they received many favorable comments, their real effectiveness is not known. Questions about the amount of time needed to comprehend the signs, about individual capabilities for reading plan diagrams, and about the interactions between driver, sign, and intersection were beyond the scope of this study to test.

Trailblazers
Besides districts and streets, some specific destinations should be identified. As the name implies, trailblazers mark — as the woodsman with his axe or the scout with his stone cairns — the way to these specific destinations. In this category come all the public services and pleasures: parking, hospitals, airports, rail and bus stations, subway stations; zoos, parks, museums, stadia, city hall. Paths to major commercial destinations such as department stores or shopping centers should also be blazed, at the expense of the enterprise.

For the major public services, unambiguous national symbols are desirable — letters are recommended here — accompanied by a specific legend. Other destinations which are more particular to each city (parks, museums) should employ pictographs ("logos") to express their unique identity. Some already have logos, and the trailblazer signs should use them. Where there is presently no graphic symbol, an effort should be made to develop and use one as part of the public information program.

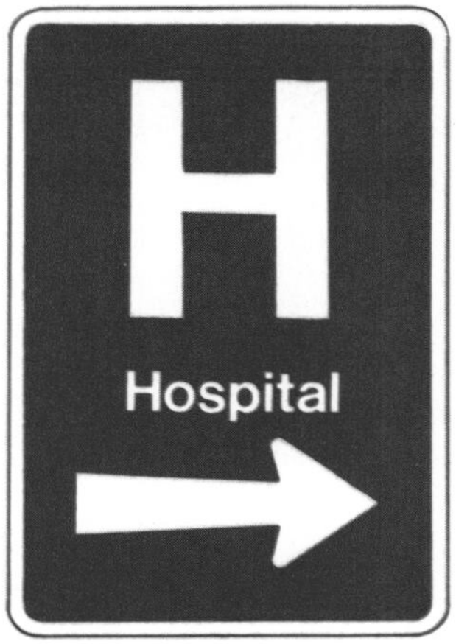

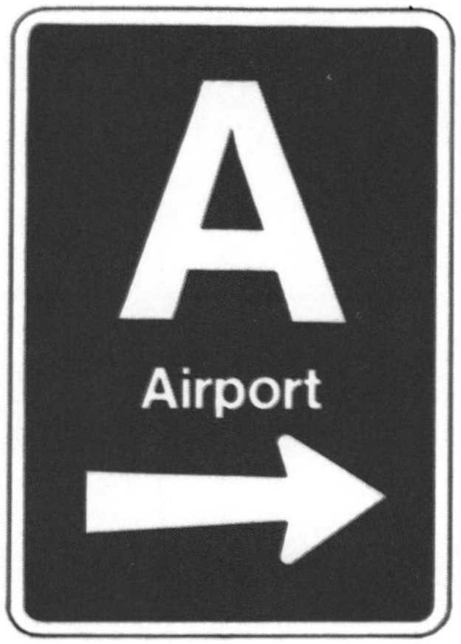

Public events trailblazers

Many short-term or seasonal events in the city should have temporary directional signing. As part of Boston's "Summerthing," musical performances and other events are staged in parks in various districts of the city. These locations are often unfamiliar to a large part of the audience. To assure legibility, correct timing, and visibility throughout the city, a temporary sign procedure should be established within the Traffic and Parking Department.

New foam-core plastic and paper combinations provide an inexpensive and sufficiently durable short-term material for such signs. Adhesive-backed, pre-cut reflectorized plastic sign face sheeting and a pre-cut standardized lettering system, like that recommended here, would allow the signs to be quickly and cheaply made. They can be temporarily attached to other guide sign assemblies.

LIGHTING FOR ORIENTATION

Beyond providing safe passage, street lighting should signal and describe things to come. Changes in the trafficway like pedestrian crossings, curves, intersections, rotaries, and interchanges should be specially lit to alert the driver to their oncoming presence and to reveal the shape of paths of movement.

All signalized intersections need additional light — at least three times the level of the intersecting streets. To signal the driver in advance, a different light color (warmer for pedestrians) should be used at intersections, provided either by a different type of source, such as high-intensity sodium vapor, or by tinted lenses. Pole spacing should be adjusted so that two or more will normally occur at corners in locations which are also appropriate for the attachment of the horizontal signal units and traffic signs. Rotaries and interchanges will require unique lighting solutions to meet the criteria of advance notice to drivers and delineation of movement paths.

Some important central streets deserve special lighting, both to identify them and to make them more pleasant. Light levels should be at least 3 foot-candles in mid-block and 10 at intersections. To give the street a strong rhythmical structure, lights should be paired and spaced more closely than normal. Intersections would have four lights; in addition, there might be special sidewalk lights, attached either to the street lights or the buildings.

City-wide master lighting plans, which attempt to specify detailed solutions for every condition, are unnecessary. Few cities will be in a position to carry out such plans all at once and the available hardware is changing rapidly. If different standards of intensity are systematically applied to different types of streets, if intersections and interchanges receive special treatment, if significant pedestrian paths and places and public buildings are lighted in unique and appropriate ways, and if private signing and lighting are regulated and enhanced, then the city will become a safer, more legible and hospitable place at night.

Pedestrian lights attached to street light poles.

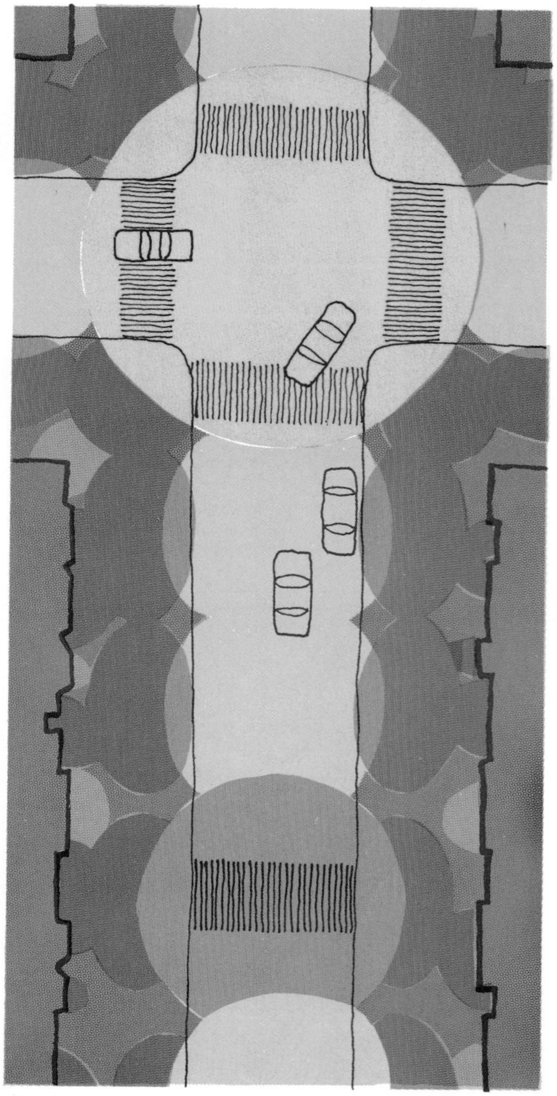

Approach to the rotary from Longfellow Bridge.

Lane choice confusion.

Approach from Charles Street.

INTERCHANGES: THE CHARLES STREET ROTARY

Interchanges between highways and city streets are typically the most dangerous and confusing points in the circulation system. Unlike rural highway interchanges, these must be fit into the existing fabric of streets and buildings. The standard gentle curves and long decision distances of highway design can seldom be achieved; instead changes in alignment are abrupt and decisions must be made with little or no time to spare. In addition, the presence of buildings or other structures often precludes an overall view of the situation. When the "normal" distractions of private signs and lights are added, the confusion can become intolerable.

The Charles Street Rotary is typical of such knots in the circulation net and adds a few special twists of its own (see Appendix 4 for a full analysis of its problems). In fast-moving heavy traffic, the rotary can be navigated only at severe risk to one's safety. Six separate streams of traffic from a bridge, a parkway, and two city streets come together in a very constricted space to sort themselves into four separate exiting streams. An elevated transit line cuts a curving diagonal path above the rotary, through a station located dead in the center. Several pedestrian bridges, like the last remaining tentacles of a landlocked giant squid, extend from the station over the traffic to the perimeter. On that perimeter, an all-night drugstore, a gas station, a parking lot, and a drive-in sandwich stand invite cars to move erratically in and out of the flow. To complete this city driver's nightmare, the guide signing is both inadequate and misleading (stating destinations ambiguously, too late, or not at all) and the scattered mercury vapor lights are both insufficient and confusing in their pattern.

The prospect for people on foot is little better. Attempting to cross the rotary at ground level is an exercise in reality testing, the more so because drivers under such stress are likely to have little attention left for pedestrians. While it is possible to move across the rotary through the MBTA station without paying, the trip is an unpleasant one, especially in winter, and there are no signs indicating that it can be done.

Untying the Knot

The Charles Rotary is a principal entry into the city from the Longfellow Bridge and Cambridge and from Boston's riverfront artery, Storrow Drive. It is a critical connection between Beacon Hill (via Charles Street) and Government Center. The immediately adjacent major hospitals are important destinations for many people coming both by car and by transit. It deserves much better treatment than it has so far received.

Besides the need for an appropriate environmental information system, there is also a formal challenge. In many places in the city, transportation systems interlock and there are likely to be more such junctions in the future as new forms of (probably elevated) center city transportation are developed. The place not only could be made to work better, it might also become an engaging event for those who pass through.

As a first critical step, lane usage must be specified. The intersection is far too complicated for such graphic devices as map diagram guide signs to be of any use. They would simply add to the information overload. Instead, a more dramatic solution — an extension of the principle of traffic channeling by islands — should be adopted: lanes leading to different exit routes (there are four) should be marked on the pavement in stripes of different colors (thermoplastic tape, which has eight to ten times the life of paint, should be used). These lanes would be keyed to equally colorful overhead guide signs, listing the destinations for each. This color coding must start far enough (at least one full block) in advance to allow cars to weave their way into the proper slot. Overhead guide signing, especially on the bridge, should come even earlier. The diagrams show how the color would be applied and indicate the flow sequence through the rotary.

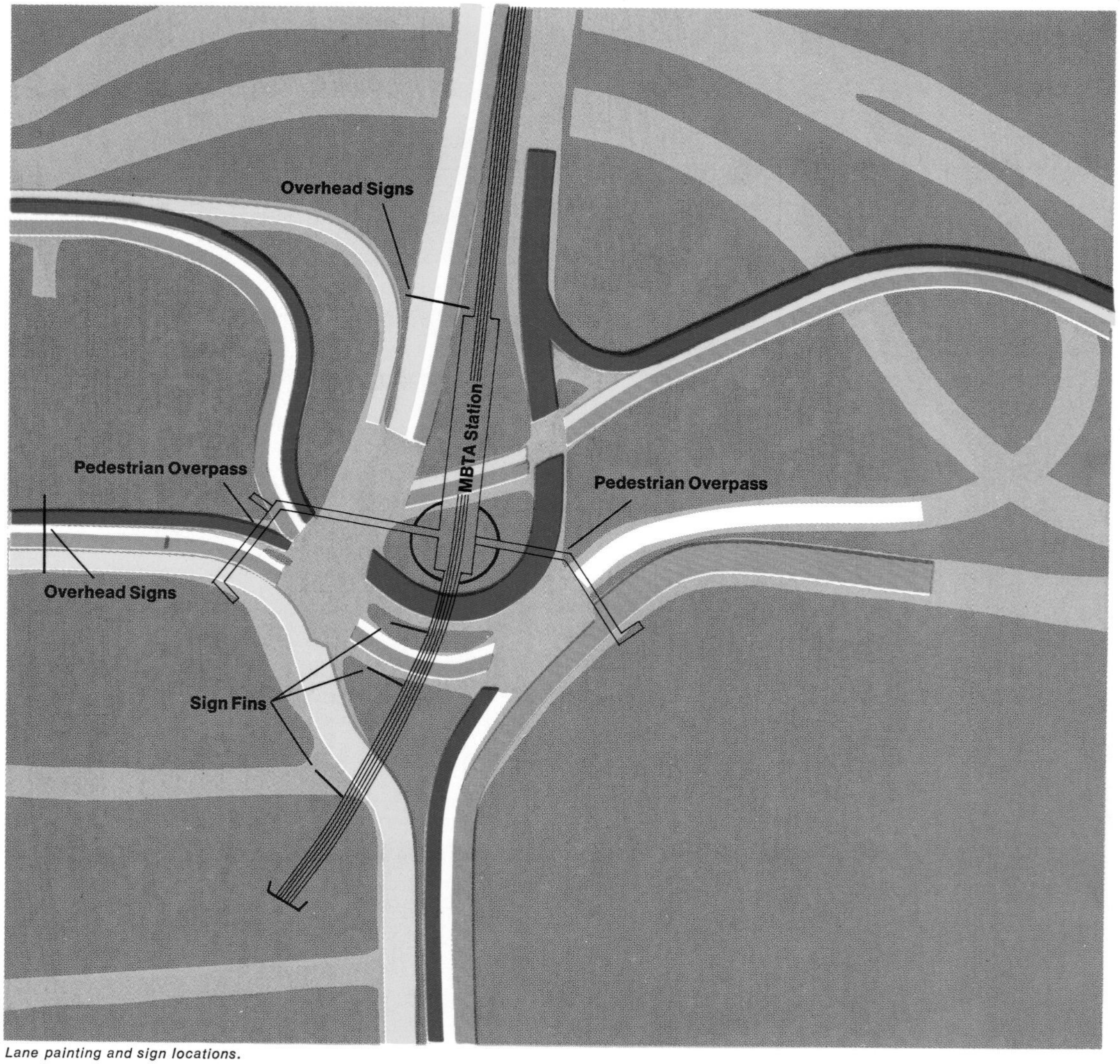

Lane painting and sign locations.

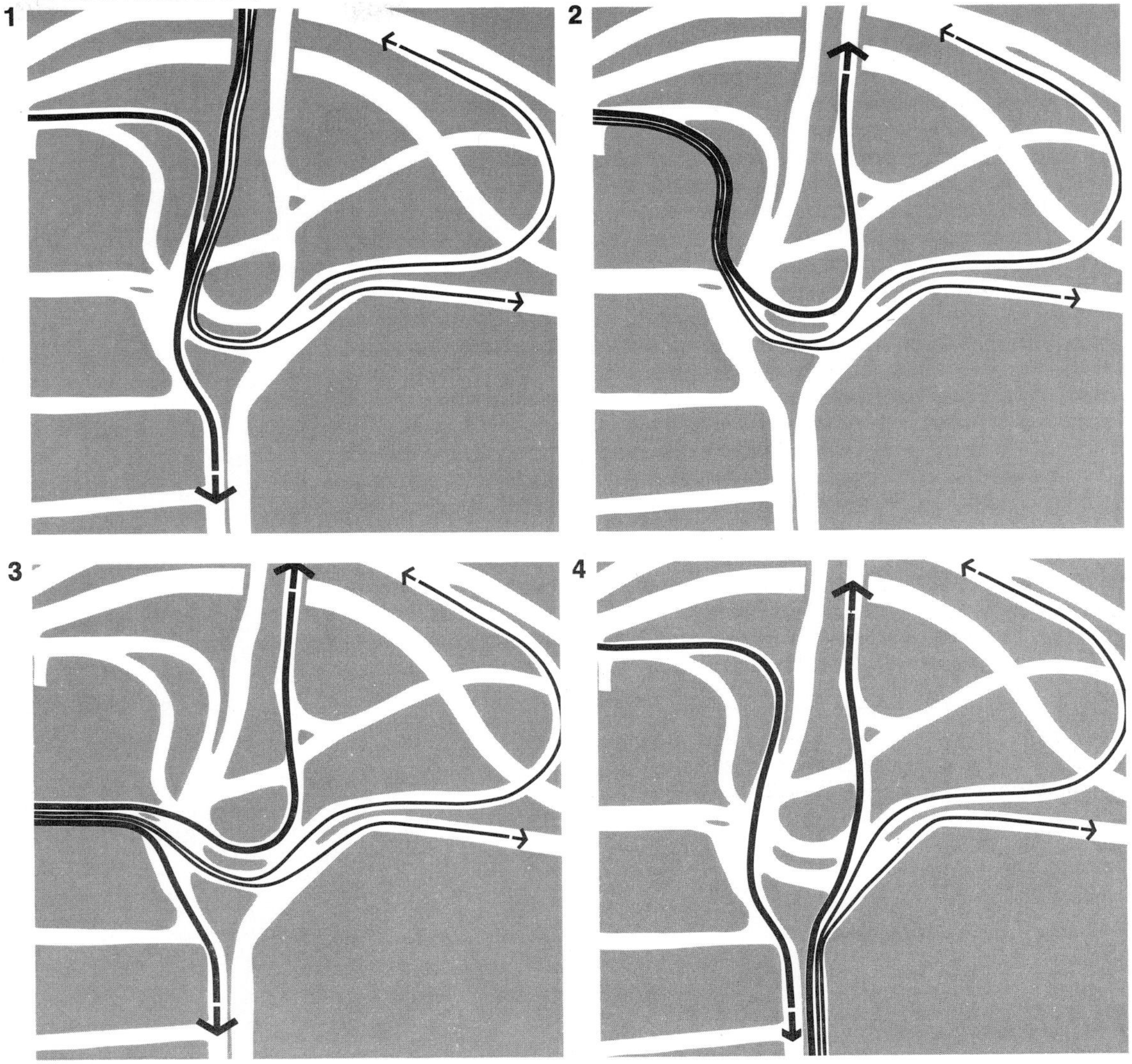

Flow sequence through the rotary.

From the ground, the new system should be equally clear. In the first sequence of drawings, the driver enters the scene as if he were coming (by heli-car) from Cambridge. He first notices the large tri-color overhead sign near the Cambridge end of the Longfellow Bridge which guides his lane choice according to destination. He finds the same three colors striped onto the pavement as he moves into the proper lane. As he approaches the rotary itself, he finds his original choice confirmed by another bright overhead sign. As he moves through the rotary, he is guided to the correct passage under the MBTA tracks by diagonal signs like huge check marks saying "yes, here!"

Approaching from Charles Street by night, a similar lane definition guides the motorist into the rotary where the color coding and signs on the train bridge enable him to choose the correct passage. These larger signs include a fuller listing of destinations. There are also new glass canopies over the pedestrian bridges which not only make them more pleasant to use, but also transform them into handsome elements in the space. New horizontal signal units are incorporated into these bridges and existing signals on ground poles are removed.

Lighting is increased and clarified. High-mounted (40 feet) high-pressure sodium lamps are located at closely spaced intervals around the perimeter of the rotary. This circular light pattern can be perceived from a distance, but close-in glare is avoided by the height of the lamps. The station itself is sheathed in a simple steel and plywood cylinder (billboard technology), painted fluorescent yellow and floodlit to glow softly at night. Each "check mark" guide sign is lit by lamps mounted on the back of the adjacent sign. Low bridge rail lighting provides supplementary illumination under the train bridge and also delineates the central passages (these rails prevent pedestrians from attempting to cross the rotary at ground level).

The sequence from Longfellow Bridge.

The sequence from Charles Street.

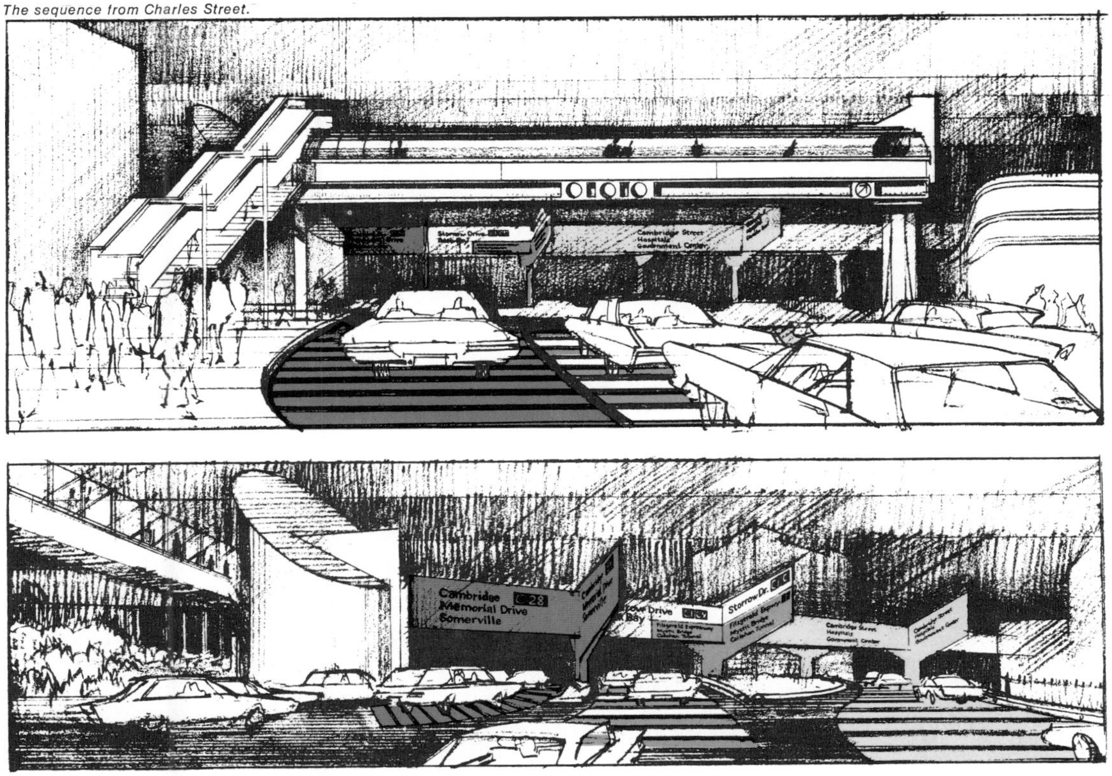

An alternative for the Charles Street Station: the big light.

The problems posed by the Charles Rotary are serious and require serious solutions. But seriousness need not be equivalent to narrow functionalism: the minimal adequate solution soberly executed. This gateway interchange could be more than tolerable; it could become a delightful and memorable experience in the humdrum routine of city driving. Why not think of the rotary as potentially an event to be anticipated with pleasure? With the addition of an air inflated polyethylene balloon or a geodesic radar dome, the station itself might become a huge light, glowing brightly from internal sources and nesting in the surrounding golden crown of sodium street lights. Perhaps the big light might change with the intensity of traffic, time of day and weather; or it might pulse rhythmically. In other cities of the world such junctions are treated as important events (see the fountain in Piazza della Repubblica in Rome, shown in Chapter 2.) Why shouldn't Boston do as well?

Summary: Information Systems for People in Cars

When streets are inadequately signed and when the signs themselves are confusing or misleading, the process of getting about becomes difficult and dangerous. People have a right to expect that this basic malfunction of the public environment will be remedied. In Boston, people were clearly pleased by the traffic sign, signal, and marking demonstrations, and many commented that the new signs should be adopted city wide.

The signing system described here is really a recommendation for national policy. What are good traffic signs in Boston will also be good elsewhere, and the only sensible traffic control system is a national one. The national Manual on Uniform Traffic Control Devices is currently in the process of revision (the first in ten years), but while there are improvements being made — including the adoption of some symbol signs — the most troublesome conceptual and perceptual inadequacies are being retained, even in the regulatory set where the most serious problems occur. Clearly there is an inertia in the present nonsystematic collection of signs which is not easily overcome.

A much larger demonstration of the proposed new system will be necessary to establish its superiority beyond doubt. At least an entire district of a city should be re-signed using this system. Before and after studies of accident rates, confusion rates, and difficulties in getting around, based on a large and diverse sample of people, would fully test the new system. It is already clear on the basis of simple logic, evidence from this project, and from other studies (see Appendices 1 and 6 that the new system is superior. Nonetheless, it will be necessary to dramatize the beneficial public effects of these changes so that they can be incorporated in the next revision of the MUTCD. The three year signing program recommended in Chapter 7 would provide for a conclusive test. Until the national manual is further revised, of course, cities must use the standard signs approved for use in the United States.

There are also conservative interests in current street lighting practice which discourage even relatively modest improvements. To validate other criteria than cost efficiency will also require a re-lighting test on a significant scale. The costs of such a program for Boston are estimated in Chapter 7. Again, the purpose is not to test whether or not the system recommended here would be an improvement. It would be. Some cities might be ready to adopt such lighting policies now, but since they would cost somewhat more than meeting present minimal standards, positive public response would be an important validation.

The policies for guide signing, pavement marking, and transit signing simply fill existing gaps in the public information system. The principles they employ are already well tested. Of course, it costs more to have these new systems (see Chapter 7), especially when there are presently very few guide signs and markings. Whether such policies can be translated into new programs will depend on the political judgment of mayors and city councils. The Boston experiments leave little doubt that the public impact will be positive.

A proposal such as that for the Charles Rotary involves an integration of all the systems — signing, signaling, lighting, and marking — and extends beyond them to deal with other aspects of the motorists' experience in passing through the city. Here, both because the problems are severe and because the potentials are so interesting, extraordinary measures and extraordinary costs may be justified. In this particular case, the changes in the rotary should be keyed to the remodeling of the Charles MBTA station, and a substantial part of the cost would be necessarily borne by the MBTA. The project would be an important test case, precisely because it would necessitate interagency coordination, not only at the city level (Traffic and Parking and Public Works) but also between city and metropolitan agencies (the Metropolitan District Commission, which is responsible for Storrow Drive, and the MBTA). Most city interchanges will require this kind of coordination.

Process: Coordination and Implementation

Policies in this chapter have been designed and presented, for the most part, so that single agencies could implement them. Limited interagency coordination would be necessary for the information centers, for some of the policies for central streets and spaces, for the combined street light and signal units, and for interchanges. However, the policies are also designed to reinforce one another such that to carry them out together would produce a qualitatively different effect than to carry them out in an uncoordinated and piecemeal fashion. It was clear in Park Square that the combination of the information center with the new signs was much more potent than either would have been by itself. The image of the whole area was changed and many people remarked on this transformation. Had it been possible to also deal with public lighting and with private signs and lights, the effect would have been even more pronounced.

One step toward coordination is to establish a process of design review by the staff of a single agency, such as planning and development. Clear and arguable criteria must stand behind such review if it is not to degenerate into a debate between designers and engineers about aesthetics versus efficiency. The staff in charge of such review would need to familiarize itself with present engineering criteria and their basis in both research and experience. Beyond expertise, the review staff would also need the support of the mayor (or city manager).

A much more significant level of coordination and funding would be necessary in planning, budgeting, and implementing a capital improvement program like that described in Chapter 7. If Boston or any other city were to implement these policies within normal (or incrementally increased) agency operating budgets, they would take anywhere from two to ten years to have city-wide impact. Some, like those for people on foot, fall outside these normal operations and would depend on special funding. But the policies in marking, signs, and signaling could be carried out, with varying effectiveness, within normal operations.

Markings are generally repainted every four to six months and consume about 10% of a city's street hardware budget.* Implementing the new system within the central city would take at least two years. In this period, other areas of the city might suffer, since the new markings are more expensive.

Signs must be replaced every four to five years and consume about 15% of the street hardware budget. Assuming the state highway department would allow it, quite dramatic changes might be possible within two years, since the recommended regulatory signs are no more expensive. Some additional corner signs are needed, but parking signs could be reduced. Guide signs would take longer to have city-wide impact, since current signs are both far too few and normally too small.

Much of the cost in signaling (about 30% of the street hardware budget) is likely to be in establishing new centrally programmed traffic activated control systems. Once a city initiates that change, it may also want to consider more effective signal units and mountings. If the new signal units can be systematically coordinated with light poles, the saving in poles and installation costs would more than offset the additional cost of the unit itself. However, signal hardware like lighting hardware normally has a long life (20 to 25 years), so that without a re-allocation of city funds in this direction, widespread change could not be expected in much less than ten years.

Most cities, including Boston, already feel compelled to spend more on street lighting to replace antiquated fixtures. Street lights are normally the most costly items in a street hardware budget (50%), but many cities have already undertaken large capital programs or will do so soon. Assuming that a city wished to bring its lighting up to the IES recommended standards, the policies suggested here should not increase the cost of this program by more than 5 to 10%.

* All information on typical street hardware costs has been obtained from a recent study conducted by Urban America for the U.S. Department of Transportation and a group of five cities. Urban America, Inc. *Improved Urban Transportation Information Systems*, Phase 1: Feasibility Study. Washington, D.C.: Department of Transportation, 1968, chap. 10, pp. 169-170.

CHAPTER FIVE

A System for Private Signs and Lights

This is The Glo
easy-to-rea
Easy to read,
Handschumacher
FRANKFURTS
Handschumacher's
FRANKFURTS
Above all oth
MANOLI
Budweiser
OFFICE SPACE
2600 SQ FT
Space Room
restaurant
lounge
LOGAN
AIRPORT
International Bldg.
NO PARKING
BUS STOP
BUTTER & EGGS
KEN

A System for Private Signs and Lights

Privately owned signs and lights are important sources of useful information. Although they are not yet treated as a system, these sources resemble public systems by being inequitable and inefficient in providing information. Private signs and lights transmit messages using the public environment as a medium; in this respect, they resemble broadcasting stations. However, whereas people can turn off electronic messages, the flow of information from signs and lights can be neither controlled nor ignored by the individual receiver. Policies for private signs and lights should give priority to the needs of people living in and visiting cities over those of commercial senders of information, while protecting legitimate rights of identification.

This chapter presents the case for systematic regulation of private signs and lights and describes an administrative process and a set of policies. A full discussion of the underlying operational and legal issues may be found in Appendix 3, along with an outline for a model sign and light code.

There are many problems that cannot be resolved and many potentials that will not be realized by a single, city-wide code. There must be different types of information zones to which different policies and procedures can apply. This chapter recommends that three types of zones be established: a small number of Special Information Districts where, by reason of high public use or significance and sensitivity of the area to the effects of private signs and lights, a set of specialized codes, guidelines, and incentives is required; General Information Districts, comprising the rest of the city, where a simple code applies; and, within General Information Districts, Local Information Districts where local groups can formulate additional special regulations.

The policies recommended here recognize the receiver's need to have information organized so that he may find it efficiently and so that messages do not interfere with one another. Several "visual channels" are needed for messages serving different purposes: one for traffic control and guidance; one for identification; and one for advertising, where it is allowed. Within the identification channel, restrictions on the attention seizing features of signs such as size, projection, letter size, motions, flashing lights, intensity of illumination, and the use of certain colors would protect the receiver and improve the transmission of information. Overall, the policies would produce a reversal in the usual visual priorities, imposing strict limits on "super-signs," such as billboards and large on-premise advertising signs, while ensuring a more equitable distribution of information sending rights.

This recommended system for private signs and lights serves several general objectives:

1 To restrict private signs and lights which overload people's capacity to receive information, which violate privacy, or which increase the probability of accidents by distracting attention or obstructing vision.

2 To encourage privately initiated communications which aid orientation, identify activities, express local history and character, or provide other educational information.

3 To increase opportunities for presently excluded individuals and groups to express themselves in the public environment.

4 To reduce conflicts between private signs and lights and between the private and public systems.

5 To increase opportunities for local groups to collectively determine policies for private signing and lighting in their areas.

These objectives and the policies, standards, and guidelines which follow are based on an analysis of the conditions, visible effects, and social costs of the present system.

CONDITIONS AFFECTING PRIVATE SIGNS AND LIGHTING

Large institutions and firms can saturate the public environment with their messages and can also use expensive alternate means to reach potential customers — television, radio, magazines, and newspapers. They can afford off-premise advertising and are often influential in public regulatory policy. Small businesses and institutions, small groups, and individuals lack resources, the options among several types of media, and political influence. Most small businesses are restricted to a street identification sign and occasional newspaper ads.

Land tenure requirements further restrict private messages. To send messages normally requires a vertical surface adjacent to the street. Ground floor activities control such space as a matter of course and the advertising industry creates it and sells it, but those who do not control such space or cannot afford to buy it cannot send messages in the environment.

Trained, competent sign and lighting designers are scarce. What few there are concentrate in large sign companies and advertising agencies. Small groups and businesses cannot afford design services and thus cannot make optimum use of their sending space.

Public policy does not acknowledge the operation of private signs and lights as an information system, nor does it adequately reflect the system's real and potential value. Policy has been minimal, merely restrictive, and has been unconcerned with encouraging socially useful communications.

Land tenure requirements and the scarcity of design services raise the cost of sending messages and restrict the number of senders. Minimal and unimaginative public policy encourages escalating competition among senders. These limitations result in the domination of the private environmental information space by the largest firms and advertisers.

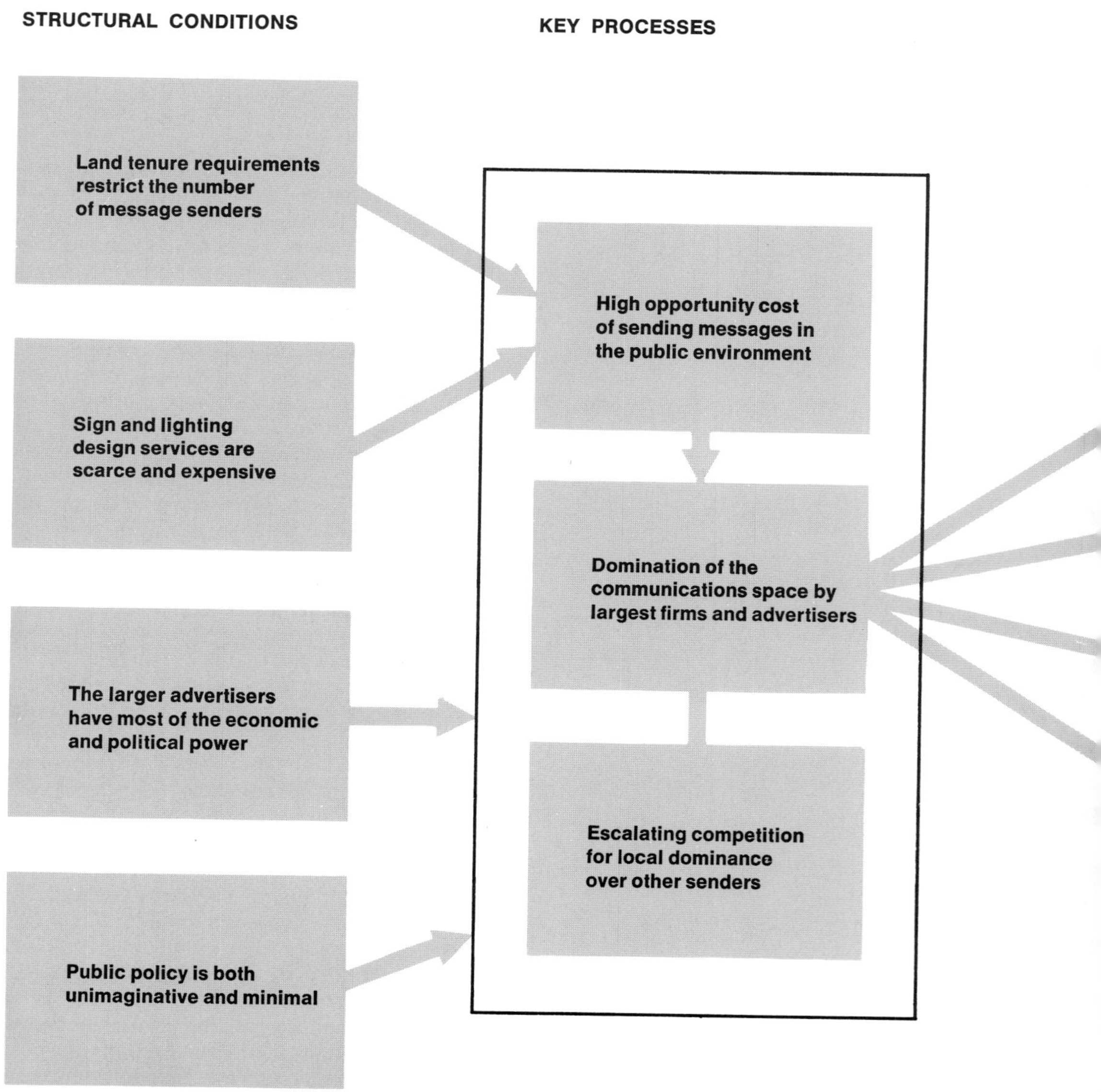
STRUCTURAL CONDITIONS
KEY PROCESSES
Land tenure requirements restrict the number of message senders
Sign and lighting design services are scarce and expensive
The larger advertisers have most of the economic and political power
Public policy is both unimaginative and minimal
High opportunity cost of sending messages in the public environment
Domination of the communications space by largest firms and advertisers
Escalating competition for local dominance over other senders

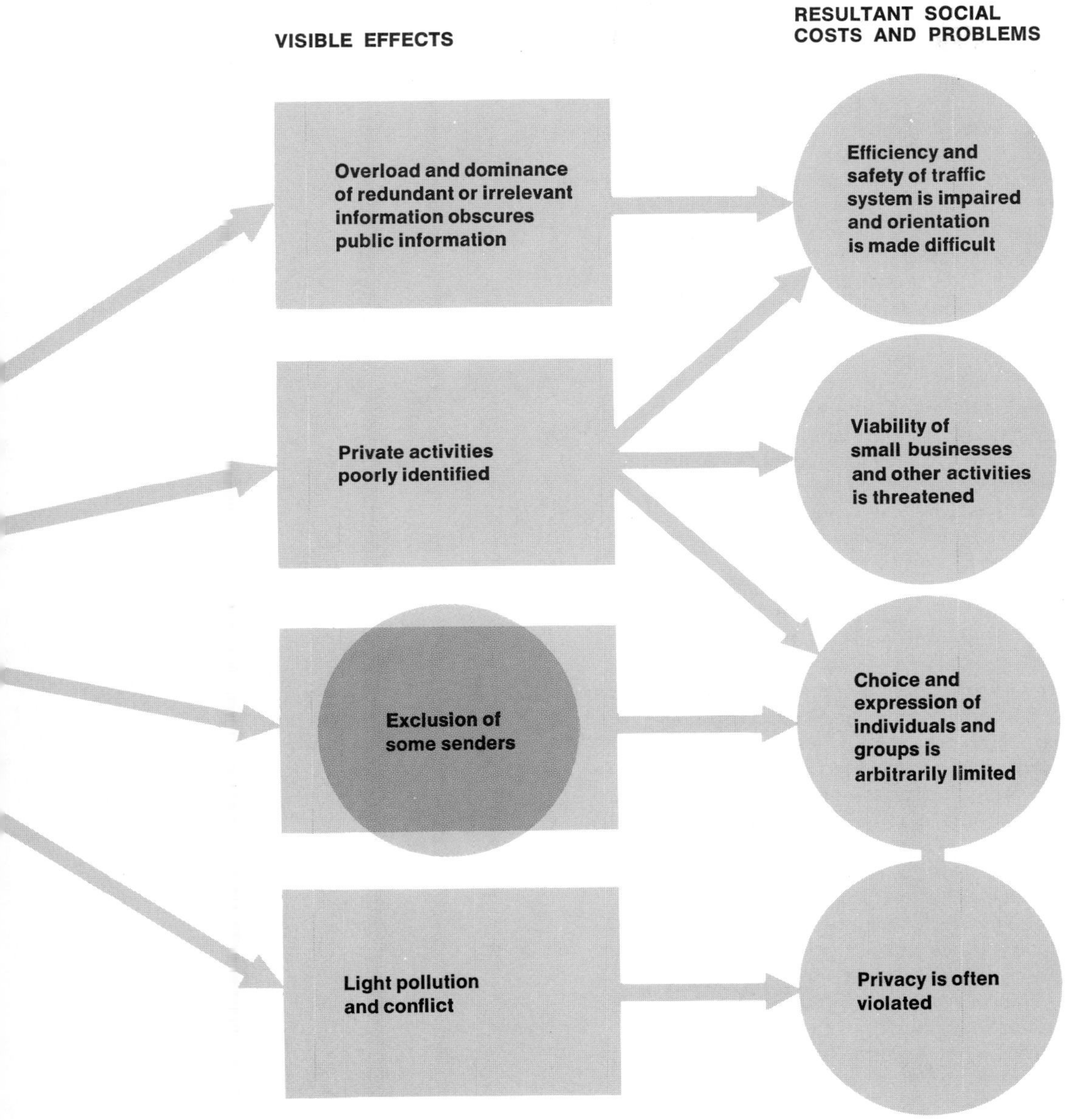
VISIBLE EFFECTS
RESULTANT SOCIAL COSTS AND PROBLEMS
Overload and dominance of redundant or irrelevant information obscures public information
Efficiency and safety of traffic system is impaired and orientation is made difficult
Private activities poorly identified
Viability of small businesses and other activities is threatened
Exclusion of some senders
Choice and expression of individuals and groups is arbitrarily limited
Light pollution and conflict
Privacy is often violated

VISIBLE EFFECTS AND SOCIAL COSTS

The landscape of private signs and lights is characterized by visual overload, redundancy, and irrelevance. Messages of national and institutional advertisers loom large in key areas; sign illumination bears little relation to actual nighttime activity. As one visible effect, essential public and traffic information is obscured.

Information about the nature and location of private activities is poorly and inconsistently presented; activity names and street numbers are missing or hard to find. Further, since many individuals, small groups, businesses, and local organizations are unable to employ signs and lights, only a fraction of the potentially useful information is transmitted at all.

Glare from brightly lit used car lots, gasoline stations, parking lots, and similar activities often spills over onto residential and other business premises. Flashing and animated signs and some illuminated vertical signs intrude on the environment of neighboring activities, especially residences on upper floors. Often, these signs conflict directly with traffic control devices.

These visible effects have important social costs. The efficiency and safety of the traffic system are impaired: drivers are often confused, traffic flow is obstructed, and the probability of accidents increases. People are unable to locate information they need to orient themselves or to find specific places and activities, and the viability of small businesses and other activities is threatened. Individual and group rights of identification and expression are arbitrarily limited. Receiver choice is narrowed and privacy is often violated by irrelevant signs and lights. Overall, living in the city is less meaningful, convenient, and pleasurable than it might be if privately owned signs and lights were treated systematically as an information source.

A System of Zoning for Private Information Systems

INFORMATION DISTRICTS

Types of Districts

The city should establish a system of information zoning with three types of districts:

1 Special Information Districts: areas with high use by the general public or recognized broad public significance, which are very sensitive — for reasons of safety, aesthetics, orientation, history, or whatever — to the effects of private signs and lights. These districts should be few in number. Here the city would exercise central control and would develop with the affected groups in each area a set of complex and specialized codes, guidelines, incentives, prototype designs, and review procedures.

The basic criterion for establishing a Special Information District is its importance to the city-wide population. This can be determined by:

a. Intensity of use of the area, measured by traffic flow, density of development, and economic activity.
b. Significance of the area, based on history, dominant activities, particular information problems, and environmental character.

2 General Information Districts: all other parts of the city. Here the city would impose a simple code, easily administered with a minimum of discretionary review, and provide certain types of design aid when asked.

3 Local Information Districts: recognized subareas such as zoning districts, wards, precincts, or model cities areas in which the city allows local groups in what would otherwise be a General Information District to formulate and administer additional regulations and guidelines, subject to legislative review of regulations and the right of central appeal. Locally initiated regulations could develop or intensify the basic city code, but could not weaken or supersede it.

Relation to Zoning

Information district zoning may be related to existing zoning in one of two ways:

1 Comprehensive information zoning, based on use and significance of districts and not necessarily co-terminous with existing land-use districts, may be established for the city as a whole.

2 Certain existing land-use zoning districts, after review of actual use, may be identified as Special Information Districts. Special regulations could then be added to existing code provisions.

In making this determination, a city should consider recent developments in state and local law, recent litigation, and alternative administrative consequences. In most cases, the existing districting system will not be appropriate, but the zoning mechanism itself should be used in order to take advantage of judicial precedent, present administration, and legislation. However, both the letter and the spirit of the new regulations will be initially unfamiliar to zoning administrators. Special technical assistance may resolve this problem; alternatively a city may transfer some existing administrative functions to a new Department of City Information.

Process of Establishing Information Districts

The establishment of information district boundaries is, ultimately, a legislative determination by the city council acting on the advice of the city's information, planning, and zoning agencies. Agency recommendations should derive from a process of study and consultation with groups whose interests are likely to be affected.

If policies for Special Information Districts are to be effective, support and participation by both senders and receivers is essential. Unfortunately, adequate representation of receivers will not be possible, for while businessmen and property owners are often organized, the same is not true of shoppers, motorists, and office workers. Receivers' interests can be imperfectly represented by advisory boards, surveys, and other devices, but they will ultimately fall to the judgment of the city council. Special Information Districts, once established by the council, should have an advisory board with which city agencies can discuss policies. Major interest groups should be represented, and a large fraction of places should be reserved for receiver groups. The board should be formed prior to the establishment of precise boundaries and should review agency decisions on districting, reporting to the city council.

The General Information Districts would be established residually. The codes applied in these areas should be easily understood and administered, allowing the city to concentrate its efforts in critical areas. Such codes would be aimed at limiting dominance by the large senders, competition, overload, and redundancy so that important identifying messages will be more effectively communicated, so that more groups can send messages, and so that drivers will not be unnecessarily distracted.

The greatest difficulties are likely to arise in establishing Local Information Districts. The problems are similar to those that accompany any decentralization of government functions. Since sign and lighting policy does not justify establishing permanent special purpose community organizations, local policy initiative might be assumed by a variety of existing community groups. In Boston, the mayor's new Local Advisory Committees would be the most likely locus of such initiative.

If in the future, other planning and development functions are delegated to elected district councils, then regulation of private signs and lights should certainly be included in these functions. Where such boards and councils already exist, in function of urban renewal or model cities programs, they should be given the power to draft the special district regulations for adoption by the city council and could also assume any continuing review functions. Alternatively, the local regulation might be made a referendum question as a part of regular district council, renewal or model cities board elections in the area, which could also give a vote to non-resident owners and businessmen. These locally adopted regulations should be subject to final approval by the city council, but the local board should be able to veto changes made by the council. (The Cambridge, Massachusetts model cities program provides an operating precedent for these principles.)

New enabling legislation will be necessary to give the required legal status to these Local Information Districts as special zoning districts. In principal this is no different from the creation of other special legislative classifications of districts as historical areas, conservation areas, or indeed renewal or model cities areas.

Ideally, these regulatory powers should be granted to a neighborhood board on a continuing basis to deal with problems as they arise. This would present further legal problems, but the courts have generally held that while governmental authority cannot be granted to individuals, ordinances which condition zoning use approval upon the consent of neighbors are valid (see Appendix 3, *Legal Issues,* for further discussion). Local boards can, by election, represent persons most affected by the regulations ("neighbors"). The legislation should be written so that if the local board disapproves a proposal, a special majority vote by the city-wide zoning board would be required to override the local decision.

Where this kind of representation does not exist and is impractical to institute, local groups may have to be content with organizing on a short term basis to initiate special regulations for adoption by the council, possibly with a continuing informal review function. The additional legitimacy of a referendum on the question would be highly desirable but very difficult to achieve within present frameworks of wards and precincts which may bear little relation to real community boundaries and, in addition, disenfranchise local businessmen and owners who are not residents within these wards but whose interests are directly affected. In this type of referendum, unless there is a major organizing effort, it might be difficult to achieve an informed vote.

CHANNELS FOR INFORMATION

Types of Channels

The central purpose of information channeling is to aid people in locating the information they need. Messages should be distinguished by the public purposes they serve, and each type should be assigned its own channel, as shown in the diagram:

1 *Traffic Channel:* traffic control and guidance information.

2 *Identification Channel:* identification of products or activities on the premises where the message is located.

3 *Advertising Channel:* advertising of products or activities on or off the premises where the message is located.

The channeling policy distinguishes two types of private sign: identification signs and advertising signs. Identification signs are those which carry any or all of the following — the name, street address, and type of business or activity conducted on the signed premises. Advertising signs are those which are designed and placed to seize the observer's attention beyond what is necessary for him to identify an establishment and take appropriate action. Public policy can make this distinction operational by establishing both a channel and a set of identification limits. Private signs which fall outside this channel or are within it but exceed the limits are, by definition, advertising.

Spatial Definition of the Channels

The Traffic Channel consists of a vertically unlimited space within the public right of way and overlapping the curb line by 3 feet on each side. The Identification Channel is a continuous volume which extends from the building line to one-third the width of the sidewalk and from the sidewalk to the third floor of a multistory building, or in the case of a single-story building, 15 feet above the sidewalk or to 4 feet above the lowest point of the roof, whichever is less restrictive. (Marquees and canopies, which should generally be encouraged for their shelter, would be exempted from the one-third sidewalk width rule.) The Advertising Channel is a series of discontinuous volumes as defined by the standards for advertising signs.

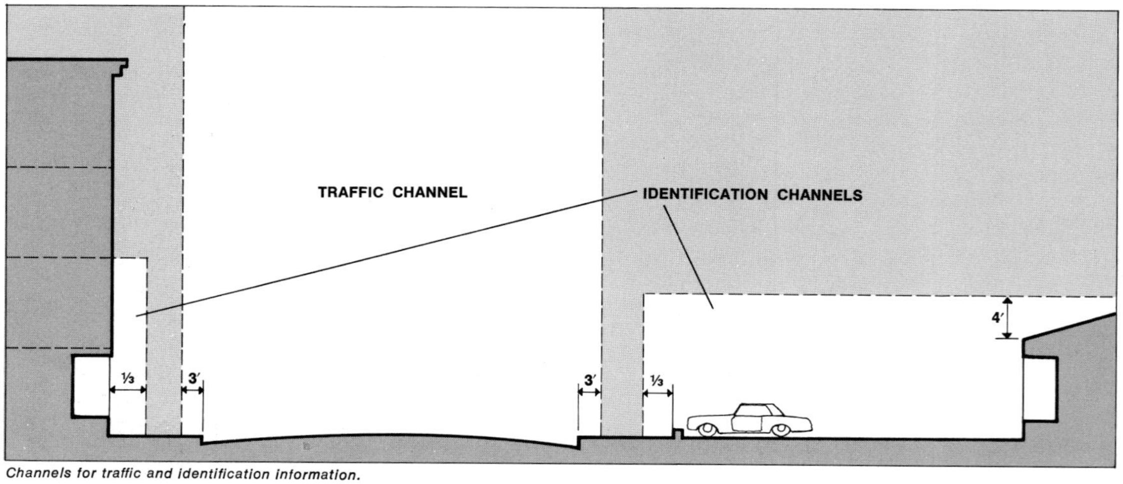

Channels for traffic and identification information.

Policies for General Information Districts

IDENTIFICATION CHANNEL

Within the variable Identification Channel, standards should constrain the attention seizing features of signs so that the intensity with which messages are conveyed will be appropriate to the identification needs of intended receivers but not in excess of those needs. The potential for dominance by any one sender should be limited so that the identification rights of other senders will be protected and their chances to send will be improved. For the same reasons, repetition of messages should be eliminated or reduced. Further limitations are necessary to prevent conflict with traffic information.

Several aspects of private signs and lights need to be limited: vertical location, projection over the sidewalk, overall size of message space, letter size for various identification purposes, motions, flashing lights, intensity of illumination, and the use of certain colors. Beyond reasonable limits, any of these characteristics can transform an identification sign into an advertising sign which diverts attention from other sources of needed information and may contribute to information overload.

The general location of signs and lights and their projection into the public right of way is controlled by the limits on the Identification Channel already described. The purpose of this channel is to assure that identification will occur in a generally predictable location within the normal field of view of people, whether in cars or on foot, and that signs will not be allowed to block views of other signs for pedestrians on the same side of the street. Additional regulation is needed to assure that both of these criteria are met, but the channel is the first necessary step in establishing an effective system of private signs and lights.

Within the channel, size limits on signs can assure more equitable identification rights. Presently these rights are often related directly to street frontage, yet frontages vary from less than 10 feet to several hundred, while the identification needs of the activities involved are quite similar. Signs of small-frontage activities bunched together obscure one another, whereas activities with larger frontages can send unobstructed identification messages. Sign control ordinances commonly reinforce this inequity by making allowable sign size a function of frontage or even more inequitably, a function of facade size. A linear relation between lot frontage and allowable sign area will not ensure that smaller shops and other activities can make themselves heard.

Greater equity of sending space can be achieved by basing sign size on the square root of frontage. Sign area measurements were made on three typical Boston blocks: a strip commercial zone, a local shopping district, and a downtown shopping street. For Boston, a reasonable formula to limit the gross area of all identification signs is: allowable area = 15 times the square root of street frontage.* On the strip commercial block, application of this formula would eliminate 44% of the existing signs while in the local shopping center only 23% would be eliminated and on the downtown shopping street only 17%. (In other cities, a different multiple than 15 may be more appropriate.)

Sign area in this formulation refers to the entire area within a single continuous perimeter encompassing all the display area of the sign. Signs at right angles to the street should be encouraged for their greater legibility, thus only one side of a two-faced projecting or freestanding sign need be counted in determining area. The allowable sign area can be distributed at the owner's will among facade signs, projecting signs, freestanding signs, or signs on marquees.

An ambiguous case arises when the sign copy is attached directly to the building without any intermediary background, or, as is increasingly the case, when whole facades are designed by sign companies to be an integral part of the sign. In these cases, judgment will be necessary to determine whether the entire facade is to be considered the sign background or only the area encompassing the sign copy (letters, symbols).

Size of lettering is a critical determinant of private sign legibility. The standard and tested

* For a shop with 25 feet of street frontage, the allowable area of identification signing $= 15\sqrt{25} = 75$ square feet.

rule of thumb for letter size in public signing is 50 feet of legibility per inch of letter height. Required legibility distance is a function of speed and mode of movement of the observer and the time required to take appropriate action. A common, near maximum, city speed is 30 miles per hour. At this speed, the observer can travel about two average blocks (900 feet) in 20 seconds. This would appear to be a reasonable maximum time required for a driver to see a sign and take appropriate action to go to that location. At 900 feet, the necessary letter size for identification signs is 18 inches.

This standard should be adopted as the maximum allowable letter size for "building identification signs," which identify the building as a whole or its predominant use. A further distinction can be made between these signs and those which identify various secondary occupants within the building. For these "occupancy signs," a viewing distance approximately one city block (400 feet) and a time of 10 seconds should be adequate to decide to stop, assuming that the viewer has already seen the building sign or, as would be typical in a shopping area, knows he is in the right general location and has slowed down. For 400 feet of legibility, 8 inches should be the maximum size for lettering on occupancy signs. Signs identifying parking areas (another kind of occupancy) should also follow this rule. In addition, the owner should be required to display the street address of each building in numerals at least 4 inches high.

A third type of identification sign is that intended exclusively for the man on foot. These should be more strictly limited to avoid redundancy with the building and occupancy signs as seen from the roadway. A viewing distance of 150 feet and maximum letter size of 3 inches should be more than adequate for such signs.* The sidewalk adjacent to the building should be an allowable surface for such signs and they should not be more than 10 feet above the sidewalk (to the top of the sign). No more than one pedestrian sign per occupancy should be allowed.

The distribution of the total allowable sign area between occupancy and building identification signs must be negotiated between the building owner and the occupants. The law, however, should protect the right of each building occupant to have an occupancy sign within the Identification Channel. To additionally ensure this right by preventing redundancy, each building or predominant use should be limited to one building identification sign and each occupant to one occupancy sign. Occupancy signs for other than first floor occupants should be limited to the area of the facade between the second and third floors.

Further constraints on size and location should be applied to signs on or within display windows. Identification through the display of products, services, and views to inside activities should be encouraged. Permanent signs should not be allowed to cover more than 10% of the window area. If it could be managed, the area devoted to temporary signs should also be limited, but monitoring such a rule would prove a practical impossibility in most cities. It nevertheless may be valuable to have such a rule on the books: 20% would be a generous limit.

Illumination of signs must be limited to what is adequate for identification. Signs should be illuminated only by steady, stationary, shielded light sources directed solely at the sign, or internal to it, without causing glare for motorists, pedestrians, or neighboring premises. Illuminated signs, including neon signs, should be limited to an intensity of no more than one foot-candle at 4 feet from the sign. In addition, illuminated signs should not be allowed between the hours of 11:00 P.M. and 7:00 A.M. unless indicating an establishment open to the public during those hours.

Other types of illumination should also be controlled to prevent violations of privacy on neighboring premises. Here a useful rule would limit the marginal increase of light as measured at the property line with any adjacent property to no more than one foot-candle. This need not apply to the public right of way which can generally benefit from spill-over light, provided that glare is prohibited.

*The foregoing analysis of letter size standards is indebted to a study by Robert E. Dyer, "Performance Standards for On-Premise Signs," Department of Planning and Inspection, City of Fresno, California, April 1967.

An allowable identification sign. Photo: Nishan Bichajian

Window signs: 10% permanent; 20% temporary.

Illumination allowable after 11:00 P.M.

Allowable temporary sign.

Several attention seizing features should be prohibited altogether in General Information Districts. No sign or light should be allowed to move, flash, or make noise. (Indicators of time and temperature can be excluded from the motion restriction.) Moving and flashing signs are clearly not necessary for identification and constitute a safety hazard for drivers. By the same reasoning, colored lights and illuminated signs employing colors in use for the traffic regulatory system (red, yellow, and green) should be disallowed, at the least within view of any signalized intersection. Words such as "stop," "look," or "danger" which may confuse or mislead drivers should be prohibited. Fluorescent colors should also be disallowed, particularly those in the yellow to red range.

Further restrictions are necessary in residence districts to protect them from commercial intrusions. Signs not exceeding 2 square feet in area should be allowed to identify each owner or occupant (or a permitted accessory use) of a residential building. Signs and lights for other permitted uses in residential areas should conform to the general identification sign requirements, except that the maximum allowable letter size should be no more than 8 inches. Temporary and seasonal house and street decorations should not be regulated, except that the same one foot-candle rule should apply to spill-over light from both decorative lights and other private sources.

Temporary signs of limited size pertaining to real estate, construction, political campaigns, community events, and legal notices should be allowed anywhere within the Identification Channel for periods of time related to the duration of the event being announced, with perhaps a maximum of one year beyond which the sign will no longer be considered temporary. Construction sites should be required to display a description of the process and provide views of it. Other temporary signs including portable ground signs and posters, display cards, or decorative signs mounted outside a building or display case should not be allowed. Public display kiosks (see Chapter 4) should provide poster space in Special Information Districts and advertising zones.

Regulation here is obviously very difficult, especially considering the large number of temporary signs. They should not be required to obtain a permit because of the administrative burden this would impose. Neighbor complaints will be the major means of enforcement, and all signs should be required to display the name and address of the individual responsible so that any costs of removal can be billed.

Other desirable permanent signs within the Identification Channel include those intended for education and orientation. These should be allowed, providing they serve a public purpose and do not incorporate advertising. The line is fine but discernible: thus a memorial plaque on Joe's Shoe Palace to identify it as the site of the first pillory in Boston is legitimate but a directional sign saying "This way to Joe's Shoe Palace, Site of the First Boston Pillory" should not be allowed.

Messages to identify and explain local history or to explain processes going on within a building but out of view, including making the processes themselves visible, should be actively encouraged. As an incentive to these educational signs, an additional increment of 20% should be allowed to the overall identification area limits and allowable letter size. Building directories should be required to be legible from outside the building. None of these signs should exceed 20 square feet in area and should meet letter size and location standards for pedestrian signs.

ADVERTISING CHANNEL

A single set of regulations should apply to advertising in the public environment, whether it refers to products, accommodations, services, or activities on or off the premises on which the sign is located. Advertising signs are defined by virtue of exceeding the reasonable limits of identification, as established in the preceding section. There are several major options to consider in the regulation of these "super-signs":

1 A complete ban on advertising signs throughout the city is one option. The case for prohibition of advertising signs is based on research studies, public opinion, legislative determinations, and court tests. A number of cities and towns and at least one state have banned billboards and are now phasing them out. The case for complete prohibition can only be summarized here. Further arguments and documentation are included in this report (Appendix 3).

Advertising signs are difficult to ignore because of factors such as size, placement in the visual field, and intense night lighting. They are systematically located to further one goal — to capture the attention of a maximum number of motorists. Not only is this practice an invasion of privacy, it also increases the probability of accidents — demonstrably on curves, at intersections, and in areas of peak traffic volume where this effect can least be tolerated.

Advertising signs frequently conflict with local rights. While some revenue accrues to the owner of property upon which an off-premise advertising sign is located, neighboring people and premises typically suffer from glare, distraction, and repeated bombardment with messages for which they can have no consistent use. These effects are scarcely more welcome in places of work than in places of residence.

Off-premise advertising signs are not effective as a means of providing tourists and drivers with activity and locational information, for they give no hint of the actual range of available choice. Their effect is both to skew the information presented in favor of certain senders and to promote more of such advertising by competitors. Vermont has instituted a state-wide travel information system as a substitute for off-premise advertising.

2 Many large cities may wish not to eliminate advertising but, in the public interest, to bar it from certain locations. The case for this option is substantially the same as for the first. The city's first priority should be to eliminate advertising signs from locations where they are particularly hazardous to motorists and/or where they tend to conflict with local values, including property values. A typical code might state:

a. No advertising sign shall be permitted where visible from portions of limited access highways wherever distances between interchanges, merges, and other decision points are less than those prescribed by present U.S. Bureau of Public Roads safety standards.
b. No advertising sign shall be permitted where visible at major intersections (defined as the intersection of expressways with all other streets, and of arterial streets with collector streets).
c. No advertising sign shall be visible from residential or institutional zones nor from other "unique" (generally historic) areas.
d. No advertising sign shall be located to extend more than 40 feet above the record grade.
e. No advertising sign shall be allowed on the roof of a building.
f. All locations for off-premise advertising signs must be approved by the Department of City Information or its equivalent.
g. Areas designated as Local Information Districts may further restrict advertising signs with the approval of the city.
h. Off-premise advertising signs may be located in General Information Districts, provided that:
   - The area is zoned commercial or industrial.
   - They are not in conflict with any of the above standards.
   - They meet all other city or state requirements.

3 A third option should be regarded as a minimal policy for city regulation of advertising signs. It retains provisions a), b), c), f), g), and h) of the second option but permits advertising signs higher than 40 feet and on roofs of buildings. The provisions retained are the most critical for road safety.

4 A fourth option would not allow advertising signs except in special locations, designated by

Restriction "a".

Restriction "b".

Restriction "e".

the Department of City Information and approved by the city council. In these locations they normally would be allowed to go wild and sky signs might also be allowed. In such locations, the city could make use of powers of "inverse condemnation" (described in Chapter 7 and Appendix 3, *Legal Issues*) to acquire sign and lighting rights and sell space with further controls on the placement of signs. Such locations might often fall within Special Information Districts, especially in entertainment zones, but would not be limited to these. Any commercial center might have its "advertising channel," located so as not to conflict with traffic safety and other values. Parking lots will often be likely locations. In some cases, an advertising design for the upper stories of a commercial block might be allowed and developed cooperatively with merchants and owners.

Recommendation on Advertising Signs

The recommended policy is the fourth option. While it represents a considerable change from existing policy, it would permit advertising signs in certain designated areas, subject to other applicable codes (such as building codes or state regulations). The choice of this policy is contingent upon the idea that the city would have Special Information Districts in entertainment, commercial, and industrial zones in which various forms of controlled advertising would be allowed.

Policies for Special Information Districts

Special Information Districts are by definition areas in which special public attention is justified — additional codes, guidelines, incentives, and assistance. It is clear that harmful communication cannot be controlled by persuasion alone, for the public interest directly conflicts with particular private practices; on the other hand, good private sign and light systems will not result from restrictions alone. Public review and design assistance are essential in Special Districts if the full potential of private systems is to be realized.

Code provisions should not be uniform in all Special Information Districts. Various types of activity concentrations have different sign and lighting needs and possibilities. Present zoning ordinances set different building standards for different land uses; sign and light codes will necessarily reflect these changing conditions.

Incentives will be particularly important in encouraging desirable sign/light developments in Special Districts. Joint public-private development is likely to be an important technique. If legislation like that recommended in Chapters 3 and 7 is forthcoming, powers of inverse condemnation combined with low interest loans and improvement grants could make a critical difference.

1. Central Retail Districts
A number of policies for central retail districts have already been outlined in Chapter 4 in the Central Streets and Spaces section. Policies for these areas should promote exposure of activity and products rather than a heavy reliance on signs. Devices like the canopy and galleria proposed in Chapter 4 can allow stores to display goods outside or to develop exterior display kiosks. Temporary signs on shop windows should be strongly discouraged in favor of displays of goods. Illuminated signs should be kept secondary to illuminated window displays. Street banners and other decorative displays should be encouraged.

2. Entertainment Areas
Entertainment areas provide a major focus for night activity in the city, attracting people from the surrounding metropolitan area. Policies for signs and lights in such areas should recognize the wide variety of personal plans which people have when they are out on the town and there is time for new kinds of action and experience. Entertainment areas should be visually lively places and be designed for people moving on foot. Large, colorful signs and lighting should be concentrated where entertainment activities are most intense. "Super-load" is desirable here. Entertainment related advertising should be encouraged by permissive regulation and incentives. Non-commercial sound and light spectaculars and other displays could be jointly developed by public and private agencies, as illustrated by the policies in Chapter 4 for lower Washington Street.

Entertainment areas are also good sites for experiments with new sign, lighting, and sound technology. Most technical innovations are used in conventional ways, harnessed to specific, static advertisements. Freed of these constraints, new developments could be used in displays open to the messages, movement, and sound of people.

Cities should not encourage sign spectaculars in places where they will raise the probability of accidents. However, traffic in entertainment areas though sometimes heavy is generally slow moving, and specially illuminated traffic signs can be used to overcome some of the distractions of super-load.

3. Industrial Areas
Since work is increasingly divorced in space and time from other parts of life, people see and use products with little understanding of how they are produced or of the people who produce them. This is much more than an information problem, but signs and lights can help reduce the visual isolation of industrial areas. Most industries project a "front office" image of order and cleanliness which is neither interesting nor representative of actual manufacturing and distribution. Plants seem increasingly identical and isolated from their surroundings. By night, industrial areas are dark and forbidding.

The problem is not "beautification" — masking, token landscaping, and color schemes unrelated to the work going on inside. Industries should be encouraged to make processes more visible, relating color and the location of lighting to the flows of materials and goods. Pedestrian guide signs and color coding could let visitors find destinations in plants and industrial parks without interfering with work or exposing themselves to undue danger. Guidelines for public signing in Chapter 4 can also be used for signs for private roads and parking areas within the industrial zone.

4. Office/Institutional Areas

Office areas appear uniform, rather lifeless, and forbidding at night. Typically, activity is visible only at peak hours of the day. Specific activities are not apparent from the building forms and are hard to find.

Signs and lights can alleviate some of these problems. Building directories could be placed outside entrance doors, and cessions of space for this in the public right of way could encourage the practice. Building names and numbers should be readable at a distance, lighted at night. Institutions could be aided in developing their own guide sign systems, using color coding and symbols as well as words. Principal entrances should be lighted at night. Thoughtfully used, floodlighting would relate to activities going on inside buildings; that is, those areas which have higher public contact would be lit more intensely or in a different color. Distinctive activities can be made more visible. Firms and institutions could, individually or cooperatively, produce displays similar to those at international fairs, explaining activities in the building or area and how they relate to activities elsewhere in the city or region.

5. Critical Traffic Areas

Some areas of the city have become critical for traffic flow, particularly where different systems come together. The Charles Rotary is an example of such a place in Boston. At these points or in these areas the city may need to exercise extraordinary controls over private signs and lights to minimize all distracting influences.

City-Wide Policies

Amortization of Non-Conforming Signs and Lights

Allowable periods for the removal of nonconforming signs in existing codes are often related to the cost of the sign. This is equivalent to a pollution abatement law which would allow those producing the most pollution the most time to do something about it. Instead, amortization periods should be related to the seriousness of the problem caused by that type of device. Thus, signs and lights which contribute to traffic or other safety hazards would be the first to go. After those would come roof signs and other advertising. (A full listing appears in Appendix 3, *Outline for a Model Code.*)

Guidelines

Most of the principles stated in Chapter 4 in relation to public signing and lighting are pertinent here and need not be repeated. These general guidelines for the design of private signs and lights may be useful in developing detailed guidelines and standards on a case by case basis for Special Information Districts. They are also intended for sign designers and as a basis for design review and design assistance services.

1 A first principle of visual communications in the city is that wherever possible the thing or activity itself should be exposed to view. Direct exposure is nearly always more vivid and expressive than a symbol. The real thing allows the observer to explore further if he wishes in a way that no symbolic statement, however poetic, can do. Where exposure is not possible or desirable, then a trace of the hidden activity — something that is a direct by-product of it — is usually more powerful than a symbolic sign. Verbal signs become necessary where the information to be transmitted is abstract.

2 Signs are most useful if they are "rooted": they are located where the activity symbolized is located and they function only when the activity is occurring. Beer signs belong on bars and should be most obvious (for instance, by lighting) when the bar is open.

3 The form of the sign or lighting should express the form of the thing or activity symbolized, if such a form exists. This may be done by direct mimicry, as when an arrow symbolizes movement in a particular direction, or by common association (usually once based on mimicry) as when a danger sign is made big, red, jagged, and flashing. Big is important, red is hot, jagged is dynamic, rapid motion signals danger, and so on.

4 Signing and lighting devices should allow for active participation of the observer. Signs which are metaphors, whether pictorial or verbal, do this by allowing for interpretation on several levels. Beyond this, it might be possible to develop signs with which the observer can actively interact, as he does with a directory. Such devices would only yield the information wanted, when it was wanted, and would shape it to the observer's needs.

5 To be easily identified, a visual element must be differentiated from its background. Sign designers normally achieve this by using bright colors, unique (and often grotesque) shapes, or flashing lights. Unfortunately, in most cases, the designer does not control the background environment and therefore cannot adequately prejudge the effectiveness of his graphic devices. In our cluttered streets these devices often weaken the impact of a sign. A simple way to achieve distinctiveness is to control the background for the message by keeping plenty of free space around the words or images. A common graphic rule of thumb is that the background area should be about three times the copy area.

6 A final principle is simplicity. To have several lettering styles, colors, and shapes in the same sign is confusing because it breaks the sign into several visual elements. Since signs appear in already complex visual environments, they are more likely to be effective when they are kept simple.

Design Assistance Services

Design services will be essential if private signs and lights are to be made into an efficient, legible information system. Design is needed at two levels:

Sign and lighting system design

The design staff of the Department of City Information or an equivalent city agency should de-

"Hidden" activity exposed.

Goods and activity on view.

Danger.

Sign as metaphor.

Background three times copy.

velop and test detailed policies for the Special Information Districts and prototypes to implement them. The staff should include people trained in city design, environmental psychology, architecture, and graphic design. It should:

1 Prepare guidelines and detailed district plans, working with district interest groups.

2 Prepare special street or block designs and seasonal or special temporary displays as requested by these interest groups.

3 Produce a handbook for general distribution to merchants, institutions, sign companies and local groups, showing new and existing possibilities for solutions to prototypical sign design problems.

4 As a joint public-private venture, design and produce prototypes of the latest sign and lighting innovations. The city could provide design services and research funds (perhaps with some federal support), while equipment makers and senders could cover hardware costs. Non-commercial sound and light environments for entertainment areas could be developed in much the same way, but with joint public-private funding of hardware costs.

Local design assistance

The same staff should also deal with requests from Local Information Districts. It should:

1 Act as design consultant to local boards, assisting them in design review and the development of guidelines, incentives, and specialized codes.

2 Provide design assistance services to those who request it, emphasizing services to small shopkeepers, small sign companies, and groups of merchants interested in block designs. As an alternative, grants to local districts in lieu of services would enable them to hire their own advocate designers. Small additional subsidies (as part of the federal incentive program recommended in Chapter 3) could enable a merchant, company, or group to hire a local designer or design student.

Space for Small Senders

In Chapter 4, policies were described which would provide public space — projection structures, kiosks, bulletin boards, parking lot display screens, graffiti walls — for inexpensive, temporary message transmission. Policy for private signing and lighting can amplify that space. Special allowances, for instance on the area of identification signs or by cessions of space in the public right of way, should be made to owners who provide and manage bulletin or display space for public use. Many supermarkets and laundromats do this now and the practice should be encouraged.

Coded Symbols for Basic Services

A final city-wide policy worth serious consideration would be the preparation of a set of coded symbols for basic private services. Chapter 4 describes the rudiments of such a system for public services. Olympic games and world fairs have used such systems where visitors of many languages had to be served (see Chapter 2). As international trade and tourism increases, the problem may become a general one. Drug stores, cleaners, laundries, hotels and motels, restaurants, bars, food stores, barbers and hairdressers, and various repair services should have such a system available if they wish to make use of it.

CHAPTER SIX

Field Testing

what do you think

Field Testing

Many of the policy recommendations in this report were at least partially tested in the field. These tests, ranging from simple opinion surveys to complex evaluations of the experimental demonstrations, were a central part of this project. The assumption behind the field testing is that people outside professional circles can make a critical contribution to the development of effective policy recommendations. Whether this assumption is correct the reader must judge for himself. The policy proposals presented in Chapters 4 and 5 were strongly influenced by the tests.

The policies for public lighting, many of the traffic signing policies, and some of the policies for private signs and lights borrow heavily from other work, but new field research was needed in all of these areas. Sometimes, as with private signing and the Information Center, little or no previous research had been done. In other cases, as with public signing, ideas in use elsewhere in the world had not been subjected to systematic field testing. Experiments in lighting public parks and buildings and in street marking were less tests of public response than demonstrations to build support for the wider use of such techniques in Boston. In a number of cases — the policies for private signs and lights and the proposals for Boylston Street, Washington Street, and Charles Rotary — time or money or both were insufficient for field experiments: policies go untested except by prototype designs on paper.

Certain problems and costs in the experimental approach appear neither in the description of the installations in Chapter 4 nor in the evaluations of public response. The time needed to design and implement a temporary field experiment can be greater than for a permanent facility. Special approvals for unconventional and temporary structures or equipment take time, even though Boston's city agencies were highly cooperative. In addition, designers want to perfect something that is to be built and installed for public use beyond the level implied by the term "temporary experiment." For both these reasons, the experimental installations became an even larger part of the project in terms of staff time than had originally been anticipated.

Not all of the tests were "successful." Sometimes the experiment itself failed to achieve the desired effects or had unanticipated and unwanted side effects; tree lighting in the Public Garden is an example. In the case of the Sound and Light Environment, most of the people who were there seemed to enjoy themselves, but the group attracted by the experiment was a small part of those who might have been reached by other means. Still, as much or more can be learned from "failures" as from "successes," and these two experiments were not by any means a waste.

This chapter describes four sets of tests:

1 evaluative studies of the prototype information center erected in Park Square;

2 evaluative tests on the impact of the public signing demonstration;

3 evaluations of two public lighting demonstrations;

4 two experiments and two surveys on the impact of private signs.

More detailed descriptions of these tests and their results appear in Appendices 5 to 8.

INFORMATION CENTER: EVALUATIVE STUDIES

There were five tests of public reaction to the Information Center; a short-questionnaire interview, an open-ended interview, tube interviews, an opinion scale, and unobtrusive observations.

Short-Questionnare Interviews

In the short interviews, people were asked whether they were visiting the Information Center for the first time, if they would like to return, and if they would suggest that others visit the Center; how they found out about the Center, why they were in Boston and the Park Square area, how long they stayed at the Center, and about their general attitude toward it. The interview recorded the respondent's sex, age, occupation, and place of residence, but there were no consistent differences in answers attributable to these variables.

One-fourth of the 70 people interviewed had been to the Center before. About 80% said that they would like to come back again and nearly everyone (97%) agreed that other people should visit the Center when in Park Square.

Three-quarters of those interviewed came upon the Center by chance; the remainder learned about it from friends or the local news media. People gave a variety of reasons for being in Park Square; only ten had come expressly to see the Information Center. Most were on foot when they spotted the Information Center and once they had walked to it spent between 10 and 50 minutes viewing the displays, the average falling between 20 and 25 minutes.

Ninety-two percent of the people interviewed liked the Center somewhat or very much, based on a rating of answers to the whole interview.

Open-ended Interviews

This study documented detailed visitor reactions to the Information Center and its components. Forty-one people were interviewed at different times of the day during the first two weeks of the demonstration. Their answers were tape recorded.

Again, the interviewer rated each respondent's overall degree of favorableness toward the Center. Feelings toward the Center were overwhelmingly positive: 37 of the 41 respondents liked it and only 4 disliked it (no one felt neutral

Pedestrian Guide System/Experimental Demonstration
Park Square/Boston, Mass./April 25–May 25, 1969

PURPOSE. Signs/Lights/Boston, a project of Ashley/Myer/Smith Inc., is experimenting with a number of systems of communication in the public environment. The information center on Providence Street and Arlington Street is part of a system designed for pedestrians, to be tested for a period of one month starting in late April, 1969. This experimental center is designed to gather information as well as give it, and will help develop the information content and presentation methods for a permanent city-wide Pedestrian Guide System to encourage people to learn about Boston and how to use the city. The system is currently seen as a network of information centers located at major transfer points where people begin and end journeys or transfer from one mode of transportation to another. These centers would be supplemented by map kiosks at all major exits from public transportation terminals and parking garages. The user will thus have guide information available to him as he leaves his vehicle and begins to walk in the city. □ **DESCRIPTION.** The center is designed to attract pedestrians and to provoke public reaction through its exciting form and vivid graphics. Large cardboard tubes, normally used for forming concrete, are transformed into information kiosks on which are mounted huge plastic balloons. (These tubes and balloons provide inexpensive temporary construction materials to demonstrate the information center concept, but are not necessarily intended as the structural system that might eventually be used.) A dynamic and colorful graphic pattern unifies the visual elements and creates a vibrant pedestrian place. Information content is designed to explain the activities of the city within easy walking distance of the center and to relate the user to the city as a whole. □ Pictorial maps give a pedestrian's sense of the city, and the slides, sound tracks, and movies give a visual and audial image of Boston and the local area. Revolving directories give descriptions of activities in the area and are keyed to local maps. Activities described include a wide range of shopping; entertainments such as restaurants, bars, theaters, ticket agencies, etc.; public service agencies; clubs and associations; travel services such as car hire and tours; churches, hospitals, and schools. □ Instant news is provided by a teletype machine; a question/answer machine prints out information under the headings of: **Untangling Boston, Excursions Out of Boston, Boston History, Directions to Important Destinations, The New Boston,** and others. □ **RESPONSE AND EVALUATION.** Opportunities for immediate public reaction include: a response phone which accepts messages from anyone and will replay these messages the following day; a response panel which invites written messages; and a poster kiosk on which small groups and individuals advertise events of interest. More formal responses will be gathered through interviews and questionnaires. Changes in average information levels will be assessed by before-and-after telephone and map surveys. Patterns of use will be measured quantitatively and qualitatively to evaluate each information kiosk and the center as a whole. Findings from these tests will lead to recommendations for the design of a permanent, city-wide pedestrian guide system, to be included in the final report of the Signs/Lights/Boston project.

Designed and developed by Signs/Lights/Boston, a project of Ashley/Myer/Smith Inc., 14 Arrow Street, Cambridge, under a demonstration grant contract from the U.S. Department of Housing and Urban Development through the Boston Redevelopment Authority. □ Built and erected by Donnelly Advertising and the Center for Communications, Inc. Electrical service donated by Boston Edison Company. Film and movie projectors loaned by Ealing Corp.

Hand-out used to explain the Park Square information center.

about it). Thus, 9 out of 10 people interviewed liked the Center.

A majority of people thought that the Center was in a good location, mostly because there are so many people in the Park Square area. All of the respondents thought similar information centers should be constructed in other parts of the city such as the Boston Common, the Prudential area, and Government Center.

Most people liked the appearance of the Center. They remarked that it was "eye-catching" or "attractive." Several dissenters thought it looked "gaudy."

One-third of the respondents said they had learned something from the Center. Nearly two-thirds were critical of some aspect of the information presented; most of these would have liked more information or felt that the presentation was repetitive. Other frequent criticisms were that the exhibit was confusing, crowded, and failure-prone.

These interviews recorded many strong opinions on the Center: "Well, it attracts the eyes of people and gets people over here to find out what it is".... "It's the type of thing that makes the city more livable".... "It's pretty freaky looking".... "Thank God they finally did something, instead of someone sitting in a booth that said 'information.' " Comments are reported more fully in Appendix 5.

Tube Interviews

People were interviewed at random as they looked at the various displays. These interviews were conducted periodically during the day and evening throughout the four-week demonstration.

There was substantial agreement among the small number of interviews on several questions concerning the usefulness of the tube displays and their relative popularity. The question/answer machine was the most popular; it was judged useful for both tourists and natives. The "talking" map of Boston and the maps and directories of the travel, shopping, and entertainment tubes drew favorable comments from a majority of both tourists and non-tourists — the dissenting voices came from people who either don't generally use maps or considered the information center maps unclear. The teletype machine was also popular, and several people suggested that the print-out should be projected onto a large screen.

The comments from these interviews which appear in Appendix 5 are a rich source of critical ideas. Here is a small sample: "That push-button directory [question/answer machine] is fantastic. Very clever. I think particularly for anyone new or for anyone who's wondering what's going on. They're all down-to-earth questions that average, everyday people would ask."... "Well, for me it isn't helpful [maps and directories] because I get all mixed up and I know every place in Boston 'cause I'm walking all the time" ... "I like that music, calliope-type, [from slide shows] because it isn't consciously 'mod,' 'today,' 'real with it.' That I think is what you should stay away from, because this should be for anybody from weaning age to 99."

Opinion Scale

During the first few days that the Center was open, an opinion scale was handed out to visitors to be filled out on the spot. Most of those approached cooperated, and 116 opinion scales were completed. The opinion scale consisted of 12 statements. Each described a different aspect of the Center, either favorably or unfavorably. The visitor circled one of five numbers to indicate whether he agreed very much, agreed somewhat, was neutral, disagreed somewhat, or disagreed very much with each statement.

People tended to agree with the favorable statements and disagree with the unfavorable ones, regardless of sex, age, or occupation. However, younger people liked the Center more than older people.

The opinion scale questionnaire also provided space for comments: "Creates a festive atmosphere needed in our complex urban life" .... "Trees and a fountain with light and music and a pretty girl behind a rustic booth would be more Bostonian" .... "Many people can't be bothered to go to tourist agencies or information centers. This information center cannot be avoided by anyone who is in the least bit curious. What would McLuhan think?"

Unobtrusive Observations
Another assessment of public response to the Center was made by observation without direct contact with the visitors. There were several unobtrusive measures: the number, age, and sex of people at the Center; the number of people attracted into the Center as contrasted with the number who passed by; and the popularity of various kiosks.

The observations revealed that people visited the Center at an average rate of 240 per hour, during working hours. By extrapolation, more than 80,000 visited during the month of its operation. More than half of the visitors were men (63%); 41% were young adults. Middle aged adults (25% between 35 and 55) and teenagers (19%) made up most of the remainder. People over 55 (9%) were slightly more common than children (6%).

Of all people observed walking by, 40% actually entered the Center. In the evening the Center attracted a higher percentage of people (47%) than during the day (39%). Also, more visitors came at the beginning (42%) than during the middle (36%) of the demonstration period.

The question/answer machine attracted the largest audience. The movie tube and the entertainment slide show appeared to be the second and third most popular displays by this measure.

Conclusions
The most significant result of the tests of the Information Center was the overwhelmingly positive character of the public response. People liked the Center and felt others should visit it; many wanted to come back, a quarter had already done so. They were particularly intrigued by the more animated media: the question/answer machine and the slide and film presentations. Whatever the usefulness of the specific information provided in the Center, it was clear from observation of the people there and from their own comments that the Center was a very attractive place to be; and people spent quite a long time there.

The short questionnaire interviews indicated that publicity was not a major factor in informing people of the Center. Rather, the visual distinctiveness and interest of the Center, easily seen from other parts of Park Square, drew most of the visitors. This was a measure of success, since the Center was designed to serve the Park Square area.

The open-ended interview results suggest that the construction of information centers in other areas of the city would be a well-received project. However, judging by some of the criticisms, other centers should be highly responsive to the unique needs of their visitors, and especially those of the residents of the area. According to these evaluative studies, future centers should define their purpose for the public more clearly, expand the information coverage, and provide better explanation as to how to use the information available.

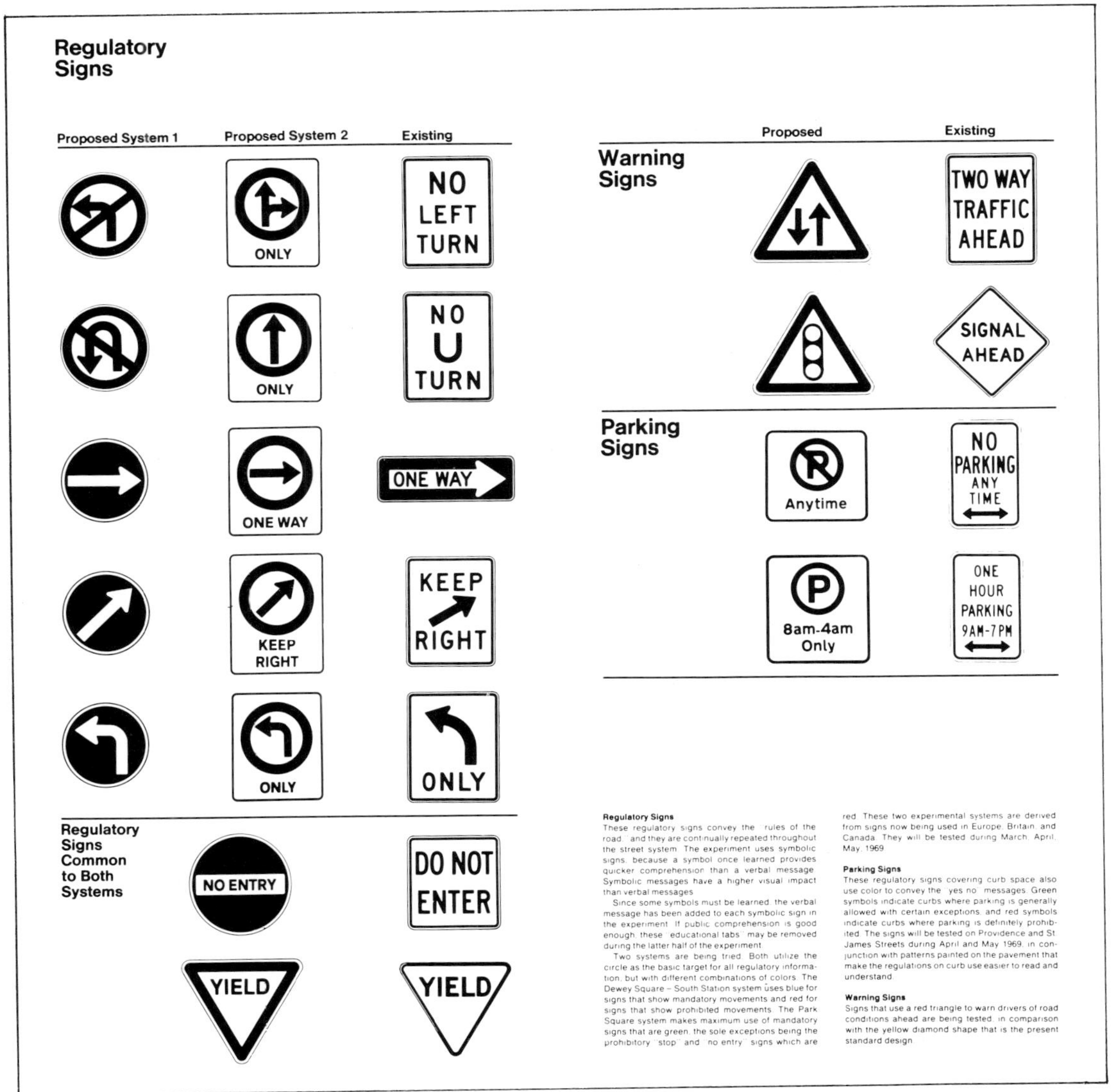
Regulatory Signs
Proposed System 1
Proposed System 2
Existing
ONLY
NO LEFT TURN
ONLY
NO U TURN
ONE WAY
ONE WAY
KEEP RIGHT
KEEP RIGHT
ONLY
ONLY
Regulatory Signs Common to Both Systems
NO ENTRY
DO NOT ENTER
YIELD
YIELD
Proposed
Existing
Warning Signs
TWO WAY TRAFFIC AHEAD
SIGNAL AHEAD
Parking Signs
Anytime
NO PARKING ANY TIME
8am-4am Only
ONE HOUR PARKING 9AM-7PM
Regulatory Signs
These regulatory signs convey the "rules of the road," and they are continually repeated throughout the street system. The experiment uses symbolic signs, because a symbol once learned provides quicker comprehension than a verbal message. Symbolic messages have a higher visual impact than verbal messages.
Since some symbols must be learned, the verbal message has been added to each symbolic sign in the experiment. If public comprehension is good enough, these "educational tabs" may be removed during the latter half of the experiment.
Two systems are being tried. Both utilize the circle as the basic target for all regulatory information, but with different combinations of colors. The Dewey Square – South Station system uses blue for signs that show mandatory movements and red for signs that show prohibited movements. The Park Square system makes maximum use of mandatory signs that are green, the sole exceptions being the prohibitory "stop" and "no entry" signs which are red. These two experimental systems are derived from signs now being used in Europe, Britain, and Canada. They will be tested during March, April, May, 1969.
Parking Signs
These regulatory signs covering curb space also use color to convey the "yes no" messages. Green symbols indicate curbs where parking is generally allowed with certain exceptions, and red symbols indicate curbs where parking is definitely prohibited. The signs will be tested on Providence and St. James Streets during April and May 1969, in conjunction with patterns painted on the pavement that make the regulations on curb use easier to read and understand.
Warning Signs
Signs that use a red triangle to warn drivers of road conditions ahead are being tested, in comparison with the yellow diamond shape that is the present standard design.
Hand-out used to explain the traffic sign demonstration.

PUBLIC SIGNING: EVALUATIVE TESTS

The new signs were evaluated by tests in the laboratory (regulatory signs only) and in the field: laboratory tests dealt with the legibility of symbolic vs. existing traffic signs; evaluations of symbolic traffic signs were made by postcard questionnaires; and evaluations of the guide sign system were made by observation of driver behavior.

Symbolic vs. Existing Traffic Signs: Laboratory Tests

The first laboratory test investigated how well people could comprehend the new symbolic traffic signs, without any previous exposure and after a brief learning period. The results indicate that most of the symbolic signs, even without legends or helpful contextual clues, were readily understood. Thirteen of the 22 signs were understood by more than half of the 35 subjects without previous exposure. After the symbols had been explained, there was nearly complete comprehension of the signs.

In two other experiments, responses to slides of photographed intersections with both symbolic and existing signs were compared. When compared with signs of the existing system in their natural settings, the symbolic signs were correctly identified more frequently than were the old signs. The symbolic signs were also better understood than were those from the existing system. This was the most rigorous test of the signs, because the intersections pictured were confusing and subjects had to indicate all allowable turns.

Evaluation of Symbolic Traffic Signs: Postcard Questionnaire

One thousand drivers were given self-addressed questionnaire postcards while stopped at red lights in both experimental areas. Of the 500 postcards which were distributed in Park Square, 110 were returned; of the 500 distributed in Dewey Square, 70 were returned.

Motorists reacted extremely favorably to the signs. On the 110 Park Square postcards, 330 positive responses were checked, 15 fair responses, and 71 negative responses. There were 221 positive responses, 9 fair responses, and 21 negative responses on those returned from Dewey Square.

However, the spontaneous comments on the postcard questionnaire were more significant: "If we could do this at strategic spots in Boston—hurrah!".... "Some signs are a bit obtrusive... 'No entry' sign is not easy to understand. Definitely too many signs".... "Cab drivers read signs 12 hours a day. I am a cab driver. New signs, Common-Charles Street, etc., are excellent".... "Great! Fantastic! Cover the city with them!".... "Finally Boston does something about direction problems".... "Take down all the old signs. New Signs are very attractive—they help to make streets look cleaner and less cluttered" ... "I think that the color scheme and design of the new signs is elegant and beautiful. Reminds me of London. Gives Boston a cosmopolitan air" ... "Easy to understand except 'no left turn' arrows—traffic light should be larger".... "More clear, general-type directions *before* choice has to be made would be welcome".... I hope you are taking *down* as many as you put *up*. Too many signs at many intersections are confusing because drivers stop or almost stop to read every sign".... "I think they are very nice but I think they should be placed all over Boston as I have never been in a city with so many unmarked streets".... "These signs are a step in the right direction in traffic control and are more in tune with universal traffic signs (European)." Further comments appear in Appendix 6.

Evaluation of Guide Sign System: Observation of Driver Behavior

Observers counted the number of drivers who appeared to be confused in both Dewey and Park Squares before and after installation of the new signs. Behavior counted as "confusion" was defined according to narrow criteria.

In Park Square, there were — on the average — 18 instances of confusion per hour "before" and 11 "after." In Dewey Square, there were 27 instances of confusion before and 11 after the new directional signs were installed.

It is not possible to separate the impact of the guide signs from that of the new regulatory and street-name signs. Clearly, the installation of the *total* new signing system resulted in less driver confusion at these intersections.

Conclusions

Tests of public signing indicated that in nearly all cases the new signs were a significant improvement over the old. These results strongly suggest that a large-scale demonstration of the complete system recommended in Chapter 4 is in order.

The laboratory tests also indicated that the symbolic signs are fairly well recognized when seen for the first time and very well recognized after a brief learning period. They are also better recognized than existing signs when viewed briefly in natural settings on the street or in the context of a total intersection.

The field test results are equally supportive of the new sign system: response to the postcard questionnaire was decidedly favorable. In addition, the observed decrease in driver confusion suggest that the new system would increase driving safety.

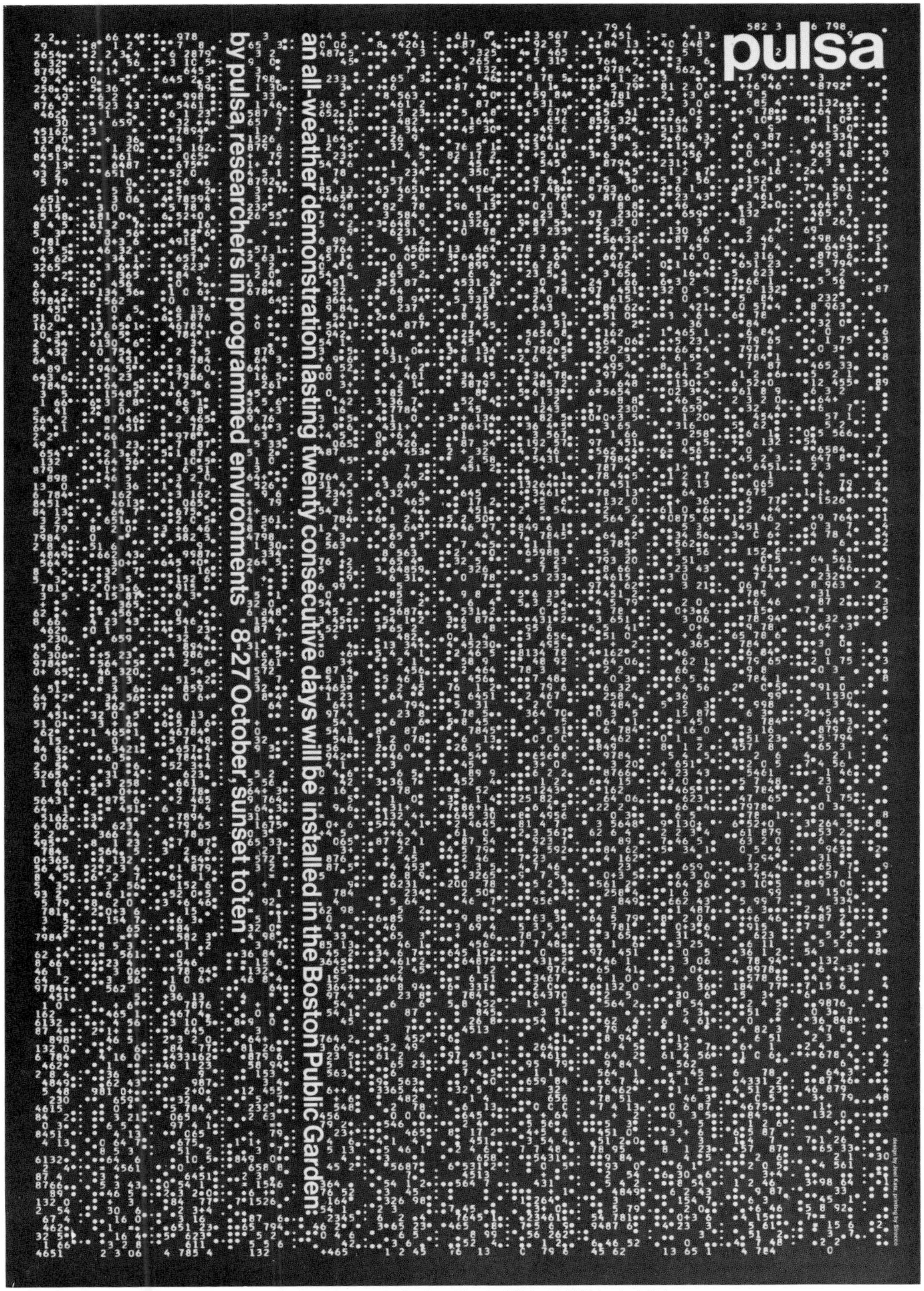

Poster used to publicize the PULSA light and sound concert *Designed by Joel Katz, © 1968 by Joel Katz.*

PUBLIC LIGHTING DEMONSTRATIONS

Evaluation of the Light and Sound Environment

Five methods were used to determine attendance rates and attitudes toward the Light and Sound Environment: visitor count, spatial location of visitors, an adjective check-list, short interviews, and open-ended interviews.

By extrapolation from sample counts, between 6,000 and 7,000 people saw the demonstration. Most people seemed to gather at the bridge or stand on the Beacon Street side of the pond to watch the demonstration, probably because there was less ambient light there.

Thirty-three people checked a list of adjectives as to how appropriate or inappropriate each one was for characterizing the Light and Sound Environment. The results suggest that most people (67%) liked the demonstration.

Of the 48 visitors to the Light and Sound Environment who answered the short interview questionnaire, most (63%) came upon the demonstration by chance. At the time of the interview, 64% of the respondents had been at the demonstration under 20 minutes. However, 74% said that they intended to stay some time longer.

The people who didn't like the demonstration often remarked that it was somewhat interesting but very "confusing," "noisy," or "uncomfortable." For the people who liked it, the demonstration was also quite confusing and noisy — but "promising," "very interesting," or "exciting."

Visitor opinions on this experiment differ sharply (see Appendix 7): "Obviously the sounds represent frogs and the light lightning bugs." . . . "It sort of synthesizes the unreal daily experience with city noises and sounds." . . . "It's not exactly that I don't like it, but sometimes the sounds sound like somebody is dying or groaning in agony."

The Public Library and Copley Square

Another demonstration involved lighting the Boston Public Library. No formal evaluations were made, however; a group of professionals viewed the trial lighting alternatives and expressed their individual opinions. A more detailed discussion of this demonstration and suggestions for additional lighting of the privately-owned buildings in Copley Square can be found in Appendix 7.

PRIVATE SIGNS: TESTS

Private signs are familiar objects in the cityscape. Store or "on-premise" signs are erected to attract the attention of motorists and pedestrians. They announce the name of an establishment and frequently state its function. They are also used to advertise specific goods, services, and costs. Off-premise signs normally advertise goods, services, and establishments which are located at some distance from the sign. Billboards are in this category.

Several experiments and surveys assessed public feelings about both on and off-premise private signs. These included: a recognition experiment, an opinion survey, a test of the influence of private signs on assessment of street attractiveness, and another opinion survey on billboards.

Recognition Experiment

This study investigated the attention that people give to commercial signs on Washington Street in downtown Boston. It used 32 slides of Washington Street signs, windows, and buildings; and 8 slides of signs, windows, and buildings on other streets.

After a walk down Washington Street, 25 subjects looked at the series of 40 slides and indicated on an answer sheet whether or not they "recognized" the slide being shown. "Recognized" meant that the subject was certain that he had seen the sign, window, or building during his walk.

Signs were recognized better than windows or buildings; subjects familiar with Washington Street correctly recognized Washington Street signs more frequently than subjects who were strangers to the area; signs shown without their backgrounds were correctly recognized more frequently than signs shown with their backgrounds; and men made slightly more correct sign recognitions than did women. There was also a positive correlation between correct recognition of signs and a preference for those signs.

Opinion Survey

On three different streets in downtown Boston — Washington, Boylston, and Newbury Streets — people were asked whether they considered commercial signs to be a problem and whether

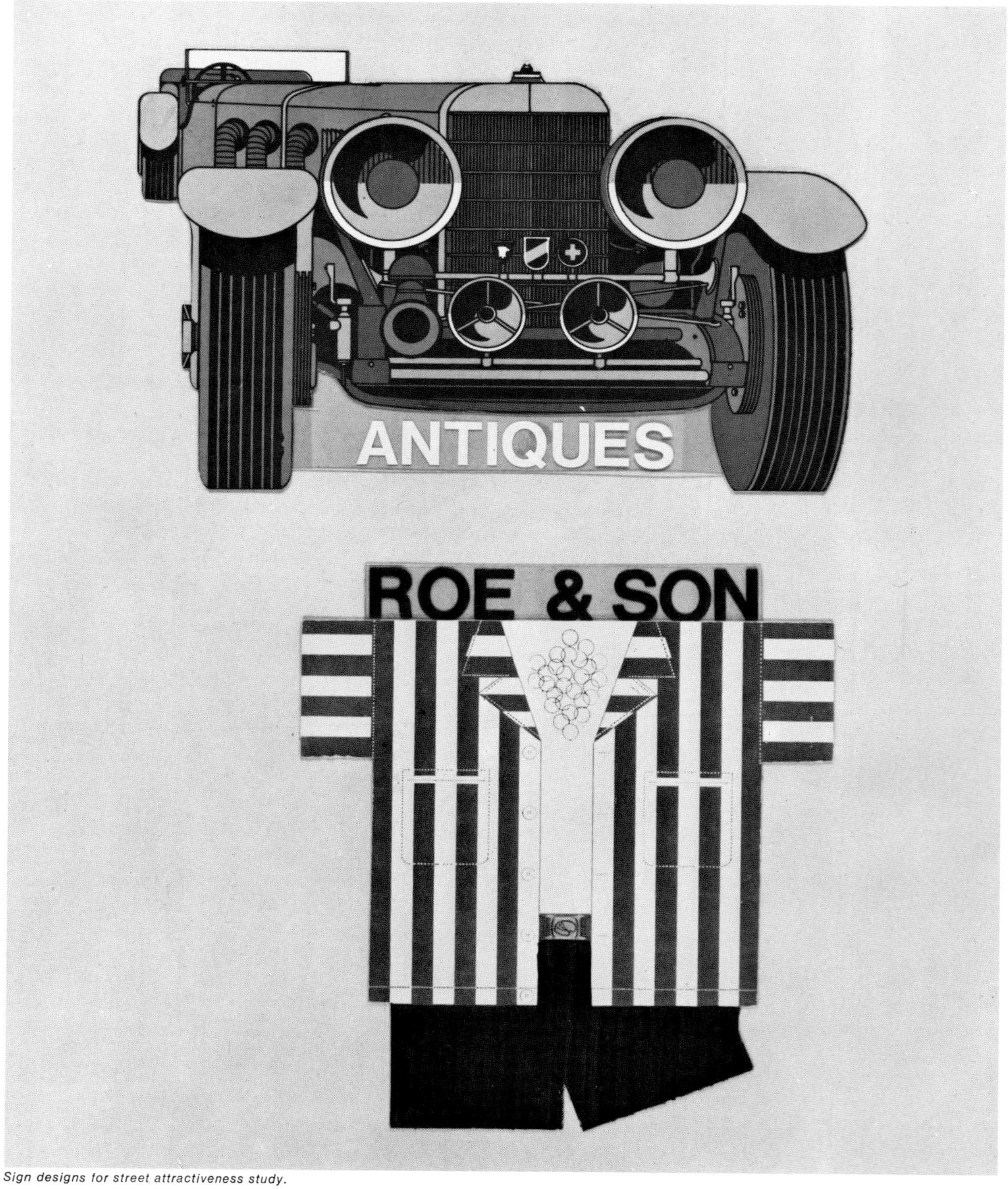

Sign designs for street attractiveness study.

Washington Street

Boylston Street

Newbury Street

sign controls would be an effective way to improve the streetscape. In all, 83 people were interviewed. Answers were recorded as Favorable, Unfavorable, and Neutral.

Each respondent first ranked several "problems" according to their importance — "car exhaust," "gaudy commercial signs," "traffic," "noise," "congested sidewalks," "run-down buildings." Almost all respondents ranked "gaudy commercial signs" as the least important problem and "run-down buildings" and "traffic" as the most important.

Forty-five people were asked: "What do you think of the signs on this street?" People on Newbury Street were overwhelmingly favorable, on Boylston Street about half were favorable, and on Washington Street fewer than 20% liked the signs.

To get a better idea of what people thought about specific signs, the interviewer pointed to four signs on each street and asked people how they liked them. On Washington Street, no signs were overwhelmingly liked or disliked; on Boylston and Newbury Streets the examples were generally liked. On Boylston and Newbury Streets people talked about the aesthetic qualities of the signs, whereas people on Washington Street mentioned such things as the condition of the signs.

When asked whether they would like to have an administrative agency controlling the size, style, and position of private commercial signs, over half of the respondents said that they were in favor of some kind of control.

Influence on Assessment of Street Attractiveness
The influence of "good" or "bad" signing was investigated to see if evaluations of settings could be changed by changing a sign. The study explored the effects of three different variables, each of which was defined according to specific criteria (see Appendix 8):

1 background quality — "orderly" vs. "disorderly"
2 sign quality — "good" vs. "bad"
3 sign size — "small" vs. "large"

The experiment was divided into four sessions with a different group of subjects participating in each and viewing a different set of slides. The slides, 80 in all, differed according to the three variables above and were grouped as follows:

Session 1: Large Signs—
good sign/disorderly setting;
bad sign/orderly setting

Session 2: Large Signs—
good sign/orderly setting;
bad sign/disorderly setting

Session 3: Small Signs—
good sign/disorderly setting;
bad sign/orderly setting

Session 4: Small Signs—
good sign/orderly setting;
bad sign/disorderly setting

It should be emphasized that each group of subjects saw the same "orderly" and "disorderly" settings and the same "good" and "bad" signs. In all, 10 "orderly" settings and 10 "disorderly" settings were used. Each setting paired with 10 "good" signs (large and small) and 10 "bad" signs (large and small).

Each group of subjects was shown 20 slides in random order and asked to indicate on a 10-point scale whether and how much they liked a particular setting (10 = like very much). The signs themselves were never mentioned.

The results indicated that:

1 When the background is "orderly," small signs are preferred. On the other hand, when the background is "disorderly," large signs are preferred.

2 "Orderly" backgrounds were, almost consistently, preferred over "disorderly" ones, regardless of the size or quality of the sign. However, subjects preferred to have a "disorderly" background rather than an "orderly" one, when the sign shown in the slide was large and "bad."

3 Whether a sign was "good" or "bad" was unimportant when the sign was small. However, when the sign was large, the subjects preferred the "good" signs on an "orderly" background and the "bad" signs on a "disorderly" background.

Billboards: Opinion Survey

Another survey investigated attitudes toward billboards. Billboards in this study were "large advertising signs which can be seen over rather large areas." The questionnaire dealt with the importance of signing problems in the city, control of signing by the city, form and content of billboards, attention value of billboards, and aesthetics and appropriateness of billboards.

Fifty-five people completed the questionnaire. More than half the respondents felt that billboards present important problems in the city and that they should be controlled by the city. Most people also expressed general disfavor with the form and content of billboards. Women were the most outspoken critics of billboard appearance.

Slightly less than half the sample said that billboards did not provide them with useful information. Of those people who felt that billboards do provide useful information, most said that this was in the form of "driving information" (i.e., information about rest stops, motels, restaurants, and gasoline stations).

Although the results indicate that the respondents disliked billboards, a substantial minority agreed that people do pay attention to them. Despite the fact that most people felt that billboards were too distracting, less than half thought that billboards cause traffic accidents.

The respondents had clear ideas about where billboards are and are not appropriate. Almost 95% said that billboards are not appropriate everywhere; three-quarters said that billboards are not located in the right places with respect to buildings and views. The subjects had particularly negative reactions to billboards placed in areas that may interfere with their driving or detract from the scenery. Billboards placed in essentially commercial areas were considered least objectionable.

Conclusions

People interviewed in this study did not normally think about private signs as a significant urban problem. Before being questioned specifically, many people spontaneously remarked that they had never thought about signs before and that they did not pay much attention to them. While slightly more than half of the respondents in the billboard survey felt that billboards are an important problem in the city, only about one-third rated other commercial signs as an important problem. There is no way to know, of course, whether the attitudes of this small sample are more widely held.

The recognition experiment respondents said that they looked at windows and stores most and signs least during their walk down Washington Street. (The recognition rates conflict with their statements, however.) When asked whether they remembered looking at private signs at all, all but one subject said that they had spent some time doing so; a majority, however, said that they glanced at them only briefly. In contrast with the opinion survey, slightly more than one-quarter of the respondents of the recognition experiment ranked signs as a serious problem (one problem among many that are equally bad); slightly less than one-quarter felt that signs ruin the looks of a street. In the opinion survey the first question asked for a ranking of city problems, but in the recognition experiment this question was held until the end. Thus, in the latter, the commercial sign orientation was clear to the respondents, and perhaps they became more sensitized to signing during the course of the interview. By the end of both experiments, a majority of people expressed support for the idea of sign controls.

The findings are suggestive only. It may be that bad feelings about commercial signing are widespread but that they surface only when the problem becomes extreme, as with billboards, or when people recognize that there may be a real possibility of doing something about signs. The development of city policy should not proceed without a thorough program of public analysis.

The results of the billboard survey gave some indication of locations where people most oppose billboards and where they are more permissible. The people interviewed disapprove of billboards most strongly when they are likely to interfere with driving (i.e., at road intersections, along major roads, and on highways approaching the city) or to detract from the scenery (on the skyline and along water edges). It is significant that all of the least objectionable areas for billboards are essentially commercial in nature: shopping areas, entertainment districts, and parking lots or used car lots.

In scenic areas, there is an obvious mismatch between billboard and environment. In commercial areas, billboards may not be especially disliked because a match exists. The experiment on the influence (of private signs) on assessment of street attractiveness supports this notion. "Orderly" backgrounds were, almost consistently, preferred over "disorderly" backgrounds. However, people preferred the "disorderly" background over the "orderly" one when the sign was large and "bad," as opposed to small and "good." Thus, people again tended to like backgrounds and sign combinations most when a match existed. These results suggest that people may harbor a secret wish for a harmonious environment.

These findings have implications for policy: billboards and other super-signs seem to be considered a more important problem than other types of signs; people appear to prefer signs which are consistent with their context, regardless of the character of the sign. The recommended policies emphasize strict control of super-signs and the maintenance and development of unique street and district character in private signing and lighting.

Overall, field testing was an indispensable part of this study. The tests are suggestive rather than conclusive in many cases. Limited as they are, they provide strong support for building such evaluative processes into future city information programs and for further uses of field experimentation. No final policy should be based on these field tests without further public discussion and debate of the issues.

CHAPTER SEVEN

A Program for Action

A Program for Action

What actions are necessary to organize an environmental information program in city government? In particular what must be done to establish a Department of City Information as proposed in Chapter 3? How can the new agency acquire the necessary administrative powers and funding to become an effective part of city government?

In the long run the city council and, in states like Massachusetts, the legislature will need to authorize a new Department of City Information, giving it the stature to deal with other city departments and business groups whose interests are at stake. While proposals are being drafted for such full-scale action, however, a great deal of useful work can and should be done. The mayor could use his existing powers to create a city information office within his present staff. While the support of the mayor (or city manager) will always be crucial, initial staff work and coordination might also be contributed either by civic organizations or by an existing public agency with a special interest in the problem, such as a renewal authority or a legislative study commission. One full-time professional, with one or two assistants and the aid of the General Counsel of the city, should be able to put together the basic structure and tools for the new program in less than one year.

Sources of financing for the new information programs must also be explored in advance, presumably by the same staff. Improvement of traffic signs is one of the aims of the "TOPICS" urban traffic improvement program of the U.S. Bureau of Public Roads. Other types of public signs can be financed as part of an Urban Beautification program. All investments in public signs and lighting are eligible within renewal projects. A license and fee system, such as now supports the operations of the Massachusetts Outdoor Advertising Board, could be used to pay for the administrative costs of regulation of private advertising signs. Grants for new street lights can be obtained from the federal Department of Justice under the Crime Control and Safe Streets Act of 1968. The general administration of a Department of City Information will require a number of new positions, and these costs must be borne by the city unless a pilot project grant can be obtained for the first years.

Prior to this initial staff work, some group of citizens will probably need to take the initiative in bringing the potentialities of such an agency to the attention of city officials and the public. The composition of the organizing group would vary from city to city but might typically include politicians, businessmen, and professionals. The organizing group will first need to build public support for the program, and this report is intended to aid in that effort. This chapter describes the necessary first public actions in Boston and then, in more detail, a recommended three-year program for the new agency.

AN ADVISORY COMMITTEE

In Boston and other cities, an organizing group might work with the mayor's staff to build support for the new program and agency. All those who currently control the design and placement of signs and lighting in the city should be consulted; they will have a major stake in the new program and will make their interests known to the city council in any case. Some of the strongest views will come from the traffic department, renewal project managers, the electric power company, and firms who install sign or lighting structures. To begin the discussion, this report might be circulated to each of these parties for review and comment. Chambers of Commerce and Boards of Trade should also be consulted; they have often brought together business interests around the issues of sign and lighting improvement.

In the early stages, the sponsors of the new program can begin to test the idea of Local Information Districts with neighborhood groups. Local merchants' associations may have the strongest interest; they in turn may look to the Chamber of Commerce or Board of Trade. In Boston, the network of "little city halls" provides one contact point with the city's residents. In some cities, certain areas may already have neighborhood associations or elected neighborhood boards, like those organized for many model cities or renewal project areas, which can consider the special district idea.

Endorsement of the new program by an advisory committee representing these various interests would obviously be an asset when the proposals are submitted to the city council. The organizing group and the mayor's special staff should work with such an advisory committee from the outset. Whether this committee should include representatives of the sign building industry, whose activities it will be seeking to regulate in the program, is a decision that must be made by the mayor himself. Past experience suggests that industry representation can be useful in a study group but that it must not be given a dominant voice.

Use of Existing Programs

Many steps to effectuate the new policies can be taken by existing city agencies as part of the general effort to get the new program underway. These will need only instructions from the mayor and will not have to wait for new legislation and budgets.

Perhaps the most obvious of these steps, in Boston at least, is to tighten requirements for signs in the public airspace — typically for those overhanging the sidewalk beyond the property line. In Boston, permits for such signs have traditionally been issued by the Public Works Department using standards relating mostly to size and method of lighting. These could be directly amended to incorporate the requirements for information content related to visual channels of the street, as described in Chapter 5. Issuance of the permit should be preceded by a design review, in anticipation of the entire permit issuing process being transferred later to the Department of City Information.

The urban renewal program obviously provides an opportunity to put the new sign, lighting, and information policies into effect; each time a parcel of land is sold, the policies can be included as deed restrictions. Other, more positive incentives should be possible in the renewal program; Boston's present requirement that one percent of the cost of each new commercial building be devoted to art could be satisfied by design costs of exterior signs, symbols, and lighting which make a contribution to its artistic quality. The builder might also be permitted to count certain sign and lighting equipment or materials as part of his investment in art.

If the zoning ordinance makes special provisions for review and approval of planned unit developments, a detailed plan for signs and lighting that follows the guidelines recommended in Chapter 5 could be made a requirement. In Boston, "planned development areas" may be approved for parcels of one acre or more, and use of this option could result in a well-coordinated design for signs and lighting for substantial street frontages. (Note, though, that most ordinances require much larger land areas.)

In a number of cities, historic districts have been established for which a design review board is given special approval powers over alterations or new construction. In Boston, such boards have been established for Beacon Hill and for the residential area of Back Bay. By adopting guidelines that relate to the city-wide policies described in Chapter 5, such boards can put these policies directly into effect for their areas. These boards can also form the nucleus of Local Information Districts and act to formalize any controls that may be needed to preserve the qualities of their particular areas.

Model cities agencies are in the unique position among public offices of having a clearly identified neighborhood constituency, the need to build communication links with this constituency in regard to a wide range of new program opportunities, and budgets that are not initially tied to operating program categories. An information center can be much more for a model cities agency than simply a service to its neighborhood — it can be a source of information from constituents on current progress or new program proposals. Such a center could follow the general format for the district centers described in Chapter 4, though it would need an even greater emphasis on person-to-person communications, and should employ and train local people as information specialists. This would seem a logical use of model cities program resources, even during the planning phases, and could be an important continuing operation as well. Model cities areas should, of course, be given high priority as prospective Local Information Districts in the new city information program.

New Administrative Powers

If it is to carry out a program for private signs and lights approaching that outlined in Chapter 5, the new Department of City Information will need to have at its disposal at least four additional powers beyond those provided to municipal agencies in typical enabling legislation. The organizing group could undertake the necessary legal studies, which would be a major part of the proposal for the creation of the new office. Other municipal functions or other levels of government have had similar powers, but they have not before been brought together under a single city office.

Most of the model code provisions described in Chapter 5 for the centrally-controlled Special Information Districts and General Information Districts can be enacted under standard zoning enabling legislation. However, off-premise advertising signs, mostly billboards, should be licensed on an individual basis by the proposed city agency, and the licensing fee should be sufficient to defray an appropriate share of the total cost of the program, including district-level administration. This is a new power for municipalities.

In Massachusetts, such licensing powers are now exercised by a special board of the state government, which only recently has been required to keep the billboards it licenses within the restrictions of local zoning. State exercise of such powers may be appropriate for signs on major inter-city highways, and strong incentives for such control are provided in the Highway Beautification Act of 1965. However, for lands abutting major highways in densely built-up areas, local interests should predominate. It will be necessary to define state as opposed to city jurisdictions; for instance, the boundaries of the "urbanized area," as drawn by the U.S. Census Bureau, could be used to identify locations where billboard licensing fees should go to the municipality. In these places, the role of the state or regional agency would be to resolve disputes over signs or lights affecting land in an adjoining city or town.

The second new power involves the formation of Local Information Districts, where localized zoning provisions and an administrative structure involving local representatives can be established. The question of which authority will be given the power to adopt local zoning provisions will be a central issue in the enabling legislation for Local Information Districts. The boundaries of the district will need approval by the city-wide zoning authority, presumably the city council; zoning provisions within that district could also be adopted by the city council, but it would be preferable for adoption to be locally based (see Chapter 5 for a discussion of alternative mechanisms for this).

The third new tool recommended for the Department of City Information is the power to make incentive payments to property owners for bringing their properties up to the standards of the new zoning codes. This could be seen as a kind of roadway rehabilitation; grants and low-interest loans are now available for similar purposes under the "concentrated code enforcement" programs. The payments would permit more rapid improvement of signs and lighting; using zoning powers alone, extended amortization periods would be needed. Aid of this type is not presently available in the Urban Beautification Program of HUD. Until new federal legislation is passed, there would be little overall impact from any attempt to use incentive payments city wide. However, in the Special Information Districts, where visible results are needed in the first few years of the program, city funded incentives for early action by private property owners could be decisive.

A fourth power, which could be vital to the success of the program, is that of condemnation of the rights of a property owner to install signs or lighting in certain specified ways, with compensation only upon petition of the owner. This would secure the controls more firmly than does the police power exercised in zoning. The extent of the condemned rights would have to be carefully designed and located so as to avoid conflict with too many existing structures or with too many immediate development plans of property owners. If so designed, and especially if a deadline were established for filing of claims by owners, condemnation should result in only limited claims by property owners for compensation, as compared with eminent domain takings which presently require immediate compensation in this country. The types of districts where such "inverse condemnations" might be most effective include residential areas, older commercial areas that still retain some unique style through private efforts (as do many downtown areas today), and vacant lands. (See Appendix 3, *Legal Issues,* for further discussion.)

Powers of inverse condemnation would probably be most useful in the Special Information Districts. For example, the sign building and lighting rights of merchants abutting a major traffic interchange area (see, for example, the Charles Rotary in Chapter 4) should be limited more than those of similar businesses outside the District. Ownership of those rights by the city would be justified by the public purpose of keeping those particular business frontages relatively free from distractions. Sign and lighting requirements would be tailored to special traffic situations. Inverse condemnation would also be effective in conserving older established commercial areas with some unique style, especially if most of the property owners were in sympathy with the restrictions. Such powers could also be used to establish areas where the city could actively promote and sell sign space — for off-premise ads, spectaculars, and other special displays — as recommended in Chapter 5.

A Three-Year Agenda

The public actions discussed so far are necessary preliminaries. The rest of the chapter describes a possible action agenda for the new agency during the first years of its life. While these are all rightly matters for public debate and decision, this set of recommendations shows how the Department of City Information might use its new authority and gives some idea of what resources it would need to do the job. Staff and funding requirements and suggested sources of funds are listed for each program element; an estimate of the total cost of this three-year capital improvement program and the overall staffing requirements appear at the end.

The first priority of the Department should be to obtain legislation giving the city at least the power to license billboards and to organize and designate information districts. Then the Department should select one or two centrally located and highly visible pilot development areas for the first large-scale implementation of the new public systems and the first designation of each kind of information district. The area should be large enough to include the full range of typical sign/light information districts. The ordinance for General Information Districts should also be included in the initial program, but since it is city-wide in application it will involve a coordination of interests far beyond the pilot development areas.

The following criteria should be used to draw the boundaries of the pilot area or areas:

1 Include at least one obvious prototype of each of the five types of Special Information Districts outlined in Chapter 5.

2 Include some example of each category of the proposed General Information Districts (e.g., major commercial, neighborhood commercial, industrial, multi-family residential, one or two-family residential, etc.).

3 Include locations that require the full range of public sign/light information systems described in Chapter 4.

4 Identify the areas of interest of existing local business and neighborhood associations, including elected neighborhood councils or boards if possible, as incipient Local Information Districts.

5 Include prospective Local Information Districts that are likely to provide a strong resident constituency to support the program in the future and to help maintain backing by elected officials.

6 Make the new developments highly visible to a large portion of the city's population, both by location of the areas and by the opportunity for dramatic improvements over existing conditions.

In Boston, the downtown area would meet most of the above criteria if there were included three entire urban renewal project areas (Downtown plus South Cove plus New York Streets), plus parts of the Back Bay north of Stuart Street, and the Prudential Center. A total of about one square mile of the city would be involved.

A second recommended development area for the three-year program should include outlying strip-commercial uses and one and two-family residences not found in the downtown area. In Boston, this might be Dudley Square and the adjacent neighborhood, plus the adjoining new light industrial area that is part of the Washington Park urban renewal project, a total of about one-half square mile. This area has the advantages of an organized model cities board with neighborhood delegates, an existing "little city hall" at its center, a strong traditional commercial base, and a potential for widespread new sign and lighting improvements when the elevated line is removed and relocated.

The recommended three-year programs in public signs, public lighting, and city information are designed to cover the initial development areas, so that all of the components may be seen and tested together in their mutual effects. Simply to supplement existing unrelated components or to install only parts of the new systems would be insufficient. To generate sufficient support for their city-wide use, the systems must be given a chance to demonstrate their full effects, particularly considering the level of investment needed.

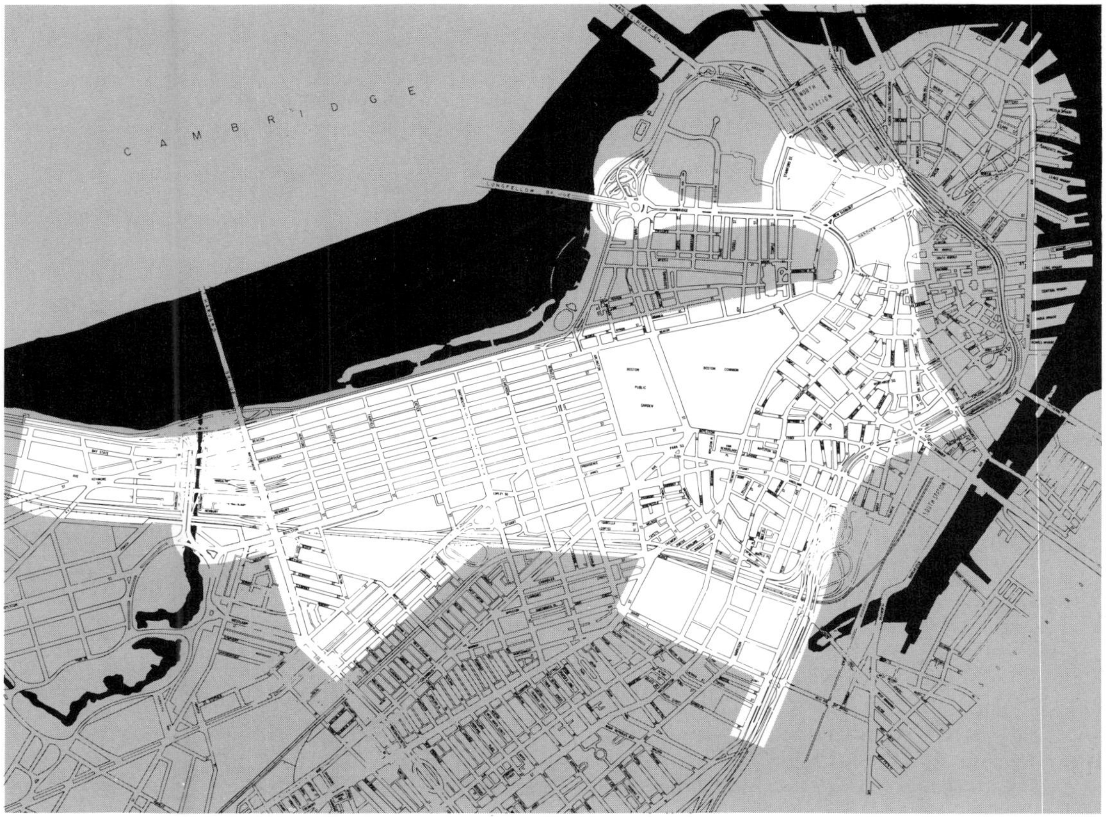

Development area for the initial three-year program.

PUBLIC ROAD SIGNS AND SIGNALS

The new system of public road signs and signals described in Chapter 4 replaces an existing system, which in Boston is installed and maintained by the Traffic and Parking Department. In the proposed three-year program, that Department should continue in this role. The Department has been sympathetic to such improvements but has lacked the funds and authority to put them into effect city-wide. It will require some form of grant-in-aid contract with the Department of City Information and will need authorization from the state to proceed with a system that deviates from federal and state standards. Also, authorization for the Department to proceed on a pilot installation would have to be obtained from the U.S. Department of Transportation. The application could draw support from successful tests of some of these components in the present project, plus other studies of new sign systems now being completed under the auspices of the National Joint Committee on Uniform Traffic Control Devices.

The estimated cost of the three-year program of sign and signal equipment installation in Boston is $1,300,000. This figure is based on costs of the experimental demonstrations and includes $500,000 for traffic signs, $700,000 for new signal units (coordinated with the new intersection lighting), and $100,000 for new information signs for pedestrians. Agency staff to manage this part of the program should cost no more than about $40,000 per year, assuming that working drawings, specifications, and supervision of installation are carried out by the Traffic and Parking Department. About $500,000 of this program cost should be available from existing or future federal sources like the "TOPICS" program of the U.S. Department of Transportation.

PUBLIC LIGHTING

Roadway lighting on all major streets in the pilot area should be brought up to the standards outlined in Chapter 4, including glare cut-off for any high intensity fixtures and both an increase of light intensity and a change of color at all significant street intersections. If high intensity lights on separate poles have already been installed in the area, the cost of new equipment suggests that new additions be limited to external glare shields, plus new luminaires to achieve a color change at intersections. One or two additional poles at each major intersection will probably also be required for the desired brightness. The Public Works Department, which in Boston installs and maintains the street lights wherever public capital funds are involved, could well continue in this role, but it will need substantial financial aid to meet the new requirements.

In Boston, about 40 percent of the 60 miles of arterial connector streets in the pilot areas has been equipped with high intensity lights. Another 30 percent need not be lit during this initial period. Glare shields for the existing lights, plus new lights and poles to bring the remaining 30 percent up to standards recommended in this report, would cost an additional $1,000,000. Another $400,000 would be needed for other public lighting, including $100,000 for park lighting, $200,000 for lighting public buildings in the area, and $100,000 for lighting special intersections and areas. Agency staff and overhead might add $20,000 per year to the cost, assuming the Public Works Department gets the contracts and supervises installation. At least $250,000 of the street lighting costs should be available through code enforcement and urban renewal programs and another undetermined percentage from the U.S. Department of Justice under the Crime Control and Safe Streets Act of 1968. Some part, up to 50 percent, of other lighting costs might be covered by Urban Beautification funds.

PUBLIC LOCAL INFORMATION SYSTEM

The major new facility built directly by the Department of City Information, rather than through agreements with other agencies, will be the system of information centers, following the outlines suggested in Chapter 4. To show the pattern for the city-wide system, at least one of each of the two major types of information centers should be built — one for a concentrated downtown commercial district similar to the center demonstrated in this project and one for a local residential district. Each center should serve as the focal point of an information network that reaches various other points in the area it serves, as outlined in Chapter 4. In Boston, the "little city halls" should serve as the starting point for the system for residential areas. These rely on neighborhood councils and personal contact for communication and are located at 16 activity centers throughout the residential areas of the city (as of the winter of 1969-1970). Management of the information centers should be closely coordinated with the Local Information Districts.

The estimated cost of two information centers, each having the general scope of the experimental guide center described in Chapter 6, with their accompanying networks of kiosks in neighboring blocks of the city is $300,000. A large part of this cost will be for staff of the Department of City Information to compile the information content, transfer it to film, tapes or printed sheets, and then to man each information center at least 12 hours a day starting in the second year of the program. Continuing maintenance costs are also included. Staff for planning and management might cost an additional $40,000 per year. There is some evidence that listings of establishments in the information center has sufficient commercial value that a local merchants' association might be willing to pay as much as one-third of the installation cost of the centers. Limited institutional advertising might also be used to support the centers, under strict control by the city.

PRIVATE SIGN AND LIGHT PROGRAM, CITY-WIDE

The Department of City Information must make heavy commitments of staff time at the outset to gain adoption of revised zoning for General Information Districts incorporating the kinds of private sign and light control provisions outlined in Chapter 5, and to set the ground rules for Special Information Districts. Assuming enactment of the enabling legislation for such districts, the DCI could ask the earlier formed organizing group or the mayor's advisory committee to manage review of detailed code provisions by the important local interest groups. Extensive coordination will be needed among the state, regional, and local agencies responsible for land development planning, zoning and building codes, and traffic engineering. Staff work for this effort for a period of six months might cost $50,000. Administration of the city-wide code thereafter, including organizing a succession of new Special Information District requirements, could cost about $100,000 per year.

The equivalent of installation costs for this phase of the program would be the property improvement grants and low-interest loans recommended as incentives for sign rehabilitation and the compensation payments for loss of condemned sign or lighting rights (it is assumed that both of these new tools will have been enacted). Anywhere from $50,000 to $500,000 per year might be invested in such payments, depending upon how quickly the target areas are to be improved. A budget of about $200,000 per year would seem reasonable for a program of the size recommended for Boston. At present there are no sources of financial aid in sight for this portion of the budget, although the potential benefits of such improvements in critical traffic zones might warrant a grant of highway research funds. Federal highway construction funds might conceivably be used to compensate owners of billboards within 660 feet of primary federal aid highways, if any such areas fall within Special Information Districts. Alternatively, the city may prefer not to recognize any rights of compensation to off-premise advertisers for signs lost under new zoning, other than a brief amortization period.

PRIVATE SIGN PROGRAM FOR LOCAL DISTRICTS

The most innovative task in the control of private signs and lighting will be the organization of Local Information Districts, initially within the pilot area. Although this work may begin slowly, it will expand continually as districts are organized to cover more and more of the city's neighborhoods.

The first step will be to contact groups that can provide locally accountable leadership in the development and adoption of special sign and lighting controls. If the district is part of an urban renewal or model cities project, or if it has an elected district council, these channels may be well established, otherwise an organizing effort will be necessary. The general identity of the district, including its dominant activities, its boundaries, and the political body which will have local authority, must be established for recognition by the city council.

Once the district is identified, its sign and lighting controls can be drafted. Staff from the Department of City Information will need to work together with local residents, businessmen, and property owners if the proposals are to meet the test of local adoption. Local residents should be hired by the local authority to work with DCI staff on surveys, analysis, and design of the controls.

The speed with which the new local regulations can be developed will depend in part upon the resources committed. Total staff and neighborhood resources of between $10,000 and $20,000 would seem adequate to organize a district and design its special set of controls; there should be an additional $5,000 per year for continuing administration. A large share of this might be contributed by local business associations in those districts that include a commercial area. Yearly, the total program might cost about $50,000, with about one-third covered by local contributions.

STAFF AND BUDGET FOR THE THREE-YEAR PROGRAM

Suggested staff for the Department of City Information for the three-year program (by end of first year) includes:

General Staff
- Agency Director
- Legal Counsel
- Public Relations Officer
- Administrative Officer
- Accountant
- Head Secretary
- Project Secretaries (4)

Sign and Lighting Program Staff
- Projects Coordinator
- Sign Designer (half-time)
- Designer-Draftsman (half-time)
- Field Assistant

Information Systems Program Staff
- Information Systems Developer
- City Information Specialist (half-time)
- Designer-Draftsman (half-time)

Private Improvements Program Staff
- Code Development Coordinator
- Sign Designer (half-time)
- Designer-Draftsmen (2)
- City Information Specialist (half-time)
- Zoning Administrator
- Community Organizer
- Field Assistants (2)

Annual Budget Summary

Staff Salaries	$265,000
Consultants	30,000
Staff Benefits and Travel	40,000
Rent, Equipment, Supplies, etc.	65,000
Total Annual Staff Budget	$400,000

For the first three-year period, the five program components described above would total approximately $3,300,000 for signs, lights, and information system improvements, plus about $250,000 per year for direct staff services in the planning, design, and supervision of these programs. In addition, there would be staff costs for central management and general services, such as legislative counsel, fiscal management, public relations, space rental, etc., which could approach $150,000 per year for the agency. A total annual budget of about $1,500,000 is indicated for the scope of program outlined here; prospects for grants from sources other than the city would be about $600,000 of this yearly amount.

PROSPECTS AND PROBLEMS OF THE THREE-YEAR PROGRAM

The result of this level of investment over a three-year period would be a reorientation of expectations for the typical information content of the environment in non-residential portions of the city: a brighter, more informative, and more useful urban landscape in an area of one and one-half square miles. Even modest changes like those in the demonstration experiments had dramatic visible impact. It would cost somewhat less to do another one and one-half square miles, though the savings in start-up costs might be partially offset by further increases in performance expectations and other contingencies.

Perhaps the greatest problem of the Department of City Information will be to produce visible results quickly enough to convince the city council of the continued need for a substantial budget for all of its operations. An early victory in establishing new enabling legislation should help. Also, it would be wise for the department to concentrate on those projects that can be done quickly. Indeed, the question of scope is crucial; it may be that greater concentration of resources on a smaller number of the highest visibility improvements would be the best three-year strategy. The new urban road sign system is an example: the new designs have already been tried and tested, make use of multiples of standard components that are small and hence not too costly, and can be applied quickly to existing conditions by the city's traffic engineering staff.

The relationship of the new program to the outdoor advertising industry will be another problem, at least until city-wide controls of supersigns are adopted. The industry is organized at a national scale to take advantage of the landscape for commercial ends; it is bound to lose some profitable locations if the new program is successful. Considering the effectiveness with which industry representatives often plead their case with local governing bodies, the pattern of their relationship with the city will need to be established from the outset by the mayor. On the other hand, the local companies that build and maintain on-site advertising signs should be more sensitive to local conditions, more likely to make positive contributions to the development of sign regulations, and may even benefit from a resulting rush of rebuilding signs to meet the new requirements.

The Department of City Information must build a strong constituency among the voters of the city if it is to maintain the political backing and budget required for its long-range program. Careful selection of sign districts in the initial areas will help, for it is here that the most direct assistance to individual citizens will be given. If publicity stresses the city-wide applications of the new program, dramatic improvements in private signing can lead to requests for the work of the new Department in other parts of the city.

Like other recommendations in this report, this three-year action agenda is designed for Boston but is intended to be useful to other cities. To carry out a similar program in another city of comparable size is likely to cost as much and have similar benefits and problems. These costs are low by comparison with other physical improvement programs and the benefits appear significant, both for the people of the city and for politicians who initiate the program. All our cities suffer the same confusing and incoherent public information systems and the same dreary commercialism: that endless urbanized world we never made. Far more fundamental changes are needed than the assertion of public control over environmental information systems; yet such a step may have great symbolic value beyond its immediate benefits. For many people, public neglect of the form and appearance of the city must symbolize the "natural order" of city life: comfort and convenience for a few, hardship and inconvenience for the many. This project demonstrates that at least for one important aspect of urban life, the balance can be shifted.

Appendices

CONTENTS

Public Signing Review

Various aspects of sign visibility and legibility have been tested over the years. These include shape, color, lettering, arrow forms, and symbolic vs. verbal signs.

SHAPE

The shapes of European signs convey information. Warning signs are triangular, signs giving orders (mandatory or prohibitory) are circular, and directional and informatory signs are rectangular. In an experiment done by Moore and Christie, the class of sign, indicated by shape, was recognized at a greater distance than the detailed meaning of the sign.[1] In another study, they found that certain shape-color combinations are more easily recognized than others. The most distinct colored shapes are: red-bar, octagon, square, and pentagon; blue-bar, and pennant; and green-bar, and octagon. The least distinct colored shapes are yellow-hexagon, trapezoid, circle, and pennant. These differences, however, are not dramatic and all shapes and shape color combinations tested can convey information in extremely brief observation periods.

An experiment by Markowitz and Dietrich investigated the relative ease of recognition of various shapes. They found that "the shapes that appear to be most distinct and recognizable . . . are those with the most acute angles — triangle, pennant, and trapezoid." [2]

In another study, drivers were tested to assess the importance of shape as opposed to color in the recognition of American traffic signs.[3] They had to infer the meaning of a variety of traffic signs from *a.* color alone, *b.* shape alone, and *c.* shape and color. They were also asked to guess the color from the shape and legend. Overall recognition was quite low because of the inconsistent use of shapes and colors in the American system but the triangle, octagon and diamond, which are consistently used, had higher recognition rates.* European signs not only have consistent, meaningful shapes but also each shape is associated with a color.

Birren has shown that a consistent pairing of shape and color can be more important in the recognition of a particular sign than its letter legend.[4] For example, when the letters on the octagonal red and white stop sign were jumbled, making TOPS out of STOP, the change went unnoticed by 86% of the drivers passing the sign. Results such as this argue for the adoption of a consistent shape-color code for American signs.

1. R. L. Moore and A. W. Christie, "Research on Traffic Signs," *Engineering for Traffic Conference,* London, 7/1963 (July 1963), 113-122.
2. Bolt, Beranek, and Newman, Inc., *An Investigation of the Design and Performance of Traffic Control Devices* (December, 1968), 4-29.
3. W. S. Ferguson and K. E. Cook, *Driver Awareness of Sign Colors and Shapes,* Virginia Highway Research Council, 1967.

* The test results showed that only where a color is both precisely defined and restricted in its usage (e.g., red and yellow) is recognition of its meaning generally high.

4. F. Birren, "Safety on the Highway: A Problem of Vision, Visibility and Color," *American Journal of Ophthalmology* 43 (1957), 265-270.

COLOR

Several experiments have investigated the effects of color on the legibility of print in books. In one study, which has a direct application to the legibility of signs, measurements were made of the maximum distance at which legibility of copy was possible.[5] In general, it was found that legibility depended upon brightness differences between symbols and background. The three most legible combinations were blue on gray, black on gray, and black on yellow. The three least legible ones were black on blue, yellow on white, and blue on black. In another experiment, Tinker found the three best combinations to be blue on white, black on yellow, and green on white; the three worst ones were black on purple, orange on white, and red on green.[6] Markowitz and Dietrich, in studying differences in image to background visibility, found that dark messages on a light background are superior to light messages on a dark background.[7]

Birren applied this type of experimentation to the investigation of the legibility of colored reflectorized traffic signs.[8] Using the standard octagonal stop sign shape and different combinations of the letters O, W, and N, he found that during the day, black on white was legible at a greater distance (404 ft.) than white on red (361 ft.), black on yellow (358 ft.), or white on green (358 ft.). During the night, the order was slightly reversed; black on yellow was more legible (341 ft.) than white on green (337 ft.), black on white (316 ft.), or white on red (312 ft.). The differences in legibility, however, are so small that threshold points for the most and least legible signs for a driver approaching at 50 mph under daylight conditions would be only 0.627 seconds apart and under nighttime conditions only 0.395 seconds.

Birren's interpretation of these results is that since "In both instances the time element (at 50 mph) is less than the 0.75 second 'reaction time' so often mentioned in driver's manuals as the normal moment of hesitation between an external visual stimulation and a physical reaction to it . . . it is perhaps fair to state that slight differences in the legibility of traffic signs are of no great consequence. If black on white has minor advantage, it would be impractical to keep adding more and more combinations of it anyhow, because clear identity and differentiation through color would be lost and a meaningful code sacrificed." Moreover, Birren continues, "A thorough investigation of research on color, visibility, recognition, and safety would seriously question black as a suitable color for sign backgrounds — despite the high legibility it gives to white legends or characters." Black is a passive, emotionally negative, and "empty" color. "Like space itself, black is hard to localize or to judge as to distance. It therefore sets up a poor target even though the letters placed upon it may be easily seen." Birren recommends replacing the white on black directional signals with white on green ones, and suggests specific colors to be incorporated in a comprehensive color code. The results and suggestions of Birren's study were incorporated into the

5. Cited in M. S. Tinker, *Legibility of Print* (Ames, Iowa: Iowa State University Press, 1963).
6. Ibid.
7. Bolt, Beranek and Newman, op. cit., p. 3-31.
8. Birren, loc. cit.

recommendations of the Special Committee on Color of the National Joint Committee on Uniform Traffic Control Devices.[9] The members of the Committee were less concerned with legibility and visibility of signs than with selecting easily discriminable colors (even by color blind and weak-sighted persons). Drawing from the current research on color perception, they concluded that although it might be possible for the average human being to differentiate between 7 to 10 million different colors and shades, not more than 10 to 15 could be successfully included in a meaningful and applicable color code. Twelve colors were selected for the color code of American traffic signs and the meanings of 9 of them were specified. These are:

RED	Stop or prohibition
GREEN	Movements permitted as indicated
BLUE	General commercial services
YELLOW	Warning
BLACK	Part-time regulation
WHITE	Full-time regulation
ORANGE	High danger
PURPLE	School area
BROWN	Public recreation
BRIGHT YELLOW-GREEN	Unassigned
LIGHT BLUE-GRAY	Unassigned
CORAL-BUFF	Unassigned

The visibility of signs placed against different backgrounds was investigated by Forbes.[10] In two laboratory experiments, a highway scene was shown to subjects who were required to carry out an auxiliary task while viewing. Test signs were flashed on the highway scene for about one second to measure their visibility against different colored backgrounds. In a field experiment, observers reported when they first saw signs while driving along an urban route and a freeway route. Forbes found that:

1 Relative brightness and contrast, of sign-to-background and of legend-to-sign, are of primary importance for visibility and attention value.

2 Hue contrast can enhance the brightness effects, but color is most important and effective for transmitting coded meanings.

3 For best visibility, a sign should be darker against a bright day background, but brighter against a dark day or night background.

The visibility of a sign is a function of its "target value," the combined effect of size, shape, and color. Odescalchi found that different colored signs can have the same target value, depending on their size.[11] The following color-areas of signs have a roughly equivalent target value at a range of 250 yards: 14 sq. ft. yellow, 16 sq. ft. white, 18 sq. ft. red, 20 sq. ft. blue, 22 sq. ft. green, 36 sq. ft. black. There are, therefore, disadvantages in using blue, green or black backgrounds, especially for small signs; large signs, like those on highways, are conspicuous because of their size alone.

The results of these studies are inconclusive. Many variables, which are difficult to control, can distort experiments which attempt to determine optimum sign color combinations. Among these there are the characteristics of color itself: Different rank orders of visibility and legibility of color combinations can result from the use of different hues and brightness values of the same color. Light may also influence the results substantially. A dimly-lit laboratory room may affect color vision quite differently from a brightly-lit one. In outdoor investigations, weather and daylight conditions are likely to have varying and unpredictable effects, as are varying backgrounds. Based on these findings, only limited statements can be made about the influence of color on sign legibility:

1 The degree of brightness contrast between message and sign background and between sign and general background is the most significant single factor.

2 While dark images on light backgrounds are generally better, the consistent use of different colors for different classes of sign is a more important factor in determining overall legibility.

3 The target value of a sign is determined by color, size, and shape together.

9. National Joint Committee on Uniform Traffic Control Devices, *Report of the Special Committee on Color,* January 1967.
10. T. W. Forbes, R. F. Pain, R. P. Joyce, and J. P. Fry, "Color and Brightness Factors in Simulated and Full-Scale Traffic Sign Visibility," *Highway Research Board,* in press.
11. P. Odescalchi, "Conspicuity of Signs in Rural Surroundings," *Traffic Engineering* 2 (1960), 390-393.

MESSAGE FORM

Upper and Lower Case Lettering

The results of investigations concerned with the legibility of upper and lower case letters are by no means conclusive. The following factors, which frequently vary from one experiment to another, may interfere with the establishment of significant differences between upper and lower case: The use of serif vs. sans-serif type faces; individual letters vs. single words vs. phrases; spacing; letter height and width; and stroke-width.

It does seem, however, that individual capital letters are more legible than lower case letters.[12] Hodge [13] and Berger [14] have found that, regardless of various height-to-stroke width ratios, upper case single letters were legible at a greater distance than lower case letters. In another experiment by Hodge, the relative legibility of words printed in upper, lower, and mixed upper and lower uniform stroke width letters was investigated. Words printed in all upper case letters were significantly more legible than those in mixed or lower case.[15]

In contrast to this, all the research done on commercial type has shown that printed passages in mixed lower and upper case can be read and understood considerably faster than material presented in all upper case letters.[16] A number of experiments and textbooks, however, explicitly favor lower case print. Paterson and Tinker in an eye-movement study on the effect of typography on the perceptual span in reading found that, as compared to lower case, 12.4% more fixations for reading a standard text in all capital letters were required, that the number of words read per fixation was 12.5% less, and the number of characters per fixation was 13.6% less.[17] These differences are statistically significant.

Chapanis *et al.* in their textbook on applied experimental psychology maintain that material in capital letters is read much more slowly than material in lower case printing.[18] Referring to research done on this topic (but without giving specific references), they state that most readers definitely do not like to read material printed in capitals — the reason being the destruction of the word form.

Neisser has also concurred with these findings. He writes, "One relevant fact — known since the dawn of the tachistoscopic age — is that a word printed all in capital letters is harder to identify than one printed in normal lower case type." [19]

An experiment by Christie and Rutley revealed that "when the results (recognition rates) for individual types of signs were examined it was noted that there was a tendency for the lower case lettering to be relatively less effective on signs with written messages such as 'Stop' and 'Ice' than on signs with place names such as Metropolis Utopia — Exit 1 Mile. Possibly people are more accustomed to seeing upper-case lettering used for warnings and instructions and on that account find them easier to read in upper-case lettering." [20]

In a study of the perception and recognition of highway signs, Forbes and his co-workers found that lower case had a slight advantage over upper case when the names on the signs were familiar to the subjects.[21] When the place names on the experimental signs were unfamiliar, upper case letters gained a slight advantage.

These differences in results can perhaps be explained by adopting Neisser's concept of word recognition. Applying the results of tachistoscopic experiments to distance legibility, one can argue that when a subject approaches an experimental sign with a familiar name on it from beyond legibility distance, he will first perceive the shape of the word and then will be able to fill in the name, without having perceived it completely. Lower case lettering is a help in recognizing familiar sign legends, as it provides more cues which the subject can use to infer the words. If the legend is unfamiliar, however, the subject has to read it completely — and for long enough not to make any mistakes — before being able to call out the name. Here, upper case letters are helpful. Because of their larger size they are legible from a greater distance. Since this variable (i.e., familiarity of the word) has not been controlled in most experiments, it may account for differences in results.

The British Ministry of Transport has installed "lower case lettering with initial capitals for traffic signs because we prefer it and because we think its outlines are more familiar to the reading eye." [22] This pragmatic approach appears justifiable. Conclusive statements about the comparative legibility of upper and lower case letters cannot be made until further research is done.

Stroke Width of Lettering

Several studies have been carried out to investigate the influence of the letter height and width-to-stroke width ratio on the legibility of signs. One of the earliest studies was done by Uhlaner who, by studying 3-inch high block letters, found that the optimal stroke width was 18% of letter width or height (ratio approximately 6:1).[23] Another study by Kuntz and Sleight using numerals, 7 height-to-stroke

12. Tinker, loc. cit.
13. D. C. Hodge, "Legibility of a Uniform Strokewidth Alphabet, Part 1: Relative Legibility of Upper and Lower Case Letters," *Journal of Engineering Psychology* 1 (1962), 34-46.
14. C. Berger, "Grouping, Number and Spacing of Letters as Determinants of Word Recognition," *Journal of General Psychology* 55 (1956), 215-228.
15. D. C. Hodge, "Legibility of a Uniform Strokewidth Alphabet, Part II: Some Factors Affecting the Legibility of Words," *Journal of Engineering Psychology* 2 (1963), 55-67.
16. D. G. Paterson and M. A. Tinker, "The Effect of Typography upon the Perceptual Span in Reading," *American Journal of Psychology* 60 (1947), 388-397.
17. Ibid.
18. A. Chapanis, W. R. Garner, and C. T. Morgan, *Applied Experimental Psychology: Human Factors in Engineering Design* (New York: Wiley, 1949).
19. U. Neisser, *Cognitive Psychology* (New York: Appleton, 1967).
20. A. W. Christie and K. S. Rutley, "Relative Effectiveness of Some Letter Types Designed for Use on Road Traffic Signs," *Roads and Road Construction* 39 (1961), 239-344.
21. T. W. Forbes, K. Moscowitz, and G. Morgan, "A Comparison of Lower Case and Capital Letters for Highway Signs," Highway Research Board *Proceedings* 30 (1950), 355-373.
22. Ministry of Transport, *Traffic Signs 1963*, Report of the Committee on Traffic Signs for All-Purpose Roads (London: Her Majesty's Stationery Office, 1963).
23. J. E. Uhlaner, "The Effect of Thickness of Stroke on the Legibility of Letters," Iowa Academy of Sciences *Proceedings* 48 (1941), 319-324.

width ratios, 3 levels of illumination, and different color contrasts indicated that the optimal height-to-stroke width ratio lay between 4:1 and 6.1.[24] Legibility increased with brightness but there were no differences between black numerals on white background and white numerals on a black background. On the basis of the research in this area, the British Ministry of Transport chose a standard alphabet for the new British traffic signs having a height-to-stroke width ratio of 6:1.[25]

Letter Height, Width, and Spacing

The question of letter height and width is related to the height-to-stroke width ratio. Forbes and Holmes found that average legibility of narrow and wide letters was 33 and 50 ft. per inch of letter height, respectively.[26] Berger showed, by varying the width and height of the numerals 5 and 0, that narrow, condensed letters are less legible than wide letters.[27] In Germany, three alphabets, with different letter widths but the same height-to-stroke width ratios (7:1), are in use, and a different legibility distance is quoted for each.[28]

Similarly, the legibility of signs can be increased by increasing the space between letters. Solomon found that in certain American reflectorized signs maximum legibility was obtained when the width of a place name was 40% greater than normal; however, even greater improvement could be obtained by using the extra area to accommodate larger letters at normal spacing.[29] Berger found that the distance threshold of words increased with increasing space between single letters, up to a maximum which is above the average letter width.[30] Christie and Rutley, in their experiment on different types of upper and lower case letters, found that the largest observed effect on reading distance was produced by a change in spacing: a lower case script with narrow spaces between letters was much less legible at a given distance than the same script with wider spaces.[31]

Type Faces

Research on the effects of different type faces on the legibility of signs is scanty. Using familar words as well as nonsense letter combinations as stimuli, Hurd found that rounded letters were recognized 8% better than block letters.[32] Neal obtained similar results. With close spacing rounded letters were more legible, with wide spacing legibility for a round or a narrow letter was equal.[33] Lauer, while trying to improve the stop sign, found rounded letters superior to block letters.[34]

In 1944, Mackworth changed minor but significant details of an existing type face and observed striking differences in legibility of the letters.[35] Changes made emphasized the important aspects of the letters (i.e., openings, slashes, etc.) thereby improving their perceptual qualities. The modern sans serif type faces such as Helvetica and Univers, currently preferred by most graphic designers, appear to emphasize many of these same aspects.

Arrows

The Bolt, Beranek and Newman study referred to earlier revealed that the tapered arrow is the best. The report states that "No doubt its advantage lies in the fact that direction information is carried not only by the arrow head but by the shaft as well. As a consequence, necessary processing of the figure is reduced. For example, it is no longer necessary to 'find' where the arrow head is located — any small slice is sufficient to tell exactly the orientation." [36]

In investigating the position of arrows, relative to place names, Bolt, Beranek and Newman found that place "names with directional arrows to the right should be avoided in favor of a staggered, or all-left arrow, placement."

Comparison of Symbolic, Pictographic, and Verbal Messages

Studies which have compared accuracy in recognizing European and American signs, have found that European signs, which make use of pictures and abstract symbols, are superior. In a study conducted by Walker, Nicolay, and Stearns, even the most difficult abstract symbolic signs (no left turn, no right turn, no entry) were more easily recognized than their verbal American counterparts (despite familiarity of the American signs).[37] The experiments suggest that the symbolic sign is perceptually simpler than the verbal sign; the symbol is more visually integrated, whereas the letters of the verbal signs are more fragmented. However, the authors warn that before generalizations can be made about the superiority of the European system more comparative research should be done.

In another study, which directly compared the European and American signs, British investigators found that European signs of all types could be successfully identified at a greater distance than their counterparts in both the American system and the British system.[38] However, they also found that the class of sign (warning, mandatory, prohibitory, or informatory) was recognized sooner when the sign was from the American system. This result, (although less pronounced and less important than the former) is somewhat surprising and points out the need for further investigation.

24. J. E. Kuntz, and R. B. Sleight, "Legibility of Numerals: The Optimal Ratio of Height to Strokewidth," *American Journal of Psychology* 63 (1950), 567-575.
25. Ministry of Transport, op. cit.
26. T. W. Forbes and R. S. Holmes, "Legibility Distances of Highway Destination Signs in Relation to Letter Height, Letter Width and Reflectorization," Highway Research Board *Proceedings* 19 (1939), 321-335.
27. C. Berger, "Some Experiments on the Width of Symbols as Determinants of Legibility," *Acta Ophthalmologica* 30 (1952), 409-420.
28. Deutscher Normenausschuss, *Normblatt DIN 1451* (Berlin and Cologne, 1951).
29. D. Solomon, "The Effect of Letter Width and Spacing on Night Legibility of Highway Signs," *Traffic Engineering* 27 (1956), 113-120.
30. Berger, "Grouping, Number and Spacing of Letters."
31. Christie and Rutley, "Relative Effectiveness of Some Letter Types."
32. F. Hurd, "Glance Legibility," *Traffic Engineering* 17 (1946), 161-162.
33. H. E. Neal, "The Legibility of Highway Signs," *Traffic Engineering* 17 (1947), 525-529.
34. A. R. Lauer, "Certain Structural Components of Letters for Improving the Efficiency of the Stop Sign," Highway Research Board *Proceedings* 27 (1947), 360-371.
35. Mackworth, cited in: Chapanis, Garner, and Morgan, *Applied Experimental Psychology.*
36. Bolt, Beranek and Newman, op. cit., p. 3-39.
37. R. E. Walker, R. C. Nicolay, and C. R. Stearns, "Comparative Accuracy of Recognizing American and International Road Signs," *Journal of Applied Psychology* 49 (1965), 322-325.
38. Cited in Moore and Christie, "Research on Traffic Signs."

Several studies indicate that pictorial signs are generally understood better than abstract signs. A Swedish survey in 1953-1954 found that pictorial representations in their system were understood by nearly all drivers while only 8 out of 11 signs with abstract symbols were understood.[39] A survey of drivers who had driven on the continent, carried out by the British Road Research Laboratories in 1962, showed a similar picture.[40] These findings are corroborated by an American laboratory study.[41] Subjects had to guess the meaning of 30 European signs, and, again, the least abstract signs were easiest to understand. The European signs, however, were understood moderately well on first presentation, and after one exposure to the correct meaning of each sign comprehension approached 100%. The researchers concluded that certain European signs could be used in the United States without any instruction to drivers; the majority of the signs, however, could not be used without a minimal degree of familiarization. (The Bolt, Beranek, and Newman study has rated 44 conventional pictographs currently in use or proposed for road signs, for both recognizability and clarity of meaning.)[42]

In sum, studies to date suggest that changing to a traffic sign system similar to the European (International) system would have several definite advantages:

1 Most important, since symbols are easier to recognize than words, the new signs would lead to greater safety on the roads for drivers and pedestrians; they would minimize the amount of time that the driver's attention is diverted from the road itself.

2 Driving would be made easier for non-English speaking people living in the United States and for international visitors.

3 American drivers would have an easier time driving in foreign countries which use the International sign system.

39. Cited in British Road Research Laboratory, *Research on Road Traffic* (London: Her Majesty's Stationery Office, 1965).

40. P. G. Gray and P. Russell, "Drivers' Understanding of Traffic Signs," Central Office of Information, *Social Survey 347* (London: Her Majesty's Stationery Office, 1962).

41. R. W. Brainard, R. J. Campbell, and E. H. Elkin, "Design and Interpretability of Road Signs," *Journal of Applied Psychology* 45 (1961), 130-136.

42. Bolt, Beranek and Newman, op. cit., pp. 3-116 — 3-121.

Public Lighting Review

2

RESEARCH ON STREET LIGHTING

In a paper on visibility in lighted streets, A. W. Christie writes:
It can be argued that the standard of visual performance required in lighted streets is lower than that required in lighted interiors as a driver need not have to do anything akin to reading fine print or threading a needle. Nevertheless, his task is not simply one of detecting the presence of the various objects in his field of view; he has also to estimate their position, their direction of motion and their speed — all of which have to be done very quickly. There is, therefore, a widespread belief that a higher standard of street lighting will be required in the future than has been provided in the past.[1]

A number of factors must be considered in determining this "higher standard of street lighting," all of which may have a different weight in lighting cities than they do in lighting highways. Most of the research on light sources, pavement reflectance, problems of glare, the effects of mounting height and spacing, and the relation between lighting and accidents has been done in the context of highway lighting. Thus, the findings reviewed here cannot be accepted uncritically as being applicable to city lighting, and in the second part of this appendix guidelines for urban lighting fixtures are stated.

Type of Light Source

Ketvirtis, in *Highway Lighting Engineering,* states that, "from the point of view of visibility, the most effective light source is sodium vapor."[2] According to J. B. deBoer, up to 35% more mercury vapor is required for an effectiveness comparable with that of a sodium source.[3] However, the sodium vapor source has several disadvantages: short lamp life, difficulties in precise light control, and a garish yellow color which many find objectionable. (New high-pressure sodium sources have improved color.)

The fluorescent lamp is the second most effective light source for visibility. Differences in color rendition and difficulties in light control make direct comparisons with other light sources impossible. Nevertheless, research on this problem has shown that at least 10% less fluorescent light can be tolerated for equivalent visual conditions compared with mercury vapor.

Field studies[4] comparing the mercury vapor lamp with high-pressure sodium vapor lamps have also yielded interesting results. For example, Walton and Rowan found that the 400-watt high-pressure sodium vapor lamps mounted at 50 feet and spaced at 300 feet produce approximately the same photometric values as 1000-watt mercury vapor units mounted at 50 feet and spaced at 300 feet. However, they also point out several shortcomings of high-pressure sodium

LIGHT SOURCE COMPARISON

	Uses and Advantages	**Limitations**
Incandescent	First major step in the technology of illumination. Mostly used for residential and commercial illumination.	Less efficient than other sources for street and highway lighting.
Fluorescent	Highway lighting. Increased efficiency over incandescent lamps. Second most effective light source for visibility.	Expanded tubular lamp limits the effectiveness of the reflector and refractor in controlling the light. Particularly difficult to regulate lamp efficiency under varying temperatures, conditions. High maintenance costs due to short lamp life. High installation costs.
Mercury Vapor	Highway lighting. Long lamp life. Good lumen maintenance. Reliable operation — low cost. Small light-producing area sizes (near point source) have enhanced the development of effective optical systems for a variety of light distribution patterns.	Color quality is limited to narrow wave bands in the zone of green and blue. While color can be improved by coating the outer lamp, this results in loss of precision in light control.
Low-pressure sodium lamp	Highway lighting. Most efficient light-producing device.	Short lamp life. Yellow color.
High-pressure sodium lamp	Highway lighting. Relatively small lamp size and linear shape offer good light control. High lighting efficiency. Improved color rendition.	Short lamp life. Pink-yellow color.

1. A. W. Christie "Visibility in Lighted Streets and the Effect of the Arrangement and Light Distribution of the Lanterns," *Ergonomics* 6, No. 4, (October 1963).
2. Antanas Ketvirtis, *Highway Lighting Engineering* (Toronto, Canada, 1967), p. 23.
3. J. B. deBoer, "Lighting of Traffic Routes," *Public Lighting (Philips,* Holland, 1965).
4. N. E. Walton and N. J. Rowan, Texas Transportation Institute, *Interim Progress Report on Supplementary Studies in Highway Illumination,* Research Report 75–7 (October 1967), p. 24.

lamps: the initial cost of the equipment is high and the lamp has a relatively short life (6000 hours). (A recent study by General Electric suggests that on both initial cost and operating costs, high-pressure sodium may now be competitive with mercury vapor.) [5]

DeBoer also points out that, although the mercury vapor lamp is not as effective as sodium or fluorescent sources, it offers many important advantages: longevity of lamps, constant light output over wide temperature ranges, and precise light control characteristics.

One further point concerning the effects of different light colors should be considered. DeBoer and Van Heemserck Veeckens found that, "for constant road-surface luminance, constant degree of discomfort glare and other unvariable conditions, the luminous intensity in the direction of the observer's eyes when using sodium lighting, may be 1.3 times higher than when applying light from fluorescent tubes and from incandescent lamps, and 1.4 times higher than when using high-pressure mercury vapor lamps with fluorescent bulbs." [6]

Pavement Reflectance

Road brightness is dependent upon the type of light source, the angle of viewing, the angle of incidence, and the color and texture of the pavement. As one might expect, the reflectance qualities of pavement change with use. In one study, according to Ketvirtis, "... a good concrete surface initially can reflect approximately 25% of incident light but its reflectance qualities are reduced to approximately 16% to 18% by the gradual accumulation of carbon, oil, and chemicals. Black asphalt, on the other hand, has approximately 10% to 11% initial reflectance. Later, due to polishing, its reflectance is increased to 12% to 14%...." [7]

Under wet road conditions, asphalt and concrete pavements have different reflective qualities. For example, a smooth asphalt pavement when wet reflects a considerable amount of light, mostly in the form of continuous streaks or large patches. On the other hand, a concrete surface under wet conditions produces only subdued specular reflections. Ketvirtis writes, "When the pavement is wet, specular reflections are created. Specular reflection is detrimental to the driver's visibility. For most cases it consists of extremely bright spots or streaks, blinding the motorist's eyes." [8]

The reflective characteristics of the road surface can be improved by using light colored materials in the pavement. In Great Britain chips of white flint rolled in the asphalt surface have been used for this purpose. However, an economical light-colored compound which can enhance pavement reflectance has not been developed.

Glare

Much of the research concerning the effects of glare on motorists has been done by British investigators. DeBoer and Schreuder suggest that there are two ways for establishing requirements for limiting glare: measuring the decrease in visual performance due to glare (disability glare) and measuring the influence of glare on visual comfort (discomfort glare). DeBoer and Schreuder chose to study only discomfort glare for the following reasons: "1. An unequivocal border between permissible and non-permissible glare can be given for discomfort glare but not for disability glare; 2. avoidance of discomfort glare usually imposes more exacting demands on the lighting installation than the avoidance of disability glare." [9]

In a series of laboratory experiments on discomfort due to glare, they found no significant difference between a sodium light source and a high-pressure mercury vapor fluorescent lamp coated. They conclude that "no correction for colors need be applied in respect to road-surface luminance." They also add that "the average intensity of the sodium light sources could be 40% higher than that of mercury light sources at equal road-surface luminance and equal degree of glare." [10]

As a result of these experiments, deBoer and Schreuder developed a formula for calculating the discomfort glare emitted from a light source. Field studies showed a very high degree of correlation between a number of independent glare appraisals by lighting experts and the degree of discomfort glare calculated by the formula.

Commenting on disability glare, Christie writes, "disability glare is probably ... the more important from the point of view of safety. Its main cause is believed to be scattering of the glare light within the media of the eyes to form a veiling luminance which reduces the apparent contrast between an object and its background. It is not surprising, therefore, that the effect of disability glare is greatest for objects seen against the darker parts of the background. . ." [11]

During 1961 and 1965 the Road Research Laboratory in England conducted a series of experiments using cut-off, semi-cut-off and non-cut-off installations with medium-angle beam distributions. Four-hundred watt mercury lamps were used and the spacing in all three installations was 120 feet. To avoid dark patches on the road, greater mounting heights had to be used in the cut-off and semi-cut-off installations than in the non-cut-off installations: 35 feet, 30 feet, and 25 feet respectively.

The results indicated that "The general level of revealing power, so far as objects seen against the road is concerned, was much the same in all three installations. On the other hand, the revealing power for objects seen against the backgrounds beyond the road itself was highest in the cut-off installation and lowest in the non-cut-off installation. . ." [12] The subjective appraisals revealed an overall preference for the cut-off distribution: 88% of the observers preferred it when compared with the non-cut-off distribution and 64% of

5. R. E. Faucett, *An Evaluation of Higher Mounting Heights for Roadway Lighting* (No. Carolina: Outdoor Lighting Department, General Electric Co., 1967).
6. Cited in J. B. deBoer and D. A. Schreuder, "Glare as a Criterion for Quality in Street Lighting," *Trans. Illum. Eng. Soc.* 32, No. 2 (1967), p. 123.
7. Ketvirtis, op. cit., p. 28.
8. Ibid.
9. deBoer and Schreuder, op. cit., p. 117.
10. Ibid., p. 123.
11. A. W. Christie, *Research on Street and Highway Lighting with Particular Reference to Their Effect on Accidents,* Paper presented at the Annual Conference of the Institution of Municipal Engineers, Blackpool, London: Road Research Laboratory, June 1966.
12. Ibid.

the observers preferred it when compared with the semi-cut-off distribution.

Subjects found no difference in the level of road brightness produced by the three installations. However, concerning the visibility of objects, the cut-off installation was rated equal to the semi-cut-off installation but much better than the non-cut-off installation. The subjects also felt that the cut-off installation was nearly free from glare while the semi-cut-off installation was rated poor with respect to this variable.

Christie concludes that these results provide further evidence that the change from the non-cut-off installation with medium-angle-beam distribution (specified in the British Standards code of 1952) to the semi-cut-off distributions (specified in the 1963 code) was indeed wise.

Further discussing the results of this experiment, Christie and Fisher explain why their results are at variance with the conclusion of previous investigators that glare has a negligible effect on revealing power. These researchers, they say, did not consider backgrounds other than the road surface. "Pedestrians stepping off the footways and cyclists riding near the curb are seen against other backgrounds which, except in shop-lined streets, tend to appear darker than the road surface. It is therefore in these regions that the effect of disability glare on revealing power is greatest." [13]

Walton and Rowan made photoelectric measurements comparing the performance of the British glare cut-off luminaires with the American highway standard Type III luminaires at various heights and spacings. They found that increased mounting heights and spacings for the 400-watt and 1000-watt Type III luminaires (40-50 feet spaced 200-220 feet apart) can reduce glare levels to approximately those for the cut-off units (which must be mounted no higher than 40 feet at 160 foot spacings for similar illumination performance). Thus, they conclude that there are no serious problems of glare when using Type III luminaires in a system design with the higher mounting heights.[14]

Mounting Height and Spacing

It is clear that the choice of light source and problems of glare are directly related to questions of mounting height and spacing.

The general practice in the United States, recommended by the American Association of State Highway officials, is that lighting systems provide between 0.6 and 0.8 maintained foot-candles. In the G.E. study conducted by Faucett, mounting heights and spacings required to achieve these levels, with acceptable uniformity of illumination, were established for three different bulbs: 400-watt mercury, 400-watt high-pressure sodium, and 1000-watt mercury. For example, for 400-watt clear mercury lamps, the spacing required to produce 0.6 and 0.8 foot-candles at a 30 foot mounting height is 195 and 142 feet respectively. If the mounting height is increased to 35 feet, the spacing must be reduced in order to maintain the specified 0.6 and 0.8 average foot-candle levels, but the uniformity ratio is significantly improved. "This suggests that higher lumen output [lamps] might conceivably go to higher mounting heights and also longer spacings, resulting in significantly fewer poles and therefore less overall cost."[15] The paper goes on to analyze initial investment costs and annual maintenance costs for standard performance levels for the three types of luminaire at various heights and spacings. The tables presented strongly favor higher mounting heights and indicate that G.E.'s newer sources — high-pressure sodium and "multi-vapor" — are to be preferred over mercury vapor (see Part II of the report). The author states, for example, that "the initial investment as well as the total annual costs are significantly less for 0.8 foot-candles utilizing a 400-watt [high-pressure sodium] lamp at 50 feet than it is to install 0.6 foot-candles utilizing the 400-watt mercury lamp at 35 feet."

In their studies on light distribution (employing full-scale field simulations), Walton and Rowan found that:

1 "The initial average illumination on the roadway was inversely proportional to the mounting height and longitudinal spacing of the luminaires, and to the width of roadway considered.

2 "The uniformity of illumination on the roadway was directly proportional to the mounting height of the luminaires, i.e., higher mounting heights provide better uniformity.

3 "The systems of 1000-watt luminaires provided more illumination and greater uniformity than the 400-watt systems when compared for similar spacing-mounting height ratios (for mercury vapor lamps)." [16]

The authors also suggest that uniformity of illumination is very important to visibility. Indeed, they say that "visual evaluations of these systems have suggested that any reduction in visibility due to a lower average illumination can usually be more than compensated for by an apparent increase in visibility due to improved uniformity of illumination, as in the case of systems with luminaires at higher mounting heights." They conclude that current standards for average intensity may be higher than necessary (for highway lighting) and that more emphasis should be placed on uniformity.

In some applications, especially on bridges, ramps, and rotaries, where delineation of the roadway is important and poles are difficult or objectionable, low fluorescent rail mounted lighting offers some advantages. The literature is strangely silent on the subject. However, one study done in 1966 by Charles J. Mitch, a lighting engineer, analyzes advantages and disadvantages of a continuous bridge installation utilizing four lines (two for each direction) of continuous 6-foot, 300 Milliamp, 40-watt fluorescent tubes mounted in the rails at 40 inches above the roadway as compared to the normal, overhead 400-watt mercury vapor luminaires mounted at 30 feet. Mitch asserts that the low level system

Effective* reductions in injury accidents during dark hours on 64 urban "single-carriageway" road on which light was improved.

From Christie, "The Night Accident Problem"

Severity	**Effective Reduction**
Fatal	50%
Serious	33%
Slight	27%
All Severities	30%
Type of Road User Injured	**Effective Reduction**
Pedestrian	45%
Other Road Users	23%
All Road Users	30%

*An effective reduction means the percentage by which the observed number of accidents in dark hours after the change was less than the number expected on the assumption that without the lighting change, the number of accidents in the dark would have changed in the same proportion as the number of accidents in daylight.

13. A. W. Christie and A. J. Fisher, "The Effect of Glare from Street Lighting Lanterns on the Vision of Drivers of Different Ages," *Trans. Illum. Eng. Soc.* 31, No. 4 (1966), p. 6.
14. Walton and Rowan, op. cit., p. 23.
15. Faucett, loc. cit.
16. Walton and Rowan, op. cit., p. 11.

Improved lighting on urban street (total numbers of injury accidents in comparable before and after periods at 64 sites where improved lighting replaced poor lighting)

From Christie, *Research on Street and Highway Lighting*

ACCIDENTS CLASSIFIED ACCORDING TO TYPE OF ROAD USER INJURED.

	Pedestrian	Other	Total
Daylight			
Before	319	929	1248
After	334	1091	1425
Darkness			
Before	159	346	505
After	91	312	403
After/Before			
Daylight	1.05	1.17	1.14
Darkness	0.57	0.90	0.80
r*	0.55	0.77	0.70
Whether significantly different from 1.0	yes	yes	yes

ACCIDENTS CLASSIFIED ACCORDING TO SEVERITY.

	Fatal	Serious	Slight
Daylight			
Before	16	224	1008
After	17	244	1164
Darkness			
Before	28	123	354
After	15	90	298
After/Before			
Daylight	1.06	1.09	1.16
Darkness	0.54	0.73	0.84
r	0.50	0.67	0.73
Whether significantly different from 1.0	no	yes	yes

* r is defined as the ratio of the actual number of accidents in darkness after the improvement to the expected number (of accidents).

utilizes light output more efficiently, with a higher component of vertical illumination (unclear assertion), more uniform longitudinal pavement brightness, a low glare factor (not explained why this should be so, since the lights are nearly at driver's eye level), and improved visibility during periods of fog, rain, or snow.[17] Other more obvious advantages include improved delineation of the roadway, the elimination of poles, and convenience in maintenance and cleaning. Disadvantages include higher initial cost (some experience indicates 4 to 5 times as much), higher power consumption, the need for more frequent cleaning, and reduced visibility of the surrounding environment at night.

Lighting and Traffic Accidents

"Before and after" studies would seem to be the most reliable means of assessing the effects of improved public lighting. In these studies the numbers of accidents or casualties which occurred on a length of road in a period after a change in street lighting are compared with the numbers which occurred in a corresponding period before the change. Several studies of this type have established a relationship between street lighting and frequency of traffic accidents.

Under the direction of the British Road Research Laboratory, the lighting of 64 urban sites was improved. The reductions were greater for accidents involving injuries to pedestrians than for accidents in which other road users were injured and greater for accidents involving serious injuries than for accidents involving slight injuries (see tables).[18] Although improved lighting was only tested on urban all-purpose "single carriageway" (two-lane) roads and streets, reductions in accident rates are also being found when other types of roads are illuminated (i.e., rural two-lane roads and rural and urban four-lane roads. There are as yet no British data relating to the effect of lighting on expressways).

Christie also mentions that there was a reduction of 38% in all reported accidents after part of the Autoronte de L'Ouest in Paris was lighted in 1954.

In this country, considerable attention has also been focused on the relationship of lighting to traffic accidents. In September, 1965, the U. S. Senate became particularly interested in acquiring information concerning the effect of lighting on the reduction of traffic accidents and night crimes. In response, the Institute of Traffic Engineers and the Illuminating Engineering Society appointed a special joint committee to study these problems.[19]

17. C. J. Mitch, *Excerpts from a Study of a Low-Level Lighting System,* Prepared for the Milwaukee County Expressway and Transportation Commission, Howard Needles, Tammen and Bergendoff, Consulting Engineers, Milwaukee, Wisconsin, 29 December 1966 (mimeo.)
18. A. W. Christie, "The Night Accident Problem and the Effect of Public Lighting," *Journal of the Association of Public Lighting Engineers* 33, No. 141 (June 1968), p. 99.
19. "Public Lighting Needs – A special report for the committee on Public Works, U.S. Senate and U.S. House of Representatives," Joint Committee of the Institute of Traffic Engineers and the Illuminating Engineering Society, *Illuminating Engineering,* September 1966.

The committee found that:

1 "The provision of adequate lighting, designed, installed and maintained properly, effects a significant reduction in night accidents.

2 "Roadway lighting materially aids the driver by improving his efficiency and by alerting him in advance of hazardous encounters. The cost of modern lighting can be justified by the accident savings to the nation's economy.

3 "On urban arterial streets, the major benefit of lighting is in the saving of pedestrian lives. Reductions of 30 percent to 80 percent have been found in various cities, following modernization of lighting. Significant reductions in the range of 10 to 44 percent have been found for all types of night accidents."

And also:

4 An analysis of 17,060 accidents occurring during more than five billion vehicle miles of travel on nearly a dozen different freeways was made. "Beneficial results were found, and night-to-day accident ratios tended to be lower on the better and more uniformly lighted freeways."

5 The Committee examined more than 18,000 fatal and injury accidents on city streets and over 96,000 property damage accidents in numerous cities. Major accident reductions by improved lighting were found.

Several specific studies are cited concerning the decreased traffic accident rate following improved illumination:

1 Chicago Arterial Street Fatal Accident Comparison — "This study compared fatal accidents on 533 miles of streets lighted during 1952 to 1958. In 1952 there were 156 fatal night accidents on these routes, vs. 81 in 1958, a reduction of 48 percent."

2 Pedestrian Fatalities, Kansas City, Missouri — "In 1945 a master relighting program commenced. During the three-year period 1945 through 1947, there were 94 pedestrians killed, 70 at night. An average of 3 percent of the streets had modern lighting during this period. As the lighting program progressed, the number of pedestrians killed was steadily reduced . . . During the three-year period, 1954 through 1956, only 44 pedestrians were killed, 13 at night. An average of 90 percent of the streets was relighted by this time. This is a reduction in night pedestrian accidents of 81 percent. Furthermore, traffic volume studies found 25 percent of travel at night for the city as a whole.

"At the beginning of the lighting program, nearly 80 percent of the pedestrian deaths were at night, vs. less than 30 percent in the 'after' period. By 1956, the figure dropped to only 19 percent at night . . . During the entire 12 year period, an estimated 140 pedestrian lives were saved by the modern lighting."

3 Fatal and Injury Accidents, New Jersey — "During the period 1946 to 1960, the City of Trenton improved the street-lighting system by a 36 percent increase in average illumination. Pedestrian night accidents (injury and fatal) were reduced by 30 percent. The effective reduction, based on day to night accidents was 37 percent. For all types of injury and fatal accidents, the overall night reduction was 10 percent compared to day rates."

Based on their investigations, the committee made a series of recommendations for lighting standards:

"For the lighting of residential side streets, an average illumination of 0.2 foot-candle . . . is specified. This level will provide reasonable traffic safety on low-volume and low-speed streets . . . On major arterial streets traversing business areas, a level of 2.0 foot-candles is needed to compensate for greatly increased traffic, pedestrians and background distractions. Various other levels between these limits are needed for intermediate degrees of traffic, volume, speeds and abutting land use . . .

"In order to minimize the number of freeway accidents that occur at night, lighting levels have been specified which are felt to be appropriate to the traffic and seeing task problems facing the freeway driver. For urban freeways, 1.4 foot-candles is recommended and for rural freeways, 1.0 foot-candle. At interchange locations, these levels should be increased 50 percent. . . .

"In addition to the level of lighting needed for traffic safety, the uniformity (even coverage) of surface illumination is important. For all but residential streets, a uniformity no poorer than 1 to ½ is specified. This means that at no point should the illumination be less than ½ the average illumination."

In several cities, officials have become persuaded that even these standards are inadequate, at least for central business districts, and are installing systems which create levels of 10 foot-candles or more. St. Louis, for example, has recently illuminated an area of 144 blocks at 20 foot-candles. The expense is justified on grounds of safety (see the *Crimes and Lights* section of this appendix) and attracting people back downtown.

GENERAL GUIDELINES FOR STREET LIGHTING FIXTURES

Performance requirements for the qualities of light in different parts of the city should be based on the effects of public and private lighting combined. To develop detailed requirements, a series of experiments must be conducted which test public response to a variety of lighting levels, types, and conditions in the field.

If the only operational performance standard was minimum strength of light flux striking the pavement in a sufficiently uniform pattern (as it presently is), then the current fixtures being installed in Boston and other cities probably represent a least-cost compromise. The standard 400-watt mercury vapor luminaire, mounted at a height of about 30 feet on alternate sides of the street at 110 foot centers, provides a system that is thoroughly tested and has relatively high reliability and low maintenance cost. Before considering other systems or modifications to that system, thorough testing of full-scale prototypes against new performance standards for light quality will be necessary. The following characteristics should be considered in screening or developing new systems:

Distribution of Light Emitted

The directional pattern of the light emitted from the fixture should relate to the widths of street and sidewalk, the site-line of drivers, the height of building facades, the use and lighting of the buildings, and the reflectivity of the surfaces that are to be lighted. The fixtures should incorporate reflectors, refractor lenses, and shields to direct the light where it is desired. The number of fixtures needed, and thus the total cost, are in direct proportion to the effectiveness of each fixture in accomplishing this. Information on current standard fixtures is available from the manufacturers who have developed routine methods of measuring and charting light distribution. However, fixtures can most efficiently be adapted to the different requirements of different locations if their light distribution can be adjusted by changes in reflector, lens, or shield; otherwise a city will need a number of "standard" fixtures.

Type of Source

There is a trade-off between control of distribution and quality of light. Color corrected (coated) mercury lamps are clearly much less objectionable in their color rendition (though far from daylight) than are clear mercury vapor lamps, but distribution is much more difficult to control. In many contexts, high-pressure sodium sources may be desirable and can be better controlled, but here the trade-off is with lamp life and thus maintenance costs. Some improvement in color might be accomplished by tinted lenses, and best of all would be a lens which changed color with the temperature to produce a warmer light in winter and a cooler light in summer. A pleasant light color can be achieved through a mixture of sodium and mercury sources, but to maintain distribution control at the same time would require a separate reflector and refractor lens for each lamp — obviously a more costly solution.

Apparent Size and Brightness

The appearance of the lighted fixtures themselves is affected by both the mounting height and spacing and the design of the light source. Clear mercury vapor lamps at 30 feet produce quite uncomfortable glare. As mounting height is increased, and when bulbs are coated or refractor lenses are present, the apparent size of the source is increased, which in turn increases the "softness" of the light. Thus, glare is reduced (accompanied by some loss in control over distribution), although not nearly as effectively as with the introduction of glare shields.

Mounting Height and Spacing

Both mounting height and spacing in combination with light distribution affect the uniformity of the light flux striking the pavement. In general, higher mounting heights and wider pole spacing, combined with more powerful sources (in terms of lumen output), can produce the same intensity of illumination with better uniformity and less glare at less cost. However, these higher mounting heights can create problems in urban installations. Violation of privacy in upper stories through light spill-over is increased, and light distribution is more difficult to control. Also, the wide spacing implied by higher mounting heights is likely to fit less well with the typical pattern of blocks and intersections (see Chapter 4).

Contribution of Lighting Mountings to the Daytime Structure of the Street

If light poles are spaced regularly and fairly close together, they can help create visual rhythms with other elements of the streetscape, such as trees or parking meters. Where such rhythms cannot be achieved, the poles will add to visual clutter. Other solutions should be considered:
1. Mounting the lights on the walls of buildings, where the street is fairly narrow and the building line fairly regular (This has been done successfully in the renewal of Yonge Street in Toronto following the subway construction, and is common practice in Europe.); 2. clustering strong lights on high, widely-spaced poles (The lighting at the parking lots at Expo in Montreal is an example and this "high mast" lighting is becoming popular for plaza lighting in Europe.); and 3. combining lights with other fixtures, such as guard rails and traffic lights.

Safety

Light poles, as with any street furniture, should be designed and located so as to reduce the likelihood and damages of collision. Except in areas of high pedestrian use, where the falling pole would itself be a danger, poles should be "frangible," designed to break easily upon collision.

Cost of the System

All of the design factors described above, and several additional factors as well, will affect costs. If a fixture is not available, there are costs of development and testing. Costs of power and maintenance must be considered. Costs can be substantially cut if existing poles, and especially pole bases that are already wired, can be used in new lighting systems. Also, standardization of design can produce economies of scale.

CRIMES AND LIGHTS

Introduction

The assertion is often made that brighter street-lighting fights crime. According to J. Edgar Hoover, "It is axiomatic that darkness is an ally to crime. The thief, the arsonist, the rapist, the peeping tom, and all other perverse individuals often depend on darkness to cloak their misdeeds and conceal their identities." Articles in *Nation's Cities* (March 1967), the *Police Chief* (May 1962), the *Boston Sunday Herald* (4 June 1967), the *Christian Science Monitor* (27 June 1959), and electrical trade magazines support this hypothesis without offering statistical proof. A research report assembled by the Library of Congress Legislative Reference Service, "The Impact of Street Lighting on Crime and Traffic Accidents," is of similar dubious validity, since it uncritically relies on statistically crude studies and newspaper editorials to prove the point.

In an attempt to obtain reliable data on which to found conclusions about the function of street-lighting in crime prevention, letters were sent to the police chiefs of cities which had been cited as test-cases in crime-preventative lighting — Gary, Indianapolis, Detroit, St. Louis, and Chicago. The raw data from these cities and several others are reported below.

Reported Studies

1 *Gary, Indiana:* During a two-year period (1953-1955) more than 5,000 new lights were installed along every street in Gary. The number of reported criminal assaults declined more than 70% and the decrease in robberies was 60%, even though Gary's population increased 27% during this period.

2 *McPherson, Kansas:* Illumination level in residential areas was increased sixfold. The incidence of nighttime prowling, window peeping, and burglary in these areas declined 92%.

3 *Chattanooga, Tennessee:* A twelve-block district with a high homicide rate was relighted; major crimes in that district were reduced 70%.

4 *Indianapolis, Indiana:* One thousand new lights are installed each year in areas with the highest traffic accident and crime rates. In 1960, there was a 60% reduction in nighttime crime on streets with new lighting. Two hundred twenty-five fewer crimes against property were reported by five squad cars cruising in the relighted area; in the still-dark area, 102 more crimes against property were reported by two cars during that period.

5 *New York, New York:* In 1957, an 111-block area with a high crime rate received 125% more light. During the three-month period following the program of relighting, 71% fewer crimes were reported than during the three months before. In the course of the next two years, the number of murders, assaults, and rapes dropped 49%, and juvenile complaints declined 30% in that area.

6 *Boston, Massachusetts:* In 1959, a neighborhood committee in the South End pinpointed the exact locations in their neighborhood of 104 offenses — from purse snatching to assault — which were committed between August and December. And according to the *Christian Science Monitor,* this study conclusively showed that fewer crimes were committed on streets with modern lighting.

7 *St. Louis, Missouri:* Illumination in the 144 square block downtown area was raised from 1-2 to 10-12 foot-candles. Statistics show that after relighting, all crimes in that area were down 13%, while crimes in all of St. Louis decreased only 2%. In the downtown area, aggravated assault was down 80% and purse snatching down 66%. Auto thefts increased 14% during the same period, but St. Louis's Captain Camp feels that this increase probably occurred during daylight hours. The relighting program was conducted in conjunction with a massive downtown renewal.

8 *Chicago, Illinois:* In April, 1966, a study done by the police department concluded that 9.2% of all murders, rapes, robberies, burglaries, thefts, and serious assaults were committed in (or near) alleys at night. It was assumed that installing street lights in alleys would reduce the incidence of night crimes. Fifty-one thousand new lights were installed in 2,300 miles of alleys throughout the city. A comparison was then made between crimes committed during the first three months of 1966 and of 1968 (i.e., before and after relighting).

In Chicago, statistics were available for alley crimes for both day and nighttime. During the 1968 time period citywide serious crimes (day and night) increased 32.7%, with increases of individual categories ranging from 19.2% for burglary to 93.2% for assault. In alleys, total serious crimes (day and night) decreased 20.4%. Nighttime crimes in alleys decreased 30.3%, significantly better than the daytime decrease. But surprisingly, some individual categories of alley crimes did not decrease significantly more during nighttime hours than during daytime hours. For example, rape and serious assault in alleys showed a greater decrease *overall* than for darkness hours alone. (Rapes in alleys decreased overall 48.3%, but only 39.9% during the nighttime; the corresponding figures for serious assault are 39.1% and 34.5% decreases.)

Conclusions

All studies other than the one in Chicago failed to observe differences between daytime and nighttime crime rates, and since only the latter are affected by lighting, this failure lessens the value of the other studies. The Chicago study shows that several categories of crime were reduced by improved lighting of certain areas, but none of the studies gives a firm answer to several crucial questions:

- How can these data be interpreted when crime reporting and recording procedures are not standardized and when levels of enforcement may also be changing?
- Does increased lighting in one district of a city merely shift crime to another district?
- How and why does relighting have a different effect on different kinds of crime?
- Is relighting more effective in alleys than on major streets?

These questions are in line with the conclusions of the President's Commission on Law Enforcement and Administration of Justice, *Task Force Report: Science and Technology* (1967):

There is no conclusive evidence that improved lighting will have lasting or significant impact on crime rates, although there are strong intuitive reasons to believe it will be helpful.

Improved street lighting may reduce some types of crime in some areas, i.e., given a light and dark street to commit a crime, a criminal will probably choose the dark street.

Improved street lighting accompanied by increased police patrol can reduce crime rates in an area.

When new lighting programs are instituted, police departments should be encouraged to maintain records of crimes in the relighted and adjoining areas. With information on past, present, and projected crime rates, it may be possible to assess better the impact of lighting on crime.

It is likely that better lighting helps the police and others to spot offenders; that greater use of streets by people on foot (especially when they are known to one another) will discourage crime; and that the increased feeling of safety with increased illumination (particularly in areas where other people are scarce or where people are strangers) may be as important as whether safety is in fact increased. (A Central Business District study of St. Louis done by graduate students in business administration supports the last point.) Also, the color of the light may have important effects. It can be argued, for example, that the depersonalizing effects of mercury vapor make bystander help less likely and that this unpleasant light may even drive people off the streets in some areas, thus undermining any positive effects of more light. Of course, even if a tenfold increase in street illumination were shown to reduce crime significantly in any area, the question would still remain whether the cost-effectiveness of lighting compares favorably to that of other deterrents; and whether the damage done to the street life of residential neighborhoods by such high levels of illumination — especially when accomplished by unshielded mercury vapor lights — would be accepted by local people as the necessary price of "safer streets." But these questions can be postponed until the "strong intuitive reasons" (above) are borne out by experience. It is worth remembering that these intuitive conclusions usually rely on the fact that serious personal crimes occur about 40% more frequently during nighttime hours. But the significance of this fact depends on what more there is to nighttime than darkness and what more there is to crime than statistics show.

Private Signing and Lighting Review

OPERATION OF THE INDUSTRY:
ON-PREMISE SIGNS AND LIGHTS

Purchasing
On-premise signs and lights are used to identify and advertise almost every kind of commercial establishment. However, the needs and capabilities of these establishments vary. The great variations in sign expenditures among wealthy enterprises show that while all businesses need a sign for identification, some are much more dependent than others on advertising. Gas stations rely on signs and lighting more than large department stores do. A prestigious department store could easily afford a giant sign hovering high above its building but generally prefers something rather modest. Discount houses put relatively more of an investment into signs than enterprises which aim to attract the affluent. Merchants on an auto-dependent commercial strip want to be identified from a great distance so that motorists have ample opportunity to make necessary parking and turning decisions. Roughly speaking, the size and intensity of signing seem to be inversely proportional to the uniqueness and prestige of the establishment.

There are also great differences in the ability of merchants to pay for new signs. For many shopkeepers, a sign represents a relatively large investment, particularly if it is illuminated and requires a large support structure. The merchants who erect large illuminated signs do so because they believe the investment is wise — it results in returns more than adequate to pay for the sign.

A sign becomes a trademark and in some cases a recognized national symbol. Merchants have great faith in their logos and in the identification policy used during their early business years; athough, when these merchants wish to attract a broader market, sign policy becomes flexible in the search for a change in image.

Design
On-premise signs are usually poorly designed. The services of trained graphic designers or architects are not available at prices that most merchants can afford to pay. The "package deal" offered by sign companies and contractors is attractive to many small businesses — the sign company designer includes an entire new store front with the sign — but most of these designers are untrained, and the results are conventional at best. The character of the area is seldom considered and consequently districts begin to look more alike, making it harder for people to orient themselves and masking the real diversity of the city.

Manufacturers
Some signs are custom-made, others are mass produced. The custom-made signs may be produced by large or small shops. Although the design capabilities of even the larger shops are limited, they offer technical skill and flexibility. For instance, a large shop will have a large selection of "true" colors for neon signs, instead of the pink-purple neon color that represents the cheapest available material. Many large manufacturers provide maintenance service which includes periodic inspection, repairs, and painting of their signs, which are expected to last ten years.

Custom-made signs cannot compete in price with the mass-produced signs which are frequently provided to local merchants by beer and soft-drink companies, laundromats, and other franchised outlets. These "stock signs" usually consist of a translucent plastic panel with the words, symbols or pictures painted on it, frequently with interior illumination. Owners install and maintain the signs, which have a life expectancy of only two to five years. The national advertiser dominates the sign message, but the cost advantage attracts many small shopkeepers. Since the national companies are paying for the sign, it would be difficult indeed to create better designed competition to these signs.

Permits
Nobody is eager to take responsibility for obtaining the public permits needed when a sign is being erected. Manufacturers try to leave the problem to their customers, though frequently the customers insist that the manufacturers obtain the permits. Not surprisingly, there is occasional confusion. One sign manufacturer in Boston has a large collection of signs in storage that were custom built but never installed because the expected permits were not granted. At present, Boston is regarded as being fairly consistent and easy to deal with in this respect. The greatest uncertainties over approvals are in the suburbs.

Typical stock sign.

OFF-PREMISE SIGNS AND LIGHTS

Most of the conspicuous off-premise signs are poster boards and painted bulletins maintained by the outdoor advertising industry. People in the industry refer to such signs collectively as "Outdoor." The public knows them as billboards. Two types of advertisers who use "Outdoor" on a large scale are advertisers selling their products on a nation-wide basis and wealthy local businesses such as banks.

Industry Attitudes

The outdoor advertising industry directs its attention almost exclusively to reaching people riding in automobiles. "The automobile has brought about the most phenomenal social and economic revolution this country has ever seen," explains one industry publication, and suggests that an advertiser can participate in this revolution by hiring space on billboards. The industry's orientation towards the automobile greatly simplifies the task of predicting "circulation." When an advertiser hires a group of billboards, he is guaranteed that a certain number of automobiles will pass his billboards every twenty-four hours, regardless of how many people in these cars look at his message. The amount that he pays is based upon the number of cars.

Because of the outdoor advertising industry's overriding concern with automobile circulation statistics, almost all billboards are located along the relatively small number of thoroughfares that carry a great deal of traffic. In Boston, for example, many of the prized locations are along the Fitzgerald Expressway and the Southeast Expressway. Other types of locations are sometimes regarded as valuable for special reasons. Some advertisers seek to locate billboards near shopping centers or supermarkets, because outdoor advertising at such locations "is often the last contact between the advertiser and the prospect before the point of purchase." There is also some interest in busy downtown areas where there is heavy pedestrian traffic. The potential for advertising in such areas is regarded as limited, however.

Having settled on locations that have high rates of traffic flow, the industry's next concern is visibility. Billboards must be designed and positioned in such a way that they catch the eye of the passing motorist; for example, at an angle rather than parallel to the road and with sufficient spacing between so that each can capture a moment of the motorist's undivided attention. It is considered particularly good to position a billboard so that an approaching motorist will see it from a great distance. If the only objective is to attract the motorist's attention, all of this is good common sense. Outdoor advertising companies do not consider whether there are some places where a driver can better afford a distraction than others.

Size, of course, is important to visibility. It is also regarded as something of a virtue in itself. "As big as all outdoor" [*sic*] is an industry slogan. "Only in Outdoor," explains a trade publication, "can you display an automobile full size and in full color, or a cake, or a glass of beer, or an aspirin tablet, thousands of times actual size. . . Size has impact." In spite of this enthusiasm, the industry has placed restraints on the size of most billboards in order to enjoy the advantages of nation-wide standardization. National advertisers use a standard 12′ x 25′ board for mounting paper posters throughout the United States, enabling them to produce a single set of designs for use everywhere. The major outdoor advertising companies contend that this standardization has raised the standards of design in outdoor advertising. It has also had the incidental effect of driving their smaller, non-standard competitors out of business.

The attitude of most of the outdoor advertising industry towards innovation in government regulation is hostile: "Whenever anybody mentions government," said one executive, "I begin to see red." Most people in the billboard business are happy with current levels of regulation and probably would make major changes only under the threat of an anti-billboard law such as exists in Vermont. They feel that if they put up a modern, standard-size billboard, keep it in repair, and change the posters once a month, they have discharged any obligation they may have to the public. One executive described an unfortunate series of events in California: When one town prohibited billboards in its commercial district, the outdoor advertising companies were "forced" to ruin a beautiful landscape outside the city limits by erecting an almost continuous series of billboards for several miles.

Plant Operators

The outdoor advertising companies (known in the business as "plant operators") build the billboard structures, maintain them, and rent space on them to customers. Large plant operators purchase the sites of the billboards whenever they can. When that is impossible, they lease them. Large plant operators normally have the facilities for fabricating the billboards they erect.

The plant operators rent a "showing" (i.e., space on a group of billboards) to each advertiser through his advertising agency. The posters are designed and printed by the advertiser's agency. They are then sent to the plant operators, who install them on the poster boards. In many cases, the National Outdoor Advertising Bureau, which is a non-profit organization run by the agencies, acts as a clearinghouse for billboard "showings." This reduces the burden on the individual agencies to deal with a large number of plant operators throughout the country.

In dealing with both the Massachusetts government and the federal government, the plant operators have been extremely effective and resourceful lobbyists against any proposed billboard legislation.

CRITICAL ISSUES IN THE REGULATION OF OUTDOOR ADVERTISING

Billboards and Safety

Billboards are generally immune from any controls which are applied to other industries where health, safety, or personal freedom of the individual is involved. Safety restrictions such as those on the automobile, airlines, railroad, and drug industries do not affect the advertising industry, although some studies indicate a relationship between accident rates and the frequency of roadside signs:

The Minnesota Department of Highways, in cooperation with the federal Bureau of Public Roads, conducted a two-year study on 420 miles of two-lane and 90 miles of three- and four-lane roadways (parts of U.S. 52 in Minnesota with traffic volumes of less than 5,000 vehicles per day) to analyze the effect of advertising signs and access points on highway accidents. The study, completed in 1951, stated that "The basic concept of roadside advertising conflicts with one of the fundamental principles of safe driving. This phase of advertising depends on the ability of roadside signs to capture the attention of and convey impressions to motorists who should direct their constant attention to the progressively changing roadway conditions. The success with which this is accomplished may be measured by the continual increase in the number of signs. Because this competition for the motorists' attention is successful, it seems axiomatic that accidents should be related to the frequency of these signs." [1]

Another study was released in February, 1963, by the New York State Thruway Authority. Madigan-Hyland, Inc., a New York City engineering firm, analyzed accidents on the Thruway over the preceding two-year period. "Advertising devices" were visible to drivers on only about one-eighth of the Thruway's 1100 miles of roadway; yet, almost one-third of all accidents "attributed to driver-inattention" occurred on the one-eighth of the Thruway mileage upon which motorists were exposed to advertising devices. The engineers found that "there was an annual average of 1.7 accidents/mile due to driver-inattention on the portions of the Thruway Mainline where advertising devices were visible; and only 0.5 of an accident/mile for this cause on stretches where advertising devices were not visible." [2]

Thus, an argument may be constructed to show that billboards placed in critical locations, especially on curves, distract the driver's attention and also obscure official warning and direction signs, thereby constituting a safety hazard.[3] Some safety officials disagree, however.[4] No one has conclusive evidence on their effects in urban situations, although the dangers of distraction are obviously greater in cities. It is clearly a matter of legislative choice as to whether traffic safety shall be made a factor in any billboard regulation.

Legislation and the Public Interest

State legislatures and courts have begun to recognize the detrimental aspects of outdoor advertising. The Vermont Legislature has authorized a state-wide ban on billboards. The General Assembly made the following "findings of fact":

1 "The proliferation of outdoor advertising is hazardous to highway users," *and*

2 "The scattering of outdoor advertising throughout the state is detrimental to the preservation of those scenic resources and so to the economic base of the state, and is also not an effective method of providing information to tourists about available facilities." [5]

The Vermont Travel Information Council established by the legislation administers the anti-billboard law and also has the authority to regulate size, shape, color, lighting, lettering, and how official business directional signs are displayed. When these signs become too numerous at one location or highway safety requires it, panels or tiered signs are employed (see Chapter 2).[6]

Outdoor advertising which undermines the traffic informational system of signs and lights and detracts from the natural landscape is not in the public interest. The Federal Highway Beautification Act of 1965 recognizes the need to control "outdoor advertising signs, displays, and devices . . . adjacent to the Interstate System . . . to protect the public investment in such highways, to promote the safety and recreational value of public travel, and to preserve natural beauty." [7] The act provides incentives to states if they do not allow billboards along interstate routes. By 1967, twenty-seven states had elected to accept this bonus.[8]

An ordinance passed by the City Council of Cleveland in 1964 states, in part, that ". . . the unrestricted and unregulated erection or maintenance of advertising devices adjacent to a controlled access highway and parkway creates

1. *Minnesota Rural Trunk Highway Accident, Access Point, and Advertising Sign Study,* conducted by the Highway Planning Survey, Minnesota Dept. of Highways (Rev. 1952), provides statistical evidence that billboards are a safety hazard ("To obtain a measure of the association between accident rate and sign frequency, two statistical tests were applied to the data. The first produced a correlation coefficient of 0.97 and the second produced a standard error or estimate of 0.13. The results of these two tests practically eliminates the probability that this association is due to chance. It may be assumed that an increase in the number of signs per mile will be accompanied by a corresponding increase in accident rate.").
2. Madigan-Hyland Inc., *Signs and Accidents on New York State Thruway.* Report prepared for New York State Thruway Authority, February 1963.
3. Curve locations are particularly attractive to outdoor advertisers as the line of vision of the oncoming driver is almost sure to include the advertising message. "The frequency of advertising signs per mile on curves was nearly half again as great as that found on tangent sections." *Minnesota Rural Trunk Highway Accident, Access Point, and Advertising Sign Study.* Bertram Tallamy, former federal highway administrator, testified before the Gore Committee Senate Hearing on Control of Advertising on Interstate Highways (1957), that intensification of outdoor advertising at turnoffs to and from the highway seriously impairs efficiency of official signs: "I am convinced that a mixing of outdoor advertising signs and of official signs would be very detrimental." For further reference, see R. T. Shoaf, "Are Advertising Signs Near Freeways Traffic Hazards?" *Traffic Engineer 26* (1955), 71-73.
4. For statistical evidence that billboards are not a safety hazard, see Planning and Traffic Division, Michigan State Highway Dept., *Accident Experience in Relation to Road and Roadside Features* (1952). Also see Lauer and McMonagle, "Do Road Signs Affect Accidents?" *Traffic Quarterly* (July 1955), 322-329; and testimony of J. Carl McMonagle, 1957 *Hearings* 309.
5. 1967, No. 333 (Adj. Sess.), Sec. 2, eff. March 23, 1968.
6. 1967, No. 333 (Adj. Sess.), Sec. 10, eff. March 23, 1968; amended 1969, No. 92, Sec. 7, eff. April 19, 1969.
7. U.S., Congress, Senate, *Highway Beautification Act of 1965,* 89th Cong., S. 2084, Public Law 89-285, 22 October 1965, p. 1.
8. U.S., Department of Transportation, *First Annual Report of the Department of Transportation,* Part 1, Fiscal Year 1967, p. 73.

traffic hazards and unnecessary unsightly conditions which are incompatible to the public interest." The Massachusetts Supreme Judicial Court upheld a regulation of the defendant in *General Outdoor Advertising Co. v. Department of Public Works* which prohibited billboards near highways where, in the authority's opinion, "having regard to the health and safety of the public, the danger of fire and the unusual scenic beauty of the territory, signs would be particularly harmful to the public welfare." [9]

An opinion survey conducted by this project (appearing in Appendix 8), also found negative public attitudes toward large advertising signs. Respondents made such statements as: "billboards should be inconspicuous or nonexistent where attention is important" and "indiscriminate placement of them is distracting, dangerous," which indicate awareness of a traffic hazard. A majority of respondents agreed that billboards are distracting. Perhaps related to this, the respondents pointed out locations where billboards are inappropriate: at major road intersections in the city, along major roads in the city, and on the highways approaching the city. Respondents also pointed out, however, that some information of value, which they described as "driving-information," was supplied by billboards — location of rest stops, motels, restaurants, and gasoline stations, occasionally consumer goods and entertainment information. And there are areas where distractions are tolerated and billboards as well: entertainment districts, some shopping areas, and parking lots.

In a study of human response to the roadside environment, sponsored by the Outdoor Advertising Association of America and conducted by Arthur D. Little, Inc., observers were asked to evaluate the character of selected visual environments (presented in photographs) as objects (billboards, utility poles, and other signs) were removed from the pictures. Slide sequences of commercial and landscaped routes were initially rated by observers as being monotonous, depressing, complex, and ineffective. However, "when billboards alone were removed from both routes, the routes were rated as more varied and lively, simple and effective." [10]

Limitation of Choice and Invasion of Privacy

A distinction among various types of private signs and lighting is necessary in order to separate information-giving from purely advertising functions. The 1965 Highway Beautification Act recognizes the need for "signs, displays, and devices giving specific information in the interest of the travelling public." Location of public services and private activities, aid to orientation, and route directions are acknowledged to be functions of signs in the city and along the highway; outdoor advertising, however, does not present information on the real range of available choice. Also it is difficult to ignore, and in the process of seeking specific information, the public is overwhelmed by irrelevant signs. In the words of one advertising executive, "A billboard is there for the sole and express purpose of trespassing on your field of vision. Nor is it possible for you to escape . . . is this not an invasion of privacy?" [11]

The Massachusetts Supreme Court ruling, in *General Outdoor Advertising Co. v. Department of Public Works,* characterized commercial advertising as a "forcible" intrusion by solicitors of business upon the motorist and an invasion of his right to use the roadways: "The object of outdoor advertising in the nature of things is to proclaim to those who travel on highways and who resort to public reservations that which is on the advertising device, and to constrain such persons to see and comprehend the advertisement. It does not appeal to the desire or consent of such persons; it is forcibly thrust upon the attention of all such persons, whether willing or averse. For such persons who strongly desire to avoid advertising intrusion, there is no escape; they cannot enjoy their natural and ordinary rights to proceed unmolested." [12]

In sum, courts are aware that unrestricted outdoor advertising interferes with the public use of roadways in the demands it makes on the attention of motorists,[13] but the assertion that billboards contribute to the incidence of accidents cannot be conclusively demonstrated. However, both common sense and the small amount of statistical evidence strongly suggest that they are a safety hazard, and there can be no doubt that billboards do conflict with other values such as aesthetics, information choice, and individual privacy.

9. *General Outdoor Advertising Co. v. Department of Public Works,* 289 Mass. 149, 168, 193 N.E. 799, 808 (1935).
10. Arthur D. Little, Inc., *Response to the Roadside Environment,* Report to the Outdoor Advertising Association of America (Cambridge, Mass., 30 January 1968), p. II-4.
11. Howard Gossage, "How to Look at Billboards," *Harper's Magazine* 220 (February 1960), 12-16.
12. *General Outdoor Advertising Co. v. Department of Public Works,* 289 Mass. 149, 168, 193 N.E. 808 (1935), appeals dismissed, 296 U.S. 543, 297 U.S. 725 (1936). See also Gardner, "The Massachusetts Billboard Decision," 49 *Harvard Law Review* 869 (1936); 36 *Michigan Law Review* 666 (1938).
13. For recognition that interference with normal highway uses is inherent in the billboard advertising business, see *Fifth Avenue Coach Co. v. City of New York,* 194 N.Y. 19, 30-31, 86 N.E. 824, 827 (1909); *General Outdoor Advertising Co. v. Department of Public Works; Churchill & Tait v. Rafferty,* Collector of Internal Revenue, 32 Phil. Is. 580, 609 (1915).

LEGAL ISSUES

The legal basis for public control of private signs and lighting (whether through zoning, licensing systems, or special procedures as for historic districts) is primarily the generally recognized "police power" to make reasonable regulations to promote public health, safety, morals, and general welfare. In some states support may also be found in specific constitutional provisions. Massachusetts, for instance, by a 1918 amendment provided that, "Advertising on public ways, in public places and on private property within public view may be regulated and restricted by law."

Promotion of safety provides a strong basis for exercising powers to regulate signs and lighting. Legislative bodies and courts have frequently found that billboards interfere with the public use of the highways, distract drivers through the demands on their attention, and obscure traffic signs, as indicated in the previous section of this appendix. Promoting ease of identification of premises and occupancies also serves public convenience.

Public welfare may encompass general economic well-being. Courts have held that unsightly or discordant development will affect the economic welfare of a community and influence general prosperity by causing blight.[14]

Although there was long reluctance to recognize aesthetics and the promotion of the beautiful as within the concept of general welfare, many courts particularly since the ringing statement of Justice Douglas in 1954[15] now do recognize aesthetics as sufficient to justify regulatory ordinances, either as a sole basis or when buttressed with economic or safety factors. Ordinances so upheld have included design controls even more extensive than those involved with signs and lights.[16]

The American Law Institute's proposed Model Land Development Code includes within the definition of development to be controlled by ordinance, "commencement or change in the location of an advertising structure or use of land, and the commencement or change in location of advertising on the external part of a structure."[17]

The constitutional validity of public regulations of private signs and lighting is therefore assumed, so long as reasonable. In proposing and discussing a model ordinance, it is also assumed the state has or will enact a general or special enabling act delegating the constitutional power sufficiently, or that the state constitution gives the municipality sufficient home rule powers. Any municipality considering enactment of control ordinances should of course make careful independent legal review of these assumptions in the light of the particular state constitution, statutes, and case law.

Legal issues of equal and perhaps greater practical importance may be involved in determinations of reasonableness. In general, reasonableness requires objective standards and fair and even-handed procedures for their application to particular circumstances, both well calculated to meet the objectives. The main thrust of this work is on developing such standards and procedures.

Reasonableness of requiring removal of existing uses is more difficult to establish than for control of new uses. But there are useful precedents whereby non-conforming signs and lights may be barred under the police power without compensation either after a period for amortization, or immediately as a nuisance, or barred by acquisition of rights therefor through purchase or exercise of eminent domain and payment of compensation.

Amortization is the compulsory termination of a non-conformity at the expiration of a period of time. The state laws or zoning ordinances using the amortization theory provide that land uses lawfully in existence on the date of enactment of the law and which do not conform to its provisions shall be required to be removed at the expiration of a designated period of time. Sometimes it is, in effect, a grace period for relocation or liquidation corresponding to the degree of violation or commensurate with the investment. A zoning ordinance that provides for eventual liquidation of a non-conformity within a prescribed period commensurate with the investment is valid in California and elsewhere.[18] Enabling acts in at least five states (Colorado, Georgia, Kansas, Utah, and Pennsylvania) permit enactment of local zoning ordinances using the technique of amortization.[19] Boston's special Zoning Act before 1956 had a 37 year amortization clause (c. 448 Acts of 1924, 9) not in its present special enabling act (c. 665 of 1956).

14. On general welfare including the protection of property values, see *City of Miami Beach v. Ocean & Inland Co.*, 147 Fla. 480, 3 So. 2d. 364, 367 (1941); *Hav-a-Tampa Cigar Co. v. Johnson*, 149 Fl. 148, 5 So. 2d. 433 (1942); *Murphy v. Westport,* 131 Conn. 392 40 A. 2d. 177, 179 (1944)

15. 348 U.S. 26 (1944)

16. Hershman, Beauty as the Subject of Legislative Control, *The Practical Lawyer* (Feb. 1969), 20-35; Wilson, in American Bar Association National Institute on *Junkyards, Geraniums and Jurisprudence: Aesthetics and the Law* (June 2, 3, 1967), 327-345, and related articles in the same institute; Ells, *Open Space Law* (1969), 34-35 (Conservation Law Foundation, 44 School Street, Boston, Massachusetts 02108); Cases recognizing aesthetics as a valid basis for police power regulations include: *Merritt v. Peters*, 65 So. 2d 861 (Fla. 1951); *Ware v. Wichita,* 113 Kan. 153, 214 Pac. 99 (1923); *City of New Orleans v. Pergament,* 198 La. 851, 5 So. 2d 129 (1941); *Cromwell v. Ferrier,* 19 N.Y. 2d 263, 225 N.E. 2d 749 (1967) overruling *Mid-State Advertising Corp. v. Bond*, 274 N.Y. 82, 8 N.E. 2d 286 (1937); *Commonwealth v. Trimmer,* 53 Dauph. 91, 34 Mun. 37 (Pa. Quar. Sess. 1942), in conflict with *Liggett's Petition*, 291 Pa. *109*, 139 Atl. 619 (1927), but see, *Walnut and Quince Street Corp. v. Mills*, 303 Pa. 25, 154 Atl. 29 (1931); *Connor v. City of University Park*, 142 S.W. 2d 706 (Tex. Civ. App. 1940), in conflict with *Spann v. City of Dallas*, 111 Tex. 350 (1921); *State v. Wieland*, 269 Wis. 262, 69 N.W. 2d 217 (1955); *Cromwell v. Ferrier,* perhaps the leading case recognizing aesthetics as a sole justification, says, "the offense to the eye must be substantial and be deemed to have material effect on the community or district pattern."

17. Tentative Draft No. 2, April 24, 1970, s. 1-202 (2) (h)

18. See *Livingston Rock and Gravel Company v. County of Los Angeles,* 43 Cal. 2d 121, 272, P. 2d 4 (1954): *County of San Diego v.* McClurken, 37 Cal. 2d 683, 234 p. 972 (1951) Martin & Nelson, Land Use Control and the Billboard, *Calif. L. Rev.* 46 (1958) 818, conclude that California enabling legislation should provide for amortization of any non-conforming billboards which are presently located within the protected area. Ann Arbor's Sign Ordinance calculates the period of amortization according to either the original sign cost or renovation cost — a perod from 3-15 years from the date of installation or most recent renovation (Ch. 61, *Ann Arbor City Code,* 5:518).

19. The Colorado enabling act allows for termination . . . either by specifying the period in which the non-conforming uses shall be required to cease, or by providing a formula whereby the compulsory termination of a non-conforming use may be so fixed as to allow for the recovery or amortization of the investment in the non-conformance. The Kansas enabling act, amended in 1937 merely states . . . that reasonable regulations may be adopted for the gradual elimination of non-conforming uses.

Nuisances may be abated under police power without compensation. A sign can be prohibited as a nuisance if the extent of its intrusion and its place of erection at the edge of a store front interferes with the view of a sign on the adjacent store. Lighted signs interfering with occupants of adjacent property have been legally prohibited. A few states have enacted legislation using the expanded doctrine of nuisances.[20] Typically, these statutes determine that a particular use of land constitutes a public or private nuisance. The owner is notified to comply with the statute or abate or remove the non-conforming use. If he does not comply within a specified period, the government agency is authorized to remove, obliterate, or abate the nuisance.[21] Any off-premise sign erected in Massachusetts without authorization of the OAB is deemed a nuisance.[22]

Eminent domain requires a public purpose to justify its exercise. A number of cases support condemnation for billboard control purposes.[23] If enabling acts or home rule authority so permit, condemnation may be of advertising rights only, reducing compensation accordingly.[24] It is possible that legislation could be devised along lines of the Massachusetts Wetlands Act whereby compensation would be paid only if an owner objected to a regulation, and the regulating authority elected to pay rather than rescind.

A further legal issue which will require checking in any instance is whether the state and municipality have powers to authorize neighborhood participation or special district procedures. Delegation of zoning authority to neighborhood boards, officers, or consenting neighbors has been upheld in the field of urban redevelopment.[25] The cases that uphold the requirement of consent agree it is valid to allow regulations "to be modified with the consent of the persons who are to be most affected by modification."[26]

20. The Court upheld billboard regulations that applied to billboards already in existence, without requiring compensation, in *Ghaster Properties, Inc. v. Preston,* 110 N.E. 2d 328 (1964). Also relevant are: *Ohio Rev. Code,* sec. 5516.04; *Wash. Rev. Code* Annot. sec. 47.42.080; *N. Hamp. Rev. Code* Annot. sec. 249-A:7.
21. In Re Opinion of the Justices, 169 A. 2d. 762 (1961), court upheld the legislative determination that as a general proposition billboards in proximity to a highway are nuisances. However, if an individual feels that in his case his sign is not a nuisance, he may contest this general proposition and receive compensation.
22. *General Laws,* Chap. 93, Sec. 30A.
23. E.g., *Commonwealth v. Boston Advertising Co.,* 188 Mass. 348, 74 N.E. 601 (1905); *Kansas City v. Liebi,* 298 Mo. 569, 252 S.W. 404 (1923).
24. Nichols, *Eminent Domain,* Sec. 5.72 (1958); Wilson, Billboards and the Right to Be Seen From the Highway, *Georgetown L.J.* 30 (1942) 723. *State v. Kamrowski,* (Wisc) 142 N.W. 2d 793, 1966.
25. *Zisook v. Maryland-Drexel Corp.,* 3 Ill. 2d 570, 121 N.E. 2d 804 (1954); *Redfern v. Bd. of Comrs. of Jersey City,* 137 N.J.L. 356, 59 A. 2d 641 (1948). Cf. Edward M. Levin, Jr., "Citizen Involvement in Zoning: A Decentralization Proposal," *Land-Use Controls Quarterly* 3 (Summer 1969), 14-22.
26. *State ex. rel. Standard Oil Co. v. Combs,* 129 O.S. 251, 194 N.E. 875, 877 (1935); *Robwood Adv. Assoc. v. Nashua,* 102 N.H. 215, 153 A. 2d 787 (1959).

PRESENT REGULATION: LOCAL AND STATE AUTHORITIES

Zoning

The Boston Zoning Code adopted pursuant to its special enabling act (c. 665 of 1956) contains provisions (Article 11) regulating signs in residential and local business districts. Signs on private property in other types of districts are completely unregulated. In residential areas, each building is permitted a single two square foot sign identifying the occupant or street number. Also permitted are signs advertising a property "For Rent" or "For Sale," church or institutional signs, contractor's signs, and signs related to lawful non-conforming uses.

In local business districts, permitted signs include the on-premise signs allowed in residential districts plus billboards, signs, or other advertising devices licensed by the Outdoor Advertising Board.[27] When a piece of property in a local business district adjoins a residential district, the occupant is permitted to erect signs facing the residential district so long as the aggregate area of all signs does not exceed 10 percent of the area of the wall parallel to the lot line or one square foot for each foot in the length of lot line, whichever is greater.

The Boston Zoning Code is enforced by the Building Department, which refuses building permits for structures that it believes to be in violation of the Code. State and municipal officers refuse a permit or license for a new use of a building they consider to be in violation of any zoning regulation.

Adverse decisions of the Building Department may be appealed to the Board of Appeal to obtain a variance on the basis of undue hardship or some similar ground. After a hearing, the Board may reverse or affirm the order or decision. A four-fifths concurring vote is necessary to reverse any decision, decide in favor of the applicant, or to effect any variance.

Public Works Department

The City of Boston's Public Works Department is empowered by the state to grant permits "for the placing . . . of signs, advertising devices . . . and other appurtenances . . ." projecting more than 12 inches over the public way.[28] Boston has adopted an ordinance to govern the granting of such permits in accordance with this section. City regulations limit the size of projecting signs. The Commissioner of Public Works makes the decisions as to granting of sign permits on behalf of the Public Improvement Commission. The Commissioner reserves the right to reject a permit for a smaller sign (within the size limitation) "if, in his opinion, conditions so warrant."[29] The PWD's principal responsibility is to keep the public way open and safe.

Enforcement of the regulations is difficult. The small inspection staff is primarily concerned with seeing that size regulations have not been violated and that signs have not been erected without permits. Little effort is made to force permit holders to maintain their signs in good repair.

27. Subject to Sections 29 through 33 of Chapter 93 of the *General Laws.*
28. *General Laws,* Chap. 85, sec. 8.
29. Boston, Mass., Department of Public Works, *Rules and Regulations,* Part One, 1 Jan. 1955, p. 10.

Building Department
The City of Boston Building Code sets standards for the structural safety of buildings and other structures erected in the city. All signs, except those that are located on the ground and those that are less than one square foot in area, must comply with these general standards. In addition, the Code sets forth regulations regarding the use of combustible materials in signs. The Building Code is enforced by the Building Department as part of the same permit-review procedure that is used to enforce the Zoning Code.

Parks and Recreation Department
City ordinances require that anyone seeking to erect or alter a sign within 300 feet of a public park or parkway must first obtain permission from the Parks Department. The Department receives a few such applications each year, and deals with them on a case-by-case basis. Many changes for which Parks Department approval is technically required are never brought to the Department's attention. Other agencies like the PWD and the Outdoor Advertising Board are in the habit of issuing permits without consulting the Parks Department. Nor does the Department have the personnel necessary for enforcement. The interests of the Parks Department might be better protected if its authority were transferred to an agency concerned primarily with sign control.

Urban Renewal
The BRA controls signs on its urban renewal lands through restrictions in the deeds by which it grants the land to private developers. The BRA also offers an informal review and design service within its urban design section.

Historic Districts
The Back Bay and Beacon Hill Architectural Commissions exercise very strict control over any changes in the exterior appearance of buildings within their jurisdiction. Rather than promulgating regulations, they deal with cases on an individual basis. The Commissions require an application for a certificate of design approval for proposed construction or alteration of any structure or exterior architectural feature.[30] A certificate of appropriateness as required by the Beacon Hill Architectural Commission must accompany any sign permits issued by the Public Improvement Commission or any other city agency.

Metropolitan District Commission
The MDC has power over private signs projecting into its rights-of-way similar to that exercised by the Public Works Department over projection into the public way.[31] Occasions for the exercise of this power are rare.

Outdoor Advertising Board
The principal control over off-premise signs in Massachusetts is administered by the Outdoor Advertising Board, an agency of the state government with the power to license and regulate outdoor advertising throughout the state. The OAB has worked closely with the billboard industry and is held in high esteem by the industry's representatives.

The Outdoor Advertising Board prescribes standards of size, setback, and clearance, and grants permits for the erection of billboards and other signs only in areas of a business character.[32] A recent amendment to the rules and regulations of the OAB (eff. August 15, 1969) deals with the location of signs within a city or town in relation to local ordinances. This amendment states that any local ordinance or bylaw shall be consistent with the rules of the Board even if such ordinance or bylaw prohibits billboards, signs, or other advertising devices, which in the absence of such local law would be in conformance with the OAB rules and regulations. City and town sign ordinances can therefore be more restrictive than the OAB.

30. Area boundaries and certificate requirements are defined in secs. 2 & 8 of Chap. 625 of the Acts of 1966 and secs. 1, 1A-C, of Chap. 616 of the Acts of 1955.

31. *General Laws,* Chap. 97, sec. 95A.

32. *General Laws,* Chap. 93, sec. 29.

OUTLINE FOR A MODEL CODE*

1. General Objectives

1.1 To restrict private signs and lights which overload the public's capacity to receive information, which violate privacy, or which increase the probability of accidents by distracting attention or obstructing vision.

1.2 To encourage signing and lighting and other private communications which aid orientation, identify activities, express local history and character or serve other educational purposes.

1.3 To increase opportunities for presently excluded individuals and groups to express themselves in the public environment.

1.4 To reduce conflict among private signs and lighting and between the private and public environmental information systems.

1.5 To increase opportunities for local groups to collectively determine policies for private signing and lighting in their areas.

2. Definitions

2.1 *Sign Districts:*

a *Special Information Districts:* areas with high use by the general public (as indicated by traffic flow, density of development, and economic activity) and/or with recognized broad public significance (based on history, type of activity, or environmental character), which are particularly sensitive to the effects of private signs and lights (for reasons of safety, history, aesthetics, orientation or whatever). In these districts, the city shall exercise central control of private signs and lights and develop with the affected groups in each area a set of detailed and specialized codes, guidelines, incentives, prototype designs, and review procedures. These controls and incentives would vary from city to city and area to area and cannot be dealt with in this outline. Any or all of the provisions of this outline code might be inapplicable in a Special Information District.

b *General Information Districts:* all other parts of the city. *This model code applies to General Information Districts only.*

c *Local Information Districts:* a ward, precinct, model city sub-area, or other recognized spatial unit, within a General Information District, in which the city allows local groups to formulate additional regulations and guidelines for area signs and lights, subject to legislative review of regulations and the right of central appeal. Locally-initiated regulations may develop and intensify the provisions of the code but may not weaken or supersede them. (See Chapter 5 for discussion of how these districts may be established.)

2.2 *Sign:* Any letters, pictorial representation, symbol, flag, emblem, illuminated or animated device, displayed in any manner whatsoever, which directs attention of persons off the premises on which the sign is displayed to any object, subject, place, person, activity, product, service, institution, organization, or business.

2.3 *Surface area (of a sign):* the surface area of any sign is the entire area within a single continuous perimeter enclosing the extreme limits of lettering, representations, emblems, or other figures, together with any material or color forming an integral part of the display or used to differentiate the sign from the background against which it is placed. Structural members bearing no sign copy shall not be included. Only one side of a freestanding or projecting double-faced sign shall be included in calculating surface area, providing that the two display surfaces are joined at an angle no greater than 60°. All sides of multi-faced signs, visible from any one street, shall be included in the calculation of surface area.

3. Allowed Signs

Signs whose subject matter relates exclusively to the premises on which they are located, or to products, accommodations, or activities on those premises, shall be allowed as follows:

3.1 *Number of signs*

3.1.1 Each building may have one *building sign* oriented to each street on which the premises have frontage, identifying the building as a whole or its predominant use.

3.1.2 In addition, there may be one *occupancy sign* and one *pedestrian sign* oriented to each street on which the premises have frontage, relating to each occupancy within the building. There may also be certain signs listed in Sections 3.3.2.2. and 4.

3.2 *Location of signs*

3.2.1 No sign shall overhang the public way to within 3 feet of the curb line. No sign, except on a marquee or canopy providing shelter, shall overhang more than 1/3 of the sidewalk width.

3.2.2 No sign shall extend more than 15 feet above record grade or more than 4 feet above the lowest point of the roof of the single story building with which it is associated, whichever is less restrictive, nor above the third floor of a multi-story building, except that motels, hotels, and other transient lodgings may display such signs up to 40 feet above record grade.

3.2.3 The top of *pedestrian signs* shall be no higher than 10 feet above the sidewalk.

3.2.4 For other than first floor occupants *occupancy signs* shall be located between the second and third floors.

*Not to be used without detailed legal review. The code assumes the existence of a Department of City Information, or equivalent set of functions within city government (see Chapter 3), and of a sufficient general or special enabling act or home rule constitutional provision to permit the city to adopt such a code.

3.3 *Sign Area*

3.3.1 With the exceptions below, the total surface area of all signs oriented to any street shall not exceed 15 times the square root of street frontage on that street, and the combined area of all signs shall not exceed 15 times the square root of the combined street frontage:

Street Frontage	Allowable Area
20 feet	67 sq. ft.
25	75
30	82
35	89
40	95
50	106
60	116
70	126
80	134
90	143
100	150
125	168
150	185
175	198
200	212
250	237
300	260
400	300
500	336

3.3.2 Sign Size Exceptions

3.3.2.1 No sign on a residence shall exceed 2 square feet.

3.3.2.2 The following are allowed in addition to signs as limited by Sections 3.1 and 3.3.1 above:

a Names of buildings, date of erection, monumental citations, and commemorative tablets up to 10 sq. ft. in area, when made a permanent and integral part of the building.

b Building directories, up to 20 sq. ft. in area if located outside.

c Educational signs of up to 20 sq. ft., providing bulletin or poster display space, identifying or explaining local history or processes going on out of sight within the building, meeting letter size and location requirements for pedestrian signs, if approved by the Department of City Information. *Establishments displaying such signs are, in addition, allowed a 20% increase in size and letter height of building and occupancy signs.*

d Traffic control and guidance signs, in conformance with public traffic sign standards, but located on private property, and orientational signs up to 2 sq. ft. in area, displayed for purposes of direction or convenience, including signs identifying rest rooms, freight entrances, and the like.

3.3.3 Permanent signs on the surface of or inside display windows shall cover no more than 10% of the display window area.

3.4 *Lettering Size*

3.4.1 *Building Signs* shall not employ letters exceeding 8 inches in height in Residence Districts as defined in the Zoning Ordinance, or 18 inches in height elsewhere.

3.4.2 *Occupancy Signs* shall not employ letters exceeding 8 inches in height.

3.4.3 *Pedestrian Signs* shall not employ letters exceeding 3 inches in height.

3.5 *Illumination*

3.5.1 Signs shall be illuminated only by steady, stationary, shielded light sources directed solely at the sign, or internal to it, without causing glare for motorists, pedestrians, or neighboring premises.

3.5.2 Illuminated signs, including neon signs, shall not produce more than one foot-candle of illumination 4 feet from the sign.

3.5.3 Signs shall not be illuminated between the hours of 11:00 p.m. and 7:00 a.m. unless related to an establishment operating during those hours.

3.5.4 All permanent outdoor lights such as those used for area lighting or building floodlighting shall be steady, stationary, shielded sources directed so as to avoid causing glare for motorists, pedestrians, or neighboring premises. The marginal increase in light, as measured at any property line other than a street line, shall not exceed one foot-candle.

3.6 *Temporary signs*

The following signs are allowed for a period up to one year without a permit.

3.6.1 Construction signs: one unlighted sign of up to 20 square feet identifying parties involved in construction on the premises where the sign is located; one illuminated sign of up to 40 square feet identifying the owner's name and the activity for which the building is intended and describing the construction process, but not including the advertisement of any product. These signs must be removed within 14 days after the beginning of the intended activity.

3.6.2 Real estate signs: one unlighted sign of up to 20 square feet pertaining to the sale, rental, or lease of the premises on which the sign is displayed, to be removed within 14 days after sale, rental or lease.

3.6.3 Event signs: unlighted signs of up to 32 square feet displayed on private property and limited to one per each premise, announcing a campaign, drive or event of a political, civic, philanthropic, educational or religious organization, to be removed within 14 days after the event.

3.6.4 Display window signs: signs on the surface of or inside display windows, lighted only by building illumination and covering no more than 20% of the display window area.

4. Required Signs

The following are required:

4.1 The name and street address of any non-residential building and the names of all current occupancies of the building must be identified on or legible from the exterior of the building.

4.2 Off-street parking facilities for 10 or more cars must be identified by a sign displaying the letter "P" in a size between 8 and 18 inches high, and a directional arrow indicating ingress. Such a sign may also identify the building (or its principal occupant) to which the parking is accessory in letters not to exceed 8 inches in height.

5. Prohibited Devices

5.1 No sign or light shall move, flash, or make noise. (Indicators of time or temperature may move.)

5.2 Colored lights and illuminated signs employing colors in use in traffic signal lights are prohibited within view of any signalized intersection.

5.3 Any imitation of official traffic signs or signals and the use of such words as "stop," "look," "danger," "go slow," "caution," or "warning" are prohibited.

5.4 Fluorescent colors in the yellow to red spectrum are prohibited.

6. Exceptional Signs

In certain areas (within General Information Districts) designated by the Department of City Information and approved by the City Council, signs larger, brighter, more numerous, or located elsewhere than those allowed in Section 3, or signs whose subject matter does not relate to the premises on which they are located, may be allowed when so located and controlled that they will not constitute a traffic hazard or conflict with other environmental values.

Regulations in these designated areas will necessarily vary from area to area and city to city and cannot be dealt with in this outline. (For an alternative set of rules for such exceptional signs, see Chapter 5, "Advertising Channel.")

7. Non-Conforming Conditions

Signs and lights shall be made to conform to the requirements of this Code within the following periods of its effective date:

Violation of Sections **5** and **3.6**: *within 60 days*

Violation of Sections **3.1**, **3.2**.1, **3.2**.2, **3.3**.1, **3.4**, **3.5**, or **4**: *within one year.*

Violation of any other Section: *within three years.*

8. Administration

8.1 No sign, except those specifically exempted by this ordinance, shall be erected without a permit issued by the city building official, application for which shall be accompanied by such scale drawings, photographs, and other information as the building official may require. All signs shall display a tag supplied by the building official as evidence of the permit.

8.2 Fees for sign permits shall be as fixed from time to time by the city council.

8.3 A city-wide inspection shall be carried out upon enactment of this code and every two years thereafter by the Department of City Information Inspector or a city building official to determine compliance with this code and the structural provisions of the building code. Every sign owner shall pay an inspection fee as determined by the city council to defray expenses connected with inspection by the first day of May of each inspection year.

8.4 Non-conforming signs shall be removed by their owner within 10 days of the period set forth in Section 7, or else the building official shall cause their removal at the expense of the owner.

8.5 Appeals may be made to the Zoning Board of Appeals (or equivalent) by the same rights and procedures governing other zoning appeals. Appeals shall be reviewed by the Department of City Information which shall advise the Board of its findings.

APPENDIX FOUR

Field Analysis

GENERAL PROCEDURE

Field analyses were done to identify and describe significant problems and potentials of existing signs and lights. This information helped to: 1. determine the types and locations of specific improvements needed; 2. formulate city-wide and local-area policies for signs and lights; and 3. identify the problems which need additional design and research investigation.

Two types of analysis were done: Some areas were generally analyzed, with a view to developing prototype design solutions; in two areas selected for demonstration of experimental solutions to sign and light problems, detailed inventories were done. This appendix describes the general analysis method and reproduces one example analysis in full.

The Selection of Areas for the Field Analyses
The field analysis areas illustrate typical sign and light problems and potentials of American cities. Each area has a different class of problems and potentials, with a minimum of overlap.

Areas selected for possible prototype design solutions were:

1 *Central Boston "Spine" Zone: Boylston Street to Washington Street to Waterfront:* The public and private signing and lighting in this critical area need improvement. Public lighting is especially inadequate and private signs and lights as well frequently fail to inform about the diverse places and activities which exist along this route. Potentials of the area relate principally to strengthening the various aspects of its diverse character.

2 *Brighton Avenue, near Harvard Street:* This area represents one of the most typical for private signing problems — a commercial strip where private signs compete with each other to produce a disordered and confusing streetscape. The analysis attempted to identify particularly severe problems which require attention in private sign policy.

3 *Charles Rotary, at Storrow Drive:* Charles Rotary is both an entrance to the city and a typical "confusion node." An expressway meets city streets; there is conflict between pedestrian and automobile usage; it is also an important transit stop. This jumble of uses has created severe information problems, leading to driver anxiety and hazards which might be resolved by improved graphics and lighting.

4 *Freedom Trail:* Boston's Freedom Trail is a marked pedestrian route that conveys information about the history of the city — mostly buildings and monuments. Studies of this trail from the user's point of view indicate many areas of potential improvement of signs and, especially, of lighting. It is also possible that the trail could be extended to cover parts of the redeveloped Boston waterfront.

The following four areas selected for demonstration projects were studied in great detail; complete inventories were made of the existing signs and lights in each area:

1 *Park Square:* An area close to downtown shopping, transportation, offices, hotels, and entertainment. It suffers from traffic confusion, supplies no information for pedestrians, and lacks identity.

2 *Dewey Square:* An extremely confusing, major intersection. It requires quick decisions by the motorist; it is the meeting point of a number of city streets and an expressway entrance and exit.

3 *Copley Square:* A major downtown area with a number of important and imposing buildings, unnoticeable at night because they are not illuminated.

4 *Public Garden:* An important recreation area in the heart of Boston. Like most public parks, it has poor nighttime lighting and little nighttime use.

Criteria of the Analyses
A major step in field analysis was the formulation of criteria for evaluating the performance of city signs and lights. Signs and lights are viewed as systems in the public environment which inform people about aspects of the city — its activities, people, places, anatomy, products, history, and future. Performance criteria are specified in detail in Chapter 3 and listed here along with the corresponding types of analysis:

1. *Reduce overload* — identify points or areas of extreme competition for the observer's attention, especially where he must make critical driving decisions.
2. *Respect privacy* — identify cases of violation of privacy of individuals or groups.
3. *Clarify control information* — identify points or areas of confusion in traffic control and potentials for clarification.
4. *Orient in time and space* — analyze problems and potentials in identifying locations in space and time and in way-finding.
5. *Express city functions* — evaluate the extent to which signs and lights inform people of local activities, products, and processes.
6. *Encourage diverse and responsive communication* — analyze the range and expression of social diversity in a place or area and the degree to which individuals and groups can send and control messages.
7. *Seize opportunities for education* — identify special opportunity areas for educating people about the environment, its structure, function, history, or possible future development.
8. *Establish priorities* — evaluate the apparent priorities among various types of information presented by means of signs and lights.

Structure of the Analyses
The analyses normally included:

1. *Summary observations, both day and nighttime.*
2. *Activities:*
   a. local activity
   b. flow patterns
   c. major destinations/purposes of persons in the area
3. *Form:*
   a. spatial form
   b. signs
   c. lighting
4. *Problems and potentials of signing and lighting*
5. *Initial proposals for signs and lights*
6. *Historic places and events in the area (where applicable)*
7. *Identification of various groups using the area (only in the demonstration areas)*

CHARLES ROTARY EXAMPLE

Analysis of an Area for Development of Prototype Design Solutions

There are many reasons for studying Charles Rotary:
1 It is a major entry into Boston from Cambridge (via the Longfellow Bridge).
2 It is a critical connection between two of Boston's most interesting and most visited areas, Beacon Hill and Government Center.
3 It is a major interchange for automobiles entering and exiting the city via Boston's riverfront artery, Storrow Drive.
4 It poses the problem of conflict between pedestrian access to public transportation (the Charles MBTA Station) and private transportation (automobiles) at an important node.

General Observations

Day

1. Orientation signs for pedestrians and motorists are inadequate; they are incomplete, unclear, hard to see, and are not located far enough in advance of decision points.
2. Automobile paths through the rotary are confusing.
3. The MBTA station is a visual barrier to comprehending the structure of the rotary.
4. The facade and underside of the MBTA station and tracks are oppressive.
5. Pedestrian overpasses are unpleasant to look at and to use.
6. Private signs around the rotary and on Cambridge Street are disorganized and distracting to motorists.
7. Space around the rotary is chaotic.

Night

All points of the daytime analysis apply at night also, plus these additional points:

1. The rotary and station are very dark and ominous.
2. Signs are hard to see.
3. Cambridge Street is very spottily lit.
4. There is the "normal" unpleasant color of mercury vapor lamps.
5. Traffic signals and lighting along the paths are confusing; the correct route is difficult to find.
6. Nearby visible landmarks — Massachusetts General Hospital, Museum of Science, Longfellow Bridge, Charles Station — are poorly lit.
7. Private signs around the rotary are dominant, distracting, and ugly.

Activity Analysis

On the edges of the rotary are the Suffolk County Jail, several shops, including a drug store, a liquor store, a drive-in sandwich shop, a small gasoline station, and a parking lot. Most pedestrians enter or exit the rotary by means of overpasses from the elevated Charles MBTA Station which is situated in the center.

The rotary is at the foot of Beacon Hill whose main street, Charles Street, enters from the east. On the west lies the Charles River and entrances from the Longfellow Bridge and Storrow Drive. The rotary is bounded on the northwest by the Massachusetts General Hospital and the West End

Redevelopment Project. Cambridge Street, which leads to Government Center, enters the rotary from the east.

Traffic flow patterns and destinations can be seen in the diagrams. The flow of traffic through the rotary is nearly continuous and very heavy at rush hours. Pedestrians, too, use the rotary throughout the day, though in smaller numbers than motorists.

Form Analysis

The rotary is a no-man's land where people, whether drivers or pedestrians, are bound to be anxious and confused. The area through which the traffic moves is a complex mass of islands and passages in which no one path is clear. The MBTA station, tracks, and columns act as visual barriers across and around the roadway. This acute lack of access view necessitates effective guide signing.

The approaches to the rotary vary in character. On Charles Street, four-story brick buildings crowd close to the edge of the sidewalk on both sides. The street is not narrow — there are three lanes of traffic plus two of parking — yet its feeling of order, density, and smallness of scale is in marked contrast to the rotary.

Compared to Charles Street, Cambridge Street is very open. It is much wider — there are four moving lanes, two in each direction divided by a central island. The street is lined by numerous gasoline stations and parking lots, interspersed with buildings, so that spaces are irregular and unpredictable.

From the Longfellow Bridge approach, on the opposite side, one funnels down into the rotary — blindly, because of the station. The rise at the entrance to the Longfellow Bridge also withholds later views of MIT high-rise buildings and the river.

The exit from Storrow Drive is a simple, slowly curving ramp, but the entrance to the drive on the north side of the rotary is confusing since the driver must go in nearly the opposite direction from that in which he eventually joins the drive.

Upper Charles Street is hardly visible from the rotary, due to its sharp curve to the right which is hidden by the jail wall. From the rotary, it appears as a funnel-like enclosure.

All the pedestrian overpasses, both from the station and to the embankment, have interesting views. For instance, on the north side pedestrians look to the Museum of Science and the Sonesta Hotel, Massachusetts General Hospital, the jail, up Cambridge Street to Government Center, and across the embankment fields to the Charles River. The sky is above, the traffic below.

Signing Problems

A pedestrian in Charles Station must choose between two exits, marked only as:

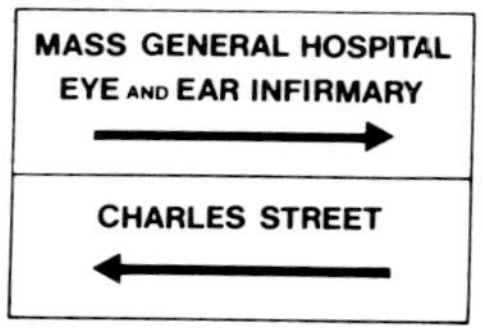

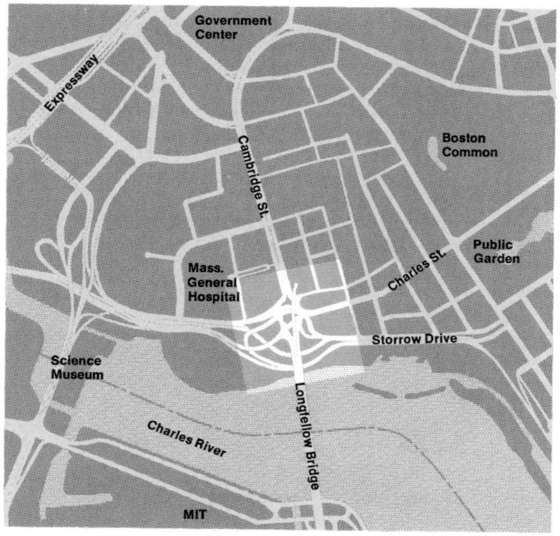

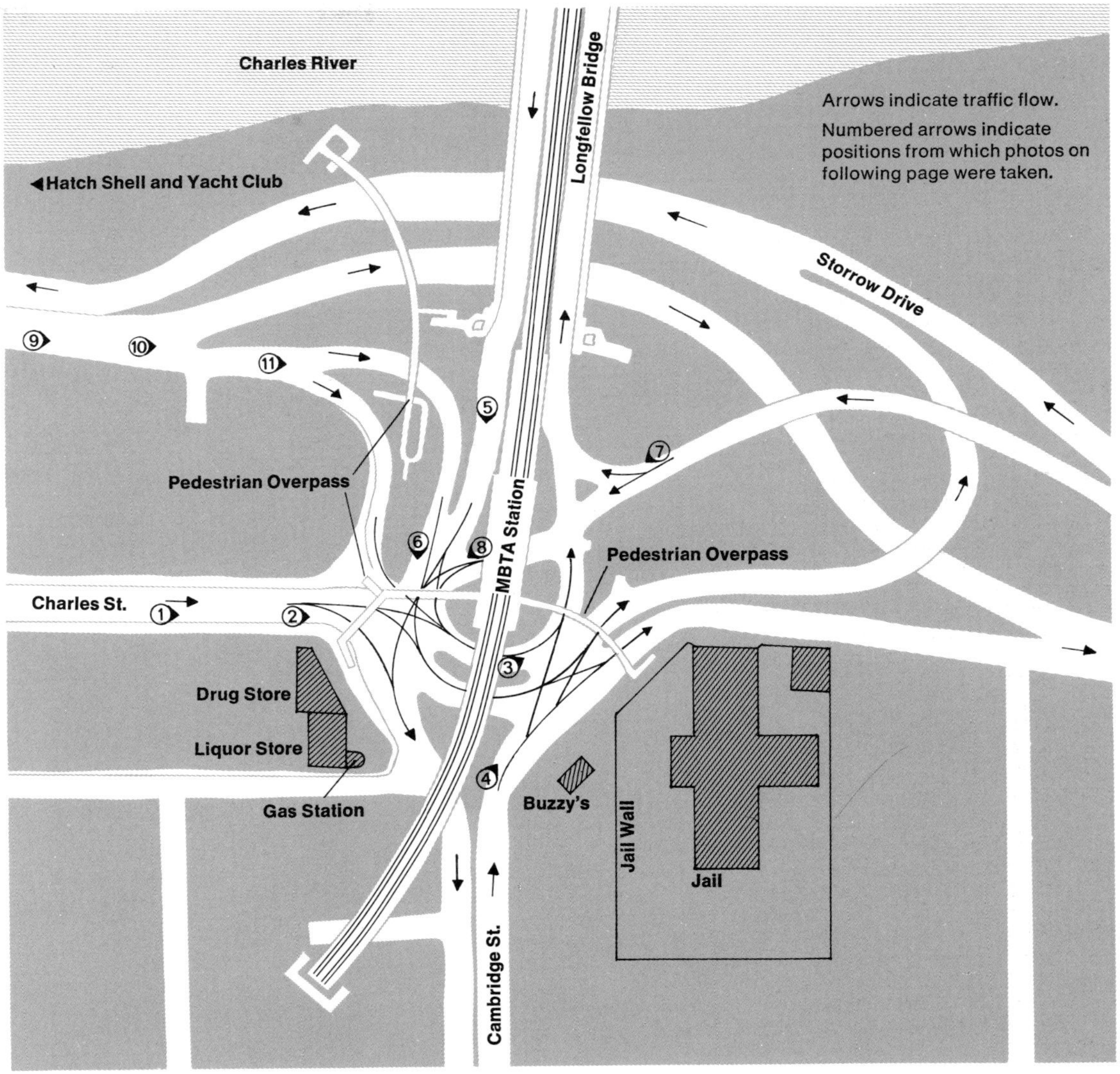
Charles River
Longfellow Bridge
Arrows indicate traffic flow.
Numbered arrows indicate positions from which photos on following page were taken.
Hatch Shell and Yacht Club
Storrow Drive
Pedestrian Overpass
MBTA Station
Pedestrian Overpass
Charles St.
Drug Store
Liquor Store
Gas Station
Buzzy's
Jail Wall
Jail
Cambridge St.

The information is both insufficient and misleading. Other major pedestrian destinations are not indicated: the Hatch Memorial Shell and the Charles River Shopping Plaza, to name two. (The third overpass, which leads from upper Charles Street *specifically* to the embankment and the Shell, has no signing at all.) Charles Street, in fact, is on both sides of the rotary: at Beacon Hill and at the Massachusetts General Hospital. Once the pedestrian has chosen his route, there is no further signing on the ramps or at their bases.

For pedestrians approaching the intersection, trying to get to the MBTA station, there is no sign to show the name of the station or even that the structure is an MBTA station. There are no signs that say the pedestrian can cross the entire intersection by following the ramps through the station and out.

Signing for motorists is more extensive, but is also inadequate, inconsistent, and in one instance, incorrect. With the aid of photographic sequences, the various auto paths can be traced to find the problem areas.

From Charles Street — Motorists entering the rotary from Charles Street first see a set of overhead signs designating two lanes: C28/Cambridge/Memorial Drive, and C1-C9/Mystic Bridge/Callahan Tunnel (photo 1). There is no sign to indicate the third direction to Cambridge Street and Government Center. There is no mention of Storrow Drive, which is an important destination for cars entering from Charles Street.

The next set of signs guides drivers under the MBTA tracks, repeating the two above (photo 2). There is still no overhead sign for Government Center or Cambridge Street Two low-mounted signs ambiguously indicate the continuation of Charles Street, another mentions the Mystic Bridge again, but also Somerville, Storrow Drive, Government Center, and the Hospital — all too late.

The next set of signs, on the other side of the tracks, is at one of the most difficult points in the rotary sequence. Overhead, from left to right, the signs read: Cambridge, Memorial Drive; and C1-C9-C28, Storrow Drive. At the same place, other low-mounted signs with smaller lettering read C1-C9-C28S/Storrow Drive; C1-C9-C28N/Mystic Bridge; and, in still smaller letters, Museum of Science (photo 3). Routes C1-C9 and C28 here appear on the same sign and indicate the same road, rather than indicating separate paths. Here too, is the first overhead sign to say Storrow Drive. There is no follow-up overhead sign for Callahan Tunnel-Mystic Bridge, though there is adequate space to do so; in fact, there is no more mention of the Callahan Tunnel at all. At its present scale, the Museum of Science sign is almost unreadable.

From Cambridge Street — Motorists entering the intersection from Cambridge Street first see a set of low-mounted signs which read, from left to right: Mystic Bridge/Callahan Tunnel; C28/Storrow Drive/Cambridge; and Mass. Turnpike (the only mention of the Pike) (photo 4). Motorists then proceed to the last set of overhead signs described above, where they are faced with a right-left reversal of these destinations.

1

2

3

4

5

6

7

8

9

10

11

From Longfellow Bridge — On entering the rotary from the bridge, there are no guide signs until part way around where the set of signs on and about the overhead tracks becomes visible (the second set in the Charles Street sequence) (photos 5 & 6). It is extremely difficult for drivers to find the correct lane, for the decision has to be made before the information is given. They do not even have a general view of the alternatives, since the MBTA station and tracks block the view to the left. As they emerge from under the tracks, drivers experience the same signing problems as those entering from Charles Street.

From C1-C9, Storrow Drive, Southbound Exit — Motorists going to Cambridge can make a right turn over the bridge and never enter the rotary at all. This path is marked Cambridge/Memorial Drive. The only other sign reads Government Center/Hospitals (photo 7). As a driver proceeds under the station, he sees the same sign with a left-pointing arrow (photo 8). At this point his path is ambiguous; the left turn leads to a variety of places. He now faces the same difficulties as drivers entering from the Longfellow Bridge.

From C1-C9, Storrow Drive, Northbound Exit — There are presently no overhead signs on Storrow Drive for rotary destinations (photo 9). At a point where the decision must already have been made, there are signs labeled Airport, Museum of Science, Fitzgerald Expressway, and Callahan Tunnel, telling motorists to remain on Storrow Drive. The first two are far too small for cars traveling at a rapid speed. A "Government Center" and a "Charles Street" sign mark the exit to the rotary, though the actual desinations are several (photo 10). Not far ahead lies another fork, this time separating the cars to Government Center and Hospitals from those to Cambridge and Memorial Drive (photo 11). These signs, too, come too late. From observation, the confusion rate here is high.

Lighting Problems and Potentials

Street lights provide mediocre illumination of the rotary for drivers and pedestrians; their total lack of relation to movement patterns adds to the general confusion by the scatter of glaring lights. The dark menacing structures which border and fill the rotary — the jail, the bridge, the MBTA station, the pedestrian overpasses, and the MBTA overhead tracks — could all be clarified and improved through lighting. In addition, the guide signs are poorly lit, if at all, and could easily be improved.

At night, the movement of cars dominates the rotary. There is a minor pedestrian activity center in front of the cluster of stores (a brightly lit all-night pharmacy, a liquor store, and a Gulf Station) between Charles and Cambridge Streets. Pedestrians and some motorists use "Buzzy's," a sandwich shop with a huge illuminated sign at the foot of the jail wall.

From Cambridge Street — Cambridge Street is now lit spottily so that it has no more identity by night than by day. the Massachusetts General Hospital has a moderate-sized lighted sign; it should have a much better lighted, more clearly defined entryway.

From Longfellow Bridge — As one approaches the rotary from the Longfellow Bridge, there is a clear view of the illuminated towers of Government Center, which disappear as one enters the confusion of the rotary. The route itself would be clarified if the side walls of the MBTA station were lit, perhaps by down-lighting from above. The bridge itself could be made more dramatic by lighting its towers.
From Charles Street — With the exception of one brightly lit liquor store, the section of Charles Street near the rotary is quite dark. At the rotary, the Cambridge Street direction is hidden by the dark overhead MBTA tracks and their supports. The MBTA station and its adjoining pedestrian overpasses look dark and uninviting. Buzzy's across the intersection is the dominant lighted object. The traffic signal lights, changing from red to yellow to green, seem to change the entire nature of the intersection.
From Storrow Drive entrances and exits — Entering Charles Rotary from Northbound Storrow Drive, the roadway is dimly lit and the signs difficult to read. Both the entry and exit on the north side of the rotary are comparatively well lit, but the large parking lot between these two ramps is also brightly lit, which confuses its entrance with the roadways. Lighting in the parking lot could be improved by using a scheme which is entirely different from that which lights the roadway.

Initial Proposals
Although the major street configurations will not be changed in the near future, changes in signs and lights at the rotary can clarify the paths through it, guide the pedestrian or motorist to his destination with less confusion, and generally improve the place.

1 *Guide signing*
a. All Scollay Square signs should be replaced with Government Center signs.
b. A sign for Government Center should be included to the right of the C1-C9, etc., sign on the south side of the overhead MBTA tracks.
c. An overhead Mystic Bridge/Callahan Tunnel/Expressway sign should be added on the south side of the northeast pedestrian overpass.
d. All Logan Airport, Museum of Science, and Mass. Turnpike signs should be larger and more conspicuous, and there should be more of them.
e. Logan Airport signs and/or symbols should always appear with signs for Callahan Tunnel.
f. A set of signs should be placed on the west side of the south pedestrian overpass; these signs should read from left to right: Cambridge; Mystic Bridge/Callahan Tunnel/Logan Airport; and Government Center/Cambridge Street.
g. A set of signs should be placed on the north side of the west overhead MBTA tracks; from left to right they should read: Charles Street, and Cambridge Street/Government Center/Hospitals.
h. Drivers entering from Storrow Drive going north should see, before the fork, signs which read: bear left for Government Center/Cambridge Street; bear right for Charles Street.
i. Signs to Beacon Hill are needed.

2 *Pedestrian signing*
a. The MBTA station structure should be signed. If it were repainted as well, it could become an effective landmark.
b. Orientation signs within the MBTA station should include at least the Hatch Memorial Shell and the Charles River Shopping Plaza and Theater.
c. There should be signs at the base of all pedestrian overpasses, telling where they go.

3 *Other proposals*
a. The station should be opened up, glazed, and illuminated at night. This would improve it both for MBTA riders and people passing through the rotary.
b. The pedestrian overpasses might be covered by glass or plexiglass roofs. This would make them less windy and slippery as well as providing a feeling of safety.
c. The undersides of the MBTA tracks should be used to light the paths under it. This could be combined with low rail lighting which would emphasize the direction of movement.
d. Since the ground floor of the station is unused, when it is remodelled it could be raised on pylons to substantially improve traffic visibility.

APPENDIX FIVE

Information Center: Evaluative Studies

The Information Center was made up of seven brightly colored, balloon-topped kiosks located near Park Square, Boston. They displayed maps, films, and other relevant information about activities and points of interest in the Boston area. But the Information Center was designed to gather information as well as to give it. Responses of visitors to the Center were obtained in the following ways:

- Short Questionnaire Interviews
- Open-ended Interviews
- Tube Interviews
- Opinion Scale
- Unobtrusive Observations

General conclusions from these studies are in Chapter 6.

SHORT QUESTIONNAIRE INTERVIEWS

Purpose

Interviews were conducted to ascertain: 1) whether the respondent was visiting the Information Center for the first time, 2) if visitors would like to return, 3) if visitors would suggest that others visit the Center, 4) how people found out about the Center, 5) why they were in Boston and the Park Square area, 6) how long they stayed at the Center, and 7) the respondent's general attitude toward the Center.

Procedure

Seventy-nine people were interviewed during weekdays at the Information Center. Subjects were selected haphazardly and therefore cannot be said to represent the visitors as a whole. Data were collected in three ways using a printed questionnaire: either respondents filled out the questionnaire themselves, or an interviewer wrote down answers to the questions, or responses were tape-recorded by an interviewer.[1]

Data were obtained from each respondent regarding sex, age, occupation,[2] and place of residence (Table 1). However, no consistent differences in responses to the questions were attributable to these variables.

1. Data for the third group were obtained from Questions 1, 2, 3, 4, 5, 6, 19, 20, 22, 23, and 24 of the Open-ended Interview questionnaire. These are identical with the short questionnaire.
2. All social class distinctions in the field tests and evaluations were determined from the Hollingshed Scale of Occupational Prestige. See A. B. Hollingshed and F. C. Redlich, *Social Class and Mental Illness* (New York: John Wiley and Sons, 1958). The distinctions are intended to give some indication as to how various policies may affect different groups in the city.

Results

Of the 79 people interviewed, one-fourth had been to the Center before. Those who were coming back for a second visit said that they wanted to see more, that they wanted to show it to a friend, or just said that they liked it. About 80% of all respondents said they would like to come back to the Information Center, and gave such reasons as: wanting to see more, to get information, or because they considered the Center interesting. People who did not wish to come back gave as their reasons: all could be seen in one visit, the presentation was bad, or the atmosphere unpleasant. Ninety-seven percent of all respondents felt that others should visit the Information Center when they were in the Park Square area. The chief reason given was that there was good information for both tourists and residents. Even people who did not expect to return themselves recommended that others visit the Center.

Despite the fact that the opening of the Information Center was covered by major Boston newspapers, television and radio stations, only 11% of the respondents had heard about the Center from the mass media. Three-quarters of those interviewed had come upon the Information Center by chance. A few people had heard about the Center from friends or had seen it when it was being constructed and came back to see it when it was completed. Thus, it seems that appearance was the most effective factor in attracting visitors.

Most of the respondents (80%) were Boston residents, 13% were in Boston for business purposes, while another 6% were tourists. There were a variety of reasons given for being in Park Square, such as shopping, school, or sightseeing. Ten people, all residents of Boston, were there expressly to visit the Information Center.

The average length of time that people spent at the Information Center was 20 minutes.[3] Forty-eight percent of the respondents stayed 15 minutes or less and 52% of the respondents stayed between 15 and 50 minutes. The largest increment of people (24%) stayed between 5 and 10 minutes.

3. The average actual time spent at the Information Center was calculated by adding the average time that was already spent and the average additional length of time that the respondents indicated they would stay at the Center. Unfortunately, this data is complete for only 54 respondents, and therefore these percentages are based on a total (N) of 54.

TABLE 1: BREAKDOWN OF SAMPLE ACCORDING TO SEX, AGE, CLASS, AND PLACE OF RESIDENCE (Short Questionnaire Interview)

		N	%
SEX	Male	51	67
	Female	25	33
	Total	**76***	**100**
AGE	Under 35	40	73
	35 and over	15	27
	Total	**55****	**100**
CLASS	Lower and Lower Middle	16	20
	Middle and Upper Middle	47	60
	Student	16	20
	Total	**79**	**100**
PLACE OF RESIDENCE	Resident	63	80
	Tourist	5	6
	Business	10	13
	Other	1	1
	Total	**79**	**100**

* Sex of 3 respondents not recorded
** Age of 24 respondents not recorded

SHORT INTERVIEW QUESTIONNAIRE

1. Is this your first visit to the Information Center? _____Yes _____No

   If this is not your first visit, when were you here before?

   How long did you stay?

   Why did you come back?

2. Why are you in Park Square today?

3. Do you live in the Boston area? _____Yes _____No

   If you do not live in the Boston area, why are you here?

   _____Tourist _____Business trip
   _____Other. Please state: ___________________________

4. How did you find out about the Information Center?

   _____a. Heard about it from friends.
   _____b. Newspaper, television, radio.
   _____c. I came upon it by chance.

   If you checked "C" (that is, you came upon it by chance), where were you coming from when you saw the Information Center?

   _____a. Bus Terminal _____d. Common, Public Garden
   _____b. Statler _____e. Other. Please state where:
   _____c. Subway ___________________________

5. How much time have you spent at the Information Center?

   _____a. 5 minutes or less _____d. 15-20 minutes
   _____b. 5-10 minutes _____e. 20 minutes to a half hour
   _____c. 10-15 minutes _____f. over 30 minutes

6. Do you intend to stay any longer? _____Yes _____No

   If so, about how much longer?

7. Would you like to come back to the Information Center again? _____Yes _____No

   Why or why not?

8. Do you think people should come to see this when they're in Park Square?

   _____Yes _____No

   Why or why not?

9. What is your age? _____

10. What is your occupation? ___________________________

11. _____Male _____Female

ACTUAL LENGTH OF TIME AT INFORMATION CENTER

Minutes	N	%
0-5	6	11
5-10	13	24
10-15	7	13
15-20	6	11
20-30	9	17
30-40	7	13
40-50	6	11
Total	**54**	**100**

Each respondent's overall opinion of the Center was rated, based on the tone of the answers to the total interview. A 5-point scale, ranging from +2 (I like it very much) to —2 (I dislike it very much), was used. Ninety-two percent of respondents fell into one of the "liking" categories.

OPEN-ENDED INTERVIEWS

Purpose

The aim of this study was to learn how visitors responded to the Information Center as a source of information, as a useful part of the city, as technology, and aesthetically.

Procedure

The intent of these interviews was to obtain detailed, in-depth responses. The questionnaire served a double purpose. In part, it duplicated the short questionnaire interview form, and those questions were then used for that analysis. The rest of the questionnaire consisted of general, open-ended questions,[4] which were used in this analysis.

As in the first analysis, answers to the questions were analyzed in reference to four characteristics of the respondents: sex, age, social class, and familiarity with Boston (Table 1). Of the 41 respondents, 27 were males, 27 had lived in Boston more than two years, 21 were middle class, and 30 were under 35. The analysis by these variables did not, except in a few instances, reveal any consistent differences.

4. *Open-ended* — "having no fixed set of alternative replies and permitting spontaneous and unguided responses for expression (as of attitudes, opinions and intent)," *Webster's Third New International Dictionary.*

TABLE 1: BREAKDOWN OF SAMPLE ACCORDING TO SEX, AGE, CLASS, AND FAMILIARITY WITH BOSTON
(Open-ended Interviews)

		N	%
SEX	Male	27	73
	Female	10	27
	Total	**37***	**100**
AGE	Under 35	30	73
	35 and over	11	27
	Total	**41**	**100**
CLASS	Lower and Lower Middle	10	25
	Middle and Upper Middle	21	50
	Student	10	25
	Total	**41**	**100**
FAMILIARITY WITH BOSTON	Familiar	27	66
	Unfamiliar	14	34
	Total	**41**	**100**

* Four interviews were conducted with groups of males and females

OPEN-ENDED INTERVIEW

*1. Is this your first visit to the Information Center?
*2. How did you find out about it?
*3. How much time have you spent here today?
*4. Do you intend to stay any longer?
*5. Would you like to come back to the Information Center again?
*6. Do you think this is something people should come to see when they're in the area?
7. What kinds of people would you recommend this Information Center for? For whom do you think it would be helpful? [Do you think this is good for people who are familiar with Boston as well as strangers?] Why?
8a. Do you think information centers similar to this one could be put up in any other parts of the city? [If so: Where?]
8b. Do you think this Center is in a good location?
9. What do you think of the appearance of the Information Center? Is there any aspect in particular which you like or dislike [colors, balloons, pavement markings]?
10. Have you learned anything new about Boston from any of the information here? [If so: What?]
11. What do you think about the kinds of information offered and the different ways in which they are presented (i.e., slides, maps, directories, etc.)?
12. Is there anything in the Information Center which you think should be improved? Anything you think is unnecessary? Anything you think should be included which is not now here? Any suggestion at all for improvement?
16. How many of the different tubes have you looked at?
17. Which tube did you like best? Why?
18. Which tube did you like least [least interesting, least effective]? Why?
*19. Why are you in the Park Square area today?
*20. Do you live in the Boston area?
21. If so, how many years have you been living here? OR: Are you familiar with Boston? Finally, might I ask your age and occupation?
**22. Age
**23. Occupation
**24. Sex

* Denotes questions which comprise the short questionnaire interview.
** Denotes questions which were used in both analyses.

Results

Eighty-seven percent of the respondents familiar with Boston (residents for more than two years) and 68% of those unfamiliar with Boston felt that similar information centers should be constructed in other parts of the city. Suggested locations were the Boston Common, Copley Square, Kenmore Square, the Prudential area, the downtown shopping area, Government Center, the South End, and Roxbury.

Thirty-one of the 41 respondents thought that the Information Center was in a good location. Of these, 27 said it was good because there were many people in the Park Square area. Others felt Park Square was appropriate because of its reputation as a major tourist area and its proximity to bus and MBTA lines. Respondents who did not think that the Information Center was in a good location felt that the area was not central and that not enough people lived there.

Appearance: Most of the respondents (83%) liked the appearance of the Information Center. When asked what attracted them, many said it was the balloons. Others who said they liked the appearance gave general answers such as, "I like it," and "The colors are nice." Only seven respondents said they did not like the appearance, mainly because it was "gaudy."

Information value: Thirteen of the 39 respondents who answered the question, "Have you learned anything new about Boston from any of the information here?" said they had. No one display was especially successful as an information source. Twenty-six respondents said they did not learn anything new. Typical explanations included: "I know the city," "I haven't been here [at the Center] long enough," "I haven't learned anything new yet, but I think I could." As a general rule, familiarity with the city did not make any difference — the Information Center was almost as informative for people familiar with Boston as for people who were not familiar with the city. Another interesting finding is that fewer working and middle-class people learned new things than students (50% of the students did learn new things, as opposed to 32% of the middle-class people and only 20% of the working-class people).

Criticism: Thirty-two percent of the respondents were dissatisfied in one way or another with the information offered or the way in which it was presented. About 60% said it was good. Several commented that more information was necessary and that the presentation was repetitive. Slightly more than one-third of the males were critical of the information while only 18% of the females expressed criticism. Also, one-third of the middle-class people and one-third of the students were critical, while only 23% of the working-class people had criticisms.

Question 12 invited criticisms of the Center as a whole. Sixty-one percent of the responses were suggestions for improvements or dealt with weaknesses in the Center. The main criticism was that the exhibit, as a whole, was confusing. Other criticisms were that it was too loud, too crowded, failure-prone, and not protected from vandalism and bad weather conditions. Middle-class people under 35 were more likely to have at least one criticism (80%) than were students (50%), working-class people (30%), and older people (10%). People who were not familiar with Boston were more critical of the Information Center than those who were familiar with the city.

Popularity of various tubes: Question 17 asked which tube was liked most. The question/answer machine which most directly involved the user was the most popular display, "most liked" by 79% of the respondents. The films, maps, and slides were the three next most popular displays. Males liked the maps and the films more than females did. Nearly half of the students liked the question/answer machine best, while almost one-third of the working-class respondents liked the films best.

Over half of the 30 people who answered question 18, "Which tube did you like least," either said they liked them all or couldn't say. Although the frequencies in all the other categories are too low to be meaningful, it is interesting to note that no one disliked the question/answer machine. In addition, several other visitors to the Information Center were asked specific questions concerning the tubes that they had examined (see Tube Interviews report).

Overall degree of favorableness: Each respondent's overall degree of favorableness towards the Information Center was rated by the interviewer on a five-point scale (Very Favorable, Favorable, Neutral, Unfavorable, Very Unfavorable). The basis for this rating was the attitude the respondent conveyed in the entire interview. The percentage of people liking the Information Center as a whole is higher than the favorableness expressed in answers to various specific questions. (In many cases people who were generally favorable criticized particular aspects.) Sixty-three percent of the interviews conveyed a Very Favorable impression. When the first and last pairs of categories are combined so that the scale becomes three-point (Favorable, Neutral, Unfavorable), a strong positive opinion of the Information Center is observed:

	N	%
Favorable	37	90%
Neutral	0	—
Unfavorable	4	10%
TOTAL	41	100%

Of the four people who did not like the Information Center, all were male, under 35, and three were students.

Comments from Open-ended Interviews

Responses to questions 7 through 12 of the open-ended interviews were tape-recorded. A proportionate sample of positive and negative comments are included for each of these questions.

Question 7: Good for what kinds of people?

People who aren't used to something like this. I think it's more entertaining for what it is than for what it tells.

For tourists, for people who are passing through. I think it'd be fun to bring the kids here.

It's fun for people who know the city already.

I think it'd probably attract everybody. I'm new in the city and I'm amazed about how many people who actually live here who don't really know the city. I find that I know more about it, having been here only a year and a half than people who have lived here a long time. Yes, it'd be just as good for the natives, really.

Tourists, I'd say. I think tourists, because not being a native of Boston this would be quite appealing to me and that's why when my family comes up from the South this is one of the first places we'll probably come.

Business people, people that are walkin' in the streets.

Anyone who has time, to come on his lunch hour or something, or somebody who's just looking around Boston. It's an interesting attraction, something you don't see too often.

Especially strangers. This would help them out a lot. I think it's a wonderful thing. [Also good for natives] because a lot of people who come from Boston don't know too much about Boston. If they'd come here it'd help them out a lot, because they have everything here.

Question 8a: More information centers in other parts of city?

Yeh, I think they help people a great deal.

They really should. I think over on the Common someplace over there nearer the shopping centers.

It might be a good idea. It'd be nice to know how to have access to other sights of interest.

Sure. The middle of Roxbury — anything would brighten up that place.

I suppose around Park St. station. It'd be interesting, if there was a place for it, in Logan Airport. There's hardly any one place where everybody comes together in Logan, though. Maybe miniature stations like this around some of the different crosswalks in Logan, where people get off the airplanes.

I think it'd be an interesting sort of thing. . . . It's just an interesting type thing. . . . I never come in this area too often. I just happened to stumble into it. I think up on Boylston St. would be better, maybe over in Kenmore Square; somewhere in Cambridge, maybe Harvard Square.

Question 8b: Is this a good location?

Yeah, all the bus terminals are right around, so it's a good location.

From the population here, I would say yes.

Yes, I think it's very good. It's right in the middle of everything.

Very good location. Right in the center of Boston.

This is sort of a central part of the city, there are a lot of out-of-town people. It would be something that Bostonians would come to see. But I think they'd pale if they were everyplace.

For lack of knowledge of any other good place, I would say that it is good.

Yeah, it's in a great location because the hotels are there and the MTA is over there and a lot of people work around here.

Question 9: Appearance? (positive)

Great. It's the best. How can you top it? It's beautiful. It's eye-catching and comes across well. It shows definite imagination.

Oh, I think it's very avant-garde. I think it's tremendous. I like the design very much. In some sense, it's very pop art in a way, and it's very apropos for this generation. I like the design very much — the shape and form.

That's what drew me to it, the appearance of the center — the big white balloons and the shiny silver paper.

It's nice. There's nothin' I don't like. It's all set up nice.

It looks kinda freakish at first. I thought something landed here during the night, I wondered what it was all about. It is nice though. It draws a lot of attention, something like this. Otherwise you'd walk right by it. You'd think it was a telephone booth or something! I think the whole thing is good. I like the set up. It's very nice.

It's attractive enough to attract people. That's what you want. That's what it will do.

Well, it's eye-catching. It sort of looks like a miniature Expo.

That's another reason I come over, wonderin' what the big balloons were there. It's attractive, it attracts people, it attracted me, anyway. Average people go for it. It don't have to be neat no more, just as long as it's put up and works.

It's a lot nicer than the rest of the city. There's nothing really particularly great about it. It's just sort of ordinary, but compared to the buildings around it which are bad . . .

For the purpose of art, it's great, but it's also environmental art. It completely surrounds you. It gets you into the entire feeling of Boston . . .

Question 9: Appearance? (negative)

It looks good, except I noticed that already today things are looking a little bit worn.

I think it's extremely gaudy and unnecessarily so. Now I suppose one can locate it from a distance because of the balloons, but the idea of being mod and "with it man" and "I dig it" like the other fellow you interviewed here said is ridiculous.

I think maybe some of the exhibits could be arranged so that maybe more people could see.

It's weird. It's strange. I don't know. In a way, it looks like it's make-believe.

Question 10: Learned anything new? (positive)

Yes, I could learn new things about the city, definitely.

We could. We haven't seen it all yet. If you spent a little time here you could learn a lot. You have to kinda push through the crowds to get to everything.

I know most of it. But it's still interesting.

I did. I learned about the cruises around the island, the schedule.

Well, I got a few of those cards [Question and Answer] to find out about the history of the city and how to get to Martha's Vineyard by boat.

I learned about the Boston symphony from the question and answer machine.

Well, I'm an old Bostonian. I learned how the name was formed, and I learned a few other things.

The only new type thing is just sort of looking at the streets. I found out where Chinatown was. I've heard people talk about where it was, but I never saw it clearly labeled.

Yes, I hate to admit it, but I learned something about the North End by just looking at these maps here.

Question 10: Learned anything new? (negative)

No, not really.

Well, actually I don't think so because I've been aware of things in the city. Being new here I explored the city already. As to the information here, I know most of it. But it's still interesting.

No, but I know the city pretty well. I'm above average people, because I have to know the city because I do deliveries around the city and I've been in Boston quite a while.

Question 11: Information presentation (positive)

I'd have to really cautiously say that from what I can see in the short time I've been here that it's very informative. I think that all of these things here have some aspect of it that's very helpful, depending on what you're looking for.

I didn't see any [information] that was superfluous. To me it all seemed important — to someone or another, perhaps not to me or to you.

I think just about any problem you have about where to go, you can find out.

Well, I've seen all these kinds of information in various things like BAD [Boston after Dark], these tourist things in various hotels and stuff. [This is] much more interesting, especially for illiterates.

Oh, it's presented real good. You got your phone, you got your televisions, you got your telegraph or whatever it is over there. It's presented in a good way.

Question 11: Information presentation (negative)

You have the human element to reckon with, because this is out of paper and has been for some time [Q & A machine]. I work in the Education Department in New York State and we find the computers break down every day and you need the human element.

I would suggest maybe a referral, a list of other social service agencies and things like other information centers that would give more kinds of direct counseling and tell people exactly what they're looking for. . . . There might possibly be a referral like "if you don't find an answer here, try such-and-such." Some centers are open and can give you a personal twist whereas the machine is programmed.

You could have some more information, sure.

Well, I think what's there is good [information]. But I think for instance about what's going on in Boston, there isn't enough of that. And there should be perhaps a way of finding out about movies and theaters. I don't know if it could be done but that would be very helpful. Perhaps if you could have something like movie schedules and so forth that would be helpful.

I think there's a definite need for a directory, a street directory. One of the drums here listing all the streets in alphabetical order and giving the grid coordinate. This is the major thing this area should provide, that is, direction. If someone was looking for a shop or something and they don't really know the area, if there were grid coordinates giving the numbering, I think that would be helpful.

Question 12: General criticism

The music is a little loud, but it may draw people to it. That's about the only thing.

I would like to get to some of the stores and I have no idea what time it is. That's what you need, a clock, in the center of the whole thing.

What I dislike about it is its focus. It's built for people of middle- and upper-class backgrounds. This is what the Authority is trying to do in all the neighborhoods — in the South End, Dorchester, Roxbury. Suddenly they're trying to build up these neighborhoods for middle-income and upper-income people; they're simply just ignoring lower-income people.

One problem that I saw was that I wasn't quite clear what the objective was. You see this thing and you think "Well, what are they up to?" You're not quite sure what's going on. If the objective is to be an information center for pedestrians, I think it should be more clearly stated before you walk up to it.

As far as I can see anybody can pick up a map. This stuff here . . . I don't see the purpose. There's no commentary, there's nothing you can understand. It looks to me like just another pork barrel thing. Somebody has gotten a grant and so they pass it on to their friends, and I don't see any good benefits to it.

TUBE INTERVIEWS

Purpose
Visitors to the Information Center were interviewed to assess their reactions to each of the seven tubes. The interview questions attempted to discover the usefulness of the tube displays and also which tubes were particularly well liked. (For a description of the form and content of each tube, refer to Chapter 4.)

Procedure
The interviewers talked to people at random while they were looking at the individual tubes — no representative selection is implied. The responses were tape-recorded. Interviews were conducted at spaced intervals during the day and evening throughout the four-week demonstration period. A list of questions served as a guideline for the interviews: not all the respondents were asked every question. Demographic characteristics are listed in Table 1.

Results
As indicated in Table 1, only a small number of people were interviewed. There was substantial agreement on many questions. For example, people emphasized the novelty and helpfulness of the question/answer machine (Directomat) and the "talking" map of Boston. The directories of the travel and associations, shopping, and entertainment tubes drew favorable responses from tourists, and the teletype machine was considered most unusual by several. (Detailed comments on each tube are included at the end of this section.)

The enthusiasm for the question/answer machine is reflected in the overwhelmingly favorable response to the first question ("What do you think of the question/answer machine"?). This tube was certainly the most popular.[5] Ten of the 12 people interviewed agreed that the machine is useful for both tourists and natives. Two respondents felt that the topics were limited and suggested more information should be included about Cape Cod and about the countryside itself.

The "talking" map of Boston was also quite well liked with 7 out of 10 people interviewed commenting that the map was better and easier to use than an ordinary map.

Most people answering the question thought that the travel, shopping, and entertainment directories were helpful to both tourists and non-tourists. A respondent mentioned that directions to clinics and hospitals were missing. Only one person, at the travel and associations tube, felt that directory was not helpful. Two other people commented that the entertainment directory and map would be helpful to tourists but that they personally "get all mixed up" by maps.

Comments were generally favorable regarding the movie tube. A technical problem hampered the functioning of the six films and limited opportunities for interviews. The one film singled out by two people for praise was about the pilgrims at Plymouth Rock.

The teletype machine drew enthusiastic response from all 14 people interviewed. Eleven considered it interesting and a "good idea." One respondent pointed out the machine's limited viewing capacity and suggested it "should [be] put on a big screen, like in Times Square." Two others also mentioned the possibility of projecting onto a large screen.

Chapter 4 describes the categories of questions offered by the question/answer machine. The following list is a sampling of the 15 most popular and 10 least popular of the 120 questions:

How many pennants and World Series championships have the Boston Red Sox won?	4,035
Where did Boston get its name? What was the Indian name for the area?	3,266
What would be a good 20 minute drive to begin to know the city?	2,697
What is happening to Copley Square?	2,593
Where can I eat good seafood?	2,098
How can I reach the historically interesting parts of "old Boston?"	1,803
How could I take a boat trip to the offshore islands of Martha's Vineyard and Nantucket?	1,671
Does Boston have a developed waterfront area?	1,544
Why is it necessary to keep water beneath Copley Square?	1,538
How does Boston usually vote in the national elections?	1,532
What Boston street is the longest in America?	1,513
What is the schedule of the Boston Symphony?	1,487
What are the best views of Boston from tall buildings?	1,307
Where is Boston's Negro Community?	1,271
How does the Chinese Community maintain its institutions?	1,264
Directions to Old Downtown	128
Directions to Copley Square	158
Directions to Dock Square	165
What changes have occurred in the building and denomination of King's Chapel since 1689?	167
What choices are open at the Charles Street Rotary, the traffic circle linking Storrow Drive and the end of Charles Street?	173
Directions to Back Bay	183
Where are Boston's famous swan boats?	232
Directions to Beacon Hill	235
Directions to Huntington Avenue	241
How many sides does the Common have? What streets make up its border?	246

5. Popularity of the various tubes is discussed more fully in the Open-ended Interviews section of this appendix; also the Unobtrusive Observations section lists the order of popularity of each tube as determined by location of visitors.

TABLE 1: BREAKDOWN OF SAMPLE ACCORDING TO SEX, AGE, AND CLASS

	TUBES	1. Question/Answer Machine	2. Talking Map of Boston	3. Travel and Associations	4. Shopping	5. Entertainment	6. Movie Tube	7. Teletype Machine
		N	**N**	**N**	**N**	**N**	**N**	**N**
SEX	Male	4	6	4	10	6	4	10
	Female	8	4	6	1	4		4
	Total	**12**	**10**	**10**	**11**	**10**	**4**	**14**
AGE	Under 20	7	3	3	2	4	1	5
	21-34	4	4	7	8	3	3	6
	35-54	1	3		1	1		2
	55 & over					2		1
	Total	**12**	**10**	**10**	**11**	**10**	**4**	**14**
CLASS	Lower and Lower Middle	2	1	1	1	1	1	3
	Middle and Upper Middle	5	7	7	6	7	2	5
	Student	5	2	2	4	2	1	6
	Total	**12**	**10**	**10**	**11**	**10**	**4**	**14**

Tube Interview

The tube interview questionnaire below was used as a guide for the interviewer. Responses were tape-recorded. A representative sample of positive and negative comments organized by tube number follows the interview questions.

TUBE 1: Question / Answer Machine (Directomat)

1. What do you think of the question/answer machine?
2. Did you use the machine at all?
   Did you have specific questions or did you just pick them for the fun of it?
   How many questions did you ask?
3. Do you think this machine covers enough topics?
   Which other topics should be included?
4. Does it have the right questions?
   Which kinds of questions are most interesting?
   Are the answers sufficient?
5. For what kinds of people can the machine be useful?
   Do you find it useful for yourself? Why?
6. How much time have you already spent at this tube?
   How much longer do you think you will stay?

TUBE 2: Talking Map of Boston

1. Do you think this kind of map can be used easily?
   Is a pictorial map like this one easier or more difficult to understand than an ordinary map of Boston?
   Would it be helpful to have more maps like this one in central Boston?
   Imagine you had looked at it to find a certain place in Boston, do you think you could have found your way after having looked it up on this map?
2. Do you think the map includes all important things?
   Could it be improved?
3. Do you think people in general like to use maps?
4. Did you use the map for any specific reason (to find your way, etc.)?
5. What do you think of the recording of the day's events?

TUBES 3, 4 & 5: Travel & Associations, Shopping, Entertainment

A. *Map and Directory*

1. What do you think of the directory? It is useful?
   Is there anything wrong with it?
   How could it be improved?
2. Did you use the directory?
   Did you intend to find something specific or did you just look up something for the fun of it? What did you look up?
   Did you learn something new?
   Could you find the things on the map you had looked up in the directory?
   [At Shopping only: Do you normally shop in this area?]

B. *Slide Show*

1. Did you look at the slide show in the back of this tube?
2. Did you watch the whole show? What did you see?
3. Did you find it interesting?
4. Was there something you did not like about it? Could it be done better?
   How?

TUBE 6: Movie Tube

1. How long have you been watching these films?
2. How many have you seen entirely? Which ones?
3. Did you like them?
4. Which did you like most and which least?
5. How much time have you already spent at this tube?
6. How much longer do you think you will stay?

TUBE 7: Teletype Machine

1. What do you think of having a teletype machine in an information center for pedestrians?
2. Do you find it interesting?
3. How long have you been reading the print-outs?
4. Do you think you will stay longer? How much longer?

Comments from Tube Interviews

Tube 1: Question/Answer Machine (Directomat)

I think it is very good because we are foreign people and I think it is very interesting.

They should be all over Boston.

A lot more about Cape Cod should be on that. A lot of people are looking for routes down to the Cape and since you have something like this you should use it wholly.

I haven't checked too many [for accuracy], but just the scope of offerings is very wide and I think it should please almost everyone.

Now I just wanted to find out about Copley Square. They're fixing it up there. Things like that you don't know because you don't see it in the paper everyday, and like this you get information that you don't get otherwise unless you just happen to see it at the right time. I think it's really helpful.

This is really only good for someone that's new to Boston and this isn't the ideal location for it either. Logan Airport probably [better].

I endorse this because thousands and thousands of people will come here. Many questions on the chart are what a good many strangers will ask. Many are what a lot of Bostonians are really not acquainted with and it gives them the answer.

Tube 2: Talking Map of Boston

For a special point of interest, it's good, but if you're looking for minor detailed streets, you probably don't have them here, do you? Just the major thoroughfares and so forth. I guess each one would serve its own purpose. This one here gives tourists a good hand on where to go, approximately how far.

It's much easier to read, although I'd sooner see it on a flat surface than on a rounded surface. I guess what I'm trying to do is get an overall perspective and it's difficult to do when it's rounded like that.

We have been lost in Boston for about two hours. This is a very comprehensive map. Now we know where we've been. We know now where we are and we're finding out where we can go.

A lot of people get lost in Boston. They need stuff like this around. I get lost myself and I been livin' here a long time. [They should be] scattered out so if you're lost, you're bound to bump into one if you walk 10 more minutes.

I was particularly pleased with the "Events of the Day" tape which presented clearly and succinctly the various activities of the metropolitan area . . . perhaps introducing tapes in one or more of the major foreign languages may be helpful.

I think the map is very prejudiced, once you get over to Roxbury and say "show me where you live" and we couldn't find street names. If you have all the questions that you can ask about how do you find Bunker Hill or what are the Negro areas of Boston, it seems that if you're going to have that kind of question answered and it is part of the area on the map, then you should also have the street names.

Tubes 3, 4, & 5: Travel and Associations, Shopping, and Entertainment

a. Maps and directories

I got my bearings. I found out where the traffic areas are — from the map.

We tried to see where we started from. We came off the train station down in here, I imagine it would be. Then we came up here, up to the Parker House, and then back down. We could find ourselves, how far we've travelled, and everything else.

I get all mixed up with this stuff (grid map). I think it's more confusing than it is to grab a cab and say "take me to such-and-such." I've been coming here for a long, long time and if there's a place I want to go and I don't want to walk I just grab a cab and go. I can't even be bothered with the subway. You get out there and you get on the wrong bus.

The map is very good. I think it's very helpful. I think for what people are looking for here, these are the best kinds of maps. Of course if you want to find something in more detail you can always buy a map. But I think these are good for what they're meant to be.

Some of the maps aren't really very clear. They're not very good guides. You really can't tell where things are by looking at them. It's a very confusing sort of city. I think these maps don't really help much. It looks good but it doesn't really help. I think it's better to have just a regular sort of map that people are used to.

This is similar to the kinds of maps they have down in the Arlington Street subway and this is what I think they should have more of, in the city, because people don't know where they're going. Something like this is very helpful to a lot of people coming to Boston or going out. A lot of people from the suburbs came in from the subway and they don't know where they are, except for the "downtown shopping district" and they're lost anywhere else. I think they'd find this type of map easy to use. Generally they know exactly what they're going to do and they go do it and that's it.

Probably a grid map is better if you've never been in a city before, because it gives you the blocks and numbers.

I think it would be terrific to have one down on Tremont Street. I think especially for the old people; there are quite a few older people around the park and I think it would be helpful to them.

I myself like to wander, but I know Boston anyway. I don't like to go by maps.

I use maps most of the time, unless I'm in a strange city and I just want to walk around.

I think the directory is fine, but one thing that's missing is how to get to the hospitals and clinics. I imagine a lot of people would want to know that. Last week we were here and we were looking for that information and it isn't there.

I think it's useful to know where, in my case, bookshops might be and I was rather interested in restaurant possibilities.

I haven't had a chance to look it over yet. I'm interested to know how they select which markets to put down here. They're not all here. In general I think the whole thing is quite a good idea. So far, I haven't learned anything that I didn't know.

I think it's quite clear as long as you're ready with pencil and paper to copy down the exact address, because once you get to that area you really don't know which end of Newbury Street, for example, the English Room is.

The restaurant information is just thrown in without any order. It's not in alphabetical sequence, it's not in type of hard to find. You could put them in three groups, you could food sequence. If you're looking for something specific it's arrange them by section, by alphabetic order, and by types.

I'm not particularly crazy about these drums that you spin around and they don't really tell you anything. Maybe if you had some kind of captions underneath each one, quotations or something like that, sort of funny quotations, instead of just addresses and names and stuff like that, it might be interesting.

I think it's useful information. I like the drums. You can go up and twirl the thing around and look for things that . . maybe something you're looking for. I don't know that people would as much there — the nightclubs — because you'd probably look in the paper for them. But, maybe, like I see here "youth clubs." That may be good because a kid might come in here and see that and might not even think of going to one; maybe that's something to think of when he sees it on there.

The map and directory relate one to another. This is excellent.

They're nice (the directories). They'd be helpful for a tourist. I live here so I know my way around pretty good.

I just spotted one [directory comment] over there on one of the restaurants; it told the price range. That's tremendous. You get somebody who's on a budget and you want a fairly reasonable place to go — this helps.

b. Slide Shows

I think it shows what Boston's really like.

They seem to indicate the kind of shopping in the area, things thrown in such as the mailman to indicate that mail is delivered in the area. It certainly gives the impression that this is a fine shopping area. It's amusing. Slides add interest. I think there's no harm in having something for people to look at.

I thought they were excellent photographs.

The sounds tend to run if you're trying to listen to one, and then to another. But that's not really that important. If you're close to it you can discern, but if you back away because of the crowd then you do have problems listening and confusing the sounds from one another.

I dug that thing (entertainment). The only thing though, it was out of synch. If it was kept in synchronization, it would really be groovy, because it's really a good presentation, with the music and the slides.

Well, they're (the slides) sort of elegant. They didn't seem very realistic. And I know I've been to some of the places that they show but I think some of the slides would scare people away unless you had a lot of money and knew you could get along very well, like the theater and the restaurants. But otherwise it's very good.

This one here looks sort of commercial. It seemed to be advertising, which I don't think is necessary. The one showing the airlines (Travel tube): it showed National Airlines and then American, and it appeared to be advertising.

It was okay, kind of middle class, but that's . . . it's a middle class exhibit, I guess.

Tube 6: Movie Tube

At this point, the one with the films [I like least], because some are labelled wrong and if that were to be improved, that would be alright. I think that could be the best part of the exhibit if that were functioning properly.

You can see the things, you really don't know about them, like the bridges and the churches and stuff like that and here it's like you hear different sounds that you never realized before. You probably understand it more . . . you see all this . . . there is something in Boston you'll appreciate.

Interesting, different things. We just came over here to this Redevelopment Authority. I think it's an excellent idea.

Very good, I guess. Amazing how they do this junk, stuff, I mean. It's pretty good about the Plymouth Rock, the pilgrims. It's amazing how they do all this stuff, though.

Tube 7: Teletype Machine

Oh, this is great, especially if you want to get some quick news. I am interested in finance. I major in economics at U. Mass. and right now they're giving stock quotations. In fact Dow Jones is up 1.23.

I kind of like the little chute into the garbage can. That's probably where the United Press should go.

I like the teletype. I just read on it about President Nixon, what he's plannin' on to do, what he's gonna do. It's very interestin' for the people to know.

They should put it on a big screen, like in Times Square. They have a news headline thing done by one of the local newspapers, a strip that goes around the building. It would be just as easy to take that and take the positions of the keys from here and convert them into an electronic force. And even if it didn't have to be the size, say the length of a building, it would be 10 x 10 or 20 x 20. Then 100 people could watch it, whereas this way only 3 or 4 people can watch at a time. So it's really a very limited use.

I think it's a very interesting idea. Now the next step would be to get permission of the Park Square Building people to put an electric sign with the latest news ticker on it. In the meantime I think the teletype ticker is very interesting.

Response Phone Comments

The response phone (recording and playback devices linked to an ordinary telephone handset, as decribed in Chapter 4) was part of the travel and associations tube. Only a few of the many comments can be included here: the following is a proportionate sample organized into three sections of positive, negative, and miscellaneous.

Positive

Well, I think this is great. I've never seen anything like this. It's really tremendous.

The best thing that's ever happened to Boston.

Well, I've been here for about a half hour now ladies and gentlemen. My name is Bill P_____ and I'm from Charlestown and what I've seen here is very interesting. I imagine it would be more interesting for an out-of-town person. This is Bill P_____ signing off. Thank you for your attention.

This place is a real trip and everybody should come down and dig it.

Hi, I really think this is the grooviest thing we've had in Boston in a long time. It really blew my mind coming in here and seeing all these big lights and tubes, and I'd like to thank you for doing a really nice thing.

Well, I think the program all in all is a worthwhile expenditure. However, I think a few more things should be added. I don't know what. I mean things like pertaining more to the younger generation. That's the generation that would be out and about.

Actually, I think this should be a regular internal part of Boston's Redevelopment Authority. Congratulations.

Although I think it's a little pretentious, I think there should be more of these around. They're a very good idea and the thing it helps you with, is when you can't find where you are.

This gives a foreign visitor a chance to see what Boston is all about. This is a great thing of communication with Bostonians. I think it should remain permanently here in Park Square. Thank you.

I think it's lovely, and really has a great deal of charm.

Boston's great. I love Boston.

Fascinating little gadget.

I really dig this; I think it's a great idea and I really think you should spread these out in the community. It's a great idea.

I think this effort on the part of Boston is very commendable. It will be good for tourists and it's an ideal way to stimulate interest of the people that live here.

It's really great; I think they should have them in every city in the country.

This is the last day of this thing and the beginning of the tourist season. This should be held on all through the summer.

I think it's a good experiment, not to be extended.

Negative

I find it incredible that the school system is so poor that instead of investing in that, the city council has chosen to invest in such a Coney Island enterprise as this. Thank you.

Why are people spending money on things like this and not worrying about putting people in houses?

Record? I want to put in a complaint. I think it's an idiotic figure, a waste of money. I think this whole thing is a waste of money. The taxpayers are losing money on this thing.

This whole thing's for the birds.

I think it would be wonderful if we could program the machine to answer our own questions rather than looking them up on the board and I think it would also be better to have a map without the buildings and with a better street layout of Boston. Thank you.

It's terrible you know, like everything else is around here. It's really a down, you know, understand what I mean?

I think this thing is a good idea but the way it's built is kind of ridiculous. It doesn't belong on this side of town. They're trying to overdo it I think, and they make a mess out of it but I still like the whole idea of the thing, except the stuff like the balloons and things.

The area is dirty, the equipment isn't working correctly.

I think it's the ugliest thing I've ever seen in my life and I hope they never put another one up when they tear this one down!

I think you're out of your mind, you're crazy!

I think quite possibly the taxpayer's money could have been spent in a better way.

Miscellaneous

The world is in a pretty sad mess.

This should include something about the Black section of Boston.

I, well, think it's really nice, but I hope I haven't picked up any diseases from those phones.

Boston is my favorite city and you are my favorite people. Oh, yes, you are my favorite people. Just keep in mind you are my favorite souls and this is my favorite city and you're still my favorite people.

I think you should do something about pigeons. They're really a nuisance.

Boston is a town that needs a lot of development. It's rather old, rather dirty. It's got some nice seafood stores and most of the people are nice.

Boston is a cool city, and I'd like to see more improvements.

TABLE 1: BREAKDOWN OF SAMPLE ACCORDING TO SEX, AGE, AND CLASS (Opinion Scale)

		N	%
SEX	Male	71	62
	Female	43	38
	Total	**114***	**100**
AGE	Under 20	24	21
	21-34	63	56
	35-54	22	20
	55 and over	3	3
	Total	**112****	**100**
CLASS	Lower and Lower Middle	24	23
	Middle and Upper Middle	44	42
	Student	37	35
	Total	**105*****	**100**

* Sex of 2 respondents not recorded
** Age of 4 respondents not recorded
*** Class of 11 respondents not recorded

OPINION SCALE

Purpose
To determine the general attitude toward the Information Center, an opinion scale was handed out to a random selection of visitors during the first few days that the Center was open.

Procedure
Most of the people who were approached cooperated and filled out the opinion scale on the spot; 116 completed scales were obtained. Each printed sheet also requested information about sex, age, and occupation so that the relationship between these variables and opinions about the Center could be analyzed (Table 1). General comments were also solicited.

Construction of the Opinion Scale
A modified Thurstone technique was used in developing the opinion scale. First, the research staff wrote 38 statements about the Information Center, ranging from very favorable to very unfavorable. Some statements referred to its physical appearance, others to its usefulness to particular types of people, others to the informational content of various parts of the Center. Ten "judges" (employees of Ashley/Myer/Smith) were then asked to rate each statement in terms of its "favorableness" (degree to which a statement indicated a positive attitude towards a certain aspect of the Center). An 11-point scale was used, with 11 meaning Highly Favorable and 1 Highly Unfavorable. The 10 ratings for each statement were averaged, and the resulting number was called the statement's "scale value." The researcher then selected 12 statements whose scale values extended fairly evenly over the range of favorableness (1-11) and on which the judges had agreed fairly well. These 12 statements, arranged in random order, constituted the opinion scale. (A copy of the scale is shown in Table 2. For purposes of identification, the scale value of each statement is written at the left.)

The visitor at the Information Center read each statement and then circled one of 5 numbers to indicate whether he agreed very much, somewhat, was neutral, disagreed somewhat, or disagreed very much. Thus, a visitor who liked the Information Center very much would generally agree with the favorable statements and disagree with the unfavorable ones.

Results
From the analysis of the data, it is evident that most visitors liked the Center very much. Table 3 shows the average response for each statement. For each statement, the average response value was determined by adding all responses (1, 2, 3, 4, or 5) and then dividing by the total number of responses. In this table the statements are arranged in order of favorableness, from most favorable to least, so that it is evident that people tended to agree with the favorable statements and disagree with the unfavorable ones. The only favorable statement which was not agreed with is #2, "There is a lot of good information here but I don't know how to use it." This is a confusing statement, and it is difficult to know whether a respondent disagreed with "There's a lot of good information here" or "I don't know how to use it."

The responses were also scored in such a way as to give a "favorableness" score for each individual. For each visitor it was noted with which statements he agreed (very much or somewhat), and the scale values for these statements were listed. The median scale value of these statements was determined, and this value was the individual's Favorableness Score. For example, an individual who agreed with statements 1, 3, 4, 10, and 11 would have scale value scores of 10.0, 4.5, 9.5, 8.2, and 6.7. His median or Favorableness Score would therefore be 8.2 (half his scores fall below 8.2 and half fall above 8.2). Although it was theoretically possible to have individual scores ranging from 0.0 to 10.0 the scores are all clustered at the high end of the scale. Twenty-five percent of the respondents had scores over 8.7, 44% had scores between 8.0 and 8.4, and 31% had scores under 7.9.

There were no consistent differences attributable to sex or occupation. Age did seem to affect the visitor's opinion: those under 20 liked the Information Center best, between 21 and 34 next best, and over 35 next best. Nevertheless, even those over 35, although not as enthusiastic as younger visitors, liked the Center very much. The majority of visitors over 35 agreed with each of the favorable statements (except #2).

At the bottom of the opinion scale, space was provided for comments. A representative selection follows.

TABLE 3: AVERAGE RESPONSE TO OPINION SCALE STATEMENTS

Scale: 1 = Agree very much, 2 = Agree somewhat, 3 = Neutral, 4 = Disagree somewhat, 5 = Disagree very much

Statement number*	Scale value	Mean score
1	10.0	1.405
4	9.5	1.517
7	9.2	1.871
10	8.2	1.991
12	7.5	2.397
11	6.7	1.862
2i	5.8	3.612
3ii	4.5	2.681
5	3.5	3.509
6	2.5	3.681
8	1.5	4.241
9	1.0	4.086

*Statements ranked in order of favorableness from most to least favorable

i State. 2: "There is a lot of good information here, but I don't know how to use it."

ii "Some appropriate topics are not covered here."

WHAT IS YOUR OPINION?

Just circle the appropriate number for each statement and drop your questionnaire in the box near this pad.

Answer categories: (Please form a definite opinion and avoid the neutral category as much as possible.)

Scale value	Statement	agree very much 1	agree somewhat 2	neutral 3	disagree somewhat 4	disagree very much 5
10.0	1. This information center is a very good idea. Other cities should follow this example and build similar ones.	1	2	3	4	5
5.8	2. There is a lot of good information here, but I don't know how to use it.	1	2	3	4	5
4.5	3. Some appropriate topics are not covered here.	1	2	3	4	5
9.5	4. This information center is a real asset to the Park Square area.	1	2	3	4	5
3.5	5. This information center is only useful for special groups like tourists, shoppers, and others.	1	2	3	4	5
2.5	6. Things are not taken seriously enough in this information center.	1	2	3	4	5
9.2	7. If more information centers like this one existed in Boston, I would have a much better knowledge of what is going on and I would like the city much better.	1	2	3	4	5
1.5	8. I don't see a real need for an information center like this one.	1	2	3	4	5
1.0	9. These huge tubes with their balloon tops are some of the ugliest things I've ever seen.	1	2	3	4	5
8.2	10. The information center is in exactly the right place, because so many people pass through here.	1	2	3	4	5
6.7	11. I like this information center because it is different from anything I've seen.	1	2	3	4	5
7.5	12. From the information center I learned many things about the Park Square area I had never heard of before.	1	2	3	4	5

COMMENTS:

Age____ Male____ Female____ Occupation________________________

Comments from Opinion Scale

Positive

The need for an information (tourist) center in Boston has been chronic for too long; it is very pitiful to see tourists (American and foreign alike) wandering about this city hopelessly lost and alienated from the city life.

I am a native of Boston and still find this center useful.

I didn't come for information — just to look and I think it is a lot of fun. Makes Boston a more "fun" place.

I think it's an excellent idea.

The 3-D maps are very helpful for an out-of-towner.

Please build a permanent one. It's great. Well done.

I think things like this will make Boston more important in the future.

I went to school smiling this morning, after seeing the exhibition — love the colors. It gives a fine idea of what a city has to offer.

I love the idea of a colorful CLEAN meeting place in the city. I'm not sure that the information distribution is as essential as the environment. The rotation disks and maps are excellent as is the music and vocal accompaniment. Also I like the press release. The decor should be a bit less jazzy but I like the balloons. There should be more bright spots like this in Boston.

I hope this center is a permanent addition to Boston. Only of course it would be difficult to reach during the snowstorms of the winter.

The balloons were just great and wanted to own one. The slides were interesting too.

Great idea! Pursue!!

It's the nicest thing that happened to Boston in a very long time. It's relaxing, peaceful, and fun.

It's gorgeous, your project near Park Square. One more happy detail to make Boston one of the world's most wonderful cities. Viva!

It makes the neighborhood (and hence the city) seem hospitable and interesting — and gives the "passerby" many good ideas. Would like to see information centers throughout the whole city. Information centers [should] fit into and reflect the best flavor of that area — that local civic or business groups be responsible for participating in the information and design of that neighborhood's particular center.

Please leave it there forever!

Your information center which I saw getting off a Greyhound bus from Hartford, is the nicest thing I have ever seen in any city, ever; and that includes skyscrapers, cafés, theaters, parks, happenings, restaurants, parades, airports and rivers.

Negative

An excellent idea but a lot of technical and some visual problems remain to be solved. The UPI teletype is great. The problem of vandalism seems to have been ignored.

I think it's like a small EXPO, fantastic. Only it costs far too much money and I think it's rather frivolous when you think of other more deserving users. If there is money to throw away, then it is a good idea.

I dislike the tin foil and the garish, multicolored aspect of the kiosks. The center would be much better looking and more suitable for its Park Sq. location if plain, solid colors were used. Also, voices on the recordings are hard to hear.

Boston is an old historical city. That type of architecture (aside from being ugly) does not fit in this city. Something a little more on the colonial style would have been much more suitable. Also this electronic equipment is wonderful, but when it breaks down, how long will it be before it is fixed?

A little too mod and noisy.

The carnival appearence makes me feel like I should be throwing darts at the balloons to win a "cupie doll". There's apparently no limits to the ways my money can be wasted.

Gives a very glamorous idea of Boston — omits things like government, poverty, ethnic areas, historic points.

Suggestions

This is a good idea, but it should have more publicity. The purpose of this should be more obvious to somebody just passing it.

This place is situated in too busy an area. Too much traffic around here. It should be situated in some open space on the Common where more people can benefit from it.

Information centers can be especially useful in core city areas as well, where information about the metropolitan area is lacking. Information should perhaps include more about public health or rehabilitation services.

Just novel to Mass. — this is a great idea. Information on the travel in/out of downtown Boston could be improved. It's a confusing city. People seem to enjoy this center — kids playing, adults smiling — it's good to see.

I think you should give more direct directions on the locations of these places that you are suggesting for trips, such as routes to take and stuff like that.

It should cover some places outside the Boston area like Brookline. It should tell the locations of golf courses near the Boston area and how to get there.

I think this would be better in an area with more tourists.

UNOBTRUSIVE OBSERVATIONS

Purpose

In order to verify the responses from the interviews, assessments were made of the response to the Information Center without direct contact with the visitors. Three unobtrusive measures were made: 1) The number, age and sex of people at the Center; 2) the number of people attracted into the Center as contrasted with the number who passed by; and 3) the popularity of various kiosks.

Procedure and Results

Number and type of people at the Center

During thirty-five 15-minute intervals (mainly on weekdays), an observer counted and classified everyone who passed particular locations at the Center according to age and sex (Table 1): During these periods people visited the Center at an average rate of 240 per hour. Sixty-three percent of the visitors were male. Young adults and teenagers accounted for 60% of the visitors; 25% were between 35 and 55. Children and adults over 55 together accounted for the remaining visitors.

Number of people attracted into the Center versus number who passed by

During twenty 10-minute observation periods an observer at various spots on the periphery counted people entering or passing by the Center. Observations were made during both day and evening at the beginning and in the middle of the four-week demonstration period. Of all people observed, 40% entered the Center while 60% passed by. The percentage attracted into the Center was significantly higher during the evening (47%) than during the day (39%). A larger proportion of people (42%) were attracted into the Center at the beginning of the demonstration period than in the middle of the period (35%).

TABLE 1: BREAKDOWN OF SAMPLE ACCORDING TO SEX AND AGE (Unobtrusive Observations)

		N	%
SEX	Male	1,338	63
	Female	770	37
	Total	**2,108**	**100**
AGE	Children (under 12)	137	6
	Teenagers (13-19)	398	19
	20-35	864	41
	36-55	525	25
	Over 55	184	9
	Total	**2,108**	**100**

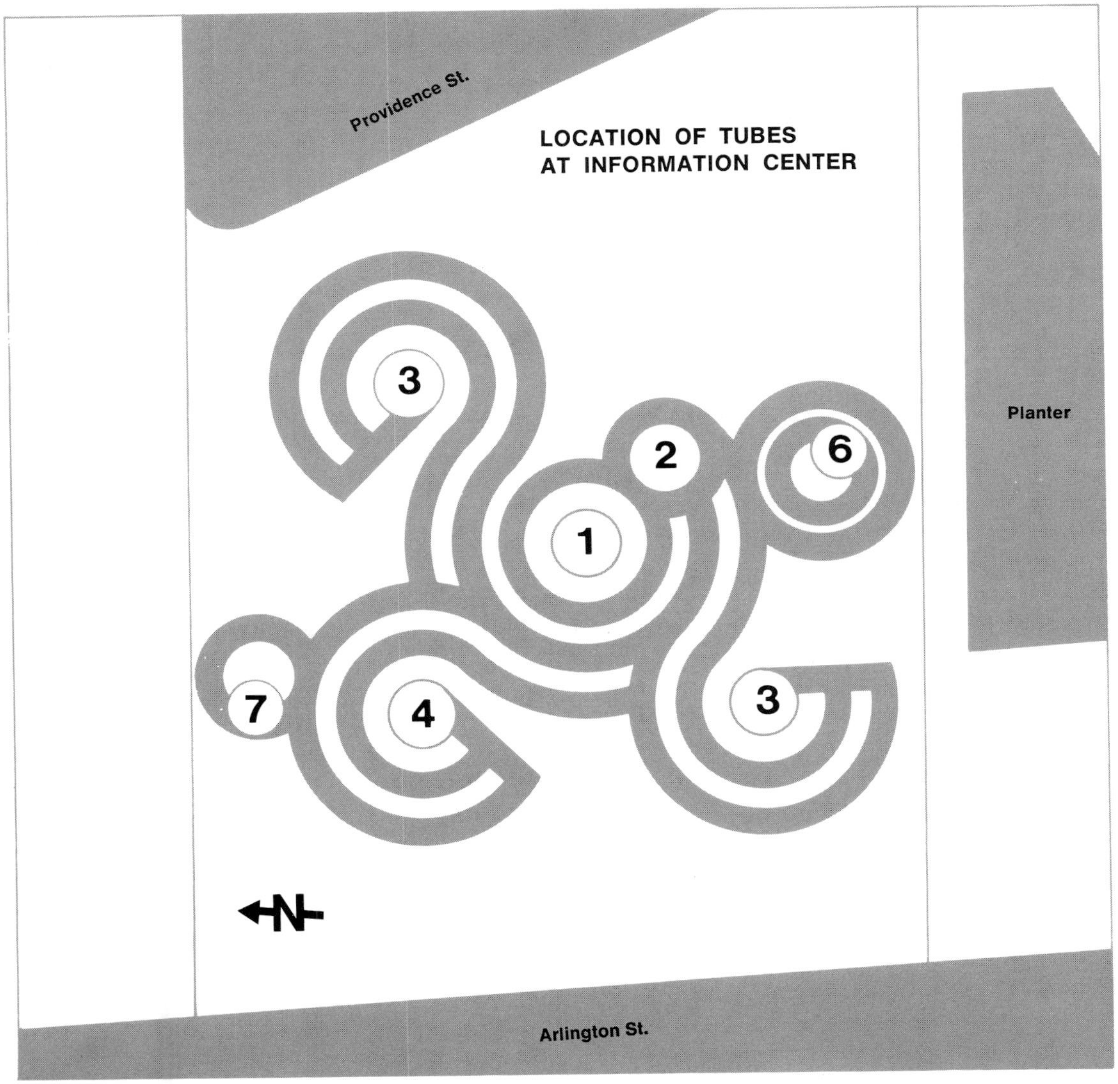

Popularity of various kiosks (Diagram 1)
During the demonstration period the observer went through the Information Center 40 times, at varying times of day, and marked the location of every person present. The results of these counts show the following preferences:

TUBE NO:	1. Question/Answer Machine	195
	6. Movie Tube	123
	5. Entertainment Slide Show	85
	7. Teletype Machine	81
	5. Entertainment Directory	60
	3. Travel & Associations	57
	3. Travel & Associations Slide Show	53
	4. Shopping Slide Show	50
	4. Shopping Directory	43
	2. "Talking" Map of Boston	39
	3. Response Phone	39

Public Signing: Evaluative Tests

6

Public road signing provides several types of information which the motorist needs. Street name signs tell him where he is. Traffic regulatory signs and signals ("stop," "one way," "do not enter," "right turn only," traffic lights) tell him what actions are allowed and prohibited. He must also know where various streets lead, information seldom provided for the city driver; guide signs fill this gap.

New guide signs, street name signs, and traffic regulatory signs were erected in Park Square and Dewey Square, Boston. Their effectiveness was evaluated in the laboratory (regulatory signs only) and in the field by:

1 Laboratory Tests

2 Postcard Questionnaires

3 Observation of Driver Behavior

The general conclusions from these studies are in Chapter 6.

EVALUATION OF SYMBOLIC VERSUS EXISTING TRAFFIC SIGNS: LABORATORY TESTS

Purpose and General Procedure

Three laboratory tests were designed to 1) evaluate the new symbolic traffic signs and 2) compare them with those in the existing signing system.

Forty-six subjects participated in the experiments. They were recruited by posters put up in Harvard Square, Cambridge, and at the Park Square, Boston, Information Center; most subjects came in response to the posters at the Information Center. Each subject was asked his age, sex, education, occupation, whether he had been abroad, whether he had a driver's license and whether he had seen the new symbolic signs in Park and Dewey Squares. Responses to the various tests were analyzed in terms of these variables.

The three tests were administered together at four different times to four different groups of subjects. (Eleven subjects in Session 1, 13 in Session 2, 15 in Session 3, and 7 in Session 4.) Because of changes in procedure, the responses of the 11 subjects in Session 1 were excluded from the analysis of Tests 1 and 2 and the 13 subjects in Session 2 were excluded from the second half of Test 1 and from Test 2. This accounts for the difference in N in the various experiments. However, although the responses were not included in the data analysis, all subjects took part in all three tests.

TABLE 1: BREAKDOWN OF SAMPLE ACCORDING TO SEX, AGE, AND CLASS (First Part of Test 1)

		N	%
SEX	Male	26	74
	Female	9	26
	Total	**35**	**100**
AGE	13-19	12	34
	20-35	22	63
	35-55	1	3
	Total	**35**	**100**
CLASS	Lower and Lower Middle	12	34
	Middle and Upper Middle	7	20
	Student	16	46
	Total	**35**	**100**

TABLE 2: BREAKDOWN OF SAMPLE ACCORDING TO SEX, AGE, AND CLASS (Second Part of Test 1 and Test 2)

		N	%
SEX	Male	16	73
	Female	6	27
	Total	**22**	**100**
AGE	13-19	5	23
	20-35	17	77
	Total	**22**	**100**
CLASS	Lower and Lower Middle	4	18
	Middle and Upper Middle	6	27
	Student	12	55
	Total	**22**	**100**

TABLE 3: PERCENTAGE OF SUBJECTS CORRECTLY IDENTIFYING SIGNS BEFORE AND AFTER LEAVING PERIOD

Signs	Meaning of Sign	Percent of Subjects Before (N=22)	After (N=22)
	2-way traffic keep right	91	100
	no right turn	40	100
	Parking Lot	63	68
	no parking	71	100
	right turn only	51	100
	traffic signal ahead	94	95
	straight ahead only	46	86
	left turn only	66	95
	pass on both sides	86	100
	2-way traffic ahead	80	95
	left or right turn only	74	100

Signs	Meaning of Sign	Percent of Subjects Before (N=35)	After (N=22)
	no stopping or standing	3	91
	keep right	34	91
	no entry	20	82
	one way	0	55
	to Parking Lot	83	100
	keep right	31	95
	no U-turn	86	100
	no right turn	49	100
	one way	0	68
	parking allowed	71	73
	straight ahead only	57	100

TEST 1 — INTERPRETATION AND LEARNING OF SYMBOLIC SIGNS

Purpose

The first laboratory test was done in order to find out 1) how well people could comprehend the new symbolic traffic signs, 2) what effect social class or having been in a country using similar signs might have on successful identification of these signs, 3) what common misinterpretations of the symbolic signs might occur, and 4) how well people could learn the meanings of the signs after a brief instruction period.

Procedure

Thirty-five subjects (Table 1) viewed 22 slides of symbolic signs without legends or backgrounds. These slides were exposed for one second and then the subjects were given sufficient time to write down what they thought was the meaning of the sign. Following this first experiment, there was a 15-minute period devoted to teaching the meaning of the signs. Subjects viewed slides of the signs *with their legends,* were given a brochure describing the sign system and a written explanation of the rationale behind the system, and urged to ask questions (Table 2). They were then shown the same slide sequence used in the first experiment, in reversed order, and again asked to write the meaning of the signs.

Results

In the first trial 13 of the 22 signs were understood by more than half of the subjects (Table 3). Only two signs, the two one-way arrows, were misunderstood by all subjects. There were no significant differences based on social class or previous exposure to a similar sign system.

There were several misinterpretations for each sign. The following is a sample of some common misinterpretations of each sign.

straight road, north-south, (two-way traffic ahead notion often missed)

intersection, blind curve, turn right, sharp curve ahead, right after rail track, turn at intersection, right turn ahead in road, coming to a bridge, curve after crossroads

pedestrians around, passing zone, (parking lot notion missed), parking allowed

blind curve, pedestrian crossing, no passing, no pedestrian cross, proceed with caution, approaching Police Station

right turn permitted, turn right, street turns right, bend in road, turn ahead, right turn with right of way ahead, right curve coming up

traffic signal intersection (ahead notion missed)

one way

left turn permitted, left curve, bear left, left turn — parking

fork in road, traffic merges ahead two ways, split lanes, divided highway, intersection, left or right (no straight ahead), double lane coming up

two-way traffic ends, two-way traffic — yield (ahead notion missed)

left and right turns ahead, road ends — divides, intersection, turn either way — danger ahead surely, street ahead has two-way traffic, dead end, road junction, curved intersection

intersection, road closed, crossing, do not enter, merging traffic

road from left, street goes right, bend (sharp), parking right hand side, hill road bears right, right turn only, right all traffic, curve, road makes sharp right turn, straight

stop, stop if making turn at intersection, do not cross, walkway, barriers, highway ahead, intersection, dead end, caution sign, stop — going in wrong direction

left turn, right angle traffic, right turn, go right, left only, road turns left, traffic entering left, bear left (left and right confused)

pedestrian crossing right, passing on right, pedestrians turn right (do not cross straight)

same as "keep right" above

hairpin, U-turn ahead after underpass, danger — road has sharp curve, U-turn, rotary ahead

side road on left, bear left, street turning off at left, road branches — junction, road with crossing, turn right, right turn

same as "one-way" above

parking, pedestrian/people, passing

one-way traffic, no passing, parking ahead, straight road, marked highway goes straight

In the second trial, following the learning period, all 22 signs were understood by more than half of the subjects and 16 signs by between 80 and 100%. Although the two one-way signs remained among the least clearly understood of the signs, they were correctly identified by 54% and 68% of the subjects.

INSTRUCTIONS FOR TEST 1

We are going to show you some slides of new traffic signs. These slides will be exposed for a very short moment only. Please look at them carefully and then write down what you think the meaning of each new traffic sign might be.

If the meaning is not clear to you, just guess what it could be; don't leave any blanks.

Please don't look at what your neighbor is writing down, rather, make wild guesses. This is very important because we are particularly interested in how drivers who had never seen these signs before would interpret them.

After each exposure you will have 30 seconds to write down your answers.

EXPLANATORY SHEET FOR SUBJECTS IN TEST 1

As you will have noticed, the signs you have just seen fall into four different categories easily identifiable by shape and color. The following outline briefly explains these categories:

I. SHAPE:

A. TRIANGLE = warning signs.

B. ROUND = mandatory signs (things you must or must not do)

II. COLOR -- Mandatory signs are in three colors:

A. BLUE SIGNS

1. Arrows indicate movements the driver is permitted to make.

2. Movements in any other direction are not permitted.

B. Signs with GREEN BORDERS

They have the same meaning as the blue signs.

C. Signs with RED BORDERS and RED SLASHES

These signs are prohibitory -- the driver is not permitted to make movements described in the sign.

D. PARKING SIGNS

They comply to the same color code as the other signs:

1. "P" in GREEN border = parking is permitted.

2. "P" in RED border = parking is not permitted.

III. SPECIAL CASE

NO ENTRY, a red disc with a white bar.

Now look at the inside of the brochure you find next in your envelope. You will see examples of the new traffic signs and their old counterparts. Please look at this brochure and the above given explanations carefully and try to memorize the meaning of the new traffic signs.

TEST 2 — COMPARISON OF SYMBOLIC SIGNS AND THEIR EXISTING COUNTERPARTS

Purpose

This experiment was designed to determine the difference in comprehensibility between the symbolic signs and their existing counterparts when viewed briefly in natural surroundings. The influences of social class and familiarity with similar sign systems were also evaluated.

Procedure

A tachistoscope was used to expose the subjects to a series of 24 random-ordered slides for 20 milliseconds each. The series was shown twice — the first time simply to familiarize the subjects with the procedure. After the exposure of each slide in the second showing, the subjects were allowed 20 seconds to write down the meaning of the sign. The responses of 22 subjects are discussed in this section (Table 2).

The slide series showed 12 symbolic signs and 12 existing counterparts to them, photographed as pairs with identical meanings, in normal street environments. The symbolic signs, installed, were photographed first. Next, black and white reproductions of the old signs were enlarged photographically, mounted on cardboard, and attached to a clear plexiglass stick. This mock sign was held between the camera and the new sign, so that the new sign was completely covered. The resulting pair of slides was thus identical in background and lighting, though the old signs appeared somewhat larger because they had to cover the new signs.

TABLE 4: PERCENTAGE OF SUBJECTS CORRECTLY IDENTIFYING SYMBOLIC AND EXISTING SIGNS (N=22)

Symbolic Signs	%	Existing Signs	%
	82		55
	64		32
	68		77
	77		91
	91		91
	18		5
	77		86
	68		36
	81		91
	91		55
	91		73
	82		9

The symbolic signs were correctly identified more frequently than were the existing signs (Table 4). (The Wilcoxon matched-pair signed-rank test yielded a result significant at the .05 level.) In 11 of the 12 pairs, more than 60% of the subjects correctly interpreted directions on the new signs. In 7 of the 12 pairs, the new signs were recognized by more subjects than were the old ones. For one pair,  the same number of subjects correctly identified both the new and old signs. There were no significant differences in responses based on social class or experience abroad. Non-students did better than students in recognizing the signs.

INSTRUCTIONS FOR TEST 2

In the following part of the experiment you will see all these signs and their old equivalents in their surroundings. They will be exposed for a very brief moment only (one second or even less). Try to identify them and write down their proper meanings (the ones you read in the brochure) as soon as possible.

There will be 30 second intervals between the exposures during which you can write down the meanings of the signs and get ready for the next slide.

All the signs will be completely mixed up, so don't worry if you think you have seen a sign twice. This may actually be possible and if it happens, it is part of the experimental procedure.

INSTRUCTIONS FOR TEST 3

Now our procedure will change somewhat. You will see slides taken from the position of a driver approaching an intersection. When looking at each slide, imagine you were driving a car and being unfamiliar with the city, you had to find out where you are allowed to turn.

For each slide, please write down which turns you were allowed to make if you were approaching this intersection in a car.

In this part of the experiment you will have more time to look at the slides and to write down your answers. When giving your responses, just write down the directions in which you are allowed to turn (right, left, straight ahead, etc.).

BACKGROUND INFORMATION

1. Sex: male _____
   female _____

2. Age: _____ years

3. How long have you been living in the Boston area?
   _____ years

4. Education: _____ years in school (starting with grammar school)
   DEGREES: (check highest)
   high school diploma _____
   B.A., B.S. _____
   other (specify) _____

5. Occupation: _______________

6. Have you ever been abroad? (year, country, length of stay)
   ____
   ____
   ____

7. When were you around Park Square and South Station for the last time?
   Park Sq. (check one) a) this week _____
   b) _____ week(s) ago
   South Station (check one) a) this week _____
   b) _____ week(s) ago

If you were in these areas during the last three weeks:

8. Did you notice the new traffic signs?
   yes _____
   no _____

If you noticed them:

9. What did you think of them when you saw them there?
   Park Square area: _______________
   ____
   ____
   South Station area: _______________
   ____
   ____

10. Do you have a driver's license?
    yes _____
    no _____
    For how long? _____ years
    From which state? _______________

TEST 3 — COMPARISON OF INTERSECTIONS WITH OLD AND NEW SIGNING

Purpose

This experiment was designed to compare the comprehensibility of the symbolic signs and existing signs when viewed in the context of a total intersection. Subjects were to determine from the signs all turns which they would be allowed to make if they were drivers approaching the intersection. The impact of social class and familiarity with similar sign systems was also evaluated.

Procedure

Forty subjects viewed slides of intersections and were directed to write down all permissible turns. The slides were made by photographing, from the driver's position, 19 intersections, first with existing signs and next with the symbolic signs. The slide series was arranged in two groups of 19 slides with no two slides of the same intersection in the same series. Half of the subjects saw one series, and half saw the other series. Each slide was exposed for 2 seconds, and subjects were given 20 seconds to record their answers.

Results

The answers were coded in two ways: Completely Correct (all possible turns listed) and Completely Incorrect (none of the possible turns listed) (Table 6). The intersections with symbolic signs were significantly better understood than those with existing ones; there were more Completely Correct responses for the new signs and fewer Completely Incorrect responses. As in Test 2, social class and having been abroad did not affect responses. Once again, nonstudents did better than students in understanding choices available at the intersections.

TABLE 5: BREAKDOWN OF SAMPLE ACCORDING TO SEX, AGE, AND CLASS (Test 3)

		N	%
SEX	Male	28	70
	Female	12	30
	Total	**40**	**100**
AGE	13-19	14	35
	20-35	26	65
	Total	**40**	**100**
CLASS	Lower and Lower Middle	13	33
	Middle and Upper Middle	7	12
	Student	20	50
	Total	**40**	**100**

TABLE 6: PERCENTAGE OF SUBJECTS GIVING VARIOUS RESPONSES TO INTERSECTIONS USING OLD AND NEW SIGNING SYSTEMS

Intersection Simulation No.	Completely Correct Old %	Completely Correct New %	Completely Incorrect Old %	Completely Incorrect New %
1	50	47	20	6
2	41	95	12	0
3	15	6	20	0
4	15	6	14	23
5	50	54	20	23
6	18	80	11	5
7	94	85	0	5
8	35	20	0	10
9	45	88	0	0
10	53	80	41	20
11	20	53	15	0
12	35	35	5	0
13	47	55	6	5
14	14	45	20	10
15	20	41	20	12
16	12	10	0	5
17	45	71	15	0
18	15	53	10	6
19	14	60	6	0
Mean	**34**	**52**	**11**	**7**
	$p < .005$		**$p < .01$**	

Before and after slide pair used in the intersection test.

EVALUATION OF SYMBOLIC TRAFFIC SIGNS: POSTCARD QUESTIONNAIRE

Purpose
The purpose of this survey was to evaluate the response to the new symbolic traffic signs in Park and Dewey Squares.
Procedure
One thousand self-addressed postcards with short questionnaires on the back were handed out to drivers stopping at red traffic lights in both experimental areas after the new traffic signs were installed; 500 were distributed in Park Square, 500 in Dewey Square. A pretest in the "before" situation had determined that a response rate of 10% could be expected, hence the relatively large number of questionnaires distributed. Perhaps because of interest in the new signs, an overall response rate of 18% was obtained. One hundred ten postcards were returned from Park Square motorists (22%), and 70 postcards were returned from those driving through Dewey Square (14%).

The following is a reproduction of the postcard format:

> We are doing an experiment on new traffic signs for the City of Boston and would like to know what you think about them. Thank you very much for your cooperation.
>
> Do you think the new traffic control signs ("Do Not Enter"; "One Way"; "Keep Right," etc.) are [check one in each row]:
>
> well placed ✓ poorly placed ____
> easy to understand ✓ difficult to understand ____
> easy to see ✓ difficult to see ____
> too few ✓ just right ✓ too many ____
> good ✓ fair ____ poor ____
>
> Comments: GREAT. FANTASTIC! Cover the CITY with Them!

TABLE 1: POSTCARD RESPONSES CONCERNING NEW TRAFFIC SIGNS IN PARK AND DEWEY SQUARES

	Park Square N=110		Dewey Square N=70	
	Number of Responses	% of Responses	Number of Responses	% of Responses
Positive Responses				
well placed	68	62	46	66
easy to understand	78	71	53	76
easy to see	70	64	45	64
too few	30	27	18	26
good	49	45	37	53
just right	35	32	22	31
TOTAL	330	50%	221	53%
COMBINED TOTAL Park Sq. & Dewey Sq.—551 (51%)				
Neutral Response				
fair	15	14%	9	13%
COMBINED TOTAL Park Sq. & Dewey Sq.—24 (14%)				
Negative Responses				
poorly placed	17	15	5	7
difficult to understand	9	8	6	9
difficult to see	14	13	2	3
too many	14	13	8	11
poor	17	15	–	–
TOTAL	71	12%	21	6%
COMBINED TOTAL Park Sq. & Dewey Sq.—92 (10%)				
No Responses*				
well-poorly placed	25	23	19	27
easy-difficult to understand	23	21	11	15
easy-difficult to see	26	23	23	33
too few-just right-too many	31	28	22	32
good-fair-poor	29	26	24	34
TOTAL	134	24%	99	28%

* Many respondents from Park and Dewey Squares did not follow the directions stated on the postcard. Instead of checking "one in each row" they checked only those descriptions with which they agreed, regardless of row position. Six respondents did not check any categories but did offer their comments. This accounts for the relatively large group of no responses.

Results
The results of this survey (Table 1) show that motorists reacted extremely favorably to the new traffic signs in Park and Dewey Squares. Among the Park Square respondents there were a total of 330 positive responses; among the Dewey Square respondents there were a total of 221 positive responses. Thus, 50% (Park Square) and 53% (Dewey Square) of all possible positive responses were checked[1] (330 positive responses/660 possible positive responses = 50%; 221 positive responses/420 possible positive responses = 53%). The new signs in Park Square elicited 71 negative responses, while the new signs in Dewey Square only elicited 21 negative responses. Thus, only 12% (Park Square) and 6% (Dewey Square) of all possible negative responses were checked (71 negative responses/550 possible negative responses = 12%; 21 negative responses/350 possible negative responses = 6%).

Combining the data from Park Square and Dewey Square, it can be seen that 51% of all possible positive responses were checked while only 10% of all possible negative responses were checked (551 positive responses/1,080 possible positive responses = 51%; 92 negative responses/900 possible negative responses = 10%).

Another way of analyzing the data is to divide the number of positive responses by the total number of all responses. For example, among the Park Square respondents there were 330 positive responses, 15 fair responses, and 71 negative responses. Thus, 79% of all responses were positive. (330 positive responses/416 total responses = 79%). Similarly, 88% of all responses from Dewey Square were positive (221 positive responses/251 total responses = 88%). Overall, 83% of all responses from Park and Dewey Squares were positive (551 positive responses, 667 total responses = 83%).

Postcard Comments about New Traffic Signs in Dewey and Park Squares
The following comments, written by respondents on the postcard questionnaire, include both Dewey and Park Square traffic signs. The comments are a proportionate sample of positive and negative responses.

Positive

Good for the city. It should have been done sooner.

The signs are better to understand . . . good change.

Best idea I've seen in years for traffic control! Good luck.

After getting accustomed to them it would be a vast improvement!

They are excellent and should be continued and expanded.

Put up some more in the State of Massachusetts.

1. A "possible" response = the maximum number of responses which would be obtained if all subjects responded in the same way. For example, if all 110 Park Square subjects checked all 6 positive categories, then there would be 660 positive responses. Therefore, there is a total of 660 possible positive responses.

I noticed them immediately and was struck by the improvement visually.

Other city signs such as "stop" ought to be coordinated to fit into the same graphic scheme.

I have driven in Europe using similar signs. Why just Boston? Why not *all* of Massachusetts and even *all* U.S.A.?

After being in Europe in September and marveling at their signs I am ecstatic to see Boston following the example. Not having driven sufficiently through the city I don't know whether there are enough signs. There could never be too many!

Much better. It is a pleasure to cooperate with you.

Negative

I can't see the value of signs when no one pays attention to them anyway. Also, how about putting route markers *before* intersections (with arrows).

Poorly placed in some places. For example, corner Boylston and Charles Streets.

Seems confusing to have a "no left turn" followed by a "one way." The "no left turn" has already told me it's "one way." I would think you could eliminate the "one way" signs.

Reflectors should be added around the "do not enter" sign.

They would be easier to see if you could *eliminate* all those *Tow Zone* signs.

In crowded and brightly lit areas, yellow (or even bright orange) poles seem preferable. Excessive number of signs is both unsightly and limits their effectiveness; e.g., duplication of "one way" signs on north side of Statler Office Building and "right turn only" sign at Boylston Street corner (in front of Avis) which duplicates traffic light. Less *"control"* signs and more directional (i.e. *destination* are needed).

Should be larger (signs) — with legend larger.

EVALUATION OF GUIDE SIGNS: OBSERVATION OF DRIVER BEHAVIOR

Purpose
To assess the effects of the new guide signs (downtown, Chinatown, Back Bay, Mass. Pike), driving behavior was observed in the two experimental areas — Park Square and Dewey Square. Observations were carried out before and after the installation of the new signs to determine whether there was any observable difference in driver confusion.

Procedure
Selection of sites for observation
The observation sites were chosen to meet the following criteria:
1 the driver had to decide which of several possible alternatives to pick;
2 the decision had to be made while actually driving, not while stopping at a traffic light; and
3 the driver had relatively few clues to guide him or enable him to proceed in the intended direction.

One observation site was chosen in each of the two experimental areas. In Park Square (Map 1), the site was at the junction of Providence Street and Columbus Avenue, at the tip of the Statler Office Building. Traffic observed came from Eliot Street and Broadway, and could turn onto either Columbus Avenue or Providence Street.

In Dewey Square (Map 2), the observation site was at the intersection of Purchase and Summer Streets. Streams of traffic to be observed came from Atlantic Avenue and Summer Street, from the Expressway Exit and from Purchase Street. Cars could proceed on either Federal Street or the Surface Artery.

Only those guide signs which would be seen by the flow of traffic under observation are shown on the maps. Thus all of the signs in Park Square are included, but not all those in Dewey Square which, because of its size and complexity, had more guide signs. At the time the guide signs were erected, new regulatory and street name signs had also been installed (see Chapter 4 of text for full description of these). These signs were placed in the positions previously occupied by their counterparts in the existing system. These regulatory and street name signs are not marked on the maps.

Observation of driving behavior
Behavior to be counted as confusion was defined according to the following criteria:
1 definite violations of traffic regulations, e.g., entering one-way street in the wrong direction;
2 lane changes made at the last minute;
3 stopping or slowing down before proceeding in one of several possible directions, at times accompanied by actively looking around or turning the steering wheel first in one direction and then in the other; and
4 expressive behavior indicating confusion, such as shaking one's head, pointing in a certain direction by the passenger, etc.

PARK SQUARE

1

2

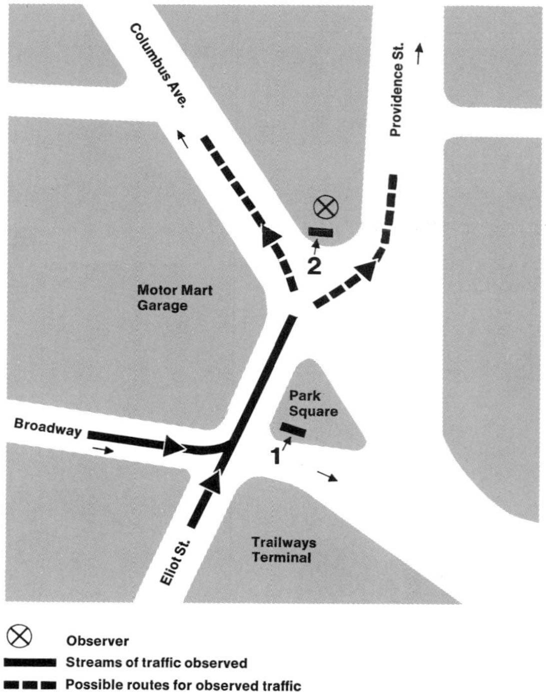

DEWEY SQUARE

1

2

3

4
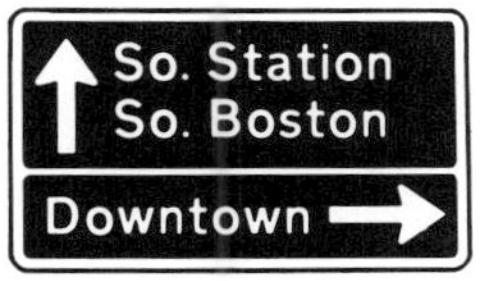

5

6

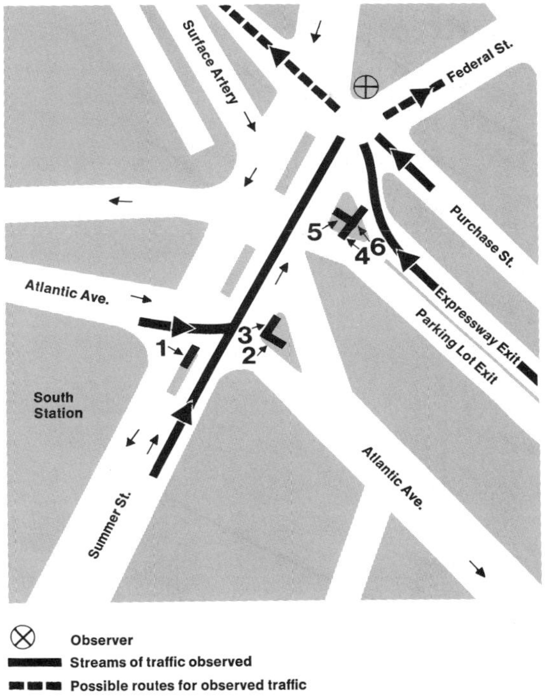

Driving behavior was rated in two categories: Definite Confusion and Possible Confusion. When the observer was certain that one of the above criteria applied to the behavior of a particular driver, he noted it on an observation pad in the Definite Confusion category. In the final analysis only the instances of Definite Confusion were used, because the two observers generally agreed on these counts. Variations in counts of Possible Confusion were more frequent and therefore not used in the analysis.

At each site, observations were evenly divided between mornings and afternoons on four days of the week (Thursday, Friday, Saturday, and Monday), before and after installation of the new signs. Thus the amount of traffic at each site was about the same during the before and after observation periods.

Results

In Park Square, there was an average of 18 instances of Definite Confusion per hour before the new signs were installed; after installation there was an average of 11 instances. In Dewey Square there were 27 instances of confusion per hour before and 11 after the new signs were installed.

It is not possible to separate the effect of the directional signs from that of the new regulatory and street name signs. It is possible to say, however, that the installation of the *total* new signing system, including guide, street name and regulatory signs, resulted in less driver confusion at these intersections.

Public Lighting: Tests

Two demonstrations of public lighting techniques were conducted. One, the Light and Sound Environment in the Boston Public Garden, was tested on a short-term basis, with no intention that it become permanent. Responses were gathered from observers and the success of the demonstration was gauged on this basis. The other demonstration involved lighting the Boston Public Library in Copley Square. In this case, a group of professionals viewed trial lighting alternatives, and the effectiveness of each was assessed by their opinions alone. The final alternative will be carried out in permanent lighting. This demonstration had the further aim of stimulating lighting efforts for the other privately-owned buildings in Copley Square — Trinity Church, Old South Church, and the Sheraton Plaza Hotel.

EVALUATION OF THE LIGHT AND SOUND ENVIRONMENT

Purpose
The Light and Sound demonstration[1] (Boston Public Garden, October 9-27, 1968) attempted to create an environment that encouraged people to see and hear the park and the city around it in new ways. A principal aim was to demonstrate that exciting events can occur in places that are generally dead and forbidding at night. In order to assess the public's reaction to the experiment, a series of surveys was conducted.
Procedure
Five methods were used for determining attendance rates and attitudes towards the Light and Sound Environment:
1. *Visitor count*
2. *Spatial location of visitors*
3. *Adjective check-list*
4. *Short interviews*
5. *Open-ended interviews*
The general conclusions are in Chapters 4 and 6.

1. For a description of the Light and Sound Environment, see Chapter 4.

TABLE 1: SEX AND AGE OF VISITORS AT THE LIGHT AND SOUND ENVIRONMENT DETERMINED THROUGH OBSERVATION (Visitor Count)

		N	%
SEX	Male	252	70
	Female	109	30
	Total	**361**	**100**
AGE	Under 12	19	5
	13-19	117	31
	20-34	209	54
	35-55	35	9
	Over 55	4	1
	Total	**384**	**100**

TABLE 2: BREAKDOWN OF SAMPLE ACCORDING TO SEX, AGE, AND CLASS (Adjective Check-List)

		N	%
SEX	Male	21	64
	Female	12	36
	Total	**33**	**100**
AGE	13-19	5	15
	20-34	19	58
	35-55	8	24
	Over 55	1	3
	Total	**33**	**100**
CLASS	Lower and Lower Middle	4	12
	Middle and Upper Middle	27	82
	Student	2	6
	Total	**33**	**100**

TABLE 3: BREAKDOWN OF SAMPLE ACCORDING TO SEX, AGE, AND CLASS (Short Interviews)

		N	%
SEX	Male	30	64
	Female	17	36
	Total	**47***	**100**
AGE	13-19	14	29
	20-34	24	50
	35-55	10	21
	Total	**48**	**100**
CLASS	Lower and Lower Middle	2	4
	Middle and Upper Middle	31	70
	Student	12	26
	Total	**45****	**100**

* One interview was conducted with a man and a woman.
** Class of 3 respondents not recorded.

Results

1. *Visitor count (Table 1)*

For 15 minutes on eleven evenings, people were counted to determine the number attending the demonstration and to assess their demographic characteristics (sex, and broad categories for age). The count was taken of people on the bridge, since it was assumed that every person interested in the demonstration would look at it at least once from there.

An average of 102 people passed one particular spot on the bridge during 15 minutes of an evening. A total number of 1,129 people passed this spot during the eleven 15 minute counting periods. Extrapolating from the count, between 6,000 and 7,000 people saw the demonstration. Most of the visitors were under 35. There were more than twice as many males (70%) as females (30%).

2. *Spatial location of visitors*

At several times during each of the eleven evenings, the spatial distribution of people attending the demonstration was recorded. The exact location of each person was marked on a map of the Public Garden. Most people gathered at the bridge or stood on the Beacon Street side of the pond. This suggests that the reflections from the Boylston Street lights may have interfered with the lights of the demonstration, thus making that side less appealing as a viewing point.

3. *Adjective check-list (Table 2)*

Thirty-three people were given a list of adjectives and asked to check how appropriate or inappropriate each one was for characterizing the Light and Sound Environment. Values of 1 to 5 were assigned to each response category (disagree, slightly disagree, neither/nor, slightly agree, and agree). Each adjective was scored so that a high value, a 4 or 5, always indicated a favorable attitude towards the demonstration.

The scores were then divided into five groups, ranging from very negative to very positive. The potential range of scores was 14 to 70, from lowest to highest.

The following distribution reveals that most people liked the Light and Sound Environment (67%).

Score	N	%
14-21	2	6
22-35	4	12
36-49	5	15
50-63	12	37
64-70	10	37
Total	**33**	**100**

4. *Short interviews (Table 3)*

Forty-eight visitors to the Light and Sound Environment answered the short interview questionnaire. Of these, 21 (44%) had seen the demonstration before; 15 (31%) had come back because they liked it, and 3 (6%) wanted to see its development and change over time. Half of the returning visitors had been to the demonstration less than three days prior to the interview, 8 of them had seen the demonstration every night. Thirteen (17%) said that they had spent more than 30 minutes at the Light and Sound Environment at their previous visit.

Most of the respondents (63%) came upon the demonstration by chance. Twelve visitors (25%) had heard about it from friends, and only 6 visitors (12%) mentioned the press or posters.

At the time of the interview, 64% of the respondents had been at the demonstration under 20 minutes. However, 74% said that they intended to stay there some time longer. Younger people spent more time at the demonstration than older people, who generally stayed for 30 minutes or less.

The people who didn't like the demonstration generally felt that it was somewhat interesting but very confusing, noisy, and uncomfortable. Moreover, they thought that it was unnecessary and pointless. For the people who liked it, the demonstration was also quite confusing and noisy, but not at all pointless, unnecessary, or silly; they found it very promising, interesting, and exciting.

5. *Open-ended interviews (Table 4)*

Several respondents who answered the short interview questionnaire (above) also participated in the open-ended interviews. Initially, each type of interview was conducted independently of the other; later it was decided that the short interview questionnaire would be a good introduction to the open-ended interview. In all cases where the open-ended interview was preceded by the questions from the short interview, the answers from the latter have been discussed in the above section. This section only discusses questions 5 to 9 from the open-ended interview questionnaire.

Since the intent of this interview was to encourage a casual conversation between the interviewer and the respondent, the interview form was used only as a guideline. Only a portion of the total sample of 47 respondents answered all questions.

Of those respondents who answered the question, "Would you like to come back here again?" 16 said that they would, while 8 said that they wouldn't. Reasons for not planning to return were that the respondent was a visitor to Boston, or simply because he did not like the demonstration. Twenty-six respondents said that they would tell their friends about the Light and Sound Environment and recommend a visit. Only 4 respondents said that they would not tell friends.

When asked in which other locations the demonstration might be attractive, most of the respondents (22) could not think of any other place besides the Public Garden. Six respondents mentioned the waterfront, the Charles River, or the Fenway — locations that also involve water. Seven others suggested having the demonstration in trees or at the Prudential Building. Thirty-five respondents were enthusiastic about having a similar demonstration in the Public Garden every year, only 2 were not.

Overall, there were more favorable comments (113) about the Light and Sound Environment than unfavorable (73).

There were more than twice as many positive general comments (referring to the newness, reaction of people, purpose, and location of the demonstration) as negative comments. However, specific comments about the light and sound aspects of the demonstration were more frequently negative.

At the end of the interview, each respondent was rated on a five-point scale, on his general attitude toward the Light and Sound Environment. The following shows the number of subjects in each category. The results are quite similar to the scores obtained from the adjective check-list.

	N	%
Dislikes it very much	6	13
Dislikes it somewhat	5	10
Neutral	6	13
Likes it somewhat	16	34
Likes it very much	14	30
Total	**47**	**100**

Although the number of subjects is quite small, the results show that working-class people were considerably less enthusiastic toward the demonstration than either middle-class or student respondents. Three of the 8 working-class respondents in the sample seemed to dislike the demonstration very much. No consistent differences were found attributable to either sex or age.

TABLE 4: BREAKDOWN OF SAMPLE ACCORDING TO SEX, AGE, AND CLASS (Open-ended Interviews)

		N	%
SEX	Male	34	72
	Female	8	17
	Questions answered by couple	5	11
	Total	**47**	**100**
AGE	13-19	8	17
	20-34	27	58
	35-55	9	19
	Over 55	3	6
	Total	**47**	**100**
CLASS	Lower and Lower Middle	8	17
	Middle and Upper Middle	32	68
	Student	7	15
	Total	**47**	**100**

ADJECTIVE CHECKLIST

Identification - Nr. _____ Respondent - Nr. _____

Here is a list of words characterizing the Light and Sound Show. Each word stands for the statement: "The show is ________". By putting a checkmark under one of the five categories beside each word, you indicate to what extent you feel that the particular statement does or does not apply to the show.

Example:	disagree	slightly disagree	neither/ nor	slightly agree	agree
amazing				✓	

Supposing you had put down this checkmark, it would show that you think of the show as being slightly amazing.

	disagree	slightly disagree	neither/ nor	slightly agree	agree
confusing					
enchanting					
promising					
interesting					
pointless					
noisy					
unnecessary					
entertaining					
exciting					
boring					
uncomfortable					
excellent					
spectacular					
silly					

TO BE FILLED OUT BY INTERVIEWER:

Date ___________ Time ______________

Day ___________ Weather ___________

S: A: O:

SHORT INTERVIEW

Identification-Nr. _____ Day: ________________

Respondent-Nr: ______ Time: ________________

Date: ________________ Weather: ______________

1. Is this your first visit at the Boston Light and Sound Show?

   yes _____ no_____

   If no:

   When were you here before?

   How long did you stay then?

   Why did you come back?

2. How did you find out about the Light and Sound Show?

   _____ press _____ posters

   _____ radio _____ friends, colleagues, etc.

   _____ TV _____ by chance, just passing by

3. How long have you been here?

4. Do you intend to stay any longer?

   yes _____ no _____

   If yes:

INFORMATION ABOUT THE RESPONDENT

male _________ under 20__________

female________ 20 - 35__________

occupation 35 - 55__________

_____________ over 55__________

OPEN-ENDED INTERVIEW

Identification-Nr: _____ Day: _______________

Respondent-Nr: _____ Time: _____________

Date: __________________ Weather: __________

1. Is this your first visit at the Boston Light and Sound Show?

yes _____ no _____

If no:

When were you here before?

How long did you stay then?

Why did you come back?

2. How did you find out about the Light and Sound Show?

from the

_____ press

_____ radio

_____ TV

_____ posters

_____ friends, colleagues, etc.

_____ by chance, just passing by

3. How long have you been here?

4. Do you intend to stay any longer?

yes _____ no _____

If yes:

How long, approximately?

5. Would you like to come back here again?

yes _____ no_____

(PROBE FOR REASONS) e.g. Why? Why not?

6. What do you think of the show?

(RECORD SPONTANEOUS COMMENTS)

(PROBING SUGGESTIONS, NOT ALL OF THEM HAVE TO BE ASKED IF TOPICS ARE COVERED IN OTHER WAYS)

Do you like it? (Why?)

Is there anything that you dislike? (Why?)

7. Do you think this kind of show could be attractive in other locations too? Would you like to have it there?

8. What do you think of the idea of having a show like this one in the Public Garden every year?

9. Would you recommend that your friends visit the show too?

(RATE THE RESPONDENT, IF HIS ATTITUDE IS UNCLEAR HAVE HIM RATE HIMSELF)

_____ Likes the show very much

_____ somewhat

_____ is neutral

_____ dislikes it somewhat

_____ dislikes it very much

(INSERT RATING LIST HERE)

INFORMATION ABOUT THE RESPONDENT

male_______ female_______

age________

occupation

____

location of interview:

bridge _____________

Boylston St. end ____

Beacon St. end ____

Comments from Open-ended Interviews

The statements which follow are a representative sample of positive, negative, and miscellaneous responses to question 6 of the open-ended interview — "What do you think of the show, do you like it, and what do you dislike?":

Positive

It's a dynamic work of art to me.

This particular work of art could produce far different reactions in people's minds than ordinary art such as paintings or statues.

This is a wonderful new art form regrettably poorly understood which serves as a catalyst in making people conscious of the natural environment around them.

It's absolutely one of the most interesting things I've seen in a long time.

It's exciting. It tells you to come and see what it is all about. It makes you want to find out.

It's something new and different which should excite people's imagination.

The water makes it a lot more interesting.

The water has a lot of effects on the lights, that's why it's so fantastic.

It's a wonderful thing, because the sound is quite subjective.

I like the sound, also I find it exciting.

I think it's great the way the sound follows the edge of the pond. You can hear it sort of receding and coming back around the sides.

The lights are nice.

As far as the lights go, the reflections in the water are much nicer. The lights are not distracting, on the contrary they help you meditate.

Negative

Nature's light shows, sunsets for instance, are definitely better.

I am more for things being the way they are than for artificial means of making things beautiful.

It's unnatural, anti-nature.

Obviously the sounds represent frogs and the light lightning bugs. That is the same as many people have plastic flowers instead of real flowers or have a big picture window and pull the curtains over their real windows. I guess the alienation of man from the rest of nature is represented here again.

Somebody who didn't know what it was might find it frightening.

I personally don't understand the whole thing.

I don't think this is supposed to mean anything.

The show is very repetitive when looking at it for a longer time.

It's boring after a while.

I doubt it will please everybody; Beacon Hill ladies certainly won't have much appreciation for it.

Ordinary people, people of the street, people of everyday life, don't get such a big kick out of this.

I think it could be expanded on, but this doesn't satisfy me.

I think it could be done much better. If I were doing it I'd have it a lot more involved like lights in the trees and different things like that.

I don't care for it too much. It's just a bunch of noises, it's not music.

Aren't those noises ugly?

The sounds simulate something that is already a bad thing — we are bombarded with too much noise anyway.

I would like it better without the sounds.

I would like a show that is more similar to an electronic concert.

The possibilities of the electronic sound are not exhausted; one could do something like Stockhausen.

The sounds could be more melodic.

As a matter of fact, I am a bit disappointed in the sense of your music.

I see certain limitations in this project. Are they afraid of including familiar real sound and music as well?

If they had more effective lights it would be better.

They ought to have the light flashing on all the time, have it go one by one all around the lake.

Unless the lights go around fast, they are useless.

Why aren't there any colors?

Miscellaneous

It gets away from the object of art, it makes art something you can't pin down — it's too fast for that.

People just don't know what to expect, so they don't know whether it is good or bad or filling its purpose.

It is strange and unusual.

It could provoke quite a controversy because it is so unusual for Boston.

It's like on another planet, like Star Trek for instance.

THE PUBLIC LIBRARY AND COPLEY SQUARE

The impressive siting and facade of the Boston Public Library and its prominent location in Copley Square invite the use of innovative lighting techniques for the building. Not only would ordinary floodlighting do much to destroy the overall atmosphere of Copley Square but also it would ignore the richness of form and detail that the building possesses. The lighting design tested in this study deployed special equipment to emphasize the important architectural and structural features of the library facade, while using ambient illumination in the square to delineate the form of the building and its setting. The elements chosen for emphasis were the 13 arched windows on the second floor and the entranceway. The lighting was designed to make the library appear as a lantern, radiating inner warmth and light through its major openings.

The illumination of the arched windows on the second floor employed unobtrusive lighting equipment. By trial and error field adjustment of the lamp distribution and positioning of the luminaires, light was confined to specified areas. The luminaires were mounted on the outside ledge at the base of each window, as shown in the photograph. They were aimed vertically to wash the window recess and allow spill light to illuminate the cornice. The result was a uniform band of light in the window recess which extended out to softly highlight the first projection of the stonework, thereby framing the opening. The carvings and inscriptions on the spandrels under the windows were also highlighted. A halo effect was achieved at each window.

The lighting equipment consisted of one 8 foot 430 milliamp fluorescent lamp mounted on the window ledge in a custom-designed weatherproof stainless steel housing with clear acrylic diffuser, and one 6 foot 430 milliamp fluorescent lamp in an identical fixture mounted on the lower ledge. The fluorescent lamp has a 12,000 hour lifetime. The energy total for the windows is 2 kilowatts. Lamps are deluxe cool white.

Initially, there was light reflection from the window glass and the mullions were highlighted, emphasizing the plane of the window. Partial shielding of the light source reduced this unwanted effect. However, since the grazing angle of the projected light caused most of the light to be reflected skyward from the window glass, the windows appeared dark. To achieve the desired lantern effect, it is necessary to increase the interior illumination until the windows appear luminous. An examination of the area inside the library showed that many lighting methods would have serious disadvantages: either the light sources would be visible, from inside or outside, or the quality of the ornate ceiling in the main reading room would be disturbed. However, proper illumination of the ceiling could provide the necessary brightness to the window and at the same time highlight the ceiling and raise the illumination of the reading room. Metal halide floodlighting should be used for achieving this effect.

The main entrance was the other element to be illuminated. The entrance is composed of three doors, each surmounted by an arch. A large wrought iron lantern stands on each side of the entrance steps. The doors themselves are fronted by iron grilles. The arches are illuminated by 4 foot fluorescent lamps similar to those in the windows. The lighting fixtures are mounted on the ledge at the spring of the arch. The ballasts are remote-mounted in the vestibule to keep the cross-section of the lighting fixture to a minimum. Besides providing general illumination, this backlighting dramatizes the grillework in front of the doors.

The Public Library is part of a total environment created by the space and buildings of Copley Square. Although only the library was used for demonstration, recommendations were developed for lighting the other important buildings and the square itself.

The Sheraton Plaza Hotel

The Sheraton Plaza Hotel cannot be floodlit in the usual sense, since it would intrude on the comfort of guests, filling rooms with light from outside and blocking the view of Copley Square by glaring lights. The bulk of the building must therefore be seen by whatever lighting the square itself generates.

The window arches on the first floor of the hotel, however, could be lighted without causing problems. Two hundred fifty or 500-watt iodine quartz single-ended lamps in suitable projectors would be used. These would be encapsulated in a specially fabricated case, which would be mounted on the window sill. It is expected that the amount of normal activity in the area would keep vandalism at a minimum, although such equipment can be designed to be vandal proof. Twenty-two luminaires would be required.

It might also be possible to mount a low-silhouette fluorescent strip on the ledge of the seventh floor of the hotel to softly illuminate the building cornice. This effect was produced by different means in the library illumination experiments and seemed desirable. As at the entrance to the library, the concentration of light at the hotel portico symbolizes welcome. This theme can be reiterated at all the major buildings of the square.

Trinity Church

Trinity Church is the most ornate and structurally complex of all the buildings in the Copley Square area. Technically, it is also the easiest to illuminate, for its complexity offers many places in which to "hide" equipment. A number of effects should be tried.

Certain windows of the church can be made luminous, as long as great care is taken to keep the lighting subdued. The five arched windows directly above the center entrance can be illuminated easily by placing crossed floods within the sanctuary and on the beam structure at the end of the nave opposite the main altar. A luminous effect can be achieved similarly within the two secondary towers at the front of the church. Intense highlighting of the inner porch of the nave entrance will effectively tie the bottom of the structure to the other three buildings in the square. The West Porch and the ascending stairs at the Parish House can form interesting patterns of light and shadow. However, to achieve this effect the back walls (as viewed from Copley Square) must be highlighted with uniformly spaced downlights.

Changing the illuminant in the large indirect bowl which

Library lighting trial.

Trinity Church.

Sheraton Plaza Hotel.

Old South Church.

lights the sanctuary in the center of the great tower from incandescent to a more efficient source should increase the brightness of the great tower windows and relate these to the lower illuminated space. Further, by hiding equipment behind the small turrets adjacent to the pyramidal tower roof structures, it may be possible to illuminate tangentially the surfaces of the roof and thus effectively cap the entire Trinity scene. This effect would also relate Trinity's tower to the tower on Old South Church.

Old South Church

The parts of Old South Church particularly relevant to the lighting of the Copley Square area are:

1. the corner entrance portico,
2. the Boylston Street loggia,
3. the tower entranceway,
4. the tower bell area,
5. the pinnacle of tower,
6. the dome over the sanctuary, and
7. the arched windows over the portico.

The building walls under the portico of the corner entrance can be highlighted to emphasize the interesting arch shapes. The color of the stonework in this area should be brought out by using a white light source with a high red component, such as a phosphor-coated metal halide lamp. The same treatment should be carried out in the Boylston Street loggia; both areas should be uniformly washed with light. The inscription in the loggia should be highlighted, preferably by incandescent spots of proper beam spread. Positioning this equipment will, of course, be a matter of trial and error.

The tower entranceway can be highlighted with the existing, unfocused, metal halide luminaire. In the bell area of the tower there should be eight 250-watt, phosphor-coated, deluxe, mercury, wide-beam projectors, cross-aimed to highlight the sides of the columns, thereby throwing the outermost portions of the columns into sharp relief. If possible, the roof of the tower should be floodlit with long-life, deluxe, mercury placed at each of the four corners of the pyramidal structure, behind the small structures. This would tie in with the proposed lighting plan for Trinity Church.

The light from the clear mercury on the surface of the dome over the sanctuary is garish; deluxe white mercury lamps should be used instead, with possible equipment modification.

This study did not examine the interior of Old South Church, and therefore concrete suggestions for obtaining the desired luminosity of the five major arched windows and the circular window on the main wall area on Boylston Street cannot be made. However, the investigation at Trinity Church showed this could be accomplished there; it is possible that the same principles may be relevant at Old South Church. This also applies to the arched windows over the portico. Here, in addition to interior light, strip lighting with fluorescent or incandescent iodine quartz PAR lamps — one on either corner of the roof line with beams crossed — would produce an effect analogous to that of the library and the Sheraton Plaza by highlighting interesting stonework, windows, and a tablet.

The Copley Square Area

Serious thought should be given to re-lighting the plaza itself and streets adjacent to the Copley Square buildings. The buildings in the square represent several architectural styles — the library is Italian Renaissance, fifteenth century; Trinity Church is French Romanesque, eleventh century; Old South Church is early fourteenth century. It is most important that the lighting should be in keeping with this rich, warm nineteenth century revival architecture.

Neither conventional mercury vapor roadway lighting nor the modern plastic globes with mercury sources, now installed in the plaza, are appropriate to the site. These systems have several negative aspects which are particularly out of place in Copley Square. Not only do they produce intolerable glare and cold light which conflicts with the warm materials, but also large quantities of luminaires are needed to produce adequate illumination. The rich, subdued nighttime atmosphere which can be created in Copley Square, primarily through careful illumination of surrounding buildings, can also be destroyed by the present glaring, mercury vapor public fixtures. Public lighting in the area should make use of shielded, high-pressure sodium sources for the streets and incandescent sources within the square.

Copley Square with mercury vapor lighting.

APPENDIX EIGHT

Private Signs: Tests

8

Private signs are familiar objects in the cityscape. Store signs, or "on-premise" signs, are erected to attract the attention of motorists and pedestrians. These signs announce the name of the establishment and frequently state its function. Sometimes they are also used to advertise specific goods, services, and costs. Off-premise signs normally advertise establishments, goods, and services, which are located at some distance from the sign. Billboards fit into this category.

Several experiments and surveys were designed to gauge the public's view towards private signs — both on and off-premise:

1 Recognition Experiment

2 Opinion Survey

3 Influence on Assessment of Street Attractiveness

4 Billboards: Opinion Survey

The general conclusions from these studies are in Chapter 6.

RECOGNITION EXPERIMENT

Purpose

This experiment investigated the amount of attention that people give to the private commercial signs on Washington Street in downtown Boston. One of the purposes was to discover the attention-getting capacities of signs as opposed to windows and buildings. Another objective was to identify those factors which most affect the recognition of signs — e.g., sex of subject, subject's familiarity with the street, and the context in which the sign is seen.

Procedure

Slides were made of 20 commercial signs (16 on Washington Street, 4 on other streets), 10 windows (8 on Washington, 2 on other streets), and 10 buildings (8 on Washington, 2 on other streets). One set of commercial sign slides showed the signs with their surroundings, while in another identical set, backgrounds were masked. The size of the signs and their positions in the slides were identical in both sets.

Twenty-five subjects took part in the experiment. They were recruited by posting notices in a wide variety of places, ranging from bulletin boards at Harvard University and MIT to laundromats and construction fences in Harvard Square. All of the participants had middle class occupations and were between 16 and 25 years of age. (A considerable but unsuccessful effort was made to recruit a contrasting group of subjects, i.e., older people or those of a working-class background.[1])

The subjects met the experimenter at the corner of Washington and Stuart Streets. They were sent down Washington Street one at a time at one to two minute intervals; they had to remain on the north-east sidewalk. The subjects were asked to walk at a normal pace and to behave as if they were on their own. At the end of Washington Street, after approximately ten minutes of walking, they crossed the street and went into the Old South Meeting House to the experiment room for the second part of the test.

No attempt was made to talk to the subjects about the experiment before it was completed. The subjects were simply told to look at a sequence of slides and to remember whether they had seen the figures shown (sign, window, or building) during their walk on Washington Street. Subjects knew that not all of the slides were taken on Washington Street and that therefore the subjects should check the "recognized" category only if they were sure that they had actually seen the object. The subjects were also asked to check whether or not they liked the objects shown in the slides. Exposure time for each slide was one second, and the time for checking the two answers, ten seconds.

There were three separate runs of the experiment, during which 13 subjects were shown sign slides without backgrounds and 12 subjects were shown sign slides with backgrounds. All window and building slides were shown to all subjects. Each subject saw a total of 40 slides in the same random order.

At the end of each session the subjects were asked to complete a questionnaire asking for opinions on private signs, some facts about their personal backgrounds, and their degree of familiarity with Washington Street.

Results

Any score sheet that indicated recognition of more than half the non-Washington Street slides was eliminated from the data analysis. One subject who made 6 false recognitions and another who claimed to recognize all 8 non-Washington Street slides were eliminated. Thus, the data analysis presented here is based on the responses of 23 subjects. Table 1 shows the division of subjects by sex, familiarity with Washington Street, and type of sign slide seen, i.e., with or without background.

TABLE 1: NUMBER OF SUBJECTS IN EACH CATEGORY

	Sign Slides Shown With Background		Sign Slides Shown Without Background		
	Male	Female	Male	Female	TOTAL
Familiar With Washington Street	2	1	3	5	11
Not Familiar With Washington Street	6	1	1	4	12
Total	**8**	**2**	**4**	**9**	**23**

1. By contacting representatives of several poverty programs and neighborhood community centers, 12 working-class participants were recruited. Of these, however, only one came to the experiment.

Typical sign slides.

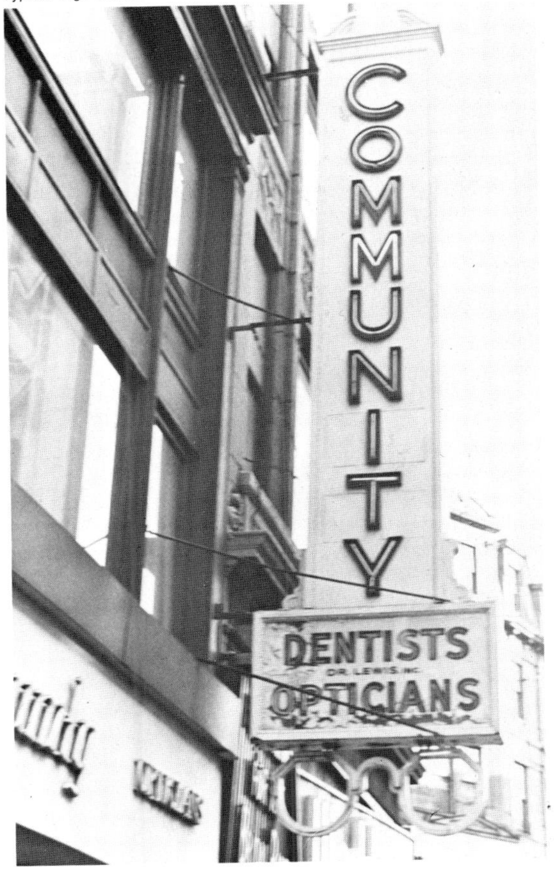

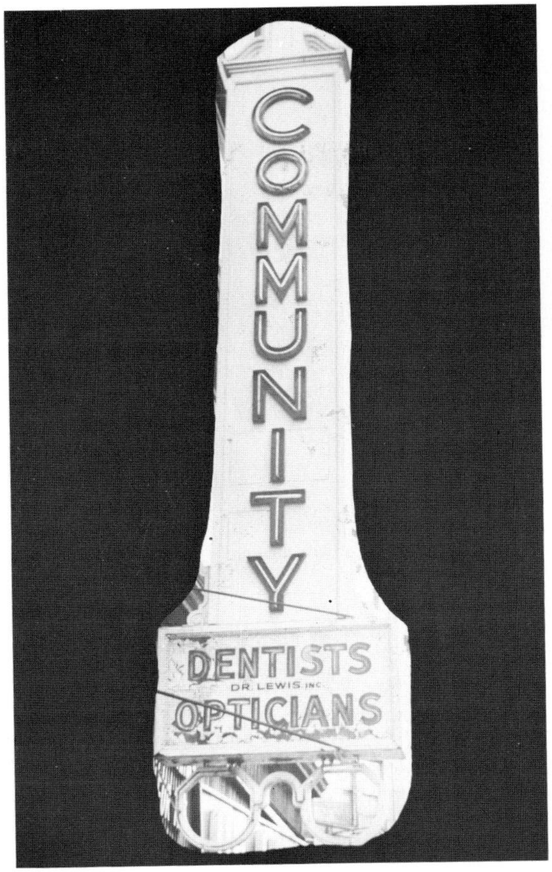

Typical window and building slides.

Since each subject looked at 40 slides, there was a total of 920 answers to be scored (23 x 40 = 920). If all responses had been correct, there would have been 736 Recognized answers (23 x 32 Washington Street slides = 736), and 184 Not Recognized answers (23 x 8 non-Washington Street slides = 184) (Table 2).

The results show that 339 of the 736 possible Recognized answers were given. This means that people frequently walked by objects which they were unable to recognize with certainty a few minutes later.

On the other hand, the non-Washington Street slides were generally correctly Not Recognized. That is, the subjects were better able to say that they had not seen the figure in the slide than they were able to say that they had definitely seen it during their walk on Washington Street.

There were only 34 instances in which a subject claimed that he recognized a slide which was not taken on Washington Street. These were defined as False Recognitions.

Length of time that signs remained in the subjects' visual field during the walk down Washington Street

The initial analysis of the data explored the possibility that the time each sign remained in the subject's visual field would determine the frequency with which it would be recognized from the slides. The signs fell roughly into two groups. In the first, the signs could be seen for only a short amount of time, one minute or less; in the second they could be seen longer, over one minute. Although there was no statistically significant difference between these two groups, the results tended to show that signs which were in the visual field longer were recognized more frequently.

Comparison of recognition of signs, windows, and buildings

For analysis, the slides were classified according to type — signs, windows, buildings (Table 3). The results show that non-Washington Street buildings were least often falsely recognized (12%), but also that slides of Washington Street buildings were identified least often (38%). On the other hand, slides of Washington Street signs were identified 50% of the time and falsely recognized only 18% of the time.

Slides of Washington Street windows were correctly recognized nearly as frequently as Washington Street signs (47%); non-Washington Street windows were most frequently falsely recognized (28%).

Taking both factors — percent of false recognitions and percent of correct recognitions — into consideration, it is legitimate to conclude both that signs were the most often successfully identified objects and that people noticed the signs on Washington Street more than they noticed either windows or buildings.

Comparison of sign recognition according to degree of subjects' familiarity with Washington Street

Subjects who claimed familiarity[2] with Washington Street

2. Familiarity was based on the respondent's own assessment of his familiarity with Washington Street, determined by answers to the questionnaire at the end of the experiment.

TABLE 2: NUMBER OF RECOGNITIONS AND NON-RECOGNITIONS OF WASHINGTON STREET AND NON-WASHINGTON STREET SLIDES

	Recognized	Not Recognized	TOTAL
Washington St. Slides	339*	397***	736
Non-Washington St. Slides	34**	150****	184
Total	**373**	**547**	**920**

* Correct Recognition: A Washington Street slide which was recognized as a slide of Washington Street

** False Recognition: A non-Washington Street slide which was recognized as a slide of Washington Street

*** Washington Street slides which were incorrectly recognized as slides of Washington Street

**** Non-Washington Street slides which were correctly not recognized as slides of Washington Street

TABLE 3: COMPARISON OF CORRECT AND FALSE SLIDE RECOGNITIONS ACCORDING TO TYPE OF SLIDE (SIGN, WINDOW, AND BUILDING)

	No False Recognitions	No Possible False Recognitions	% False Recognitions	No Correct Recognitions	No Possible Correct Recognitions	% Correct Recognitions
Signs	17	92	18	182	368	50
Windows	13	46	28	86	184	47
Buildings	4	46	12	70	184	38
Total	**34**	**182**	**19**	**338**	**736**	**46**

TABLE 4: PERCENTAGE OF WASHINGTON STREET SIGNS CORRECTLY RECOGNIZED AND NON-WASHINGTON STREET SIGNS FALSELY RECOGNIZED, ACCORDING TO SUBJECTS' FAMILIARITY WITH WASHINGTON STREET

	Familiar With Washington St.	Unfamiliar With Washington St.
Percentage of Correct Recognitions	55% *	45% ***
Percentage of False Recognitions	20% **	17% ****

* $\frac{\text{96 (correct sign recognitions)}}{\text{11 (subjects) x 16 (possible correct sign recognitions of slides)}}$

** $\frac{\text{9 (false sign recognitions)}}{\text{11 (subjects) x 4 (possible false recognitions of sign slides)}}$

*** $\frac{86}{12 \times 16}$

**** $\frac{8}{12 \times 4}$

TABLE 5: PERCENTAGE OF WASHINGTON STREET SIGNS CORRECTLY RECOGNIZED AND NON-WASHINGTON STREET SIGNS FALSELY RECOGNIZED, WITH AND WITHOUT SIGN BACKGROUND

	Sign Slides Shown With Background	Sign Slides Shown Without Background
Percentage of Correct Recognitions	42% *	55% ***
Percentage of False Recognitions	20% **	17% ****

* $\frac{\text{67 (correct sign recognitions)}}{\text{10 (subjects) x 16 (possible correct sign recognitions)}}$

** $\frac{\text{8 (false sign recognitions)}}{\text{10 (subjects) x 4 (possible false sign recognitions)}}$

*** $\frac{115}{13 \times 16}$

**** $\frac{9}{13 \times 4}$

were more likely to correctly identify the Washington Street sign slides (Table 4). The familiar group recognized the Washington Street slides 55% of the time, while the unfamiliar group recognized the Washington Street slides 45% of the time. Thus it does seem that familiarity aids correct sign recognition.

However, familiarity also slightly increased the likelihood of false sign recognitions. There are several plausible reasons why the familiar group mistakenly identified non-Washington Street sign slides more often (20%) than the unfamiliar group (17%). It is possible that subjects who were unfamiliar with Washington Street were more cautious in their responses, guessed less frequently, and may even have been more sensitive to details during their walk. It is also conceivable that people who were familiar with Washington Street may have also been more familiar with neighboring streets and may have actually seen the non-Washington Street signs on previous occasions. (All non-Washington Street signs were from nearby streets.)

Comparison of sign recognition according to sign slides shown with background and sign slides shown without background

The hypothesis that signs would be recognized much better with their backgrounds than without led to the experimental procedure with two sets of sign slides — one set with and one set without backgrounds. It seemed reasonable that the more clues presented to the subject, the easier the recognition task. However, slides shown without background had a higher rate of correct recognitions (Table 5). There were only 42% correct recognitions in the background group, while there were 55% correct recognitions in the no background group. The latter group also had fewer false recognitions.

These unexpected results are difficult to explain. However, Table 6 shows that three males who were familiar with Washington Street and who saw the sign slides without backgrounds did extremely well. Out of 48 Washington Street signs seen, they correctly recognized 39 (81%). It is also interesting to note that of these three respondents, two claimed to be very familiar with Washington Street. Thus, it is possible that familiarity enabled these subjects to recognize the signs easily even without backgrounds and was primarily responsible for the no background group's higher percentage of correct recognitions.

Comparison of sign recognition according to sex of subject

Results indicate that men had a slightly higher percentage of correct recognitions of Washington Street signs (52%) than did women (47%). However, men and women scored similarly in their percentages of false recognitions of non-Washington Street slides (Table 7).

Comparison of recognition of shop, restaurant, and cinema signs

To determine what other factors might affect recognition, sign slides were divided according to type of establishment. Signs on shops were recognized more frequently than either cinema or restaurant signs.

The data also suggest that signs of large establishments are recognized better than those of small establishments. The results, however, should be interpreted with some caution, as it is unclear what underlying factors may be involved. Is it that large establishments use larger and better signs? Or do large establishments impress people more than smaller ones and thus give more weight to their signs? There might be a third possibility: almost none of the subjects was visiting Washington Street for the first time, and it is conceivable that the names of big establishments might be recognized not only from the experimental stimuli but from past experience, no matter how transitory.

Relationship between preference and correct recognition

Although many of the preference judgments did not seem to be reliable, there were some interesting results. All answer sheets which appeared to be marked haphazardly (i.e., large number of blanks or not marked at all) were eliminated. Sixteen answer sheets remained in the final analysis.

The results show that the rank orders of signs recognized (i.e., frequency of recognitions) and signs liked were quite similar; the Spearman rank-correlation coefficient was significant at the .05 level. One possible explanation of this finding is that the very fact of recognizing something with certainty made the subjects respond that they liked the particular signs. Or, it is possible that people looked at the signs which they liked more than the signs which they disliked and thus recognition was enhanced in this process. Surprisingly, no such correlation was found in response to either buildings or windows.

TABLE 6: PERCENTAGE OF CORRECT RECOGNITIONS OF WASHINGTON STREET SIGN SLIDES, WITH AND WITHOUT BACKGROUND

	Sign Slides Shown With Background		Sign Slides Shown Without Background	
	Male	Female	Male	Female
Familiar With Washington St.	44% *	31% ***	81%†	48%†††
Unfamiliar With Washington St.	39% **	69% ****	63% ††	44% ††††

* $\frac{14 \text{ (correct sign recognitions)}}{2 \text{ (subjects)} \times 16 \text{ (possible correct sign recognitions)}}$

** $\frac{37}{6 \times 16}$

*** $\frac{5}{1 \times 16}$

**** $\frac{11}{1 \times 16}$

† $\frac{39}{3 \times 16}$

†† $\frac{10}{1 \times 16}$

††† $\frac{38}{5 \times 16}$

†††† $\frac{28}{4 \times 16}$

TABLE 7: PERCENTAGE OF WASHINGTON STREET SIGNS CORRECTLY RECOGNIZED AND NON-WASHINGTON STREET SIGNS FALSELY RECOGNIZED, ACCORDING TO SEX OF SUBJECTS

	Male	Female
Percentage of Correct Recognitions	52%	47% ***
Percentage of False Recognitions	19% **	18% ****

* $\frac{100 \text{ (correct sign recognitions)}}{12 \text{ (subjects)} \times 16 \text{ (possible correct sign recognitions)}}$

** $\frac{9 \text{ (false sign recognitions)}}{12 \text{ (subjects)} \times 4 \text{ (possible false sign recognitions)}}$

*** $\frac{82}{11 \times 16}$

**** $\frac{8}{11 \times 4}$

RECOGNITION EXPERIMENT QUESTIONNAIRE

No. _____

Sex: Male _____ Female _____

Education: High School attended _____ graduated _____

College attended _____ graduated _____

Graduate Student _____

Occupation:

Income per week:

Under $50	_____
$51 - $75	_____
$76 - $100	_____
$100 - $125	_____
$126 - $150	_____
$151 - $175	_____
$176 - $200	_____
$201 - $250	_____

Age: _____

RECOGNITION EXPERIMENT QUESTIONNAIRE

No. _____

1. How do you think you have done in this test?

   well: _____: _____: _____: _____: _____: _____: _____: _____: poorly

   Was there anything that was especially difficult?

2. What did you do when going down Washington Street?

   Can you remember looking at commercial signs?

   yes _____ no _____

   How much time did you approximately spend looking at signs?

   I don't remember looking at them at all _____

   I glanced only briefly _____

   I sometimes looked at them _____

   I spent considerable time lookin at them _____

3. So much is being said today about making our cities friendlier and nicer. How much do ugly commercial signs presently contribute to the bad looks of our inner cities?

   Their effect is negligible; _____: _____: _____: _____: _____: considerable.

   Comments:

   How important are signs compared to other features of our streets that might be improved?

4. What would you think of controlling size, style, and position of commercial signs?

   agree _____

   disagree _____

   don't care _____

   Would it make the streets look more attractive? _____

   duller? _____

   no difference? _____

OPINION SURVEY

Purpose

A survey conducted at sites on three different streets in downtown Boston explored the general public's opinion concerning private commercial signs. The primary purpose was to find out whether people consider signs to be a serious problem and whether sign control is thought to be an effective means of improving the streetscape.

Procedure

Sites of the interviews were Washington Street (in front of the Jordan Marsh Annex), Boylston Street (near Arlington Street Church), and Newbury Street (near the intersection with Clarendon on the south side of Newbury). After a few pilot interviews it became apparent that it would be best to ask passers-by only a few short questions, as time and weather were likely to limit the length of an interview. The interviewer guide, photographs of the signs, and respondent comments are included.

The interviewer had specific instructions about the number of people to interview in each of several age and social groups.[3] Filling a certain quota with people of different age groups and belonging to different social strata proved to be quite difficult for two reasons: 1) some respondents whom the interviewer had on sight alone identified as working-class were, it became clear during the interview, definitely middle class; and 2) the Newbury Street population was almost invariably middle or upper-middle class, with a higher proportion of upper-middle class than on either of the other streets.

In all, 29 people on Washington Street, 34 on Boylston Street, and 20 from Newbury Street were interviewed. Responses to the questions were recorded as Favorable, Unfavorable, and Neutral. The data in each case were subdivided and compared by sex, age, social group, and location (Washington, Boylston, or Newbury Streets) (Table 1).

3. Interesting differences in refusal rates were found. Refusal rates were highest on Boylston Street and lowest on Newbury Street, regardless of any other characteristic. Generally, working-class people, older people, and women were less responsive than middle-class people, younger people, and men respectively.

INTERVIEWER GUIDE

1. Here is a list of problems a city planner might have to deal with when trying to beautify a street. Please read through all of them first and then order them according to the importance they have in your opinion.

   (Give the list to the respondent and have him rate the problems by speaking their numbers into the microphone. Record whether he was given form I or form II.

FORM I	FORM II
Please rank these problems of the city, giving #1 to the problem you think is most serious, #2 to the next most serious problem, and so on. Simply give numbers, do not discuss.	Please rank these problems of the city, giving #1 to the problem you think is most serious, #2 to the next most serious problem, and so on. Simply give numbers, do not discuss.
car exhaust	run down buildings
gaudy commercial signs	congested sidewalks
traffic	noise
noise	traffic
congested sidewalks	gaudy commercial signs
run down buildings	car exhaust

2. What do you think of the commercial signs in this street?

   Do you feel they are a problem?

   if yes: What would you do to improve them?

   if no: But could nevertheless something be done to improve them?

3. Now look at some single signs in this street.
   (Point to the respective signs and ask each of the following questions for each sign)

   Do you like it? (very much, somewhat, neutral, dislike somewhat, very much)

   Do you think it has the right size, shape, place, color,style?

   (or, if this doesn't work)

   Do you like it? What do you think of it?

4. What would you think of controlling size, position, and style of commercial signs in this street?

   How would it affect the looks of this street?

   Would it look duller or more attractive?

occupation:

age:

TABLE 1: BREAKDOWN OF SAMPLE ACCORDING TO SEX, AGE, CLASS , AND INTERVIEW LOCATION (Opinion Survey)

		Washington	Boylston	Newbury	TOTAL
SEX	Male	18	22	10	50
	Female	11	12	10	33
	Total	**29**	**34**	**20**	**83**
AGE	Under 20	8	9	6	23
	20-35	9	11	7	27
	Over 35	12	14	7	33
	Total	**29**	**34**	**20**	**83**
CLASS	Middle and Upper Middle	17	23	20	60
	Lower and Lower Middle	12	11	—	23
	Total	**29**	**34**	**20**	**83**

Results

Ranking some selected problems of the city

Each respondent was first asked to rank the following problems according to their importance — car exhaust, gaudy commercial signs, traffic, noise, congested sidewalks, and run-down buildings. The order in which these were presented was varied to account for possible position effects. More serious problems were deliberately left out — such things as ghettos, crime, etc., would certainly have outweighed any of these relatively minor urban problems. Almost all respondents ranked gaudy commercial signs as the least important problem and buildings and traffic as the most important.

RANKING OF CITY PROBLEMS

	Average of Three Streets Mean Ranks	Overall Rank
Run down buildings	1.68	1
Traffic	1.82	2
Car exhaust	2.54	3
Noise	4.05	4
Congested sidewalks	5.56	5
Gaudy commercial signs	5.62	6

A comparison of ratings according to class reveals that both working and middle-class groups rated gaudy commercial signs as the least important problem. Only those respondents who were under 20 or were interviewed on Newbury Street generally ranked something other than signs as the least important problem — noise and congested sidewalks, respectively.

General attitudes towards signs on three different streets

Unfortunately, due to an error in the field, only 45 of the 83 subjects were asked the second question: "What do you think of the signs on this street?" As expected, the general evaluation of the signs in the streets on which interviews were conducted differed tremendously. All eight people asked on Newbury Street were favorable, on Boylston Street about half were favorable (48%), while on Washington Street fewer than 20% liked the signs. Those people who were favorable to the signs on Washington Street all had working-class occupations. In contrast, middle-class people were more favorable than were working-class people to the signs on Boylston and Newbury Streets.

Individual signs — rating of responses

To get a better idea of what people thought about specific signs, the interviewer pointed to three or four signs on each street and asked subjects their opinion of them. The underlying factor in the sample selection was variety — in each group of signs some were large and some small, some simple and unobtrusive, others complex and flashy. In the opinion of the experimenters, some signs were clearly more attractive than others.

On the following pages photographs of the signs selected from each of the three interviewing locations are presented. Along with the pictures are statements of how much each sign was liked and typical comments by the respondents about each sign. Approximately half of all the comments were such general statements as "I like it," "It's okay," etc. Most statements of that kind have not been included in the list, because they are repetitive and not as interesting as the more specific comments.

The nature of the statements differed strikingly according to the location of the interview. The feeling that "you can't expect to find beauty in the city" was rather prevalent on Washington Street but not on the more attractive Boylston and Newbury Streets. In contrast with the comments from interviews on Boylston and Newbury Streets, in which respondents talked about the aesthetic qualities of the signs, respondents on Washington Street mentioned such things as the condition of signs.

On Washington Street no signs were overwhelmingly liked or disliked. The sign which aroused the most favorable response from most people was the most clean and modern one — Rogers Jewelers. On Boylston Street people generally liked the signs, except for the Cosmetics and Vitamins sign, a large, garish sign out on the sidewalk. On Newbury Street three of the four signs were liked very much, especially the two signs with unusual designs — Alpha and Apogee; the Raleigh Restaurant sign, a gaudy, free-standing one, was judged overwhelmingly negatively.

The problem of controlling signs

When asked whether they would like to have an administrative agency controlling the size, style, and position of private commercial signs, over half of the respondents (59%) said that they were in favor of some kind of control. Older and middle-class people supported this idea more than did younger or working-class people.

A list of responses to this question is included. The types of comments made differed considerably according to the location of the interview and the social group of the interviewees. While things like order and cleanliness were important issues on Washington Street, ethical considerations such as restriction of individual choice and degree to which control would be imposed were discussed on the other two streets.

COMMENTS ON TEST SIGNS FOR SIDEWALK SURVEY

Group 1: Washington Street
Viewing position: In front of Jordan Marsh's gadget window

ROGERS JEWELERS:
This sign was liked most of the four signs on Washington Street — 25 people liked it, 4 did not. There were no striking differences between age and social groupings, except that middle-class people liked it a little less than working-class people.

More artistic than the others. I like it as signs go.

I don't see anything wrong with it . . . a pretty good sign . . . color red commands attention . . . background blends and gives contrast enough to command attention . . . not very flashy. And everyone knows Rogers. It's an established place.

It's nice, contemporary, attractive.

That's okay. At least it's a half-way decent sign. It isn't falling or anything.

That's the best one of them all. It looks new, nice, neat.

I don't know. At night maybe it's pretty bright, but right now it doesn't bother me.

MICKEY FINN:
This was the second most popular sign of the group — 13 liked it, 16 disliked it. Older people liked it less than younger people.

Like I say, it's a business district — I really don't see any harm in it.

Alright. I don't know — it's there. I don't pay any attention to signs.

That's a pretty dirty old sign. They should paint it or put a new sign up.

I don't care for it; not necessary; projects too much. They've jutted it out so that people could see it from a distance, but otherwise it's quite colorful and nice.

Not that bad, but it isn't good either.

That's nice and clean looking.

That's okay because it doesn't take up too much space on the building.

PARAMOUNT THEATRE:
This sign ranked third in popularity — 9 people liked it, 20 did not. Younger people liked it considerably less than older ones.

An old establishment . . . I think it's a good sign.

No objection. It's been there for years, is sort of a landmark.

That's alright. It's big. I notice it, I mean.

. . . It's just so pop.

A little bit old and gaudy I think.

It's part of Boston.

To be expected. You don't look for beauty here.

For the prices they charge to go into the show they could have a better sign than that.

Just needs cleaning up a bit.

Bad. Any stack lettering is bad.

Takes up an awful lot of room just to tell you the theater's there.

ADAMS HOUSE RESTAURANT:

Only 7 people liked this sign, as opposed to 22 who disliked it. Older people liked it more than younger, and working-class people liked it less than middle-class people.

Should be torn down.

Junk. Banners block other signs and look cheap.

Needs cleaning.

You can't even see it. You don't notice it.

Banners are okay. They're the easy way out.

It's very nice, Belgian-like, like on the canals in Europe.

Should be taken down. I don't like cloth signs anyway.

It seems like they couldn't afford anything better, so they had to put out a flag.

It looks more distinguished in that it's on a piece of cloth . . . Although the material it's printed on is not that classy, it gives the appearance of a very special type of locale.

Group 2: Boylston Street

Viewing position: In front of Hammond Organ Shop

CRAWFORD-HOLLIDGE:

This was the most popular sign of the group on Boylston Street — 27 people liked it, only 7 did not like it.

Unobtrusive. I do like it. Beautiful with that front.

It doesn't stand out but the windows are so that you look at it until you see it, and so it attracts you just as much if not more.

Sort of antique, doesn't look up-to-date.

Attractive, something different.

The sign itself isn't terribly effective. The whole front is tremendous.

That I might want a postcard of . . . [but] if you're shopping you don't look for a Crawford-Hollidge sign, you look for a Cosmetics & Vitamin sign and you find it because that's what you see.

No good at all. I can't even see it.

WINSHIP:

This was the second most popular sign on the street, especially among middle-class people. Twenty-five people were favorable, 9 unfavorable.

That's not bad either. That's quite a nice sign.

Successful.

You wouldn't even know it was there.

I don't object to signs of that kind at all if they're as neat as that one is. I just object to the garish ones, very much.

Rather inconspicuous, not prominent enough. From a business point of view, I'd say it's not good.

No, I don't like them hanging down. I like them on the walls.

I like that. I don't know if it belongs on this street, but I like it.

A good example of a good sign. It's small and doesn't cover up half the building.

That is a better sort. At least it's interesting to look at. It isn't just a big light speaking to you.

WILBAR'S:

This was the third most popular sign — 24 people liked it, 10 did not.

We can do without that.

Clever.

Common.

An attractive sign.

I don't see anything wrong with that in particular.

It's alright.

A little too modern for this street.

Well, it doesn't really affect me one way or another.

One thing I do like about that type is that it stays with the store — you don't have to look at it if you're just walking down the street.

I find that a rather interesting sign. It's kind of subtle.

It's pretty. I like the script.

It's large enough, but I like 'em all facing me.

COSMETICS & VITAMINS

This sign was very unpopular — 25 of the 34 respondents did not like it. Older people liked it a little less than younger people, and working-class people liked it more than middle-class people.

Terrible.

Very eye-catching. It certainly serves its purpose, I guess — to jump out and bring you in, if that's its purpose.

An eyesore, blocks your vision.

Doesn't add to the beauty of a city.

I don't approve of them being out on the walk like that at all. I think they're a menace and in the way.

It's sort of mundane. It doesn't have any class to it.

Well, I think it's a bit confusing — putting cosmetics and vitamins together in the same category. It's also rather a congested sort of sign. There could be something more simple.

. . . Just atrocious. It just sits there and glows at you.

Rather ugly. Doesn't have much taste — the red and yellow. But it doesn't bother me. If somebody wants to put it up there that's their business.

It stands out. You can see it very well, especially from the Common.

I don't like it — looks like a shopping center.

Group 3: Newbury Street

Viewing position: In front of Apogee

APOGEE:

Of the 20 people interviewed on Newbury Street, not one disliked this sign.

Quite tasteful.

That's a good one. It goes along with the Alpha.

It's eye-catching and I like it.

Very nice-looking.

Cool, really great, catches your attention.

That is interesting. That's a nice sign.

I like it. It's original — nothing that pulls you in, but if you do see it you're not taken back by it. It's good in the city.

Eye-catching. Very good — black and white.

It's elegant.

Very chic, very inventive, a good thing. There should be more like it.

Catchy, without being too big, not flashy and neon-like. It's charming.

ALPHA GALLERY:

Only two people disliked this sign.

Very excellent, very nice.

I don't have any objections to it. It's different. I guess I like it.

Kind of unique. I like it.

Artistic.

I like that, something that catches your attention, would draw you into it.

Interesting. Lots of people wouldn't know what it means. Interests people to go over. I like it.

Never even noticed it. You can't even tell what it stands for. No, I don't like that at all.

Lovely.

I like that because I like the design.

That's okay, not too gaudy; little and discreet.

RALEIGH RESTAURANT:

This sign was overwhelmingly disliked — only two people liked it.

Neutral. It's better than the old one, though.

A little too sterile.

Objectionable.

Well, it's just a sign. He has to advertise too.

Doesn't fit with street. These are all colonial-type signs and the Raleigh restaurant is sort of typical restaurant or gas station.

I hate that sign. Doesn't belong here at all.

Tells what it is.

Ought to be wiped out, obliterated.

Alright . . . kind of out of place, because all these are little shops and then it has a big fluorescent sign. Depends on what you think of Newbury St. — all boutiques and dress shops — and then a restaurant as such putting up a big sign makes it kind of out of place.

OPINION SURVEY — CONTROL OF SIGNS

The comments which follow are a representative sample of responses from question 4 (referring to sign control) from the Interviewer Guide. The comments are arranged according to physical, aesthetic, and ethical aspects of control.

Physical Aspects of Sign Control: (The statements in this group were made by people in favor of the idea of control.)

a *ORDER — an important issue on Washington Street. This category includes statements about the desirability of more uniformity, more clarity, and better visibility achieved through sign control.*

Definitely there should be more control. It gives more uniformity to the street.

Signs shouldn't obstruct views.

Synchronize signs and make them more homogeneous. Put limits on size and color.

Shouldn't be all over the street, and yet they have to be there to tell people what's there.

b *SIZE — an issue on Washingon and Newbury Streets, but not on Boylston Street, a wide street with relatively small signs.*

Would be better if size would be controlled.

I think they should all be just about the same size.

It would be a wonderful idea if they limited them to certain sizes according to the space the store had and the size of the store.

c *POSITION — mentioned frequently on Boylston Street, prompted by the Cosmetics and Vitamins sign out in the middle of the sidewalk.*

Either no signs at all or signs up against the building.

If you just kept them out of the sidewalk so they weren't blinding to traffic, I think that would be a good idea.

Just the position should be controlled.

d *SAFETY — an issue only for working-class people.*

If they're all the same size there'd be a lot less chance of them fallin' and the whole city would look a lot cleaner.

It all depends if they are any danger to pedestrians in case of strong winds or storms that they collapse over. Like that one there [Cosmetics & Vitamins]; if it's sturdy enough, and if a strong wind came along, like a hurricane, it may probably fall over, probably hurt someone.

e *CLEANLINESS — mentioned only on Washington Street, other streets have clean signs.*

If signs are run down they should be painted.

Would be a good idea. Some of these signs are dirty-lookin' and should be cleaned up.

Aesthetic Aspects of Sign Control:

a *AESTHETIC IMPROVEMENT THROUGH CONTROL OF SIGNS — mentioned only by middle-class people interviewed on Newbury Street.*

Definitely. If I want to find a place I can just find it by looking at the street number without having to look for some huge, gaudy sign. I think they generally spoil the looks of a street.

Would make streets more attractive, unless you go too far and get a very sterile look.

That would be really great if they could do that, because some of them are just too big, especially market signs.

b *LACK OF AESTHETIC IMPROVEMENT THROUGH CONTROL OF SIGNS — mostly expressed by working-class people.*

Variety is the spice of life, wonderful. Uniformity is bad, military.

Size perhaps . . . But style and design I wouldn't want to see controlled.

The street would be duller because at night they're all lit up and if they're small you wouldn't be able to see them.

Oh no! If the city controlled it, they'd all look the same — no originality or anything.

Foolish. Wouldn't affect looks of the street.

Ethical Aspects: (People in this category oppose control of signs on ethical grounds. Considerable importance on Newbury and Boylston Streets.)

a *RESTRICTION OF CHOICE*

I don't believe in a whole lot of control of things, and the more the government gets in, the more complicated things get, and there's always exceptions to the rules. If a sign got in the way of the sidewalk, there's already a law against that. It would probably make streets more attractive, but you'd get a lot more people mad about it. Does the government or anybody else have a right to do that? If a sign offends you, you can ignore it.

As long as they're on the building then it's up to the person who owns the building — his taste, discretion.

I would object to the kinds of signs that obliterate the skyline in general. Things like City Service and Kain's Mayonnaise signs are very objectionable. You can't put too much control over the shops. I don't think they interfere that much with the general appearance of a city. Control might tend to make a street too much one style, which would be a pity. I think you people tend to experiment too much with too much control.

b *KIND AND DEGREE OF SIGN CONTROL — this category includes statements from people who felt, for a variety of reasons, that certain limits and certain qualifications of sign control would have to be considered, before control could be endorsed; mentioned only by middle-class people.*

If it's done well it would make streets more attractive.

The street would look better unless you were going to do a big thing like Broadway where there are lots of signs. Then if it's gaudy it's good.

Possible general limitations might be imposed but not strict intervention. You'd have to give me a specific program before I could say whether it would be more attractive or not. People who would limit it might do a worse job than the ones out there now.

Not too good an idea. Even if you control size people could put in horrible design and it would be boring.

INFLUENCE ON ASSESSMENT OF STREET ATTRACTIVENESS

TABLE 1: BREAKDOWN OF SAMPLE ACCORDING TO SEX, AGE, AND CLASS
(Influence on Assessment of Street Attractiveness)

		N	%
SEX	Male	33	72
	Female	13	28
	Total	**46**	**100**
AGE	Under 20	17	37
	20-34	28	61
	35-55	1	2
	Total	**46**	**100**
CLASS	Lower and Lower Middle	15	33
	Middle and Upper Middle	9	19
	Student	22	48
	Total	**46**	**100**

Purpose
The influence of "good" or "bad" signs on an individual's evaluation of his environment was investigated. The goal was to see if evaluations of settings could be changed by variations in a single factor, a sign.

Procedure
The experiment was conducted immediately after (though not as a part of) the "Evaluation of Symbolic versus Existing Traffic Signs: Laboratory Tests" and used, with one exception, the same subjects. One person who came too late to participate in the first laboratory tests was included in this experiment. The total number of subjects was 47 (Table 1).

The effects of three different variables were explored:

1 *Background quality — orderly vs. disorderly*
Background quality was related to orderliness of signs in the environment. "Orderly" streets had signs with controlled variety. That is, the signs related quite well to one another and did not conflict or shout for attention. "Disorderly" streets had a wide variety of sign types, competing for attention and distracting from other qualities of the street, such as architecture, activity, or windows.

2 *Sign quality — good vs. bad*
The following are the criteria for "good" and "bad" signs:

a. *Simplicity* — "Good" signs have fewer different graphic elements and are less crowded than are "bad" signs. Graphic elements include color, decorations, letter styles, and pictures.

b. *Vividness* — "Good" signs convey messages with clarity, simplicity, and strength. They often use imagery related to the store's activity or simply word messages which are well displayed.

c. *Style* — "Good" signs have a style which is associated with favored contemporary or historic themes. For example, Early American or pop culture themes. Graphics of "bad" signs evoke negative images such as of the Depression, skid row, and cheap deals.

3 *Sign size — small vs. large*
The experiment was divided in four sessions with a different group of subjects in each session. The slides shown[4] varied according to the above factors.

Session 1: Large Signs — good sign/disorderly setting, bad sign/orderly setting.

Session 2: Large Signs — good sign/orderly setting, bad sign/disorderly setting.

Session 3: Small Signs — good sign/disorderly setting, bad sign/orderly setting.

Session 4: Small Signs — good sign/orderly setting, bad sign/disorderly setting.

[It should be emphasized that each group of subjects saw the same orderly and disorderly settings and the same good and bad signs. Only the combination of sign size, sign quality, and background quality varied from group to group.]

In all, 10 orderly settings and 10 disorderly settings were used. Each setting was paired with 10 good signs (large and small) and 10 bad signs (large and small).

A total of 80 different slides was used. Each group of subjects was shown 20 slides in random order and was asked to indicate on a 10 point scale whether and how much they liked a particular setting (10 = like very much). The signs themselves were never mentioned. For example, subjects in Session 1 viewed 10 large good signs in disorderly settings and 10 large bad signs in orderly settings.

Exposure time was two seconds, and subjects were given 20 seconds to record their responses. No subject ever mentioned the fact that some of the signs were apparently "mock signs," and nobody indicated that he understood the purpose of the experiment.

4. These signs were either "real," i.e., they actually existed, or "fake," i.e., pasted together at the office from various components like clippings from advertisements, etc. Color photographs of the "real" signs were enlarged to a standard size of the "fake" signs. These models were then mounted on a plexiglass stick and photographs were taken of the signs in the actual setting in such a way that in the final slides, these "mock" signs appeared to be real and in scale with their surroundings.

TABLE 2: MEAN PREFERENCE SCORES ACCORDING TO BACKGROUND QUALITY, SIGN QUALITY, AND SIGN SIZE (Influence on Assessment of Street Attractiveness)

		Large	Small	Mean
GOOD SIGNS	Orderly Background	4.7	5.8	5.3
	Disorderly Background	3.3	2.7	3.0
	Mean	4.0	4.3	
BAD SIGNS	Orderly Background	3.6	5.5	4.6
	Disorderly Background	3.7	2.5	3.1
	Mean	3.7	4.0	
GOOD & BAD SIGNS	Orderly Background	4.2	5.7	
	Disorderly Background	3.5	2.6	
OVERALL MEANS	Large Signs	3.8		
	Small signs	4.1		
	Orderly backgrounds	4.9		
	Disorderly backgrounds	3.1		
	Good signs	4.2		
	Bad signs	3.9		

Variations in size and background.

"Good" signs.

"Bad" signs.

TABLE 3: PREFERENCES AND SIGNIFICANCE LEVELS FOR ALL COMBINATIONS OF VARIABLES (Influence on Assessment of Street Attractiveness)

	Preference	Significance Level
Small vs. Large Signs		
Good sign, good background	Small	$p < .01$
Good sign, bad background	Large	$p < .05$
Bad sign, good background	Small	$p < .01$
Bad sign, bad background	Large	$p < .01$
Good vs. Bad Background		
Small, good signs	Good	$p < .01$
Large, good signs	Good	$p < .01$
Small, bad signs	Good	$p < .001$
Large, bad signs	Slightly bad	N.S.*
Good vs. Bad Signs		
Small signs, good background	Slightly good	N.S.
Large signs, good background	Good	$p < .001$
Small signs, bad background	Slightly good	N.S.
Large signs, bad background	Slightly bad	N.S.

* N.S. — Not Significant

Results

Small vs. large signs

The results (Tables 2 and 3) clearly indicate that when the background is orderly a small sign is preferred ($p < .01$). On the other hand, when the background is disorderly, a large sign is preferred to a small one ($p < .01$). The latter result may be an artifact of the experimental procedure. It is possible that the slide was more pleasing when the disorderly background was dominated by a large sign. Would the same effect be obtained with large signs in the normal street situation?

Orderly vs. disorderly background

Orderly backgrounds were, almost consistently, preferred over disorderly backgrounds regardless of the size or quality of the sign ($p < .01$). However, subjects preferred the disorderly background over the orderly one when the sign shown in the slide was large and bad. This suggests that a large bad sign in an orderly context was less pleasing — or more jarring — than the "blend" of a bad sign in a disorderly setting.

Good vs. bad signs

Whether a sign was good or bad was unimportant when the sign was small. However, when the sign was large, the subjects preferred the good signs on a good background and the bad signs on a bad background.

These results suggest that people want appropriateness in the cityscape. Not only do they prefer to have a disorderly background dominated by a large sign, but they would slightly prefer that sign to be bad also.

BILLBOARDS: OPINION SURVEY

Purpose
A questionnaire was devised to discover attitudes towards billboards. Billboards were defined as "large advertising signs which can be seen over rather large areas." The following are the areas of interest explored by the questionnaire (numbers in parentheses refer to the question number):

1 *Importance of signing problems in the city* (1a, b, c)
2 *Control of signing by the city* (2, 3)
3 *Form and content of billboards* (9, 10, 13, 16, 19)
4 *Attention value of billboards* (4, 6, 7, 11, 14)
5 *Aesthetics and appropriateness of billboards* (5, 8, 12, 15, 17a-k, 18)

Procedure
Two groups of subjects were given the questionnaire. One group was asked to fill it out while visiting the Information Center. The other group completed the questionnaire at the end of the laboratory tests of the symbolic and existing signs. This latter group had responded to posters which were displayed in various sections of the city asking for volunteers for a psychological experiment. Of the total of 55 subjects, 51% were between 20 and 35 years old, 69% were males; their distribution by class (inferred from the occupational prestige scale) was almost even (Table 1). Because of the small sample size, however, most of the results are not subdivided by age, sex, or occupation.

TABLE 1: BREAKDOWN OF SAMPLE ACCORDING TO SEX, AGE, AND CLASS (Billboards)

		N	%
SEX	Male	38	69
	Female	17	31
	Total	**55**	**100**
AGE	Under 20	17	31
	20-35	28	52
	Over 35	9	17
	Total	**54***	**100**
CLASS	Lower and Lower Middle	16	31
	Middle and Upper Middle	20	38
	Students	16	31
	Total	**52*****	**100**

* Age of 1 respondent not recorded.
** Class of 3 respondents not recorded.

BILLBOARD SURVEY

	Not at All				Very
1. How important are these problems in the city:					
a. Billboards: large advertising signs that can be seen over rather large areas	1	2	3	4	5
b. Commercial signs: store name signs, small advertisements	1	2	3	4	5
c. Public signs: street names, guide signs, traffic control signs					

	Agree Strongly				Disagree Strongly
2. Billboard advertising in the city should be controlled by the city.	1	2	3	4	5
3. Commercial signs should be controlled by the city.	1	2	3	4	5
4. People pay attention to billboards.	1	2	3	4	5
5. Billboards are appropriate everywhere.	1	2	3	4	5
6. Instead of spending money on billboards, advertisers should spend the money on ads in newspapers, magazines, radio, TV, or small sidewalk posters.	1	2	3	4	5
7. It would not matter if the number of billboards increased.	1	2	3	4	5
8. Billboards are located in the right places with respect to buildings, views, etc.	1	2	3	4	5
9. The shapes of billboards are good.	1	2	3	4	5
10. It would not matter if the size of billboards was increased.	1	2	3	4	5
11. Billboards are too distracting.	1	2	3	4	5
12. Billboards and other large signs are attractively lit at night.	1	2	3	4	5
13. The pictures and lettering on billboards are good.	1	2	3	4	5
14. Billboards do not cause accidents.	1	2	3	4	5

PLEASE TURN TO NEXT PAGE

	Agree Strongly				Disagree Strongly
15. The night skyline is made more interesting and attractive by billboards and other large illuminated signs.	1	2	3	4	5
16. Billboards are fine if they aren't trying to sell anything.	1	2	3	4	5
17. Billboards are appropriate:					
a. in shopping areas	1	2	3	4	5
b. in entertainment districts	1	2	3	4	5
c. on car-oriented commercial strips	1	2	3	4	5
d. along major roads inside the city	1	2	3	4	5
e. on the highways approaching the city	1	2	3	4	5
f. on the skyline	1	2	3	4	5
g. along water edges	1	2	3	4	5
h. on rooftops	1	2	3	4	5
i. at major road intersections in the city	1	2	3	4	5
j. on the sides of buildings	1	2	3	4	5
k. in parking lots/used car lots	1	2	3	4	5

18. If you think billboards are a problem, name some places in the Boston area that you consider particularly bad and explain why.

19. Do billboards provide you with any useful information? If so, what?

20. Comments.

21. Age __________

22. Occupation ______________________________________

23. Male _____ Female _____

Results by Areas of Interest

Importance of signing problems in the city (Table 2)
Public signs (i.e., street names, guide signs, and traffic control signs) were seen as the most important sign problem in the city by three-quarters of the respondents, while slightly more than half rated billboards as an important problem. Of the 15 respondents who felt that billboards do not present important problems, only one was a woman.

These results contrast with the respondents' perceptions of the commercial sign problem (i.e., store name signs and small advertisements). Only a little more than one-third of the sample felt that commercial signs present important problems in the city.

Control of signs by the city (Table 2)
A most interesting result was the correlation between the respondents' ratings of billboards and commercial signs as problems and their acceptance or advocacy of city control of these signs.

A positive correlation of .49 existed between the feeling that billboards present important problems and the belief that billboards should be controlled by the city. This means that there is a strong likelihood that someone who considers billboards to be an important problem will also feel that the city should control them. Similarly, a positive correlation of .46 existed between the feeling that commercial signs present important problems and the need for control of commercial signs.

TABLE 2: IMPORTANCE OF SIGN PROBLEM AND SIGN CONTROL

		Affirmative*	Negative**	Neutral	**Total**
Billboard problem importance (1a)	N	30	15	10	**55**
	%	55	27	18	**100**
Billboard control by city (2)	N	36	7	12	**55**
	%	65	13	22	**100**
Commercial sign problem importance (1b)	N	20	16	19	**55**
	%	36	29	35	**100**
Commercial sign control by city (3)	N	26	16	12	**54**
	%	47	29	22	**98**
Public sign problem importance (1c)	N	42	6	7	**55**
	%	76	11	13	**100**

* For questions 1a, b, c: Affirmative: important problem
Negative: unimportant problem

** For questions 2 and 3: Affirmative: agree
Negative: disagree

TABLE 3: FORM AND CONTENT OF BILLBOARDS

		Agree	Disagree	Neutral	**Total**
The shapes of billboards are good (9)	**N**	8	30	16	**54**
	%	15	54	29	**98**
It would not matter if the size of bill-boards was increased (10)	**N**	4	45	4	**53**
	%	7	82	7	**96**
The pictures and lettering on bill-boards are good (13)	**N**	10	31	13	**54**
	%	18	56	24	**98**
Billboards are fine if they aren't trying to sell anything (16)	**N**	6	38	11	**55**
	%	11	69	20	**100**
Do billboards provide you with any useful infor-mation, if so, what? (19)	**N**	19	26	—	**45**
	%	35	47	—	**82**

TABLE 4: ATTENTION VALUE OF BILLBOARDS

		Agree	Disagree	Neutral	**Total**
People pay attention to billboards (4)	**N**	21	15	19	**55**
	%	38	27	35	**100**
Instead of spending money on billboards advertisers should spend the money on other media (6)	**N**	33	6	14	**53**
	%	60	11	25	**96**
It would not matter if the number of billboards increased (7)	**N**	2	51	2	**55**
	%	3.5	93	3.5	**100**
Billboards are too distracting (11)	**N**	30	14	10	**54**
	%	54	26	18	**98**
Billboards do not cause accidents (14)	**N**	13	22	17	**52**
	%	23	40	31	**94**

Form and content of billboards (Table 3)
There was general disfavor with the form and content of billboards. This is consistent with the opinion expressed by a majority of respondents that billboards present important problems and that they should be controlled by the city.

Women were the most outspoken critics of billboard appearance. For example, a substantial majority of women indicated that they disliked the shape and graphics of billboards. On the other hand, less than half of the male respondents were critical of these factors. In general, working-class respondents tended to be more tolerant of billboard graphics and aesthetics than were middle-class and student respondents. For example, seven of the ten (70%) middle-class people between 20 and 35 and five of the nine (56%) students in this age group felt that the shapes of billboards are not good, while only two of the seven (29%) working-class respondents between 20 and 35 answered in this way. In general, students and middle-class people tended to respond similarly to a number of questions.

The questionnaire had only two questions, 16 and 19, directed toward the content of billboards. The results of question 16 indicate that a majority of people felt that even if billboards did not sell anything, they would still be unacceptable. That is, even if billboards were not used for advertisements, they would be unacceptable for other reasons. (These may relate to the form factors mentioned above.) Question 19 asked, first, whether billboards provide any useful information and, if so, what type of information. Slightly less than half the sample responded that billboards do not provide them with useful information. Of those people who felt that billboards do provide useful information, most said that this was in the form of driving information (i.e., information about rest stops, motels, restaurants, and gasoline stations). Some said that billboards provide them with consumer goods information and entertainment information.

Attention value of billboards (Table 4)
The results of questions 4, 6, 7, 11, and 14 are further evidence of dislike of billboards, although a substantial minority of respondents agreed that people do pay attention to them (38%). In spite of this (or perhaps because of it) more than half the respondents (60%) felt that advertisers would be wise to use other media, such as newspapers, magazines, radio, TV, or small sidewalk posters to display their products.

The majority of respondents (54%) said that billboards are too distracting. However, less than half the respondents (40%) indicated that they felt that billboards cause traffic accidents.

Appropriateness and aesthetics of billboards (Table 5)
The results showed that the respondents had clear ideas about where billboards are and are not appropriate. Almost 95% of the sample felt that billboards are not appropriate everywhere; 75% of the respondents felt that billboards are not located in the right places with respect to buildings, views, etc. Respondents felt that billboards were most inappropriate along water edges, at major road intersections in the city, and along major roads in the city. A majority also disliked them on the skyline, on rooftops, on the sides of buildings, and on the highways approaching the city.

TABLE 5: AESTHETICS AND APPROPRIATENESS OF BILLBOARDS

		Agree	Disagree	Neutral	**Total**
Billboards are appropriate everywhere (5)	**N**	2	52	1	**55**
	%	4	94	2	**100**
______ in shopping areas (17a)	**N**	24	19	11	**54**
	%	44	34	20	**98**
______ in entertainment districts (17b)	**N**	25	18	11	**54**
	%	45	33	20	**98**
______ on car-oriented commercial strips (17c)	**N**	16	30	9	**55**
	%	29	55	16	**100**
______ along major roads inside the city (17d)	**N**	3	46	6	**55**
	%	5	84	11	**100**
______ on the highways approaching the city (17e)	**N**	11	33	11	**55**
	%	20	60	20	**100**
______ on the skyline (17f)	**N**	7	42	6	**55**
	%	13	76	11	**100**
______ along water edges (17g)	**N**	4	49	2	**55**
	%	7	89	4	**100**
______ on rooftops (17h)	**N**	3	41	11	**55**
	%	5	75	20	**100**
______ at major road intersections in the city (17i)	**N**	2	48	5	**55**
	%	4	87	9	**100**
______ on the sides of buildings (17j)	**N**	11	33	11	**55**
	%	20	60	20	**100**
______ in parking lots/used car lots (17k)	**N**	23	19	13	**55**
	%	42	34	24	**100**
Billboards are located in the right places with respect to buildings, views, etc. (8)	**N**	4	41	10	**55**
	%	7	75	18	**100**
Billboards and other large signs are attractively lit at night (12)	**N**	11	28	15	**54**
	%	20	51	27	**98**
The night skyline is made more interesting and attractive by billboards (15)	**N**	12	32	11	**55**
	%	22	58	20	**100**
Are billboards a problem? If so, where are they particularly bad? (18)	**N**	33	22	—	**55**
	%	60	20	—	**100**

Comments from Billboard Survey

A space for comments was allotted at the end of the Billboard Survey questionnaire. A proportionate sample of these comments organized into three sections — positive, negative, and miscellaneous — follows.

Negative

Down with billboards!

I would prefer that billboards be removed from roadsides. There are other ways of getting information and advertising.

Get rid of them.

Billboards are aesthetically poor; often they distract. Often there is a self-defeating race by companies to put up more and bigger billboards; the city should step in.

Billboards usually detract from the beauty of the surrounding area. But they probably will not be taken down due to various political/economic reasons.

Billboards should be abolished.

Billboards are ugly and unnecessary. I don't think they help the companies who are trying to sell something that much. I can't stand billboards — they're cheap looking.

In general I try to ignore billboards.

Billboards should be excluded from specifically scenic spots and be inconspicuous or non-existent where attention is important. I think the Canadian sign system is very good.

The Citgo sign in Kenmore Square is the only billboard I would like to see remain in Boston.

If nothing were to be done the whole city would probably end up covered with them.

I hate billboards.

Most billboards are a waste of money — money that could be used for better purposes and is badly needed for more important things that are being put off due to lack of funds.

Positive

Well done ones illuminated, etc., actually enhance the skyline of the city, especially around Kenmore Square and along the Cambridge side of the Charles. They have a relaxing effect on drivers (i.e., me), and are helpful to those from out of town in helping them to navigate around the city. I vote for more and better illuminated billboards.

With good graphic design and proper placement, billboards can give vitality to the city scene. European cities have solved this better than Americans.

I can't generalize too much — some billboards I enjoy — especially the clever ones — some don't bother me at all — very few repel me.

The city is the city and I love it as it is. No one will ever turn the city into the country; the country is nice too.

Miscellaneous

No liquor or cigarette ads.

About the only sign I like is the Citgo sign, and if White Fuel is working properly, that too.

Municipal control is unnecessary — billboards are generally unaesthetic, but they are not a serious enough problem to warrant government interference.

Billboards are fine on highways as they break up monotony. They are tasteless in residential areas.

Billboards are an advertising medium. I think that in that respect they have a function. However, indiscriminate placement of them is distracting, dangerous, and an eyesore. There should be some municipal control.

If they were more artistically done, they would be more useful.

Billboards should be used to promote only civic information.

Billboards should only be used when absolutely necessary.

If, instead of advertisements, billboards carried paintings, e.g., similar to those that appear on some of the apartment buildings in New York's lower East and West side, then I would have a greater liking for them. It should create, or enhance, beautify, not just be there.

Selected Bibliography

GENERAL BACKGROUND ON ENVIRONMENTAL COMMUNICATION

Basic Psychology of Perception and Cognition

Chapanis, A., Garner, W. R., and Morgan, C. T. *Applied Experimental Psychology: Human Factors in Engineering Design.* New York: John Wiley & Sons, 1949.

Garner, W. R. *Uncertainty and Structure as Psychological Concepts.* New York: John Wiley & Sons, 1962.

Gibson, J. J. *The Perception of the Visual World.* Boston: Houghton-Mifflin Co., 1950.

Gibson, J. J. *The Senses Considered as Perceptual Systems.* Boston: Houghton-Mifflin Co., 1966.

Gordon, Donald A. "Static and Dynamic Visual Fields in Human Space Perception," *Journal of Optical Society of America* 55 (October 1965), 1296–1303.

Gregory, R. L. *Eye and Brain: The Psychology of Seeing.* New York: McGraw-Hill, 1966.

Hunter, I. M. L. *Memory.* Rev. ed. Baltimore: Penguin, 1964.

Miller, G. A. "The Magical Number Seven Plus or Minus Two: Some Limits on Our Capacity for Processing Information," *Psychological Review* 63 (1956), 81–97.

Miller, G. A. *Psychology: The Science of Mental Life.* New York: Harper & Row, 1962.

Neisser, U. *Cognitive Psychology.* New York: Appleton, 1967.

Vernon, M. D. *A Further Study of Visual Perception.* Cambridge, England: University Press, 1952.

Human Communication and Symbol Systems

Aranguren, J. L. *Human Communication.* Trans. Frances Partridge. New York: McGraw-Hill, 1967.

Arnell, A. *Standard Graphical Symbols.* New York, Toronto, & London: McGraw-Hill, 1963.

Arnheim, R. *Art and Visual Perception: A Psychology of the Creative Eye.* Berkeley & Los Angeles: University of California Press, 1954.

Ayer, A. J. "What is Communication," *Studies in Communication.* London: Secker & Warburg, Ltd., 1955.

Bach, Robert O. (ed.). *Communication: The Art of Understanding and Being Understood.* New York: Visual Communication Conference, 1962.

Carpenter, E., and McLuhan, M. (eds.). *Explorations in Communication: An Anthology.* Boston: Beacon Press, 1960.

Cherry, C. *On Human Communication,* 2nd ed. Cambridge: MIT Press, 1966.

Deutschmann, P. "The Sign Situation Classification of Human Communication," *Journal of Communication* 7 (1957), 2.

Frank, L. K. "Tactile Communication," *ETC: A Review of General Semantics* 16 (1958).

Hovland, C. I., Janis, I. L., and Kelley, H. H. *Communication and Persuasion.* New Haven: Yale University Press, 1953.

Kepes, Gyorgy (ed.) *Sign, Image, Symbol.* New York: George Braziller, 1966.

Krampen, M. "An Approach to Classification of Graphic Symbols." Mimeographed. For preparation survey *Communication through Graphic Symbols.* New York: Fund for the Advancement of Education (Ford Foundation), 1959.

McLuhan, M. *Understanding Media.* New York: McGraw-Hill, 1964.

Miller, G. A. *Language and Communication.* New York: McGraw-Hill, 1963.

Morris, Charles W. "Foundations of the Theory of Signs," *International Encyclopedia of Unified Science,* ed. O. Neurath, R. Carnap, and C. Morris. Chicago: University of Chicago Press, 1955.

Morris, Charles W. *Signs, Language and Behavior.* New York: George Braziller, 1955.

Pierce, John R. *Symbols, Signals and Noise.* New York: Harper, 1961.

Richards, I. A. "Structure in Communication," *Structure in Art and in Science,* ed. G. Kepes. New York: George Braziller, 1965.

Ruesch, J., and Kees, W. *Non-verbal Communications — Notes on the Visual Perception of Human Relations.* Berkeley: University of California Press, 1956.

Sebeok, T. A., Hayes, A. S., and Bateson, M. C. (eds.). *Approaches to Semiotics.* New York: Humanities Press, 1964.

Whitehead, A. N. *Symbolism, Its Meaning and Effect.* New York: Putnam, 1959.

Whitney, Elwood (ed.). *Symbology — The Use of Symbols in Visual Communication.* New York: Hastings House, 1960.

Wittkower, R. "Interpretation of Visual Symbols in the Arts," *Studies in Communication.* London: Secker & Warburg, Ltd., 1955.

Communication and City Form

Appleyard, D., Lynch, K., and Myer, J. R. *The View from the Road.* Cambridge: MIT Press, 1964.

Beinart, Julian. "The Pattern of the Street," *Architectural Forum* 125 (September 1966), 59–63.

Benepe, Barry. "Pedestrian in the City," *Traffic Quarterly* (January 1965), 28–42.

Brower, S. N. "The Signs We Learn to Read," *Landscape* 15 (Autumn 1956), 9–12.

Carr, S. "The City of the Mind," *Environment for Man,* ed. William R. Ewald, Jr., 197–231. Bloomington: Indiana University Press, 1967.

Carr, S. and Lynch, K. "Where Learning Happens," *Daedalus* 97 (Fall 1968), 1277–1291.

Carr, S. and Schissler, D. "The City as a Trip," *Environment and Behavior* (Fall 1969).

Firey, Walter. "Sentiment and Symbolism as Ecological Variables," *Studies In Human Ecology,* ed. George A. Theordorson, 253–261. New York: Harper & Row, 1961.

Jacobs, Jane. "The Uses of Sidewalks: Contact," *The Death and Life of Great American Cities,* 55–68. New York: Random House, 1961.

Kepes, Gyorgy. "Notes on Expression and Communication in the Cityscape," *Arts and Architecture* 78 (August 1961), 16–17.

Lynch, Kevin. *The Image of the City.* Cambridge: Harvard University Press & The Technology Press, 1960.

Lynch, Kevin, and Rivkin, Malcolm. "A Walk Around the Block," *Landscape* 8 (Spring 1959), 24–34.

Southworth, Michael. "The Sonic Environment of Cities," *Environment and Behavior,* (Fall 1969).

Steinitz, C. "Meaning and the Congruence of Urban Form and Activity," *Journal of American Institute of Planners* 34 (July 1968), 233–248.

Tunnard, C., and Pushkarev, B. "Part Three — The Paved Ribbon: The Esthetic of Freeway Design," *Man Made America: Chaos or Control,* 157–276. New Haven: Yale University Press, 1964.

Environmental Information Systems

Alexander, G. J., King, G. F., Warskow, M. A. *Development of Information Requirements and Transmission Techniques for Highway Users.* Vol. I. Deer Park, New York: Airborne Instruments Laboratory, November 1967.

Bison Associates. *The Center for Choice: an experiment in two-way public communication.* Boston, 1964.

Browne, K. "Streetscape with Furniture: The Attack on the Corridor Street at Nottinghill Gate," *Architectural Review* 123 (May 1958), 319–323.

Cambridge Seven Associates. *Report to the U. S. Commission of Fine Arts on the Environmental Design of Streets in Washington, D. C.* Cambridge and New York, n.d.

Helfman, E. S. *Signs and Symbols Around the World.* New York: Lothrop, Lee & Shepard Co., 1967.

Hoftiezer, Gaylord J. "Combating the Crime of the Streets," *Industrial Design* 16 (January/February 1969), 44–47.

Kahn, Alfred J., *et al. Neighborhood Information Centers.* New York: Columbia University School of Social Work, 1966.

Kato, S. "Toward an International Symbol Language," *Print* 21 (March 1967), 39–42.

Kelly, Scott. "Expo 67, Messages from the Sponsor," *Industrial Design* 13 (September 1966), 66–73.

Kneebone, Peter (ed.). "International Signs and Symbols: Special Icograda Issue," *Print* 23 (November/December 1969).

Krampen, M. "Signs and Symbols in Graphic Communication," *Design Quarterly* 62 (1965), 2–31.

Krampen, M., and Seitz, P. (eds.). *Design and Planning Two.* New York: Hastings House, 1967.

Lynch, K. and Appleyard, D. *Signs in the City.* Mimeographed. Cambridge: Massachusetts Institute of Technology, 1963.

Maldonado, T., Bonsiepe, G., and Muller, W. "Notes on Communication and Sign System Design for Operative Communication," *Uppercase* 5 (1961).

Mason, Stanley. "Towards an International Symbology," *Graphis* 20 (November 1964), 514–517.

Pitman, Sir James. "Communication by Signs," *New Scientist* 25 (March 1965), 580–581.

Plumb, William Lansing (ed.). "Graphic Design in the Human Environment," *Print* 22 (March/April 1968).

Ritter, Paul. "Urban Renewal," *Planning for Man and Motor,* 151–222. Oxford: Pergamon Press and New York: Macmillan, 1964.

Senders, J. W., *et al. An Investigation of Automobile Driver Information Processing.* Report No. 1335, Contract CPR-11-0958. Boston: Bolt, Beranek and Newman, Inc., 1966.

Senders, J. W., *et al.* "The Attentional Demand of Automobile Driving," *Highway Research Board Record* 195 (1967), 15–33.

Teltsch, Kathleen. "Subways May Get History Exhibits," *New York Times,* November 1968, p. 50.

Urban America, Inc. *Improved Urban Transportation Information Systems,* Phase I: Feasibility Study. Washington, D. C.: Department of Transportation, 1968.

PUBLIC SIGNS, SIGNALS, AND MARKINGS

Principles, Precedents, and Proposals

American Association of State Highway Officials. *Report on Uniform Map Symbols.* Washington, D. C., 1962.

Automotive Safety Foundation. *ASF Report No. 10 — Toward More Uniform Traffic Controls.* Washington, D. C., April 1961.

Automotive Safety Foundation. *Driver Needs in Freeway Signing.* Washington, D. C., December 1958.

Automotive Safety Foundation. *Summary Report: The National Conference on Highway Communications.* Washington, D. C., February 1968.

Bankley, S. "Charming But Impossible" (lack of signs in Boston), *Boston Globe,* 10 August 1967.

Brattinga, Pieter. "Signs of Life: Street Signs," *Print* 18 (March, 1964), 32–7.

Constantine, Mildred, and Jacobson, Egbert. *Sign Language for Buildings and Landscape.* New York: Reinhold Publishing Corp., 1961.

Elliot, W. G., 3d. "Symbology on the Highways of the World," *Traffic Engineering* 31 (1960), 18–26.

Froshaug, Anthony. "Roadside Traffic Signs," *Design* 178 (1963), 37–50.

"Graphic Design in the Human Environment," *Print* 22 (March/April 1968), 24–112.

Gray, Milner, and Armstrong, Ronald. *Lettering for Architects and Designers.* New York: Reinhold Publishing Corp., 1962.

Hensley, Marble J., Sr., and Volk, Wayne N. "What Revisions are Needed in Manual Signal Sections?" *Traffic Engineering* (June 1966), 59–61.

International Council of Graphic Design Associations. *Sign Information Sheets,* A1/A6.1 (Working Papers). Amsterdam, 1967.

Katzumie, M. "Design Policy for the Tokyo Olympics," *Graphic Design* (Tokyo) 17/18 (1964).

Kinneir, Jock. *Direction Signing in Great Britain.* Kinneir, Calvert and Associates, London, England, n.d.

Kneebone, P. "The Problems of Communication through Signs," Paper presented to A. Typ. I. Congress, UNESCO, Paris, 1967. *Icograda,* The First Five Years, London, 1968.

Koehler, Walter. "Those Flashing Lights on Your Dashboard Can Mean Danger," *New York Times,* 2 April 1967.

Lees, John W. *Comparative Evaluation of Signing Systems.* Cambridge: Herman and Lees Associates, April 1968.

Minneapolis Planning and Development. *Metro Center '85 — Environmental Design for Central Minneapolis;* "Visual Communication Study," 1968, "Street Name Signs," 1969, "Signs on the Streets: Design Concepts," 1969, and "Signs on the Streets: Inventory and Analysis," 1968.

Moore, R. L. "Traffic Sign Design," *Traffic Engineering and Control* (March 1962), 685–687. (British)

Neu, R. J. "Internally-Illuminated Traffic Signs," *Traffic Quarterly* 10 (1956), 247–259.

Oregon State Highways Department. *Color Coded Interchange Ramps.* January 1966.

Plumb, William Lansing. "Telling People Where to Go: Subway Graphics," *Print* 19 (September/October 1965), 13–23.

"Prospects: Magic Box," *Forum* (October 1969), 32–33.

Reid, J. A. "The Lighting of Traffic Signs and Associated Traffic Control Devices," *Public Lighting* 29 (1964), 252–261.

Research and Design Institute. *A Structure of Rules for Highway Traffic Information and Control.* Report to the National Foundation on the Arts, Washington, D. C. Providence, 1968.

Rotzler, Willy. "Public Signs and Lettering," *Graphis* 18 (November 1962), 582–609.

Solin, Arthur. "Mexico 68: Graphics for the XIX Olympiad," *Print* 17 (May/June 1968), 1–10.

United Nations. Economic and Social Council. *Draft Convention on Road Signs and Signals,* Document No. E/3999, 28 January 1965.

U. S. National Joint Committee on Uniform Traffic Control Devices. *Report of the Special Committee on Color,* January 1967.

Usborne, T. G. "International Standardization of Road Traffic Signs," *Traffic Engineering* 37 (July 1967), 20–23.

Current Practice

Advisor's Committee on Traffic Signs for Motorways. Final Report: *Motorway Signs.* London: Her Majesty's Stationery Office, 1962.

American Association of State Highway Officials. *Manual for Signing and Pavement Marking of the National System of Interstate and Defense Highways.* Washington, D. C., 1961.

American Association of State Highway Officials, Operating Committee on Traffic. *Interstate Guide Sign Policies.* Washington, D. C., June 1965.

American Automobile Association. *International Road Signs.* World Touring and Automobile Organization, n.d.

Automobile Club of New York, Traffic and Engineering Safety Service. *Directional Signing.* New York: American Automobile Association, 2 July 1968.

Deutscher Normenausschuss. *Normblatt DIN 1451.* Berlin and Cologne, 1951.

French, R. A. "Coordinated Traffic Signalling System — Sydney, Australia," *Traffic Quarterly* (January 1965), 76–88.

International Committee on Travel Signs and Symbols. *Collection of Existing Pictograms Answering to the Basic List of Informations* (Working Paper). Paris, 1967.

International Committee On Travel Signs and Symbols. *International Survey on Pictographs* (Draft report). Paris, 1969.

International Organization for Standardization. *Symbols, Dimensions and Layout of Safety Signs.* Explanatory Report of the Secretariat, January 1964.

Massachusetts, Commonwealth of. *Manual on Uniform Traffic Control Devices.* Department of Public Works, 1966.

Ministry of Transport. *Informatory Signs for Use on All-Purpose Roads.* London: Her Majesty's Stationery Office, 1964.

Ministry of Transport. *Traffic Signs 1963.* Report of the Committee on Traffic Signs for All-Purpose Roads. London: Her Majesty's Stationery Office, 1963.

U. S. Congress. House. Committee on Public Works. *Highway Safety, Design and Operations.* Hearings before the Special Subcommittee on the Federal-Aid Highway Program. 90th Cong., 2nd sess., 1968.

U. S. Department of Commerce. *Manual on Uniform Traffic Control Devices for Streets and Highways.* Bureau of Public Roads, June 1961; and *Standard Traffic Control Signs,* July 1965.

U. S. Department of Commerce. *Standard Alphabets for Highway Signs.* Bureau of Public Roads, 1966.

U. S. Department of Transportation. *Report on the Highway Safety Program Standards, Developed in Accordance with the Provisions of the Highway Safety Act of 1966.* Washington, D. C.: Federal Highway Administration, National Highway Safety Bureau, 1968.

Research Reports

Allen, B. L. "Pandas versus Zebras: Comparative Study of Control at Pedestrian Crossing," *Traffic Engineering and Control* 4 (1963), 616–619.

Allen, T. M., and Straub, A. L. "Sign Brightness and Legibility," Highway Research Board *Bulletin 127* (1955), 1–14.

Allen, T. M., Smith, G. M., Janson, M. H., and Dyer, N. F. *Sign Brightness in Relation to Legibility.* Final Report on a Highway Planning and Research Study, Michigan State Highway Commission, 1966.

Berger, C. "Grouping, Number, and Spacing of Letters as Determinants of Word Recognition," *Journal of General Psychology* 55 (1956), 215–228.

Berger, C. "Some Experiments on the Width of Symbols as Determinants of Legibility," *Acta Ophthalmologica* 30 (1952), 409–420.

Berry, D. S., Wattleworth, J., and Schwar, J. F. "Evaluating Effectiveness of Lane-Use Control Devices at Intersections," Highway Research Board *Proceedings* 41 (1962), 495–528.

Berry, D. S., and Davis, H. E. "A Summary of Development and Research in Traffic Signs, Signals and Markings," *Proceedings of the Institute of Transportation and Traffic Engineering,* 1953.

Birren, Faber. "Safety on Highways: A Problem of Vision, Visibility, and Color," *American Journal of Ophthalmology,* series 3, 43 (1957), 265–270.

Bolt, Beranek and Newman, Inc. *An Investigation of the Design and Performance of Traffic Control Devices.* Report No. 1726 Prepared for Bureau of Public Roads, U. S. Dept. of Transportation. Cambridge, December 1968.

Brainerd, R. W., Campbell, R. S., and Elkin, E. H. "Design and Interpretability of Road Signs," *Journal of Applied Psychology* 45 (1961), 130–136.

Burg, A., and Hulbert, S. F. "Predicting the Effectiveness of Highway Signs," Highway Research Board *Bulletin 324* (1962), 1–11.

Christie, A. W., and Rutley, K. S. "Relative Effectiveness of Some Letter Types Designed for Use on Road Traffic Signs," *Roads and Road Construction* 39 (August 1961), 239–244.

DeLeuw, Cather & Company. *The Effect of Regulatory Devices on Intersectional Capacity and Operation,* NCHRP Project 3-6. Chicago, August 1966.

Desrosiers, R. D. "Moving Picture Technique for Highway Signing Studies — An Investigation of its Applicability," *Public Roads* 33 (April 1965), 143–147.

Ferguson, W. S., and Cook, K. E. *Driver Awareness of Sign Colors and Shapes.* Charlottesville: Virginia Highway Research Council, May 1967.

Forbes, T. W. "Predicting Attention-Gaining Characteristics of Highway Traffic Signs," *Human Factors* 6 (August 1964), 371–374.

Forbes, T. W., Gervais, E., and Allen, T. M. "Effectiveness of Symbols for Lane Control Signals," Highway Research Board *Bulletin 244* (1960), 16–29.

Forbes, T. W., and Holmes, R. S. "Legibility Distances of Highway Destination Signs in Relation to Letter Height, Letter Width and Reflectorization," Highway Research Board *Proceedings* 19 (1939), 321–335.

Forbes, T W., Snyder, T. E., and Pain, R. F. "Traffic Sign Requirements," *Highway Research Record,* No. 70, pp. 48–56. Washington, D. C., 1965.

Forbes, T. W., Moscowitz, K., and Morgan, G. "A Comparison of Lower Case and Capital Letters for Highway Signs," Highway Research Board *Proceedings* 30 (1950), 355–373.

Forbes, T. W., Pain, R. F., Joyce, R. P., and Fry, J. P. "Color and Brightness Factors in Simulated and Full Scale Traffic Sign Visibility," *Highway Research Board,* in press.

Forbes, T. W., Snyder, T. E., and Pain, R. F. *A Study of Traffic Sign Requirements: II. An Annotated Bibliography.* East Lansing: Michigan State University, August 1964.

Gray, P. G , and Russell, P. "Drivers' Understanding of Traffic Signs," Central Office of Information, *Social Survey 347.* London: Her Majesty's Stationery Office, 1962.

Herman, R., Olson, P. and Rothery, R. "Problem of the Amber Signal Light," *Operations Research* 5 (September 1963), 298–304.

Hillier, John A., and Rothery, R., General Motors Research Laboratories. "The Synchronization of Traffic Signals for Minimum Delay," *Transportation Science* 1 (May 1967).

Highway Research Board. "Effects of Traffic Control Devices," Highway Research Board *Bulletin 244* (1960).

Highway Research Board. "Traffic Control Devices," 3 Reports, *Highway Research Record,* No. 151. Washington, D. C , 1966.

Highway Research Board. "Traffic Control Devices," 5 Reports. *Highway Research Record,* No. 170. Washington, D. C., 1967.

Highway Research Board. "Traffic Control: Devices and Delineation — 7 Reports," HRB-NAS-NRC Publication No. 105 (1966), *Highway Research Record,* No. 1515. Presented at the 44th Annual Meeting of the Highway Research Board, Washington, D. C., January 1965.

Highway Research Board. *Improved Criteria for Traffic Signals at Individual Intersections — Interim Report.* National Cooperative Research Program Report 3. Washington, D. C., 1964.

Hodge, D. C. "Legibility of a Uniform Strokewidth Alphabet, Part I: Relative Legibility of Upper and Lower Case Letters," *Journal of Engineering Psychology* 1 (1962), 34–46.

Hodge, D. C. "Legibility of a Uniform Strokewidth Alphabet, Part II: Some Factors Affecting the Legibility of Words," *Journal of Engineering Psychology* 2 (1963), 55–67.

Howard, Alfred R. *Traffic Sign Recognition.* Report presented at the 45th Annual Convention of the Canadian Good Roads Association. Montreal, Province of Quebec, 19–22 October 1964.

Hoxie, J. P. "Color and Intensity Relationships in Traffic Signals," *Proceedings of the 31st Annual Meeting of the Institute of Traffic Engineers,* 1961.

Hulbert, Slade. *Signing a Freeway to Freeway Interchange (Guide Signs).* Research Report No. 42. Los Angeles: University of California, Institute of Transportation and Traffic Engineering, September 1965.

Hulbert, Slade, and Wojcik, C. K. *Development of an Expeditious Method for Off-Site Testing of Freeway Sign Formats.* Los Angeles: University of California, Institute of Transportation and Traffic Engineering, 1965.

Hurd, F. "Glance Legibility," *Traffic Engineering* 17 (1946), 161–162.

Jackman, W. T. "Driver Obedience to Stop and Slow Signs," Highway Research Board *Bulletin 161* (1967), 9–17.

Johansson, G. and Rumar, K. "Drivers and Road Signs: A Preliminary Investigation of the Capacity of Car Drivers to Get Information from Road Signs," *Ergonomics* 9 (January 1966), 57–62.

Kermit, M. L., and Hein, T. C. "Effect of Rumble Strip on Traffic Control and Driver Behavior," Highway Research Board *Proceedings* 40 (1962), 469–482.

Kuntz, J. E., and Sleight, R. B. "Legibility of Numerals: The Optimal Ratio of Height to Strokewidth," *American Journal of Psychology* 63 (1950), 567–575.

Lauer, A. R. "Certain Structural Components of Letters for Improving the Efficiency of the Stop Sign," Highway Research Board *Proceedings* 27 (1947), 360–371.

Mackie, A. M. *A National Survey of Knowledge of the New Traffic Signs.* Road Research Laboratory Report No. 51. London: Ministry of Transport, 1966.

Michigan State Highway Department. *Interchange Ramp Color Delineation and Marking Study.* East Lansing, June 1965.

Michigan State University, Division of Engineering Research. *Research on Traffic Sign Requirements.* East Lansing: Michigan State University, 1 August 1967.

Moore, R. L., and Christie, A. W. "Direction Signs for Motorways," *The Engineer* 209 (13 May 1960), 813–817.

Moore, R. L. and Christie, A. W. "Research on Traffic Signs," *Engineering for Traffic Conference* (July 1963), 113–122.

Neal, H. E. "The Legibility of Highway Signs," *Traffic Engineering* 17 (1947), 525–529.

Odescalchi, P. "Conspicuity of Signs in Rural Surroundings," *Traffic Engineering and Control* 2 (1960), 390–393.

Paterson, D. G., and Tinker, M. A. "The Effect of Typography upon the Perceptual Span in Reading," *American Journal of Psychology* 60 (1947), 388–397.

Perkins, Stuart R., and Harris, Joseph I. *Traffic Conflict Characteristics: Accident Potential at Intersections.* Warren, Michigan: General Motors Research Laboratories, December 1967.

Powers, L. D. "Advance Route Turn Markers on City Streets," Highway Research Board *Proceedings* 41 (1962), 483–493.

Robinson, C. C. "Color in Traffic Control," *Traffic Engineering* (May 1967), 25–29.

Schoppert, D. W., Moskowitz, K., Hulbert, S. F. and Burg, A. "Some Principles of Freeway Directional Signing Based on Motorists' Experiences," Highway Research Board *Bulletin 244* (1959), 30–82.

Schwanhausser, W. E., Jr. *Visibility of Traffic Signals.* Schenectady: Illuminating Laboratory, General Electric Co., n.d.

Soloman, D. "The Effect of Letter Width and Spacing on Night Legibility of Highway Signs," *Traffic Engineering* 27 (1956), 113–120.

Spaulding, S. "An Investigation of the Factors Influencing Communication Potential of Pictorial Illustrations," *Audiovisual Communications Review* 4 (1956).

Stephens, B. W., and Michaels, R. M. "Timesharing Between Two Driving Tasks: Simulated Steering and Recognition of Road Signs," *Public Roads* 33 (December 1964).

Taylor, William C. *Colored Pavement for Traffic Guidance.* Presented at the 47th annual meeting of the Highway Research Board. Washington, D. C., 14–19 January 1968.

Taylor, William C., and Hubbell, J. Stephen. *The Evaluation of Pavement Marking to Designate Direction of Travel and Degree of Safety.* Bureau of Traffic Report No. 1-14163, Ohio Department of Highways, n.d.

Tinker, M. A. *Legibility of Print.* Ames, Iowa: Iowa State University Press, 1963.

Uhlaner, J. E. "The Effect of Thickness of Stroke on the Legibility of Letters," Iowa Academy of Sciences *Proceedings* 48 (1941), 319–324.

Utter, R. F. "The Influence of Painted Crosswalks on the Behavior of Pedestrians." Unpublished Ph.D. Dissertation, Department of Psychology, University of California, n.d.

Vaughan-Birch, Kenneth. "What Not to Expect from Crosswalk Signals," *Civic Administration* Canada 19 (May 1967), 32–33.

Vorhees, Alan M., and Associates. *Freeway Signing — Concepts and Criteria.* A Research Report Prepared for U. S. Department of Commerce, Bureau of Public Roads, Office of Highway Safety. Washington, D. C., June 1966.

Walker, R. E., Nicolay, R. C., and Stearns, C. R. "Comparative Accuracy of Recognizing American and International Road Signs," *Journal of Applied Psychology* 49 (1965), 322–325.

PUBLIC LIGHTING

Principles, Precedents, and Proposals

Allison, D. "Outdoor Lighting: An Expanding New Technology," *Architectural Forum* 113 (July 1960), 128–133.

Bonnington, J. S. *The Role of Lighting in the Britain of the Future.* Paper presented at the Five Conferences on "Lighting and the New Britain" in The Cromwell Hall, Earls Court, April 1967.

Brookes, M. J. "Street Lighting and People," *Industrial Design* 10 (June 1963), 48–55.

Derek, Phillips. "Cities by Night," *RIBA Journal* 73 (July 1966), 307–314.

Evans, Seymour. "Design of the Luminous Environment," *AIA Journal* 46 (October 1966), 50–56.

Fitch, James M. "The Control of the Luminous Environment," *Scientific American* 219 (September 1968), 191–196.

Grier, H. D. "Lighting the Landmarks of Manhattan," *Art in America* 45 (Summer 1957), 30–33.

Illuminating Engineering Society. *American Standard Practice for Roadway Lighting.* New York, 1964.

Illuminating Engineering Society. "IES Guide to Design of Light Control," *Illuminating Engineering* (November/December 1959) 722–727 (Part I: "Physical Principles"); 778–786 (Part II: "Design of Reflector and Optical Elements").

International Commission on Illumination. *International Recommendations for the Lighting of Public Thoroughfares.* Publication C.I.E. No. 12 (E — 3.3.1.), 1965.

Joint Committee of Traffic Engineers and the Illuminating Engineering Society. "Public Lighting Needs," *Illuminating Engineering* 61 (September 1966), 585–602.

Jordan, E. M. "Bristol High Mast Lighting," *International Lighting Review* 16, No. 5 (1965), 175–177.

Kepes, Gyorgy. "Kinetic Light as a Creative Medium," *Technology Review* (December 1967), 25–35.

Ketvirtis, Antanas. *Highway Lighting Engineering.* Toronto, Canada, 1967.

Kurilko, George N. "The Visual Analysis and Design of City Lighting," Unpublished Master's thesis, Massachusetts Institute of Technology, Cambridge 1962.

Lam, William M. C. "Environmental Control — Lighting," *AIA Journal* (November 1962), 88–89.

Lam, William C. "Lighting of Cities," *Architectural Record* 137 (June 1965), 210–214; 138 (July 1965), 173–180.

"Lighting for Traffic," *International Lighting Review* 18, No. 2 (1967), 35–70.

"Lighting Up Main Street," *Industrial Design* 13 (October 1966), 38–45.

Lippard, L. R. "Pulsa," *Arts Canada* 25 (December 1968), 59–60.

Middleton, Michael. *Suiting Street Lighting to its Setting.* London: Civic Trust, July 1967.

"Nightscape." *Light and Lighting* 61 (May 1968), 128–157.

"Pulsa—Light as Truth." *Yale Alumni Magazine* 31 (May 1968), 39–45.

"Symposium on Special Aspects of Street Lighting." *Transactions of the Illuminating Engineering Society* 29, No. 3 (1964), 89–98.

Toenjes, D. A. and Brewer, C. R. "Street Lighting in Action," *Progressive Architecture* 37 (August 1956), 136–141.

Waldram, J. M. "The Design of the Visual Field in Streets: The Visual Engineer's Contribution," *Transactions of the Illuminating Engineering Society* 31, No. 1 (1966), 7–26.

Wilcock, A. *Cities at Night.* Lecture presented at Two-Day Conference on "The Place of Lighting in the Urban Environment." Birmingham, England: University of Aston, November 1967.

Wilcock, A. "The World at Night," *Public Lighting* 28 (December 1963).

Research Reports

Allphin, Willard. "Further Studies of Sight Line and Direct Discomfort Glare," *Illuminating Engineering* (January 1968), 26–29.

Berla, Nancy. *Correlation Between Street Lighting and Crime.* Washington, D. C.: Library of Congress, Education and Public Welfare Division, 28 April 1965.

Blackwell, H. R., Schwab, R. N., and Pritchard, B. S. "Illumination Variables in Visual Tasks for Drivers," *Public Roads* 33 (1965), 237–248.

deBoer, J. B. "Lighting of Traffic Routes," *Public Lighting.* Philips, Holland, 1965.

deBoer, J. B., and Schreuder, D. A. "Glare as a Criterion for Quality in Street Lighting," *Transactions of the Illuminating Engineering Society* 32, No. 2 (1967), 117–135.

Christie, A. W. "The Economic Justification of Public Lighting," *International Lighting Review* 19, No. 3 (1968), 112–115.

Christie, A. W. "The Night Accident Problem and the Effect of Public Lighting," *Public Lighting* 33 (June 1968) 98–101.

Christie, A. W. *Research on Street and Highway Lighting with Particular Reference to Their Effect on Accidents.* England: Road Research Laboratory, June 1966.

Christie, A. W. "Visibility in Lighted Streets and the Effect of the Arrangement and Light Distribution of the Lanterns," *Ergonomics* 6 (October 1963), 385–391.

Christie, A. W., and Fisher, A. J. "The Effect of Glare from Street Lighting Lanterns on the Vision of Drivers of Different Ages," *Transactions of the Illuminating Engineering Society* 31, No. 4 (1966), 93–108 and 114–120.

Faucett, Robert E. *An Evaluation of Higher Mounting Heights for Roadway Lighting,* Parts I and II. Hendersonville, No. Carolina: General Electric Co., 1967.

Highway Research Board. *Bibliography No. 45; Night Visibility — Selected References.* Washington, D. C., 1967.

Highway Research Board. *Economic Study of Roadway Lighting.* National Cooperative Highway Research Program Report 20. Washington, D. C., 1966.

Highway Research Board. "Lighting, Visibility, and Driving," 6 Reports, *Highway Research Record,* No. 216. Washington, D. C., 1968.

Highway Research Board. "Night Visibility," 5 Reports, *Highway Research Record,* No. 164. Washington, D. C., 1967.

Highway Research Board. "Night Visibility," 7 Reports, *Highway Research Record,* No. 179. Washington, D. C., 1967.

Highway Research Board, Illuminating Engineering Research Institute, and Texas A & M University. *Proceedings: Symposium on Visibility in the Driving Task.* Texas A & M University, May 1968.

Illuminating Engineering Research Institute. *1965 Annual Report — A Review of Activities During the Year,* with emphasis on the relationship between colors and lighting. New York, 1966.

Illuminating Engineering Research Institute. *Annual Report 1966 — A Review of Research Activities and a View of New Goals in a Luminous Environment.* New York, 1966.

Ives, Howard. "Does Highway Illumination Affect Accident Occurrence?" *Traffic Quarterly* (April 1962), 229–241.

Mitch, Charles J. *Excerpts from a Study of a Low Level Lighting System.* Milwaukee County Expressway and Transportation Commission, 29 December 1966. Mimeographed.

"New Figures Show Lighting Does Reduce Accident Costs," *Street and Highway Lighting* 17 (Third Quarter, 1967).

Rex, C. H. "Comparison of Effectiveness Ratings — Roadway Lighting," Highway Research Board *Bulletin 298* (1961), 35–50.

Rex, C. H. *Light Distribution for the Motorist.* Paper 6, Highway Research Board. Washington, D. C., January 1966.

Rex, C. H. "Visual Data on Roadway Lighting," Highway Research Board *Bulletin 336* (1962), 61–75.

Richards, O. W. "Night Driving Seeing Problems," *American Journal of Optometry* 35 (1958), 565–579.

Richards, O. W. "Vision at Levels of Night Road Illumination," IV. Literature 1957–58, Highway Research *Bulletin 226* (1959), 56–61.

Rowan, Neilon J. and Walton, Ned E. *Optimization of Roadway Lighting Systems.* Presented at the 47th Annual Meeting of the Highway Research Board, Texas Transportation Institute, 18 December 1967.

Smith, C. C. "The Achievement of Quality in Street Lighting," *Transactions of the Illuminating Engineering Society* 32, No. 2 (1967), 136–148.

Staley, Karl A. *Fundamentals of Light and Lighting.* General Electric: Large Lamp Department, August 1960.

Tanner, J. C., and Harris, A. J. *Street Lighting and Accidents: Some British Investigations.* England: Road Research Laboratory, 1955.

Walton, N. E. and Rowan, N. J. *Interim Progress Report on Supplementary Studies in Highway Illumination.* Research Report 75-7, Texas Transportation Institute, October 1967.

west end
charles river
cambridge
back bay
south end

Massachusetts, Commonwealth of. Department of Public Works. *Rules and Regulations for the Control and Restriction of Billboards, Signs and Other Advertising Devices.* Outdoor Advertising Division, 8 December 1965.

Massachusetts, Commonwealth of. Department of Public Works. *General Laws.* Chapter 93, secs. 29–33; Chapter 85, sec. 8; Chapter 97, sec. 95A.

Massachusetts, Commonwealth of. House No. 4414; An Act to control the erection and maintenance of billboards, etc.; House No. 1568: An act requiring that permits for billboards issued by the outdoor advertising board comply with local zoning bylaws and ordinances; House No. 3869: An act granting the regulation and control of outdoor advertising to local licensing authorities; Senate No. 124: An act prohibiting the outdoor advertising board from issuing a permit for a billboard . . . whenever written objection is received, etc.

Miami, Florida. Building and Zoning Department. *Sign Law* (1965).

Ministry of Housing and Local Government. *Planning Control of Signs and Posters.* London: Her Majesty's Stationery Office, 1966.

Montgomery County Council. *Application No. F-96 for Amendment to Zoning Ordinance Text.* Maryland, 1 October 1968.

New Jersey. Department of the Treasury. *Outdoor Advertising Act* (1959).

New York. Department of City Planning. *New York City Zoning Resolution* (rev. 1966), secs. 22–30 — 42–54, Sign Regulations.

U. S. Congress. Senate. *Highway Beautification Act of 1965.* 89th Cong., S. 2084, Public Law 89-285, 22 October 1965.

U. S. Congress. Senate *1967 Highway Beautification Program.* Report of the Department of Commerce to the U. S. Congress pursuant to Public Law 89-285, Highway Beautification Act of 1965. (Part I: Cost Estimate, Economic Impact, and Alternate Methods; Part II: Standard Criteria, Rules and Regulations). Washington, D. C.: Government Printing Office, 1967.

U. S. Department of Transportation. *First Annual Report of the Department of Transportation,* Part I. Fiscal Year 1967.

Vermont. *General Laws.* Conservation, Chapter 14, Tourist Information Services, secs. 321–345.

Wagner, L. C. and Harden, V. E. *Regulation of Outdoor Advertising Along the Interstate System.* Report prepared for the Joint Fact-Finding Committee on Highways, Streets and Bridges of the Washington State Legislature, 1962.

Wellesley, Mass. Planning Board. *Zoning By-Law* (June 1967), sec. 22A — Signs and Advertising Devices.

Research Reports

Advertising Research Foundation. *Recommended Research Program for the Institute of Outdoor Advertising.* New York, 1967.

Arthur D. Little, Inc. *Response to the Roadside Environment.* Report to the Outdoor Advertising Association of America. Cambridge, Mass., 30 January 1968.

Lauer, A. R. and McMonagle, J. C. "Do Road Signs Affect Accidents?" *Traffic Quarterly* (July 1955), 322–329.

Lucas, D. B., and Britt, S. H. *Advertising Psychology and Research.* New York: McGraw-Hill, 1950.

Madigan-Hyland, Inc. *Signs and Accidents on New York State Thruway.* Report prepared for New York State Thruway Authority, February 1963.

Michigan State Highway Department. *Accident Experience in Relation to Road and Roadside Features.* Planning and Traffic Division, 1952.

Minnesota Department of Highways, Highway Planning Survey. *Minnesota Rural Trunk Highway Accident, Access Point, and Advertising Sign Study.* U. S. Department of Commerce, Bureau of Public Roads, 1951 (rev. 1952).

National Outdoor Advertising Bureau. *Highlights of Outdoor Advertising Research.* New York, 1965.

Pollack, Leslie S. *Driver Distraction as Related to Physical Development Abutting Urban Streets,* Exchange Bibliography 59. Monticello, Illinois; Council of Planning Librarians, July 1968.

Shoaf, R. T. "Are Advertising Signs Near Freeways Traffic Hazards?" *Traffic Engineer* 26 (1955), 71–73.

Singer, Inc. *The Measurement and Control of the Visual Efficiency of Advertisements.* New York, 1962.

Traffic Audit Bureau, Inc. *Standard Procedure for the Circulation Evaluation of Outdoor Advertising.* New York, 1961.

PRIVATE SIGNS AND LIGHTS

Principles, Precedents, and Proposals.

Adams, James W. R. *Posters Look to the Future.* London: The Poster Advertising Planning Committee, 1965.

Adams, James W. R. "A Town Planner Looks at Outdoor Advertising," *Building,* 19 August 1966.

American Bar Association. *Junkyards, Geraniums and Jurisprudence: Aesthetics and the Law.* Proceedings of a Two Day National Institute, Chicago, 2–3 June 1967.

Baker, Stephen. *Visual Persuasion.* New York: McGraw-Hill, 1961.

Beatrice, Mike. "Billboard Controls Seen by Rep. Dukakis," *Boston Globe,* 18 February 1969, p. 16.

Blake, Peter. *God's Own Junkyard.* New York: Holt, Rinehart and Winston, 1964.

Burtt, H. E. *Applied Psychology.* "Controlling the Prospect's Attention"; New York: Prentice-Hall, Inc., 1948.

California Roadside Council. *Signs Out of Control.* San Francisco, n.d.

Cardoso, William J. "Blight Billboard: Businessmen Fight to Banish It at Stowe, Vermont," *Boston Sunday Globe,* 8 October 1967, p. 10.

Civic Trust. *Magdalen Street, Norwich: The Story of an Experiment in Civic Design that Became Famous.* London: Civic Trust, 1967.

"Garden State Asks Removal of Signs Diverting Drivers," *New York Times,* 22 December 1968.

Gossage, Howard. "How to Look at Billboards," *Harper's Magazine* 220 (February 1960), 12–16, 21.

Hanron, Robert B. "Billboard Curbs Urged," *Boston Globe,* 4 April 1969.

Hapner, Harry N. *Advertising: Creative Communication with Consumers.* 4th ed. New York: McGraw-Hill, 1964.

Highway Research Board. *Outdoor Advertising Along Highways — A Legal Analysis.* Special Report No. 41. Washington, D. C.: Highway Research Board, 1958.

Kamekura, Y. *Trade Marks of the World.* Tokyo and New York, 1957.

Marsh, Susan. "Interstate Sign Malls Rout Billboard Clutter," *New York Times,* 22 December 1968, p. 17.

Martin, William John, Jr., and Nelson, David E. "Land Use Control and the Billboard," *California Law Review* 46 (1958), 809–823.

Natural Beauty Commission. *Sample Provisions for a Local Law to Regulate Signs.* Albany: Office for Local Government, February 1968.

Planning and Posters, PAPC Report No. 3. London: The Poster Advertising Planning Committee, n.d.

Rigolo, Arthur. *Model Sign Control Ordinance: A Weapon for the "War on Community Ugliness."* Committee on Aesthetics, AIA, 4 November 1965.

Robinson, Layhmond. "Thruway Renews Anti-Sign Battle," *New York Times,* 2 April 1963.

Selame, Joseph. "The Visual Communications Influence," *Signs of the Times,* (November 1968), 52–54.

"Signs of Life — Barbara Stauffacher's Outdoor Signs," *Progressive Architecture* 47 (June 1966), 207–208.

Sutton, James. *Signs in Action.* London: Studio Vista and New York: Reinhold Publishing Corp., 1965.

Taylor, John L. "Urban Publicity," *Building,* 13 October 1967, pp. 115–116.

U. S. Congress. Senate. Committee on Public Works. *Hearings on S. 963, S. 3041, and S. 3218, Bills Relating to the Control of Advertising on Interstate Highways.* 85th Cong., 2nd sess., 1957.

Wilson, Ruth I. "Billboards and the Right to be Seen from the Highway," *Georgetown Law Journal* 30 (1942), 723–750.

Current Practice

Ann Arbor, Michigan. *Ann Arbor Sign Ordinance.* Chapter 61 — Ann Arbor City Code (December 1966), secs. 5:500-5:521.

Association of National Advertisers. *Essentials of Outdoor Advertising.* New York: Association of National Advertisers, 1958.

Boston, Mass. Department of Public Works. *Rules and Regulations,* Part One Relating to Projections In, On, or Over the Public Ways in the City of Boston, 1 January 1955.

Boston, Mass. Building Department. *Building Code of the City of Boston* (1964).

Boston, Mass. Building Department. *Boston Zoning Code and Enabling Act* (1968).

Brookline, Mass. Building Department. *Zoning By-Law* (July 1966) Art. 7 — Signs and Illumination.

Carter, Forest C., Vredenburg, Harvey L., and Patty, C. Robert. *A Historical, Economic and Statistical Study of the Electrical Sign Industry.* National Electric Sign Association, March 1967.

Cleveland, Ohio. City Planning Commission. *Codified Ordinances of the City of Cleveland,* sec. 2500, Signs.

"A Complete System of Graphics Control for the Street Scene," *Stores* (January 1968).

District of Columbia. Department of Highways and Traffic. *Traffic and Motor Vehicle Regulations,* Part I. *D. C. Building Code* (1967), Chapter 14 — Sign Regulation.

Massachusetts, Commonwealth of. *Acts and Resolves, 1955* — Chapter 616, secs. 1-12 (An Act Creating the historic Beacon Hill District in the City of Boston and establishing in the Building Department of said City the Beacon Hill Architectural Commission and defining its powers and duties); *Acts and Resolves, 1966* — Chapter 625, secs. 1-13 (An Act Creating the Back Bay Residential District in the City of Boston and establishing in the Boston Redevelopment Authority the Back Bay Architectural Commission and defining its powers and duties).

east boston
LOGAN INTERNATIONAL AIRPORT
north end
government center
boston harbor
fort point channel
ATLANTIC AVENUE
FRANKLIN STREET
SUMMER STREET
ESSEX STREET
BEACH STREET
NORTHERN AVENUE
U.S. NAVAL RESERVATION